THE CAMBRIDGE COMPANION TO
SCIENCE AND RELIGION

In recent years, the relations between science and religion have been the object of renewed attention. Developments in physics, biology and the neurosciences have reinvigorated discussions about the nature of life and ultimate reality. At the same time, the growth of anti-evolutionary and intelligent design movements has led many to the view that science and religion are necessarily in conflict. This book provides a comprehensive introduction to the relations between science and religion, with contributions from historians, philosophers, scientists and theologians. It explores the impact of religion on the origins and development of science, religious reactions to Darwinism, and the link between science and secularization. It also offers in-depth discussions of contemporary issues, with perspectives from cosmology, evolutionary biology, psychology and bioethics. The volume is rounded out with philosophical reflections on the connections between atheism and science, the nature of scientific and religious knowledge, and divine action and human freedom.

Peter Harrison is Andreas Idreos Professor of Science and Religion at the University of Oxford, and Director of the Ian Ramsey Centre, University of Oxford. He is the author of *The Bible, Protestantism and the Rise of Natural Science* (Cambridge, 1998), and *The Fall of Man and the Foundation of Science* (Cambridge, 2007).

CAMBRIDGE COMPANIONS TO RELIGION
A series of companions to major topics and key figures in theology and
religious studies. Each volume contains specially commissioned chapters
by international scholars which provide an accessible and stimulating
introduction to the subject for new readers and non-specialists.

Other titles in the series

THE CAMBRIDGE COMPANION TO CHRISTIAN DOCTRINE
edited by Colin Gunton (1997)
ISBN 0 521 47118 4 hardback   ISBN 0 521 47695 x paperback

THE CAMBRIDGE COMPANION TO BIBLICAL INTERPRETATION
edited by John Barton (1998)
ISBN 0 521 48144 9 hardback   ISBN 0 521 48593 2 paperback

THE CAMBRIDGE COMPANION TO DIETRICH BONHOEFFER
edited by John de Gruchy (1999)
ISBN 0 521 58258 x hardback   ISBN 0 521 58781 6 paperback

THE CAMBRIDGE COMPANION TO KARL BARTH
edited by John Webster (2000)
ISBN 0 521 58476 0 hardback   ISBN 0 521 58560 0 paperback

THE CAMBRIDGE COMPANION TO CHRISTIAN ETHICS
edited by Robin Gill (2001)
ISBN 0 521 77070 x hardback   ISBN 0 521 77918 9 paperback

THE CAMBRIDGE COMPANION TO JESUS
edited by Markus Bockmuehl (2001)
ISBN 0 521 79261 4 hardback   ISBN 0 521 79678 4 paperback

THE CAMBRIDGE COMPANION TO FEMINIST THEOLOGY
edited by Susan Frank Parsons (2002)
ISBN 0 521 66327 x hardback   ISBN 0 521 66380 6 paperback

THE CAMBRIDGE COMPANION TO MARTIN LUTHER
edited by Donald K. McKim (2003)
ISBN 0 521 81648 3 hardback   ISBN 0 521 01673 8 paperback

THE CAMBRIDGE COMPANION TO ST PAUL
edited by James D. G. Dunn (2003)
ISBN 0 521 78155 8 hardback   ISBN 0 521 78694 0 paperback

THE CAMBRIDGE COMPANION TO POSTMODERN THEOLOGY
edited by Kevin J. Vanhoozer (2003)
ISBN 0 521 79062 x hardback   ISBN 0 521 79395 5 paperback

THE CAMBRIDGE COMPANION TO JOHN CALVIN
edited by Donald K. McKim (2004)
ISBN 0 521 81647 5 hardback   ISBN 0 521 01672 x paperback

THE CAMBRIDGE COMPANION TO HANS URS VON BALTHASAR
edited by Edward T. Oakes, SJ and David Moss (2004)
ISBN 0 521 81467 7 hardback   ISBN 0 521 89147 7 paperback

Continued at the back of the book

THE CAMBRIDGE COMPANION TO

SCIENCE AND RELIGION

Edited by Peter Harrison

CAMBRIDGE
UNIVERSITY PRESS

CAMBRIDGE UNIVERSITY PRESS
Cambridge, New York, Melbourne, Madrid, Cape Town, Singapore,
São Paulo, Delhi, Dubai, Tokyo

Cambridge University Press
The Edinburgh Building, Cambridge CB2 8RU, UK

Published in the United States of America by Cambridge University Press, New York

www.cambridge.org
Information on this title: www.cambridge.org/9780521712514

© Cambridge University Press 2010

First published 2010

Printed in the United Kingdom at the University Press, Cambridge

A catalogue record for this publication is available from the British Library

Library of Congress Cataloguing in Publication data
The Cambridge companion to science and religion / edited by Peter Harrison.
   p.   cm. – (Cambridge companions to religion)
   Includes bibliographical references and index.
   ISBN 978-0-521-88538-6 – ISBN 978-0-521-71251-4 (pbk.)
   1. Religion and science.   I. Harrison, Peter, 1955–   II. Title.   III. Series.
   BL241.C317 2010
   201′.65–dc22   2010016793

ISBN 978-0-521-88538-6 Hardback
ISBN 978-0-521-71251-4 Paperback

Contents

Notes on contributors

John Hedley Brooke was the inaugural Andreas Idreos Professor of Science and Religion at the University of Oxford, and served in that Chair from 1999 until his retirement in 2006. His several books include *Science and Religion: Some Historical Perspectives* (1991), *Thinking about Matter: Studies in the History of Chemical Philosophy* (1995), (with Geoffrey Cantor) *Reconstructing Nature: The Engagement of Science and Religion* (1998) and *Science in Theistic Contexts: Cognitive Dimensions* (ed. with Margaret Osler and Jitse van der Meer) (2001).

Simon Conway Morris holds an ad hominem Chair in Evolutionary Palaeobiology in Cambridge University, where he is also a Fellow of St John's College. He was elected to the Royal Society in 1990, and has won various awards. His most recent book is *Life's Solution: Inevitable Humans in a Lonely Universe* (2003), and he is currently engaged with *Darwin's Compass*. He is active in the public understanding of science and the science/religion debates. At home he can usually be found with both hands full: one with a volume of G. K. Chesterton, the other with a glass of wine.

John H. Evans is Associate Professor of Sociology at the University of California, San Diego. His research focuses on debates in the public sphere – specifically on religious involvement in politics, health policy and public bioethics. He is the author of *Playing God? Human Genetic Engineering and the Rationalization of Public Bioethical Debate* (2002) and *Contested Reproduction: Genetic Technologies, Religion and Public Debate* (2010).

Peter Harrison is Andreas Idreos Professor of Science and Religion at the University of Oxford, where he is also Director of the Ian Ramsey Centre and a Fellow of Harris Manchester College. He has published extensively in the area of early modern intellectual history with a focus on the relations among science, religion and philosophy. His books include *'Religion' and the Religions in the English Enlightenment* (1990), *The Bible, Protestantism and the Rise of Natural Science* (1998), and *The Fall of Man and the Foundations of Science* (2007).

John Haught is Senior Fellow, Science and Religion, Woodstock Theological Center, Georgetown University. His area of specialization is systematic theology, with a particular interest in issues pertaining to science, cosmology, evolution, ecology and religion. He is the author of many books on science and religion including *God and the New Atheism* (2007), *Christianity and Science*

(2007), *Is Nature Enough?* (2007), *Deeper than Darwin* (2004), and *God after Darwin* (2007). He has also authored numerous articles and reviews. He lectures internationally on many issues related to science and religion.

John Henry is a Reader in the Science Studies Unit of the University of Edinburgh. He has published widely in the history of science from the Middle Ages to the nineteenth century, but has a special interest in the Renaissance and early modern periods. He has recently published (with John M. Forrester) *Jean Fernel's On the Hidden Causes of Things: Forms, Souls, and Occult Diseases in Renaissance Medicine* (2005), and the third edition of his *Scientific Revolution and the Origins of Modern Science* has just appeared (2008).

David C. Lindberg is Hilldale Professor Emeritus of the History of Science at the University of Wisconsin, past-president of the History of Science Society, and a recipient of its Sarton Medal for lifetime scholarly achievement. He is a Fellow of the Medieval Academy of America and the Académie internationale d'histoire des sciences. He has been a Guggenheim Fellow and a visiting member of the Institute for Advanced Study in Princeton. He has written or edited thirteen books, including *The Beginnings of Western Science* (1992, 2008), recipient of the 1994 Watson Davis Prize of the History of Science Society and the 1995 John Templeton Foundation Prize for Outstanding Books in Theology and Natural Science.

Nancey Murphy is Professor of Philosophy at Fuller Theological Seminary in Pasadena, CA. Her recent books include (with Warren S. Brown) *Did My Neurons Make Me Do It? Philosophical and Neurobiological Perspectives on Moral Responsibility and Free Will* (2007) and (with William R. Stoeger, SJ) *Evolution and Emergence: Systems, Organism, Persons* (2006).

Ronald L. Numbers is Hilldale Professor of the History of Science and Medicine and of Religious Studies and a member of the department of medical history and bioethics at the University of Wisconsin-Madison, where he has taught for more than three decades. He has written or edited more than two dozen books, including, most recently, *Galileo Goes to Jail and Other Myths about Science and Religion* (2009), *Science and Christianity in Pulpit and Pew* (2007), *The Creationists: From Scientific Creationism to Intelligent Design*, expanded edn (2006) and *When Science and Christianity Meet* (University of Chicago Press, 2003), co-edited with David C. Lindberg. He is a past-president of both the History of Science Society and the American Society of Church History and the current president of the International Union of History and Philosophy of Science. In 2008 the History of Science Society awarded him the Sarton Medal for lifetime scholarly achievement.

Jon H. Roberts is Tomorrow Foundation Professor of American Intellectual History at Boston University. He has written a number of articles dealing with the history of the relationship between science and religion, as well as the book *Darwinism and the Divine in America: Protestant Intellectuals and Organic Evolution, 1859–1900* (2001), which received the Frank S. and Elizabeth D. Brewer Prize from the American Society of Church History. He has also co-authored with James Turner *The Sacred and the Secular University* (2001). He is currently working on a book dealing with American Protestant thinkers' treatment of the mind during the nineteenth and twentieth centuries.

Michael Ruse is Lucyle T. Werkmeister Professor of Philosophy and director of the programme in the history and philosophy of science at Florida State University. His new book, *Science and Spirituality: Making Room for Faith in an Age of Science* (2010), argues that because of its deeply metaphorical nature, there are certain questions that modern science does not even attempt to answer. One can be a sceptic on these matters, but the unanswered questions leave the way open for the religiously inclined person to offer solutions.

Mikael Stenmark is Professor of Philosophy of Religion and Dean of the Faculty of Theology at Uppsala University. His books include *How to Relate Science and Religion: a Multidimensional Model* (2004), *Environmental Ethics and Environmental Policy Making* (2002), *Scientism: Science, Ethics and Religion* (2001) and *Rationality in Science, Religion and Everyday Life* (1995). He has also published articles in journals such as *Religious Studies*, *Faith and Philosophy*, *Zygon: Journal of Religion and Science*, *Theology and Science*, *The Heythrop Journal* and *Environmental Ethics*.

William R. Stoeger, SJ, is a Jesuit priest and cosmologist who has been on the staff of the Vatican Observatory since 1979. He presently is based at the Vatican Observatory Research Group, Steward Observatory, at the University of Arizona. His current scientific research focuses on cosmology. His interdisciplinary research, writing and editing have focused on the interface between cosmology and philosophy/theology.

Jonathan R. Topham is a Senior Lecturer in the History of Science at the University of Leeds. Among his co-publications are *Science in the Nineteenth-Century Periodical: Reading the Magazine of Nature* (2004), *Culture and Science in the Nineteenth-Century Media* (2004) and *Science in the Nineteenth-Century Periodical: an Electronic Index* (HRI Online, 2005). His current research combines an ongoing project concerning the *Bridgewater Treatises* and natural theology in early nineteenth-century Britain with a wide-ranging study of science and print culture in the same period.

Fraser Watts is Reader in Theology and Science in the University of Cambridge, a Fellow of Queens' College, and Director of the Psychology and Religion Research Group. His recent books include *Psychology and Theology* (2002), *Forgiveness in Context* (2004), *The Dialogue between Science and Religion: an International Perspective* (2006), *Creation, Law and Probability* (2008) and *Jesus and Psychology* (2007). He is a former president of the British Psychological Society.

Introduction

PETER HARRISON

In 1939 the eminent Cambridge philosopher C. D. Broad observed that discussions of the relations between religion and science among his contemporaries had 'acquired something of the repulsiveness of half-cold mutton in half-congealed gravy'.[1] Fortunately for readers of this volume much has changed in the years since Broad offered this droll assessment and it is safe to say that the field of science and religion now offers a much more appetizing prospect. There are several reasons for the renewed vigour of discussions about science and religion. Developments in the sciences themselves have played a key role. In cosmology, the rise to prominence of Big Bang theory has led to speculations about how the temporal origins of the universe might be linked with the idea of creation. Related to this, the surprising fact that our universe seems remarkably fine-tuned for the emergence of intelligent life has, for some commentators at least, breathed new life into what had once been regarded as moribund arguments from design. Fine-tuning arguments have also found their way into chemistry and biology, raising intriguing questions about purpose, teleology and their place in the sciences. The profoundly mysterious quantum world continues to challenge commonsense understandings of matter and causation, inspiring religious and philosophical speculations about divine action and free will and, more generally, about the nature of reality itself. In the neurosciences, our increased capacity to study brain structure and function holds out the promise of laying bare some of the physical correlates of religious experience, and thus of shedding some light on the nature of religion itself. Knowledge of the physical basis of heredity with the discovery of the structure of DNA in 1953, followed by the complete mapping of the human genome in 2000, also have implications for religious views of the person, and for what it is to be a human being. Developments such as these point to the possibility of purely materialist explanations of human thoughts, beliefs and desires – explanations often judged to be at odds with religious understandings of personhood.

Leaving aside developments in the sciences themselves, another reason for heightened interest in science and religion has been the persistence, and indeed growth, of influential anti-evolutionary movements. Young-earth creationism, which rejects both macroevolution and geological evidence for the antiquity of the earth, was once associated solely with conservative Christian groups in the United States, but has now begun to enjoy international success in a variety of different religious settings. Also growing in influence is the intelligent design movement which, although it differs from young-earth creationism in important respects, also asserts that biological accounts of the adaptations of living things are incomplete unless they allow room for theistic explanation. These movements enjoy a significant public profile, partly on account of well-publicized court cases relating to their inclusion in the science curriculum of secondary schools. The activities of these anti-evolutionary movements, and the reactions which they have provoked from the scientific community, have led to a perpetuation of the common view that science and religion have been, and will continue to be, locked in perennial conflict. From a philosophical perspective, they also raise some interesting questions about what counts as legitimate science and about where the boundaries between science and religion are to be drawn. Equally significantly, these debates have inspired more general discussions about the roles of science and religion in modern liberal democracies.

Confirming Newton's third law, the rise to prominence of anti-evolutionary groups has been matched by a recent upsurge in an aggressive, scientifically motivated atheism. Many of the basic tenets of the new atheism (represented by such figures as Richard Dawkins, Sam Harris and Daniel Dennett) bear directly on science and religion questions, and it is common to hear its chief advocates claiming that science and religion represent mutually incompatible worldviews, since the former is the embodiment of reason and the latter of a dubious and credulous faith.[2] These views are attended by a historical thesis according to which science and religion have throughout history been at loggerheads. Religion, in this starkly dualistic view of the world, is the primary cause of the ills of modern society. Science, by way of contrast, is depicted as the chief engine of progress and hence as the future hope for the world. To be sure, the arguments generated by this muscular atheism, like those of many of its religious opponents, have not always been of the first rank – indeed much of the rhetoric has been redolent of the old debates that prompted Broad's 'reheated supper' remark – but their emergence has led to the renewal of public discussions of the nature of science, religion and their mutual relations.

Contributing in a less direct way to a renewed interest in science and religion is the fact that dramatic technological achievements in the biomedical sciences now present enormous challenges to traditional moral positions, many of which have been informed by religious perspectives. New reproductive technologies, stem cell research, the prospect of human cloning, along with increased capacity for human enhancement and the prolongation of life, present moral and religious thinkers with unprecedented ethical conundrums. These include not only practical questions to do with specific biomedical procedures, but also more general philosophical questions about how time-honoured religious principles such as the sanctity of human life might be applied in the brave new world generated by these medical technologies. At times, new medical policies and therapeutic techniques have met with resistance from particular religious groups. By the same token, this situation has also prompted new and creative ways of thinking about the meaning of traditional religious values and how they might be applied in these novel and unfamiliar contexts.

As we can see, the questions that cluster around the broad topic of science and religion are varied, and there are a number of different ways of approaching them. Historians are interested in the mutual interactions of science and religion in the past, and the ways in which their past relations inform the present. Philosophers have a concern to see how developments in the sciences might have a bearing on traditional arguments for the existence of God, on accounts of his activity, and on perennial philosophical questions about the nature of the human mind and free will. Also relevant to philosophy are questions about the boundaries of science and religion, and the basis of their knowledge claims. Theologians are concerned to identify features of the sciences that have theological implications, and to determine whether theology can respond to these, or indeed whether theology needs to respond. Sociologists identify patterns of belief about religion and the sciences in society, and analyse the power relations between scientific and religious institutions. Finally, scientists themselves have often engaged in speculation about what implications their scientific endeavours might have for religious belief.

All of these perspectives are represented in this collection. For convenience, however, the contributions have been grouped into three parts. The first will offer a chronological overview of science–religion relations in the West, looking at seminal periods and offering commentary on key episodes. The second will provide an account of prominent contemporary issues in science and religion. The third will explore some underlying philosophical issues to do with the nature of religion, scientific explanation, divine action, and ways of modelling science and religion relations.

THE HISTORICAL DIMENSION

The first five chapters treat historical relations between science and religion. Much recent writing by historians of science has addressed itself, in various ways, to the popular assumption that throughout history science and religion have been engaged in a perennial battle. It is now generally accepted by historians that this erroneous view, known as 'the conflict myth', was largely the invention of two nineteenth-century controversialists, John Draper and Andrew Dickson White.[3] The basic position is clear enough from the titles of their best-known works, respectively, *History of the Conflict between Religion and Science* (1874) and *A History of the Warfare of Science with Theology in Christendom* (1896). Invented or not, the conflict model would not have endured had it not enjoyed at least a superficial plausibility and if it did not play an important role in the self-understandings of those who perpetuate it. In fact, this model draws support from a number of sources: our present experience of religiously motivated anti-evolutionary sentiments and scientifically motivated atheism; well-known historical cases such as the Galileo affair that seem to exemplify conflict; the assumption that science and religion are forms of knowledge based upon mutually exclusive foundations – reason and experience in the case of science, and faith and authority in the case of religion.

When examined closely, however, the historical record simply does not bear out this model of enduring warfare. For a start, study of the historical relations between science and religion does not reveal any simple pattern at all.[4] In so far as there is any general trend, it is that for much of the time religion has facilitated scientific endeavour and has done so in various ways. Thus, religious ideas inform and underpin scientific investigation, those pursuing science were often motivated by religious impulses, religious institutions frequently turn out to have been the chief sources of support for the scientific enterprise and, in its infancy, science established itself by appealing to religious values. This is not to say that there are no instances of conflict, but rather that these instances need to be understood within a broader context. Considered in this light, celebrated cases such as the Galileo affair turn out to be atypical and highly dependent on local rather than global considerations.

Galileo's trial makes for a good story, but it is not emblematic of a larger historical picture.[5]

It is also clear from the historical record that putative instances of science–religion conflict frequently turn out to be conflicts of a rather different kind. It is often forgotten, for example, that new scientific theories almost invariably meet with resistance from the scientific community itself. At times scientific opposition to novel theories has been conflated with religious opposition. In the case of Galileo, the Catholic Church was not opposing science per se. On the contrary, it was using its considerable authority to endorse what was then the consensus of the scientific community. This course of action may have been imprudent, and it offends modern sensibilities. But it does not betray any intrinsic antipathy towards science on the part of the Roman Church. Moreover, the boundaries between science and religion were drawn rather differently in the past, and this complicates the way in which we interpret particular historical episodes. Isaac Newton, for example, contended that discussion of the existence of God was a legitimate part of the formal study of nature – a view that few, if any, twenty-first-century scientists would subscribe to.[6] The piety of scientists such as Newton (and indeed of the vast bulk of scientists who, prior to the twentieth century, were committed to theism) also gives the lie to the notion that there is some kind of scientific mindset that is inherently incompatible with religious belief.

Another important consideration in this discussion is the fact that historians have become increasingly sensitive to the dangers of projecting their experience of present events back into the pages of history. Indeed it is clear that the progenitors of the conflict myth, Draper and White, were guilty of precisely this kind of anachronism, reading history through the lens of their present experience of parochial controversies about science and religion. The historical chapters in this volume tell a different kind of story – one that resists the alluring but simplistic narrative of enduring warfare, and seeks to give due consideration to the understandings of the historical actors themselves.

In the first chapter David Lindberg makes direct reference to the conflict myth, and its application to the early interactions between the Christian church and science. It is often assumed that the patristic and medieval periods with which Lindberg deals were the dark ages, in which Christianity exercised its power to smother the science that had been inaugurated by the Greeks and nurtured by the Romans. Lindberg paints a rather different picture, acknowledging episodes of conflict, but pointing out that the more usual pattern was one of peaceful co-existence. In the patristic period, science was of value to the church at least in part because it could be harnessed to serve religious purposes. In the later medieval period, the church was patron of the universities, and thus indirectly a sponsor of science, which came to be increasingly valued as an independent activity in its own right.

John Henry takes up the story in the next chapter, which deals with the Scientific Revolution – a period which spans the sixteenth and seventeenth centuries. He begins with the Galileo affair, which occupies a special place in understandings of the history of science–religion relations. While not denying that the resources of the Catholic Church were at times mobilized against promoters of particular scientific views, he none the less points out that the circumstances of Galileo's condemnation were unique, and that it is not helpful to draw general conclusions from this single unfortunate episode. Henry also draws our attention to the fact that, like Galileo himself, virtually all of the major scientific innovators of this period were religious believers, and that many of them were secular theologians who thought carefully about the theological significance of their work. Various theories of the religious origins of modern science are also described and evaluated in this chapter. Rather than thinking about the birth of modern science as arising out of the separation of religious and scientific concerns, Henry suggests that we might regard this period as one that saw Christianity set the agenda for the emergence of modern science.

Natural theology is the topic of the next chapter, in which Jonathan Topham first explores different understandings of natural theology before offering an account of its role in the sciences from the Middle Ages to the end of the nineteenth century. Topham describes the ways in which various natural theologies were mobilized during the seventeenth and eighteenth centuries not only to provide social legitimacy for the new sciences, but to explore their theological implications and, more generally, to foster religious belief in the faithful and sceptic alike. There follows an account of the mixed fortunes of natural theology in the eighteenth century. During this period it was subjected to searching philosophical critiques by Hume and Kant, while influential religious thinkers also expressed reservations about its relevance. Topham's analysis thus points to the fact that while the advent of Darwinism in the nineteenth century is often identified as the sole cause of the demise of natural theology and especially the argument from design, religious factors themselves played a role.

Darwin and Darwinism figure centrally in chapter 4, in which Jon Roberts describes the variety of religious reactions to the theory of evolution by means of natural selection. Taking as his focus the period between the publication of the *Origin of Species* in 1859 and the Scopes 'monkey trial' in 1925, and concentrating mostly on England and North America, he offers a detailed account of the variety of religious responses to Darwinism during this period. Darwin's views provoked strongly negative reactions among many of the faithful, and for a variety of reasons: evolution and the mechanism of natural selection appeared to challenge the literal truth of the Bible, the idea of a divine plan for the creation, and the unique status of human beings. Yet, as Roberts clearly shows, the story was not simply one of uniform religious rejection. Darwin also had a number of influential religious supporters and, for that matter, some highly placed scientific critics. Then, as now, religious communities were divided on the question of Darwinism and its theological import.

The fifth chapter, by John Hedley Brooke, explores the connection between science and secularization. Here Brooke challenges the superficially plausible 'science causes secularization' thesis, demonstrating that it is difficult to sustain without significant qualification. Thus, sociologists inform us that reports of the demise of religion are premature. Positing science to account for a historical development that has not actually taken place does not make for a convincing thesis. Brooke also points out that the roots of the idea of a future scientific utopia in which religion has no place is a vestige of the dated and discredited historicism of nineteenth-century positivists. That said, in his conclusion Brooke alerts us to what he calls 'a recurring ironic pattern' in science–religion relations in the West, in which religion provides the initial foundations for a scientific enterprise that will eventually seek to displace it.

CONTEMPORARY RELATIONS

An important element of the present interest in science and religion is the controversy about evolution, and in particular the teaching of evolution in secondary schools. As we have noted, potential sources of conflict had already surfaced in the nineteenth-century debates. Evolution by natural selection seemed to call into question the literal truth of the Bible, human distinctiveness, divine providence and the foundation of moral values. But beyond these specific difficulties, which mainstream Christian denominations have largely come to terms with, is the fact that for many of its detractors, evolution is more than a scientific theory – it is a powerful medium for the propagation of materialism and atheism. In the minds of its religiously conservative critics, moreover, evolution is associated with a variety of social ills: racism, moral relativism, abortion, pornography, and the breakdown of the family unit. While these specific associations may seem far-fetched, the more general perception that acceptance of evolution necessarily entails commitment to materialistic atheism has been rendered more credible by the rise of the new atheism. A number of the new atheists thus enlist evolution as a weapon in their crusade against religion, confirming their opponents' view that evolution is not just science, but an anti-religious ideology. All of this suggests that creation–evolution debates are not instances of a more general conflict between science and religion, but are a symptom of a collision between competing ideologies.

In the first of the chapters dealing with contemporary relations between science and religion, Ronald Numbers takes up a number of these issues, offering a detailed description of the rise of scientific creationism and its recent offshoot, intelligent design. While the former takes as its point of departure the biblical account of creation and is hence committed to a young earth and the centrality of the Genesis flood, the latter seeks to establish the existence of design in nature by identifying instances of irreducible or specified complexity. Common to both groups is the conviction that their work represents legitimate scientific activity, and this explains why they do not consider themselves to be anti-science. Numbers' chapter clearly shows that these movements are not the ineradicable residue of a longstanding Christian commitment to divine creation and biblical literalism, but rather a modern movement whose origins date from the twentieth century. Moreover, while Numbers points to the importance of the US constitutional and educational factors in the growth of scientific creationism and intelligent design, he also provides evidence of the increasingly global profile of anti-evolutionary movements and of their emergence in religious traditions quite remote from the conservative evangelicalism of North America. As a global phenomenon, religiously inspired anti-evolutionism is emblematic of the deeper ideological dimensions of modern discussions of evolutionary theory.

Turning from these more general historical and sociological matters to substantive issues, we can identify as one of the core difficulties generated for religious belief by the theory of natural selection the apparent randomness of natural selection. On the standard evolutionary view, human beings are the happenstance end products of a purposeless process that did not have them in mind. Such a view is at odds both with traditional religious conceptions of the special status of human beings, and with the idea of God's providential control of nature. In chapter 7, Simon Conway Morris addresses this question, putting forward the suggestion that in spite of the contingencies of natural selection, the evolution of something very much like human beings was, in fact, virtually inevitable. His argument is that natural selection is a search engine that tends to arrive repeatedly at similar solutions. In support of this view he points to the numerous instances of evolutionary convergence. These suggest that while random events clearly have a major role in the evolutionary process, it may still be possible to speak of directionality in this context. Such a perspective (which is not to be confused with intelligent design) considerably reduces the tension between the randomness of evolutionary processes and religious assertions of purpose and directionality.

Questions of cosmic purpose are also addressed in the next chapter, which deals with the larger scale of cosmology. The now dominant Big Bang cosmological theory was first proposed in the 1920s by the Belgian mathematician and Catholic priest Georges Lemaitre, but did not achieve wide acceptance until the discovery of cosmic microwave background radiation in the 1960s. In fact, 'Big Bang' was the derogatory name proposed for the theory by the Cambridge astronomer Fred Hoyle, who at that time supported the alternative Steady-State hypothesis. One reason for initial resistance to the Big Bang theory was that, unlike the rival Steady-State hypothesis, it proposed that the universe has a beginning – a proposition that for some had unwelcome religious implications. Now that the theory is well established, discussions of its religious implications continue and they constitute one of the liveliest areas of contemporary science–religion interchange. An additional dimension has been added to these discussions with the discovery of the remarkable fine-tuning of the fundamental parameters of our universe.

In chapter 8, William Stoeger provides an account of what is at stake in these discussions. He sets out the current view of the history of the universe from the moment of the Big Bang to the present, before proceeding to discuss the possible religious implications of this story. As Stoeger points out, it has been known for some time that our universe is very special and that if any of the four fundamental forces had even slightly different values, our universe would have been simple, sterile and unproductive. On one interpretation, a supernatural intelligence predetermined the basic parameters of the universe so that it would eventually give rise to carbon-based life. On another view, our universe is simply one of a vast ensemble of universes, in which case its fine-tuned character is less remarkable. Both are legitimate interpretations, Stoeger argues, and while the first lends itself to a form of the design argument for God's existence, both are consistent with a theistic understanding of the universe as created by God. In fact, Stoeger suggests, any cosmological theory will be consistent with a theistic understanding of creation, since the idea of creation refers to the ultimate source of the being and order of the universe while cosmology seeks to provide an account of that order.

In most contemporary interactions between science and religion, including those discussed to this point, religion tends to be the silent partner. It is usually assumed that science is the authoritative voice to which religion must accommodate itself, if it can. In the cases of evolutionary theory and Big Bang cosmology, it might be claimed that religion can add a dimension that is lacking to a purely scientific perspective, but this does not amount to a substantive religious input into the science itself. In chapter 9, Fraser Watts suggests that in the case of psychology and theology a different model is possible. Theology, he contends, can offer special insights into the nature of the human person and can thus both critique and enrich psychology. It does so on the first count by contesting overly reductionistic explanations of human persons, and on the second, by making contributions that arise out of its special familiarity with such features of human experience as guilt and forgiveness. Watts also demonstrates ways in which psychology can make positive contributions to theology. Here the discussion extends to theological anthropology, biblical hermeneutics, religious experience and glossolalia. The general model he offers, then, is one in which theology and psychology can be mutually enriching. This chapter also serves as an important reminder of the difference between religion and theology. The religious life is not simply a matter of making particular propositional claims about the world which are more or less on a par with scientific hypotheses. Religion typically involves practices, behaviours and attitudes which have no direct counterpart in the scientific enterprise. These non-propositional features of religion are often overlooked in science–religion discussions, as a consequence of which religions are often reduced to their propositional contents.

Drawing a distinction between religion and theology reminds us of the fact that there is a moral component to religious belief which is lacking in the sciences. Scientific knowledge is usually considered to be value free. This does not mean that scientists are amoral or that scientific discoveries have no moral implications, but rather that determining what those moral implications might be is not the business of science itself. A case in point is the discipline of bioethics, which seeks to deal with the plethora of moral questions raised by advances in the biological and medical sciences. In chapter 10, John Evans shows how, in a relatively short time span, advances in the biomedical sciences have indirectly altered in a dramatic way the context in which public discussion of moral issues takes place. These changes have little to do with explicit philosophical or theological positions, but result rather from the necessary application of bureaucratic procedures to medical ethics. As Evans shows, this has meant that there has been an inexorable rise in the preponderance of particular styles of moral reasoning – what he refers to as thin arguments – which embody the principle of commensuration and which are incipiently utilitarian. Thin arguments concern themselves with common standards of measurement and with how to arrive at predetermined outcomes. These arguments are increasingly accepted less on account of their being more morally robust than the alternatives and more because the answers they provide match the institutional contexts in which the questions are framed. For this reason, such approaches have displaced thicker religious approaches, which have traditionally been concerned with less tractable issues of intrinsic value and the desirability of particular outcomes. In a sense, then, while the biomedical sciences represent themselves as value free, on account of the institutional and bureaucratic contexts in which they are embedded they are already bearers of a set of implicit values which forestalls the deployment of thick moral prescriptions. The general lesson of this case study is that in order to understand the relations between science and religious values, we must attend not only to the logic of arguments about moral questions in the realm of the biosciences, but also to the professional, political and bureaucratic contexts in which science and its accompanying technologies are practised and applied.

PHILOSOPHICAL PERSPECTIVES

A number of general issues in the field of science and religion fall within the ambit of philosophy. Philosophy of religion deals with the existence of God, exploring such questions as whether the scientific study of nature provides evidence for God's existence and whether scientific investigation relies on implicitly theistic assumptions about the uniformity of nature or the reliability of our cognitions. Also relevant in this context is the issue of how God interacts causally with the world (which takes in ideas about divine action, providence and miracles), the problem of evil (which for some is exacerbated by the theory of evolution by natural selection), and questions about free will and determinism (for which developments in the neurosciences are sometimes thought to be relevant). A second sub-discipline of philosophy – philosophy of mind – includes within its purview discussions about the nature of consciousness and human freedom, which have a bearing on religious beliefs about the soul and immortality. The third area of philosophy that is of direct relevance to the science and religion field is the philosophy of science. Philosophers of science are concerned with the principles of knowledge used in the sciences, the manner in which knowledge claims are justified and the explanatory scope of the sciences.

One key issue in philosophical discussions of science and religion is the extent to which scientific explanation necessarily excludes reference to the supernatural. A longstanding premise of the rational investigation of nature has been the avoidance of supernatural explanations where possible. This seems to be characteristic of early Greek natural philosophy, and carries over into the Middle Ages. Albert the Great (*fl.* 1250), the teacher of Thomas Aquinas, used the phrase *de naturalibus naturaliter* to convey the idea that it is legitimate to study nature as if God does not intervene. Aquinas and other medieval thinkers adopted a similar stance.[7] In the seventeenth and eighteenth centuries, this principle was not followed to the letter – Isaac Newton famously invoked divine action to stop the solar system grinding to a halt – but the Newtonians sought to avoid explanation by recourse to miracles whenever they could. The commitment to study the world as if God plays no part in the secondary causes of nature is now known as methodological naturalism. This expression became a term of art after its deployment in 1983 by the Christian philosopher Paul de Vries. De Vries sought to distinguish between, on the one hand, a legitimate scientific approach which excluded supernatural explanations but which was still consistent with belief on the part of the investigator and, on the other, what he called metaphysical naturalism which went beyond this to deny the existence of any supernatural entities.[8]

The issue of naturalism, then, is central to questions about the division between religion and legitimate science, and about what counts as a complete explanation. Michael Ruse addresses these issues in his chapter on atheism, naturalism and science. Here he explores the relationship between methodological naturalism and naturalism proper, where the latter is understood as equivalent to atheism. Some of the recent discussions of this question, as Ruse points out, have been prompted by claims of intelligent design theory proponents, who admit to violations of the principle of methodological naturalism but none the less claim to be engaged in legitimate science. Ruse also discusses the intriguing question, posed by the philosopher Alvin Plantinga, of whether evolutionary naturalism is ultimately self-defeating. If evolutionary naturalism has the capacity to act as a universal acid, the argument goes, then surely it is no less corrosive of evolutionary claims themselves, since these beliefs are ultimately the result of natural processes directed primarily towards our biological survival (rather than towards producing minds capable of grasping metaphysical truths). Darwin himself expressed the problem this way: 'But then with me the horrid doubt always arises whether the convictions of man's mind, which has been developed from the mind of the lower animals, are of any value or at all trustworthy.'[9] Ruse contends that naturalistic explanations of beliefs do not necessarily undermine the veracity of those beliefs, pointing out that this applies equally to religious beliefs themselves which, in the event that some plausible naturalistic explanation could be offered for them, would not thereby be rendered false. Ruse concludes that while methodological naturalism has proved itself a powerful explanatory strategy, there are important questions that lie beyond its scope. These fall into the territories of philosophy or religion.

The nature of scientific explanation is also a central concern of the next chapter by Nancey Murphy. If methodological naturalism has been one key element of modern science, another has been reductionist explanation. Reductionism is the principle according to which the best way to understand a complex phenomenon is to consider the operations of its constituent parts. Related to this general insight are two further ideas – that the scientific principles of higher order sciences such as biology are ultimately reducible to principles of lower order sciences such as chemistry and physics, and that the causes that do the real work in nature are also to be found at these lower levels. While reductionism has given rise to remarkable successes, it generates particular difficulties for our understanding of human consciousness, free will and divine action. Murphy offers a complementary explanatory model, invoking the principles of emergence and top-down causation. These principles make room for non-reductive explanations which are consistent with our intuitions that for most of the time we are in control of our actions. The case of consciousness is a key example. It appears obvious, for example, that atoms and molecules are not conscious. Neither, most of us assume, are individual neurones. But with sufficient numbers, an organization of sufficient complexity and certain external inputs, it seems that systems of neurones do give rise to the property of consciousness, and this cannot be explained simply in terms of the individual properties of the basic constituents of the system (atoms, molecules and neurones). Properties of this kind, which are not susceptible to reductionist explanations, are referred to as emergent properties, since they arise by emergence out of more basic constituents. As Murphy shows, when we add to this picture the idea of top-down causation, we can also offer an account of how the mind might be able to exercise causal power over a body. But beyond this, she suggests that the model of top-down causation also gives us a helpful way of understanding how divine action in the world might take place in a way that does not do violence to our understandings of natural causation.

In chapter 13 we return to the questions of purpose and meaning, this time considering how evolutionary thinking and the process philosophy of A. N. Whitehead might together make a contribution to new theological understandings. Writing as a Christian theologian, John Haught contends that theology has been slow to adapt itself to a world in which biological and cosmic evolution are inescapable realities. Part of its inability to do this, he suggests, is owing to its commitment to a classical deity, who lies outside of time and who is immutable and hence impassible (incapable of suffering). These commitments, in turn, owe more to the metaphysics of the ancient Greeks than to Christian sources. Haught's suggestion is that the philosophy of Whitehead, which considers the cosmos to be in process and which imagines God himself to be capable of change, is more consistent with both evolutionary theory and key assumptions of the Western religious traditions about the personal and responsive nature of God. These considerations enable Haught to propose an alternative religious metaphysics which is future-oriented, and in which all things evolve towards an ever-increasing beauty in a genuinely open future. More generally, Haught's chapter serves as an example of how different models of God might be regarded as more or less compatible with strands of contemporary science.

The final chapter, by Mikael Stenmark, addresses the important methodological issue of how best to characterize the various ways of relating science and religion. Ian Barbour's four-fold typology – conflict, independence, dialogue, integration – has long been standard in the field. Even in the present collection, this typology has been put to good use by Michael Ruse. Yet while this typology has considerable virtues, not least simplicity, questions can be raised about whether it is sensitive enough to capture the wide range of positions that various individuals and groups adopt. Is it accurate, for example, to classify scientific creationism as an exemplar of the conflict model, when its proponents explicitly claim to be pro-science? What of advocates of independence for whom peace between science and religion is bought at the cost of translating all propositional claims of religion into moral statements? Is this genuine independence, or a kind of scientistic expansionism? This chapter offers an alternative framework for mapping the relations between science and religion which seeks to be more sensitive to expressed positions of the various players while retaining the virtues of simplicity and versatility. Stenmark is particularly sensitive to the fact that the way in which we conceptualize these two entities – religion and science – makes an important difference to how we map their relations. While it is widely assumed that there is a generic religion, for example, the historical religions do not in fact share a common set of beliefs; neither do all religions stress the priority of belief. When we speak of science and religion, then, it is important to be clear about what religion we are speaking of. Similar considerations apply for the various scientific disciplines, each of which may well have different implications for particular religions.

Stenmark also introduces considerations derived from the philosophy of science, noting that while the substantive claims of the sciences are obviously relevant in science–religion discussions, so too is the stance we take regarding the truth claims of the sciences and the religions. Are scientific theories always provisional? Do they represent increasingly accurate maps of reality or are they better regarded simply as models for making predictions? While many scientists are themselves realists, in the sense that they believe that their theories and models depict reality in increasingly precise ways, there are powerful arguments for instrumentalism, according to which our scientific models are better viewed as fictional devices for making predictions about the behaviours of unseen realities. The relevant criterion for instrumentalists is not truth, but usefulness. There are also varieties of scientific realism, and a range of positions between realism and instrumentalism. Clearly, however, views about the implications for religion of various scientific theories will be different for realists and instrumentalists, and Stenmark seeks to build this into his model.

Any volume such as this suffers from inevitable omissions, and there are many other topics that might have been included. Ideally, a comprehensive treatment of science and religion would give consideration to the social sciences and religion. There is also interesting new work in the cognitive science of religion not treated here. The roles of science and religion in the environmental crisis are also a subject of great importance. Certainly, moreover, most of the topics covered in this volume could have been treated in more depth. However, the aim of this collection has been to provide some historical perspectives, some general philosophical overviews, and coverage of some of the central topics in contemporary science and religion discourse, with a view to introducing readers to some of the key issues and approaches in the field. Some compensation for its omissions is offered in the Further Reading section, which provides additional resources both for topics covered in this collection and also for the absent topics referred to above.

Readers will also have noticed that while the title proclaims this to be a collection about science and religion, most of the chapters deal almost exclusively with Western monotheistic religions, and primarily Christianity. There are good reasons for this, not least practical considerations of space. It is difficult in a volume of this size to do justice even to the enormous complexity of science–religion relations in the West without adding the further complication of a consideration of non-Western religions. Related to this is the fact that substantive questions to do with relations between the monotheistic Western religions and science cluster around a common set of issues, typically to do with God's power, his activity or his relation to the world. Non-theistic or polytheistic religious traditions raise a rather different set of questions. Moreover, modern science developed within the matrix of Western Christendom, and accordingly questions relating to the historical relations between science and religion are quite rightly discussed within this matrix. Again, the Further Reading section offers titles for those interested in pursuing the relations between science and the non-Western religious traditions.

Finally, this collection as a whole was not designed to present a single view of science and religion, and individual authors have been given licence to argue for the particular positions that they believe to be warranted. By the same token, as noted above, it does not pretend to represent the full spectrum of views about the relations between science and religion. As is probably already evident, the idea that religion and science have always been, and are of necessity, ranged against each other is not a view that will find much support in this volume. This should be taken as a sign not of bias, but rather of the fact that generally speaking those with more than a passing familiarity with both science and religion have little time for the conflict thesis (in its cruder manifestations, at least). It is probably also worth mentioning that while I have not surveyed contributors on the question of whether or not they have particular religious commitments, it is a matter of public record that our authorship includes atheists and agnostics at one end of the scale and professional theologians at the other.

Notes

1 C.D. Broad, 'The Present Relations of Science and Religion', *Philosophy* 14, no. 53 (1939), 131–54, p. 131.
2 On the new atheists, see Tina Beattie, *The New Atheists* (London: Darton, Longman and Todd, 2007).
3 Ronald Numbers (ed.), *Galileo Goes to Jail and Other Myths about Science and Religion* (Cambridge, MA: Harvard University Press, 2009), pp. 1–3.
4 See especially John Hedley Brooke, *Science and Religion: Some Historical Perspectives* (Cambridge University Press, 1991), pp. 1–15.
5 For accounts of the Galileo affair, see Ernan McMullan (ed.), *The Church and Galileo* (Notre Dame University Press, 2005); David C. Lindberg, 'Galileo, the Church and the Cosmos', in Ronald L. Numbers and David C. Lindberg (eds.), *When Science and Christianity Meet* (University of Chicago Press, 2003), pp. 33–60.
6 Isaac Newton, *The Mathematical Principles of Natural Philosophy*, tr. Andrew Motte [1792], reprinted with an introduction by I. Bernard Cohen (London: Dawsons, 1968), 2 vols., vol. II, pp. 391–2. Also see Peter Harrison, '"Science" and "Religion": Constructing the Boundaries', *The Journal of Religion* 86 (2006), 81–106.
7 See Edward Grant, *God and Reason in the Middle Ages* (Cambridge University Press, 2001), pp. 193–4.
8 Ronald L. Numbers, 'Science without God: Natural Laws and Christian Beliefs', in Numbers and Lindberg, *When Science and Christianity Meet*, p. 267. See also Edgar Brightman, 'An Empirical Approach to God', *The Philosophical Review* 46 (1937), 147–69.
9 Letter 13230, Darwin to William Graham, 3 July 1881, *Darwin Correspondence Project*, www.darwinproject.ac.uk/darwinletters/calendar/entry-13230.html, accessed 24 June 2009.

Part I

Historical interactions

1 The fate of science in patristic and medieval Christendom

DAVID C. LINDBERG

> The pagan party ... asserted that knowledge is to be obtained only
> by the laborious exercise of human observation and human reason.
> The Christian party asserted that all knowledge is to be found in the
> Scriptures and in the traditions of the Church; that, in the written
> revelation, God had not only given a criterion of truth, but had
> furnished us with all that he intended us to know. The Scriptures,
> therefore, contain the sum, the end of all knowledge. The clergy,
> with the emperor at their back, would endure no intellectual
> competition.[1]

> [O]ne finds a combination of factors behind 'the closing of the Western
> mind': the attack on Greek philosophy by [the apostle] Paul, the
> adoption of Platonism by Christian theologians and the enforcement
> of orthodoxy by emperors desperate to keep good order. The
> imposition of orthodoxy went hand in hand with a stifling of any form
> of independent reasoning. By the fifth century, not only has rational
> thought been suppressed, but there has been a substitution for it of
> 'mystery, magic, and authority.'[2]

A widespread myth that refuses to die, illustrated by these two quotations, maintains that consistent opposition of the Christian church
to rational thought in general and the natural sciences in particular,
throughout the patristic and medieval periods, retarded the development
of a viable scientific tradition, thereby delaying the Scientific Revolution
and the origins of modern science by more than a millennium.[3]

Historical scholarship of the past half-century demonstrates that
the truth is otherwise.

THE PATRISTIC PERIOD: CHRISTIANITY AND THE CLASSICAL TRADITION

The leading intellectuals of the emerging Christian church in the
patristic period (roughly AD 100–500) had access to the natural sciences
of ancient Greece through the classical tradition: the accumulated

learning of ancient Greece, in the form of Greek and a few Latin texts dealing with topics in literature, history, philosophy, rhetoric and logic, theology, mathematics, and yes, the natural and mathematical sciences. The most influential texts were those of Plato (427–347/8 BC), Aristotle (384–322 BC) in the longer run, and their intellectual offspring (the neo-Platonists and Peripatetics). Other texts represented members of the Epicurean and Stoic schools. It is with this literary heritage that the church fathers, who had assumed the task of defining Christian theological orthodoxy, were obliged to wrestle.[4]

The church fathers were drawn from the Christian intelligentsia, the educated elite, from which it follows that they had received an education in the philosophical schools and therefore, to varying degrees, in the classical sciences. These were the men who, according to the myth, waged war on the natural sciences. It is not difficult to marshal evidence in favour of the myth. Hostility towards learning surfaced before the beginning of the patristic period, in the biblical writings of the apostle Paul, who warned, in his *Epistle to the Colossians*: 'Be on your guard; do not let your minds be captured by hollow and delusive speculations, based on traditions of man-made teaching centred on the elements of the natural world and not on Christ.' Again in his *First Epistle to the Corinthians*, he warned: 'Make no mistake about this; if there is anyone among you who fancies himself wise ... he must become a fool to gain true wisdom. For the wisdom of this world is folly in God's sight.'[5]

Tertullian (fl. 195–215), a superbly educated North African, took up Paul's theme with a vengeance in his treatise *Ad Nationes*, where he argued:

> Now pray tell me, what wisdom is there in this hankering after conjectural speculations? What proof is afforded to us ... by the useless affectation of a scrupulous curiosity, which is tricked out with an artful show of language? It therefore served Thales of Miletus quite right, when, star-gazing as he walked ... he had the mortification of falling into a well ... His fall, therefore, is a figurative picture of the philosophers; of those, I mean, who persist in applying their studies to a vain purpose, since they indulge a stupid curiosity on natural objects ...[6]

In another treatise, Tertullian lashed out against harmonizers for their attempts to reconcile various claims of the classical tradition with the claims of Christian doctrine. A harmonizer, for example, could, without too much stretching, identify Plato's Demiurge, a transcendent, monotheistic divinity, by Plato's account, as an early, primitive version of the Christian God. Plato's Demiurge, moreover, was a providential god, who cared for the world that he had created. If the Demiurge's creation of the cosmos out of pre-existing materials proved to be at odds with the Christian account of creation *ex nihilo*, this detail could be brushed aside as an unfortunate mistake. This and similar harmonizing efforts provoked the following outburst from Tertullian:

> What, indeed, has Athens [meant to represent pagan scholarship] to do with Jerusalem [representing Christian religion]? What concord is there between [Plato's] Academy and the Church? What between heretics and Christians? ... Away with all attempts to produce a mottled Christianity of Stoic, Platonic, and dialectical composition! We have no need for curiosity beyond Christ Jesus, no investigation beyond the Gospel. When we believe [the Gospel], we need give credence to nothing else![7]

Tertullian has been taken as representative of the Christian response to the classical tradition, thanks to popular books by John William Draper, Andrew Dickson White, Etienne Gilson, to name only a few.[8] It is true that Tertullian was not alone as critic of the classical sciences: Basil of Caesarea (*c*.330–79) shared some of his unease, rebuking philosophers and astronomers who have 'wilfully and voluntarily blinded themselves to knowledge of the truth' – who have, consequently, discovered 'everything except one thing: they have not discovered that God is the creator of the universe'.[9] But these quotations are a few sentences extracted from very large and numerous texts, and finding corroborating passages in patristic writings is not easy. Most of the opposition to the learning of the classical tradition was directed, not towards its scientific content, but towards its metaphysics and theology – matters of much greater concern to Christian intellectuals. White, Draper, Gilson and others have built their cases largely on Tertullian because they have been unable to find another equally hostile patristic author to support their interpretation. They have failed to see that Tertullian was not representative of patristic thought, but an exception. It was St Augustine's sympathetic voice that would prevail through the Middle Ages and beyond.

Augustine of Hippo (354–430) was the dominant figure of the first two millennia of Christian history (omitting biblical figures, such as the apostle Paul), and the one who most powerfully shaped Christian attitudes towards nature and the natural sciences.[10] We know a great deal about Augustine, owing to his monumental body of writings, many of them introspective. After looking for meaning and satisfaction in a variety of quests as a youth and young adult (including stints of study and teaching in Carthage), Augustine was officially converted to Christianity (that is, baptized) in 387. Superbly educated in the classical tradition, which he had both studied and taught, Augustine was ordained into the priesthood and, in 395, became bishop of Hippo (a Mediterranean coastal town in North Africa). In his later years, he authored myriad writings on religious topics, ranging from theology and doctrine to ecclesiology, hermeneutics and heresy – the equivalent (by one estimate) of fifteen volumes of a standard modern encyclopaedia.[11]

Inevitably Augustine was drawn into the battle against heretical tendencies of the classical tradition. Scattered through his writings are worries about pagan philosophy and natural science, and admonitions to Christians not to overvalue them. But his voice was often softer, and the tone more accommodating. There was no need, he assured readers of his *Enchiridion*, to be dismayed if Christians are ignorant about the properties and number of the basic elements of nature, or about the motion, order and deviations of the stars, the map of the heavens, the kinds and nature of animals, plants, stones, springs, rivers and mountains: 'For the Christian, it is enough to believe that the cause of all created things ... is ... the goodness of the Creator.'[12]

In his *Confessions*, written about the same time, Augustine argued that 'because of this disease of curiosity ... men proceed to investigate the phenomena of nature, though this knowledge is of no value to them: for they wish to know simply for the sake of knowing'.[13]

Notice that here Augustine condemned the classical tradition not for heretical content, but solely for its lack of utility within the Christian commonwealth. This stance is increasingly evident in Augustine's later writings, according to which the study of natural phenomena acquires value and legitimacy in so far as it serves higher purposes, such as biblical exegesis. For example, only if we are familiar with serpents will we grasp the meaning of the biblical admonition to 'be as wise as serpents and as innocent as doves'.[14] Augustine also conceded that some aspects of pagan knowledge had practical value; these included history, dialectic, mathematics, the mechanical arts, and 'teachings that concern the corporeal senses'.[15]

In the writings of his mature years (the early decades of the fifth century), especially in his exegetical studies of the creation story in the book of Genesis, Augustine's appreciation of the utility of the physical sciences, as represented in the classical tradition, increased dramatically. Here, in his *Literal Commentary on Genesis*, he revealed an impressive grasp of Greek cosmology and natural philosophy, expressing dismay at the ignorance of some Christians:

Even a non-Christian knows something about the earth, the
heavens, and the other elements of this world, about the motion
and orbit of the stars and even their size and relative positions,
about the predictable eclipses of the sun and moon, the cycles
of the years and the seasons, about the kinds of animals, shrubs,
stones, and so forth, and this knowledge he holds to as being
certain from reason and experience. Now it is a disgraceful and
dangerous thing for an infidel to hear a Christian talking nonsense
on these topics; and we should take all means to prevent such an
embarrassing situation, in which people show up vast ignorance
in a Christian and laugh it to scorn.[16]

Indeed, 'If those who are called philosophers, especially the Platonists,
have said things which are indeed true and are well accommodated to
our faith, they should not be feared; rather, what they have said should
be taken from them as from unjust possessors and converted to our
use.'[17] All truth is God's truth, even if found in pagan sources; and we
should seize it without hesitation and put it to use.

Did Augustine practise what he preached? Yes, indeed! In his *Literal
Commentary on Genesis*, he discussed ideas, drawn from the classical
tradition, on lightning, thunder, clouds, wind, rain, dew, snow, frost,
storms, tides, plants and animals, the four elements, the doctrine of natural place, seasons, time, the calendar, the planets, planetary motion,
phases of the moon, sensation, sound, light and shade, and number
theory.[18] For all his worry about overvaluing the sciences of the classical tradition, Augustine applied them to biblical interpretation with
a vengeance.

We have seen that Augustine did not champion the natural sciences of the classical tradition. But he did make use of them (indeed,
he judged them indispensable) when applied to biblical interpretation
and apologetic efforts. The pagan natural sciences were to serve as the
handmaidens of religion and the church: closely disciplined, but put to
use as needed. It was this model of the relationship between the natural sciences, on the one hand, and theology and religion on the other,
that was handed down and exercised powerful influence in the Middle
Ages and beyond. Indeed, as the handmaiden proved her reliability over
the centuries, supervision by the church steadily declined to the point
where she was granted a high degree of autonomy. It was Augustine's
handmaiden formula, rather than Tertullian's rant, that shaped the relationship between Christianity and the natural sciences throughout the
Middle Ages and beyond.

Easier to treat than the case of Tertullian v. Augustine is the case of Hypatia (355–415) v. Cyril, Christian bishop of Alexandria (d. AD 444). This tale, which easily surpasses that of Tertullian for drama, accuses Cyril of engineering the murder of the brilliant mathematician and philosopher, Hypatia. The story has many different tellings, but the gist of it is that a mob of Christians, acting on instructions from Cyril (the future St Cyril), brutally murdered the charming Hypatia, whose only crime was her pursuit of classical learning. As told by Edward Gibbon, 'On a fatal day, in the holy season of Lent, Hypatia was torn from her chariot, stripped naked, dragged to the church, and inhumanly butchered by the hands of . . . a troop of savage and merciless fanatics,' thereby vividly demonstrating the depth of animosity in the Christian community towards classical learning. Unfortunately for the tale and its defenders, the only recent, reliable piece of serious scholarship on Hypatia concludes that her killing was 'a political murder, provoked by long-standing conflicts in Alexandria' and had nothing to do with either pagan philosophy or Christian belief.[19]

THE CLASSICAL TRADITION FROM MONASTERIES TO THE CAROLINGIAN REVIVAL

The slow crumbling of the *pax romana* and collapse of the Western Roman Empire in the third and fourth centuries had a profound effect on Roman intellectual life. With the loss of urban vitality, many of the Roman schools disappeared, and translation of Greek philosophical and scientific treatises (never plentiful) ground to a halt, seriously diminishing access to the literature of the classical tradition. Germanic migrations into Roman imperial territory in the fourth and fifth centuries ended, for practical purposes, the Roman Empire. The vitally important task of preserving remnants of Greek and Roman scientific knowledge was undertaken in a collection of treatises, encyclopaedic in their coverage, written by authors about whom (in some cases) we know little more than their names. These include the *Commentary on the Dream of Scipio* by Macrobius (first half of the fifth century), an influential exposition of Neoplatonic natural philosophy that included material on arithmetic, astronomy and cosmology; and *The Marriage of Philology and Mercury* by Martianus Capella (c.AD 410–39), a widely circulated allegory that surveyed the seven liberal arts (the *trivium*, comprising grammar, rhetoric and logic; and the *quadrivium*, consisting of arithmetic, geometry, astronomy and music). Early in the sixth century, Boethius (480–524), a highly educated member of the late Roman aristocracy and an Arian Christian, translated various handbooks of the liberal arts from Greek to Latin, in an attempt to save classical Greek knowledge that was fast disappearing. Written much earlier, at the height of the Roman Empire, but with limited circulation until the eighth century, was the *Natural History* of Pliny the Elder (AD 23/24–79), a broad, encyclopaedic survey of the universe and the objects (animate and inanimate) that populate it, written during a period when scholars still had relatively easy access to works in the classical tradition.[20]

Meanwhile, Christian religion was experiencing steady expansion, numerical and geographical. Literacy and learning, including access to scientific knowledge, were declining – not because of Christian opposition, but because of the loss of institutional support owing to the disappearance of Roman schools and a parallel decline in upper-class literacy and the availability of books. It was, in fact, a Christian institution – the monastery – that contributed the most to preservation and the eventual spread of the classical sciences.[21] Monastic communities demanded literacy, necessary for reading of the Bible and devotional literature. They also had very practical needs that could be at least partially met by portions of the classical tradition, for example, medical treatises, herbals, and texts (astronomical and mathematical) that made a contribution to the astronomical arts of time-keeping and the calendar (needed for regulation of life within the monastic community).[22] A particularly noteworthy event was the establishment, by an educated aristocrat, Cassiodorus (c.490–c.585), of a monastery with associated library on his estate near Squillace in the boot of Italy. There, under his direction, manuscripts were collected and copied, and an impressive library of books was built up, broadly representative of both Christian and classical culture – thus giving at least a nudge to literacy and learning during a very dangerous period in the intellectual history of western Europe.[23]

The payoff of these efforts at preservation came with the reform of education emanating from the court of Charlemagne (742–814), King of the Franks. Charlemagne was himself literate and dedicated to the spread of literacy and learning at his court and throughout the Carolingian realm (roughly, portions of modern Germany and most of France, Belgium and the Netherlands). His campaign was both religious and secular – to improve literacy among both the clergy and the laity, revitalize monastic and cathedral schools, expand and broaden educational opportunity, and encourage the copying of ancient texts. His method was to appoint abbots and bishops who shared his educational goals and would push his educational agenda. The curricula of these schools quickly extended beyond religious education to all of the liberal arts – a significant outcome of which was the copying of books. The importance of Carolingian scientific interests is to be found not so much in theoretical novelties as in the recovery and preservation of portions of the classical scientific tradition and in the evident comfort felt by this tradition within a broad cultural movement that had its roots in Christian religion.[24]

TWELFTH-CENTURY RENEWAL AND THE REFORM OF EDUCATION

A new, better sustained, more powerful, and geographically broader revival of learning in the Latin West emerged towards the end of the eleventh century and continued through the twelfth, before tapering off in the thirteenth. It differed from the Carolingian revival in several important ways. It occurred in vastly different social and economic circumstances, fuelled by a population explosion that (when it was over) had at least doubled, but may have tripled or quadrupled, the population of western Europe. This, in turn, led to re-urbanization, economic development and educational opportunity. It also benefited from western Europe's first sustained intellectual contact with an Islamic civilization that had significantly out-paced Western developments, social, economic and intellectual. And it led ultimately to a dramatic, wholesale effort, stretching through the twelfth and thirteenth centuries, to recover as much as possible of the classical tradition, major portions of which had been preserved in the Eastern cultures of Islam and Byzantium.

Serious translation began near the end of the eleventh century with Constantine the African (fl. 1065–85), a Benedictine monk who rendered into Latin large portions of the medical output of Galen (d. after AD 210), the greatest physician of antiquity; also medical works by several important Islamic authors. Translation accelerated in the course of the twelfth century, as scholars bilingual in Arabic and Latin or Greek and Latin (or occasionally a pair of scholars communicating through a third language that both shared) churned out translations on all manner of scientific and mathematical topics, including fundamental sources going back to Euclid, Archimedes, Ptolemy, Plato and Aristotle. This was a massive literary and cultural transmission of unprecedented quantity, quality and scope – the labour, primarily, of Christian scholars of the Latin West (the others Muslims, Jews and Greeks).[25]

The outcome was a revolution in literacy, learning and education, known to historians as 'the twelfth-century Renaissance'. The effect on the schools was dramatic. The newly available literature migrated quickly to universities and cathedral schools, which adapted their aims and their curricula to meet the promise of these new sources. Schools multiplied in size and number, universities were founded or emerged from pre-existing schools – the University of Bologna achieving university status around 1150, the University of Paris *c.* 1200, Oxford University *c.* 1220, another nine before the end of the thirteenth century, and a dozen more in the fourteenth century.[26] These universities provided a new stage on which the complex interactions between Christian theology and the natural sciences could be acted out.

SCIENCE AND RELIGION IN THE UNIVERSITIES

The translations of the twelfth and thirteenth centuries had a dramatic effect on the nascent universities. The newly inherited body of philosophical and scientific knowledge was overwhelming in magnitude and scope, and the process of assimilation was no simple matter. The goal was to come to terms with the contents of the newly translated texts – to digest the new knowledge, assess its significance and work out its relationship to existing knowledge. Much of this new knowledge (on mathematics and mathematical science, for example) was theologically benign and easily assimilated. But one body of translated learning – the centrepiece of which was the Aristotelian corpus of scientific and philosophical works – dramatically raised the stakes. Aristotle's works covered vast areas of human knowledge – metaphysics, cosmology, psychology, epistemology and nearly all of the natural sciences – and some of this material raised theological eyebrows or worse.

The first rumbles were felt at the University of Paris (oldest and most distinguished of the universities north of the Alps), early in the thirteenth century.[27] In 1210, a council of bishops meeting in Paris forbade instruction on Aristotle's natural philosophy, owing to alleged pantheistic tendencies. This decree, applicable only to Paris and only to the faculty of arts, was renewed in 1215 by Robert de Courçon, papal legate and former Paris theological professor. In 1231 Pope Gregory IX joined the fray, renewing the bans of 1210 and 1215, specifying that Aristotle's works on natural philosophy were not to be studied in the arts faculty until they had been 'purged of all suspected error'. He admonished the committee appointed to oversee the purging to 'eliminate all that is erroneous or that might cause scandal ... so that when the dubious matter has been removed, the remainder may be studied without delay and without offense'.[28] What is noteworthy here is the nuance evident in the Pope's letter – acknowledgement that the Aristotelian corpus had value, once dangerous errors were removed. What may at first glance appear to have been a fatal blow to Aristotelian philosophy and science can be seen, in retrospect, as a charter that gave the Aristotelian corpus a permanent position within the faculty of arts. Whatever the original force of the ban, it gradually lost its effectiveness in the next twenty-five years, and in 1255 the faculty of arts passed new curricular statutes that required the teaching of all available Aristotelian books.

A second case of Parisian conflict, larger and more celebrated than the foregoing, is the much-discussed and written-about Condemnation of 1277. The papal letter of 1231 had opened the door to the entry of Aristotle into the curriculum of the faculty of arts. But not everybody was enthusiastic. Rather, Aristotelian philosophy was accepted as a legitimate object of study, a philosophical system open to criticism and possible future rejection. The risk of going too far is obvious. By the 1270s, liberalizing tendencies within the faculty of arts had spread into the faculty of theology, finally (in 1277) provoking Etienne Tempier, bishop of Paris, to enter the fray, striking out against a faction of faculty radicals. Tempier issued a decree of condemnation, containing a mixed bag of 219 heretical propositions, many of them Aristotelian, allegedly taught in the arts faculty. Fuelling the condemnation was a conservative backlash against the inroads of liberal and radical Arisotelianism in the university. Included among the condemned articles were the obviously dangerous elements of Aristotelian philosophy, including the eternity of the world, denial of personal immortality, naturalism, determinism, denial of divine providence and denial of free will. Guilty parties were to appear before Tempier within seven days to receive penance, under threat of excommunication.[29]

What shall we make of these Parisian events? They are important for the kind of evidence they represent – not the over-the-top diatribes of a Tertullian, the contrary urging of an Augustine or the inflated narrative of a murdered Hypatia, but the nitty-gritty of mundane life in a medieval university. When the faculty of arts exercised its legal rights to determine the content of the arts curriculum, Aristotelian philosophy and science had come to stay. The result was replacement of a traditional curriculum organized around the seven liberal arts by a curriculum centred on Aristotelian philosophy and science – open to dispute, of course, but on its way to becoming the official philosophy of the

Roman Catholic Church (a status it gained in the sixteenth century).[30]
For the natural sciences of the classical tradition, this was a spectacular recovery, which led to a partnership – impermanent but none the
less significant – between the institutions of medieval Christendom
and scholarly members of university guilds, dedicated to recovery and
deployment of the classical scientific tradition.

As in the case of Tertullian in the patristic period, the Condemnation
of 1277 and other Parisian struggles were exceptions rather than the
rule. Relations between Christian theology and the natural sciences
had their rocky moments, but on the whole their relationship was
one of peaceful co-existence and sometime support. Augustine's por-
trayal of science as the handmaiden of religion was still influential and
practised, most notably by Roger Bacon (*c.*1220–92), one of its most
vocal supporters.[31] At the institutional level, the medieval church
remained the major patron of the medieval universities, endowing
hundreds of thousands of students with a basic knowledge of the natural sciences.

MEDIEVAL SCIENTIFIC ACHIEVEMENTS

What were the fruits of the Western scientific tradition whose fortunes
we have been examining? One of the most important functions of any
scientific tradition is replication of itself in the next generation. This
function of the classical tradition was performed through the medium
of books covering a wide range of scientific disciplines – books that were
employed, with the founding of the universities, to offer a scientific
education to university undergraduates who would become members
of a European intelligentsia armed with a basic knowledge of scientific
matters.

But were there instances of what we might call 'cutting-edge scientific research' – any of which were foundational for, or incorporated
into, the scientific achievements of the sixteenth and seventeenth centuries? Yes, of course! Was any of it opposed by the religious establishment? Not as far as we know. The late medieval universities became
incubators of the mathematical sciences, including the science of the
heavens (mathematical astronomy, perhaps the most robust of the late
medieval mathematical sciences) and the science of motion (both kinematics and dynamics). The latter yielded results, for example, that were
appropriated 250 years later by Galileo as the basis for the first two
propositions of his mature kinematics.[32]

Nicole Oresme (c.1320–82), judged by many historians of medieval science to have been the greatest of all medieval scientists – mathematician, cosmologist and major actor in the affairs of church and state – anticipated Cartesian co-ordinates, discussed the possible rotation of the earth on its axis, dealt with the dynamics of motion and denounced alchemy as fraud. Oresme's scientific achievements, as far as we can tell, were neither compromised nor limited by his theological loyalties and ecclesiastical responsibilities.[33]

Peter Peregrinus of Maricourt (fl. 1269) performed experiments to determine the properties of the loadstone, properties later rediscovered by William Gilbert (1540–1603) at the turn of the seventeenth century. Early in the fourteenth century, a Dominican friar, Theodoric of Freiberg (d. c.1310) undertook an experimental investigation of the cause of rainbows. Experimenting with water-filled glass globes, meant to simulate the droplets of moisture in a cloud, Theodoric demonstrated that the rainbow was caused by two refractions and an internal reflection in each of the innumerable droplets that make up the rainbow-producing atmosphere (still the modern theory). Albertus Magnus (c.1200–80), the greatest field biologist since Aristotle, wrote a magnificent book on descriptive and theoretical zoology and a smaller botanical work.[34]

And last but by no means insignificant, anatomy, physiology and medicine flourished as intellectual traditions, inspired by translations into Latin of voluminous works of the great Greek physician Galen. Developments in the practical side of medicine are represented by the professionalization of medicine and the spread of hospitals, staffed by physicians and intended not as a place to die, but as a place of healing.[35]

AN AFTERWORD

If the myth of ecclesiastical opposition to medieval scientific learning has been proved false, what shall we put in its place? If it was not the enemy, was the ecclesiastical establishment of the patristic and medieval periods a consistent ally of the natural sciences? Several scholars have responded to this latter opinion with an emphatic 'yes!' Going even farther, they argue that Christianity was the source of fundamental assumptions that, for the first time, made genuine science possible. The most emphatic of these scholars is Stanley Jaki, Benedictine priest and professor of physics. Jaki has argued, belligerently, in a couple of dozen books, that genuine science experienced a stillbirth in various ancient civilizations, and only in medieval Christendom did a viable birth occur. What made this possible, he argues, was the commitment of medieval Christian scholars to the fundamental 'rationality of the universe and denial of the celestial-terrestrial dichotomy – options not seriously open to those who were not nourished on Judeo-Christian theology'.[36] A similar case has been made more recently by sociologist Rodney Stark in his book (like Jaki's, apologetic in purpose) *For the Glory of God: How Monotheism Led to Reformations, Science, Witch-Hunts, and the End of Slavery*. Stark summarizes his chapter on science in the following words: 'Indeed, theological assumptions unique to Christianity explain why science was born only in [medieval] Christian Europe. Contrary to the received wisdom, religion and science not only were compatible; they were inseparable.'[37] And how did Christian scholars of the Middle Ages accomplish this? Stark argues, following Alfred North Whitehead, that they 'developed science because they believed it could be done'.[38] Jaki's argument does not have historical roots. Stark's argument has a historical foundation, but will leave experts in the field unconvinced; and I will not deal further with their arguments in this chapter.

How, then, shall we understand the relations between Christianity and science in the first millennium and a half of the Christian era? It would be simplistic to suppose that a complex reality such as this could be captured by a single term ('opposition' or 'support', for example). We need to acknowledge the many different currents at work and the simultaneous presence and variable degrees of opposition, on the one hand, and acceptance or support, on the other. If we must have a relatively brief covering statement on which to hang our understanding of the reality (and I judge it worth the effort), I would propose the following. The first millennium and a half of the Christian era saw episodes of both opposition and acceptance between two powerful traditions, Christianity and the natural sciences, each with its history, institutions, intellectual or spiritual traditions, clientele and inclination to defend itself. On occasion they locked horns, attempting to occupy the same intellectual ground. Each had its arguments and its stake in the outcome. But in the end, combatants (in most cases) preferred peace to warfare and found means of accommodation, compromise, satisfactory working arrangements and ultimately peaceful co-existence: Albert the Great and Thomas Aquinas (*c.*1225–74), for example, argued that there were two roads to truth, each reliable in its own realm; and Roger Bacon invoked the handmaiden formula, arguing that the handmaid (the natural sciences) had demonstrated its reliability and could be trusted, with little or no further supervision.[39]

From the thirteenth century onward, the Christian church was patron of the universities and thus, indirectly, of scientific learning. As for freedom and comfort levels of arts masters teaching in these universities (short of veering into theological territory), there were no restrictions other than those applied to the guild of arts masters as a whole. There were skirmishes, like the Condemnation of 1277, in which the bishop of Paris provoked a confrontation with the arts masters. But the late medieval scholar, including those with scientific interests, rarely experienced disapproval from church authorities and would surely have judged himself free to go where reason and observation led. His level of freedom, I should think, was at least equal to that experienced centuries later by Isaac Newton at Cambridge University.

Thus the story recounted in this chapter is not one of warfare between science and the church. Nor is it a story of unremitting support and approval. Rather, what we find, as we ought to have suspected, is a relationship exhibiting all of the variety and complexity with which we are familiar in other realms of human endeavour – conflict, compromise, accommodation, dialogue, alienation, the making of common cause and the going of separate ways. And out of this complex interaction emerged the science and the religion of the Renaissance and early modern period.

Notes

1   John William Draper, *History of the Conflict between Religion and Science*, 7th edn (London: Henry S. King, 1876), pp. 51–2.

2   Charles Freeman, *The Closing of the Western Mind: the Rise of Faith and the Fall of Reason* (New York: Knopf, 2003).

3   This chapter was commissioned at about the same time as several other articles on more or less the same topic, but with a somewhat different focus; I have also written on this subject several times in the past decade. It follows that except where I have changed my mind, I have been obliged to look for new ways of saying the same thing. I trust that I will be forgiven for having pressed several phrases into service in more than one of the articles or chapters. These other articles will be cited below, where relevant to the subject matter.

4   Edward Grant, *Science and Religion, 400 BC–AD 1550: From Aristotle to Copernicus* (Baltimore: Johns Hopkins University Press, 2004), chs. 1–4; David C. Lindberg, 'Early Christian Attitudes toward Nature', in Gary B. Ferngren (ed.), *Science and Religion: a Historical Introduction* (Baltimore: Johns Hopkins University Press, 2002), pp. 47–56; Lindberg, 'Science and the Early Church', in David C. Lindberg and Ronald L. Numbers (eds.), *God and Nature: Historical Essays on the Encounter*

between Christianity and Science (Berkeley and Los Angeles: University of California Press, 1986), pp. 19–48; A. H. Armstrong and R. A. Markus, *Christian Faith and Greek Philosophy* (London: Darton, Longman, and Todd, 1960).

5   Colossians 2:8 and I Corinthians 3:18–19, both from the *New English Bible* (Oxford University Press, 1970).

6   Tertullian, *On Prescription against Heretics*, trans. by P. Holmes, in *The Ante-Nicene Fathers*, Alexander Roberts and James Donaldson (eds.), rev. edn, A. Cleveland Coxe, vol. III, reprint (Grand Rapids, MI: Eerdmans, 1986), p. 246b. The latter half of this quotation is my translation from the Latin text in *Tertulliani Opera*, ed. by Nic Rigaltius (Paris, 1664), p. 205. Other Christian thinkers classifiable as harmonizers, to varying degrees, are Clement (150–220) and Origen (185–253), both from Alexandria in Egypt, Gregory of Nyssa (c.330–95) in (what is now) central Turkey, and St Augustine of Hippo (354–430), also a North African, to whom we will soon turn.

7   Tertullian, *Writings*, in *Ante-Nicene Fathers*, vol. III, p. 246b.

8   See Draper, *History of the Conflict between Religion and Science*, ch. 2; Andrew Dickson White, *A History of the Warfare of Science with Theology in Christendom* (New York: Appleton, 1896), vol. II, pp. 31–2; Etienne Gilson, *Reason and Revelation in the Middle Ages* (New York: C. Scribner's Sons, 1938), pp. 5–15. Also Frederic May Holland, *The Rise of Intellectual Liberty: From Thales to Copernicus* (New York: Henry Holt, 1885).

9   Emmanuel Amand de Mendieta, 'The Official Attitude of Basil of Caesarea as a Christian Bishop towards Greek Philosophy and Science', in Derek Baker (ed.), *The Orthodox Churches and the West* (Oxford: Blackwell, 1976), pp. 38, 31.

10 For Augustine's biography, see especially Peter Brown, *Augustine of Hippo: a Biography* (Berkeley and Los Angeles: University of California Press, 1967); John M. Rist, *Augustine* (Cambridge University Press, 1994). For a shorter alternative, see Vernon J. Bourke, *The Essential Augustine* (New York: New American Library, 1964).

11 Bourke, *The Essential Augustine*, lists ninety-seven works. See p. 13 for the comparison with a standard encyclopaedia.

12 Augustine, *Confessions and Enchiridion*, trans. and ed. by Albert C. Outler (Philadelphia: Westminster Press, 1955), pp. 341–2.

13 *Confessions*, trans. by F. J. Sheed (New York: Sheed and Ward, 1942), x.35, p. 201.

14 *The Gospel According to Matthew*, 10:16.

15 Augustine, *On Christian Doctrine*, trans. by D. W. Robertson, Jr. (Indianapolis: Bobbs-Merrill, 1958), II.39, p. 74.

16 Augustine, *Literal Commentary on Genesis* (2 vols.), trans. by John Hammond Taylor, SJ (New York: Newman Press, 1982), I.19, pp. 42–3.

17 Augustine, *On Christian Doctrine*, II.40, p. 75.

18 Augustine, *Literal Commentary on Genesis*, *passim*.

19 Maria Dzielska, *Hypatia of Alexandria*, trans. by F. Lyra (Cambridge, MA: Harvard University Press, 1995), pp. 83–106 (p. 104 for the

quotation). Dzielska's bibliography of past publications that deal in some way with the Hypatia story runs on for about six pages.

20 On writings covered in this paragraph, see the excellent account in Marcia L. Colish, *Medieval Foundations of the Western Intellectual Tradition, 400–1400* (New Haven: Yale University Press, 1997), ch. 4. Also Henry Chadwick, *Boethius: the Consolations of Music, Logic, Theology, and Philosophy* (Oxford University Press, 1981).

21 On medieval monasticism, see Jean Leclercq, *The Love of Learning and the Desire for God: a Study of Monastic Culture*, trans. by Catherine Misrahi (New York: Fordham University Press, 1961); Christopher Brooke, *The Age of the Cloister: the Story of Monastic Life in the Middle Ages* (Mahwah, NJ: HiddenSpring, 2003); David C. Lindberg, *The Beginnings of Western Science: the European Scientific Tradition in Philosophical, Religious, and Institutional Context, Prehistory to AD 1450*, 2nd edn (University of Chicago Press, 2007), pp. 152–7.

22 On the Venerable Bede (*c*.672–735), principal monastic practitioner of these astronomy-related activities and perhaps the most distinguished monastic scholar of the early Middle Ages, see Peter Hunter Blair, *The World of Bede* (Cambridge University Press, 1970); Stephen C. McCluskey, *Astronomies and Cultures in Early Medieval Europe* (Cambridge University Press, 1998); Faith Wallis (ed. and trans.), *Bede: The Reckoning of Time* (Liverpool University Press, 1999).

23 On the educational efforts of Cassiodorus, see Colish, *Medieval Foundations*, pp. 48–50; James J. O'Donnell, *Cassiodorus* (Berkeley and Los Angeles: University of California Press, 1979). On literacy and learning, see Pierre Riché, *Education and Culture in the Barbarian West: Sixth through Eighth Centuries*, trans. by John J. Contreni (Columbia, SC: University of South Carolina Press, 1976).

24 On Carolingian reforms, see Colish, *Medieval Foundations*, ch. 6; Rosamund McKitterick, *The Carolingians and the Written Word* (Cambridge University Press, 2005). For the scientific presence in these reforms, see Lindberg, *The Beginnings of Western Science*, pp. 194–203; and, for more detail, Bruce S. Eastwood, *Ordering the Heavens: Roman Astronomy and Cosmology in the Carolingian Renaissance* (Leiden: Brill, 2007).

25 On the translations, see Charles Burnett, 'Translation and Transmission of Greek and Islamic Science to Latin Christendom', in David C. Lindberg and Michael H. Shank (eds.), *Cambridge History of Science*, vol. II (Cambridge University Press, forthcoming), ch. 14; Burnett, 'Translations and Translators: Western European', in Joseph R. Stayer (ed.), *Dictionary of the Middle Ages*, 13 vols. (New York: Charles Scribner's Sons, 1989), vol. XII, pp. 136–42; David C. Lindberg, 'The Transmission of Greek and Arabic Learning to the West', in David C. Lindberg (ed.), *Science in the Middle Ages* (University of Chicago Press, 1978), ch. 2.

26 A useful overview of the universities and university life and structure is John W. Baldwin, *The Scholastic Culture of the Middle Ages, 1000–1300* (Lexington, MA: D.C. Heath, 1971). For the University

of Paris in particular, see Stephen C. Ferruolo, *The Origins of the University: the Schools of Paris and their Critics, 1100–1215* (Stanford University Press, 1985). And for a full history of the origins and struc-ture of the University of Paris, see Hastings Rashdall, *The Universities of Europe in the Middle Ages*, new edn by F.M. Powicke and A.B. Emden, 3 vols. (Oxford University Press, 1936), vol. I, pp. 269–584. See also Charles Burnett, 'The Twelfth-Century Renaissance', in Lindberg and Shank (eds.), *Cambridge History of Science*, vol. II, forthcoming; Lindberg, *Beginnings of Western Science*, pp. 203–15; Colish, *Medieval Foundations*, pp. 175–82. For the social and insti-tutional aspects of the universities, see Michael H. Shank, 'Social and Institutional Context', in Lindberg and Shank (eds.), *Cambridge History of Science*, vol. II (forthcoming). The count of medieval univer-sities depends on the definition of 'university'. My count is intention-ally conservative; see the map of Europe and its universities (map 9.2) in Lindberg, *Beginnings of Western Science*, p. 220.

27 Fernand van Steenberghen, *Aristotle in the West*, trans. by Leonard Johnston (Louvain: Nauwelaerts, 1955), pp. 66–77; Lindberg, *Beginnings of Western Science*, pp. 226–8. Reference to pantheism indicates that the sources of influence were Aristotle's Islamic commentators, rather than genuine Aristotelian works.

28 In fact, the committee appears never to have met, and no purged version of any Aristotelian writing has been discovered.

29 Of the ample literature on the Condemnation of 1277 and its after-math, see (for short accounts) Lindberg, *Beginnings of Western Science*, pp. 243–53; Grant, *Science and Religion*, pp. 181–202; and for a full account, Van Steenberghen, *Aristotle in the West*, ch. 9. For the full list of condemned propositions, see Edward Grant, *A Source Book in Medieval Science* (Cambridge, MA: Harvard University Press, 1974), pp. 45–50. We do not know what penance was imposed or how many members of the arts faculty put in an appearance.

30 Achieved at the Council of Trent (1545–63), under the banner of 'Thomism' – the philosophical system of Thomas Aquinas, identified by the Second Vatican Council (1962–5) as the 'perennial philosophy'.

31 David C. Lindberg, 'Science as Handmaiden: Roger Bacon and the Patristic Tradition', *Isis* 78 (1987), 518–36.

32 On the science of motion, see Marshall Clagett, *The Science of Mechanics in the Middle Ages* (Madison: University of Wisconsin Press, 1959), chs. 5–6. For Galileo, see his *Two New Sciences*, trans. by Stillman Drake (Madison: University of Wisconsin Press, 1974), pp. 165–7.

33 The best source on Oresme is Marshall Clagett, 'Oresme, Nicole', in Charles C. Gillespie (ed.), *Dictionary of Scientific Biography*, 16 vols. (New York: Charles Scribner's Sons, 1970–80), vol. X, pp. 223–30.

34 For Peter Peregrinus, see Grant, *Source Book*, pp. 368–76; for Theodoric of Freiberg, see ibid., pp. 435–41; and for Albertus Magnus, *Albertus Magnus on Animals: a Medieval Summa Zoologica*, 2 vols., trans. by Kenneth F. Kitchell and Zirven Michael Resnick (Baltimore: Johns Hopkins University Press, 1999).

35 Nancy G. Siraisi, *Medieval and Early Renaissance Medicine* (University of Chicago Press, 1990); Lindberg, *Beginnings of Western Science*, ch. 13.

36 Stanley Jaki, *The Savior of Science* (Washington, DC: Gateway, 1988). The quoted words are borrowed from my review of this book in the journal *Isis* 81 (1990), p. 538. See also Jaki's *The Origin of Science and the Science of its Origin* (South Bend, IN: Regnery/Gateway, 1979) and his *The Road of Science and the Ways to God* (University of Chicago Press, 1978).

37 Rodney Stark, *For the Glory of God: How Monotheism Led to Reformations, Science, Witch-Hunts, and the End of Slavery* (Princeton University Press, 2003), p. 3.

38 Alfred North Whitehead, *Science and the Modern World* (New York: Macmillan, 1926), p. 13. But it was a different 'they' – namely, Renaissance scientists – whom Whitehead had in mind.

39 Lindberg, 'Science as Handmaiden'.

2 Religion and the Scientific Revolution

JOHN HENRY

The Scientific Revolution has always played a prominent part in the historiography of science and religion. Historians typically use the expression 'Scientific Revolution' to refer to that period from the early sixteenth century to the late seventeenth, when something recognizably like modern science coalesced out of previously distinct traditions such as natural philosophy, the mathematical sciences and Renaissance magic.[1] The importance of this period in science and religion discussions is largely owing to the *causes célèbres* provided by the Copernican theory in general (which defied the biblical pronouncement that the earth shall not be moved[2]), and by Galileo's championing of the theory in particular. Second only to Darwinism, the Copernican revolution and the Galileo affair are all too often regarded as demonstrating clearly and irrefutably that science and religion just do not mix, and indeed are essentially incompatible with one another. But this view only came to be accepted in the late nineteenth century when science became, not a weapon to be used against religion, but a battlefield, over which both religionists and secularists fought.[3] For the vast majority of us today religious belief is a matter of personal choice, but before secularism became the norm in the West God and religion were so pervasive in social, political and intellectual life that it seems fair to say that all but a very few intuitively thought in a religious way. It was as inevitable as anything can be in history, therefore, that those concerned with studying and understanding the natural world in the early modern period were every bit as religious as the population at large. Certainly, it is true to say that virtually all of the most prominent figures in the historiography of the Scientific Revolution were religiously devout, and some of them extremely so.[4]

RELIGIOUS INSTITUTIONS AND SCIENCE

Recent research on the so-called Galileo affair has shown that it involved such a unique set of circumstances that it cannot be used to establish a general incompatibility between science and religion. After all, Galileo was given permission by Pope Urban VIII (1568–1644) to write his *Dialogue on the Two Chief World Systems* (1632). Given that this was after his predecessor as Pope had issued a ruling in 1616 against the Copernican theory, it showed that the Papacy could be flexible on the matter. Furthermore, the main issue at the trial was not so much that Galileo had defended the Copernican theory, but that he had done so after being ordered at the earlier ruling of Pope Paul V (1550–1621) not to hold, defend or teach it 'in any way whatever', and that by neglecting to mention this when asking for permission to write the *Dialogue*, he had deceived Urban VIII (although Galileo had legitimate grounds for denying the validity of the stringent 1616 order against him).[5]

There can be no denying that the churches, as formal institutions, were regularly mobilized against thinkers whose writings were deemed to be potentially threatening to the church and its authority. But generally speaking, natural philosophers, astronomers and others concerned with the nature of the physical world attracted far less attention than theologians did. Cardinal Roberto Bellarmino (1542–1621), a leading member of the Holy Office under Paul V, when the church made its ruling against the Copernican theory, had so displeased an earlier Pope, Sixtus V (1521–90), that one of his own books almost ended up on the Index of Prohibited Books, and of course, a number of printed editions of the Bible were proscribed on the Index.[6] Nobody has ever argued that this proves religion per se is unsustainable against itself; it simply makes it obvious that complex institutions, widely interconnected with other social and political institutions, must respond to many pressures, and try to anticipate a bewildering range of possible developments which might result from innovation. It is hardly surprising, therefore, that the churches sometimes acted against innovations in the sciences and in philosophy; but this should not be taken to mean that religious belief and the scientific enterprise are inherently inimical to one another.

The major example, after Galileo's, of the works of a leading innovator being prohibited is provided by René Descartes (1596–1650). The Cartesian system was proscribed by the French crown and subsequently the Holy Office, not only because of its perceived scepticism, but also because it undermined the traditional Aristotelian explanation of how transubstantiation – the official doctrine regarding transformation of the substances of bread and wine into the body and blood of Christ during the Eucharist – could occur without anyone being able to taste anything but bread and wine.[7] But long before this, the earliest would-be reformers of natural philosophy, seeking to replace Aristotelianism with their own superior systems, Girolamo Cardano (1501–76), Francesco Patrizi (1529–97), Giordano Bruno (1548–1600) and Tommaso Campanella (1568–1638), were all at some point in their careers imprisoned by the Inquisition.

This kind of policing of innovatory natural philosophy was usually conducted by the Roman Church, which had administrative apparatus for dealing with such matters, but there is evidence that the Reformed Churches might have followed suit if they had had a similar administration. Michael Servetus (1509/11–53) was burnt at the stake in Geneva, under the auspices of Jean Calvin (1509–64). Primarily a medical writer, Servetus is usually credited with being the first to realize that blood travelled from the right ventricle of the heart to the left, not by passing through the flesh of the heart between the two ventricles (as was believed), but by passing through the lungs. We now know the purpose of this is to aerate the blood, but for Servetus it was to enable the blood to take up the Holy Spirit, which he held to be all around us in the air that we breathe. This was too materialistic a notion of the Holy Spirit for Calvin to countenance and Servetus was executed by the Reformed Church for, among other things, denying the Holy Trinity.[8] Cartesianism could not be proscribed throughout the federation of states in the Netherlands, as it was in absolutist France, but it certainly encountered official opposition in Utrecht and Leiden, where powerful professors of theology swayed the city councils into ruling against it.[9]

NATURAL PHILOSOPHERS AS THEOLOGIANS

Whatever the tensions between religious institutions and science, it is a matter of historical fact that many, if not all, of the leading natural philosophers of the Scientific Revolution were devout believers. Furthermore, they did not simply maintain a routine faith as they pursued their interests in studying the natural world; many of the leading thinkers in the Scientific Revolution clearly recognized a need to turn themselves into what we might call amateur theologians and to develop their own theological positions alongside their new natural philosophies. The result was, as Amos Funkenstein has pointed out, that for a short time (throughout the period of the Scientific Revolution) 'science, philosophy, and theology [could be] seen as one and the same occupation'.[10] It is important to note that this entailed, as Funkenstein says, 'a new and unique approach to matters divine, a secular theology of sorts', because, apart from anything else, theology had been a protected profession since the thirteenth century – protected, that is, from the incursions of laymen. Furthermore, although natural philosophers prior to this had occasionally found themselves encroaching on theological matters, for the most part they avoided such areas, and they always deferred to the theologians.

Certainly, the natural philosopher was exclusively concerned to explain natural phenomena in naturalistic terms. It would have been considered a betrayal of the precepts of natural philosophy, for example, simply to invoke God as the explanation for a physical effect or process. God was always recognized as the first (or primary) cause, without whom nothing would be as it is; but the natural philosopher was concerned to understand phenomena in terms of the secondary causes through which it was assumed that God always chose to operate. This assumption was conceded by the theologians, and was considered by them to provide the *raison d'être* for natural philosophy. The only possible exceptions to this assumption were miracles, but these required careful handling by theologian and natural philosopher alike, because the claim that God intervened directly to accomplish the miracle seemed to imply lack of foresight on God's part, while the claim that he achieved the miracle by secondary causes seemed to suggest, however unusual the secondary causation was (such as a passing comet, for example), that it might not have been a miracle at all.[11]

It is misleading, therefore, to suppose, as one recent commentator has, that natural philosophy was fundamentally 'an enterprise which was about God', in contrast to modern science wherein God's 'existence and attributes are taken to be *irrelevant*'.[12] For the most part, God's existence and attributes were (although taken for granted) assumed to be irrelevant to the naturalistic aims and achievements of medieval natural philosophy.[13] Accordingly, as Funkenstein says, the secular theology developed by the so-called new philosophers of the early modern period was not only 'new and unique', but also 'of fundamental social and cultural importance'.[14] Its profound importance has been demonstrated in recent scholarship which has shown that developments in the Scientific Revolution can be properly understood only against the backdrop of the theology which inspired and supported them.

One of the most important, and most recent, contributions to this scholarship, for example, has seen the new amalgamation of theology and natural philosophy in the early modern period as foundational in establishing the scientific culture of the West today. Natural philosophy was reshaped so that 'What we find with growing momentum as the seventeenth century progresses, are repeated and increasingly successful attempts to ally natural philosophy with revelation in an attempt to share an entirely new cultural role for natural philosophy.' Stephen Gaukroger, the author of this view, like Funkenstein, believes that 'Christianity set the agenda for natural philosophy,' and played the most crucial role in the subsequent cultural success of science.[15]

Before considering the major kinds of theologizing which have been discerned in the rise of modern science, it is worth asking why theology made this sudden encroachment into natural philosophy after centuries of separation. Essentially, the answer lies in the medieval handmaiden tradition discussed in the previous chapter. The pervasiveness of this tradition ensured that early modern natural philosophers were concerned to show how their new philosophies, in spite of their unfamiliarity, continued to serve theology. This was especially important, of course, when there was more than one version of Christianity seeking support. Natural philosophers from different confessional or denominational backgrounds began to insist that their natural philosophy supported their particular brand of religion better than any other. Francesco Patrizi suggested that his Neoplatonic system of philosophy should replace Aristotelianism in the schools because it was more in keeping with Catholic doctrine and would bring erring Protestants back to Holy Mother Church; Paracelsian medical theories were used by radical sectarians to support their religious views; and the work of the Royal Society, one of the first scientific institutions, was said by its first founders to be based on the method for establishing truth first developed by the Church of England.[16]

The urgency of showing how a new natural philosophy could be used to support the faith also arose from the pervasive perception that atheism was beginning to flourish, and what was worse, that for many outside the ranks of natural philosophy, the new philosophies were regarded as instrumental in helping to spread atheism. The actual prevalence of atheism at this time is impossible to ascertain (it was perforce a very clandestine position), but what is undeniable is that it was widely perceived to be a constant threat to religion and to society. Its evident emergence in Christendom in the sixteenth century is commemorated by the fact that the word atheism was coined at that time (previously there had been only heresy). Any attempt to assess the real history of atheism is clouded by the fact that charges of atheism, like charges of witchcraft, were levelled at those who merely subscribed to a different creed, but the early modern fear of atheism was undeniable.[17]

There were good reasons, as far as the orthodox were concerned, for implicating the new philosophies in the promotion of atheism. For example, the dominant matter theory of the new philosophies developed by Descartes, Pierre Gassendi (1592–1655), Thomas Hobbes (1588–1679), Robert Boyle (1627–91) and others was essentially atomistic, which was the matter theory favoured by the newly rediscovered ancient atheists (supposedly), Epicurus (c.341–270 BC) and Lucretius (c.99–55 BC).[18] Gassendi was assiduous in his apologetic efforts on behalf of Epicurus. Boyle was apologetic on behalf of Descartes, Gassendi, and atomism in general. Others, however, demonstrated the religious credentials of their own philosophies by showing the dangers inherent in rival philosophies of nature, thereby promoting, as they tried to dissipate, the view that new philosophies tended to undermine sound religion. Henry More (1614–87), who introduced Cartesianism into Cambridge University, later saw it as perniciously irreligious, while for Isaac Newton (1642–1727) Descartes' philosophy seemed to be 'made on purpose to be the foundations of infidelity'.[19]

A GENERAL THEORY OF RELIGION AND THE RISE OF SCIENCE: PROTESTANTISM AND SCIENCE

One of the earliest suggestions that there might actually be a positive connection between religion and scientific achievement grew out of the observation by the Swiss naturalist Alphonse de Candolle (1806–93) in 1873 that Protestants seemed significantly to outnumber Catholics among the ranks of European scientists, even though Catholics vastly outnumbered Protestants in the general population. When the historian Dorothy Stimson tentatively suggested in 1935 that Puritanism was an important factor 'in making conditions in England favourable to the new philosophy', she offered no analysis as to why this might be so but relied on the claim that the majority of contributors to the scientific movement in seventeenth-century England seemed also to belong to the Puritan movement.[20] It was at this point that the sociologist Robert K. Merton proposed what came to be called the Puritanism and science thesis (1938). Merton, it has to be said, relied to a large extent on the same kind of head-counting to make the case that there must be a link between Puritanism and science. The trouble with this kind of evidence, however, is that it is endlessly open to dispute. No consensus has ever been reached as to how to determine who counts as a Puritan and who does not.[21]

Merton did, however, try to strengthen his argument by offering a theoretical explanation as to why Puritanism should have been particularly conducive to innovation in science. His explanation drew on the claims of the German historian and sociologist Max Weber (1864–1920), laid out in his *Protestant Ethic and the Spirit of Capitalism*, particularly Weber's characterization of the Protestant ethos in terms of a 'this worldly' asceticism and the notion that one can have a vocation not just to the spiritual life, but also to a secular occupation or career.[22] Unfortunately, much of Merton's argumentation was vague and ultimately unpersuasive: the experimental method, he tells us, 'was the scientific expression of the practical, active, and methodological bent of the Puritans'.[23] Even so, although always controversial among historians, the Merton thesis has never quite gone away, and it is hard, therefore, to resist the conclusion that there must be something in it.[24]

Arguably the strongest historical case for the links between Puritanism and science has been made by Charles Webster. He drew attention to the millenarianism of the period and showed that this aspect of Puritan theology played a crucial role in the promotion of scientific and technological innovation. The millennium was to be a thousand-year period of prosperity and happiness on earth, a return perhaps to the way things were in the Garden of Eden. Whether this was to take place after the Second Coming of Christ or, as some believed, before it, the fact that it was to be lived on earth meant that improvements in earthly life would be required. For the reformist thinkers that Webster discusses, it was the duty of the faithful to try to usher in the required improvements as soon as possible, and to contribute as much as possible to the amelioration of life on earth, in readiness for the consummation of these improvements during the millennium. In so doing, these reformers were taking their lead from Francis Bacon (1561–1626), who was convinced that the time was at hand when man's dominion over creation, lost at the Fall, could be restored by carefully organized and well-directed labour.[25] The Baconian Great Instauration, or restoration of the true philosophy of nature, was attempted, according to Webster, by Puritan reformers seeking to prepare for the millennium.

This is persuasive, but there remains one problem from the perspective of our attempts to assess the relations between science and religion. Webster's historical protagonists are concerned with a range of pragmatic concerns, including agriculture and animal husbandry, which do not always coincide with our notion of science. If our aim is to discover the role of religion in the origins of modern science, it is something of a distraction to look at the kinds of enterprises being pursued by Webster's group of reformers.[26]

Perhaps the problem is that we have moved away from Protestantism to Puritanism, and what is more to Puritanism in England. There have been a number of attempts to refine Merton's thesis by focusing on other religious groups in England, including orthodox Anglicans who turn to science as a pious pastime throughout the civil war period, when their religion is proscribed; and so-called Latitudinarian Anglicans, whose irenic doctrinal minimalism coupled with a liberal scepticism has been seen as going hand-in-hand with a Baconian emphasis upon gathering facts without interpretation, and cautious empiricism without theorizing.[27] There is something to be said for these alternatives, but their concern, like Stimson's, Merton's and Webster's, is only with the situation in England. There is certainly more to be said on the broader issue of Protestantism, as a European phenomenon, and science.

The unexpectedly high proportion of Protestant scientists in predominantly Catholic Europe can in part be explained by various piecemeal factors. The widely known condemnation of Galileo in 1633 perhaps made it harder for Catholic thinkers to accept Copernicanism. Doctrines of the Eucharist must have made it harder for devout Catholics to accept the new quasi-atomist matter theories which were dominant in the new philosophies (this would also have tended to discourage Lutherans from embracing the new science, but would not have affected Calvinists).[28] Perhaps these things in turn meant that Catholic natural philosophers had a greater tendency to retreat into a kind of fideism when their philosophies seemed to run counter to the doctrines of their church. Certainly, of the three famous cases of early modern natural philosophers who abandoned their secular interests in favour of a retrenched piety, two were Roman Catholics: Niels Stensen (1638–86), a convert from Lutheranism, and of course, Blaise Pascal (1623–62); and the third, Jan Swammerdam (1637–80), came under the spell of the Flemish Catholic mystic Antoinette Bourignon (1616–80).

There is, however, a much more general theory, proposed by Peter Harrison, which offers a highly plausible account of why Protestants were more pioneering in science than Catholics. The notion that God is the author of two books – the book of Scripture, and the book of nature – has a long history, but the reading of the book of Scripture underwent a dramatic change from the outset of the Reformation. Rejecting the mediation of a corrupt priesthood, the Protestants urged the faithful to read the Bible for themselves. Still forbidden to lay Catholics, the Bible began to be read by the rank and file among Protestants – and vernacular translations were rapidly made available from the printing presses. Harrison's claim, put simply, is that ensuing dramatic changes in the reading of Scripture carried over in significant ways into the reading of God's other book. The more literalist reading of the Bible favoured by the Protestants led readers of the book of nature to develop a more naturalistic reading. Rather than embellishing what they saw in nature, and investing it with allegorical or other kinds of extra significance, they noted only what could be seen, and took a down-to-earth and cautious attitude to interpreting its meaning. 'The modern approach to texts, driven by the agenda of the reformers and disseminated through Protestant religious practices,' Harrison suggests, 'created the conditions which made possible the emergence of modern science.'[29] This important realization has also been taken up by Stephen Gaukroger in his major synthesis of the role of religion in the formation of our predominantly scientific culture. 'The combination of revelation and natural philosophy – the two books superposed into a single volume, as it were – produced a unique kind of enterprise,' Gaukroger proposes, 'and one that was largely responsible for the subsequent uniqueness of the development of natural philosophy in the West.'[30]

VOLUNTARIST AND INTELLECTUALIST THEOLOGIES AND EMPIRICISM VERSUS RATIONALISM

Other theories of the relationship between religion and science have focused on particular theological positions rather than confessional allegiances – although as a matter of historical fact the theological positions can sometimes be seen to be affiliated to particular groups. The first of these positions to be discerned by historians of science, and the most extensively discussed, is what has come to be called voluntarist theology.[31] Deriving from medieval efforts to define and defend the boundless omnipotence of God, voluntarist theologians insist, among other things, that God was able to create the world in a free and unconstrained way – without having to conform to pre-existing notions of goodness, for example, or predetermined aspects of what matter, say, could be made to do. The creator, or cosmic *demiourgos*, described by Plato (429–347 BC) in his *Timaeus*, forms the world out of the chaos, but there is only so much he can do because matter is recalcitrant and unsuitable for doing everything the creator might desire. In Christian theology, however, God is omnipotent, and creates the matter he requires for the creation. Like Plato, Aristotle (384–322 BC), the supreme authority in medieval philosophy, also had a tendency to declaim what was physically possible and what was not. As was seen in the previous chapter, this brought Aristotelian natural philosophy into conflict with theology. The response of Etienne Tempier (d. 1279), bishop of Paris in 1277, to the proscribed Aristotelian propositions was effectively a voluntarist stance. Notwithstanding what Aristotle declares to be physically possible, God could, for example, make a void space if he so wished.

Voluntarist theology came to the fore once again when the new philosophers sought to show that their philosophies, far from being atheistic, went hand-in-hand with the notion of an omnipotent God. As well as the ubiquitous threat of atheism, the background to this included a revival of attitudes closer to those of Plato and Aristotle, in which God had to conform in the creation to various truths, moral or physical, which were held to be uncreated and co-eternal with him. This is usually referred to in the literature as intellectualist theology, and broadly speaking its revival was intended not to defend ancient pagan thought, but to reject various strands of Protestant thought which were seen as antinomian in morality and lacking in rational persuasiveness in natural philosophy. With regard to morality, the voluntarist believed that what God decreed to be good was good (by definition), but the intellectualist insisted that God, because of his goodness, could only decree what was good (in absolute terms). The latter position implied that God's creative power was limited by certain constraints, but for intellectualists this was preferable to the antinomianism of supposing that anything, no matter how vicious, might be considered good, if God declared it to be. For voluntarists, however, the intellectualist position arrogantly presumed to be able to know what was best, and to dictate those terms to God. Furthermore, voluntarist antinomianism was bound up with the revived Augustinian notion that salvation could be achieved only by the freely bestowed gift of God's grace – it could not be earned by doing supposedly good works.

Intellectualist theology manifested itself in natural philosophy in attempts to provide supposedly unassailable rational proofs for the existence of God. The Cambridge Platonist, Henry More, for example, based his argument on a supposed categorical distinction between the material and the immaterial. Borrowing from Cartesianism, he insisted that matter was completely passive and inert, and that, accordingly, the activity in the world (including all the motions of bodies) must be brought about by an active principle, which must be immaterial spirit. Having established that immaterial spirit must exist (otherwise the world would have no activity), it is then an easy matter to insist that God must exist, and to refute all would-be atheists.[32]

The problem with this for voluntarist thinkers was that the force of the rationalist argument made less impression than the clear implication that God was not as omnipotent as he was usually held to be. The Presbyterian churchman Richard Baxter (1615–91) wanted to know how More could be sure that God could not make matter active. The cynical answer to this question is that More could not allow this because it would completely undermine his efforts to refute atheist materialism, but of course, More argued the point by combining traditional Christian dualism with Cartesian dualism and insisting that matter was by its very nature inert, and not even God could make it active in its own right.[33]

Not every intellectualist subscribed to the same set of starting assumptions, but they all ended up relying on a supposedly rationally determined principle which they discerned in the world (analogous to More's principle that matter must be completely inert), and which pointed to the existence of God. For G.W. Leibniz (1646–1716), another leading intellectualist, the existence of God was guaranteed by the complex interconnectedness of everything in creation. He famously took issue, therefore, with Isaac Newton's suggestion that perhaps the motions of the planets were gradually slowing down and that, at some time in the future, to prevent the dissolution of our world system, God would perhaps send a comet to add a gravitational kick to the system and speed the planets up again.[34] This was all too sloppy for Leibniz, who objected to the fact that Newton's God was such a poor craftsman that he 'wants to wind up his watch from time to time'.[35] The point is that for Leibniz, Newton's God was so inadequate that dissemination of Newton's ideas would undermine religion. For Newton, however, it was important to avoid the Cartesian (and Leibnizian) scenario, in which once God had set the universe running, his presence was no longer required – all could be carried on by bodies operating in accordance with the laws of nature. A world running on its own, with an absentee God, was for Newton and others, to all intents and purposes, an atheistic world picture.

Another important aspect of this rivalry is that it has been seen as shaping the methodology and epistemology of early modern science. Intellectualists are committed to the idea that, just as there are absolute principles of morality which are co-eternal with God, so there are rational principles which dictate the kind of world that God can create. As Voltaire satirized the Leibnizian position, God, in accordance with his own goodness, must create the best of all possible worlds. Since the best world is discoverable by reason, it ought to be possible for the philosopher to reconstruct God's thinking in the creation, and to arrive at an understanding of the world simply by the use of reason. Voluntarists, by contrast, deny any such ineluctable chain of thinking which guided, or forced, God's hand in the creation. For them, the only way to discover how God created the world is to examine it closely. Only *a posteriori* knowledge of the world is possible. Accordingly, voluntarist theology has been seen as going hand-in-hand with empiricist approaches to an understanding of the world.[36] It seems likely, therefore, that voluntarist theology was revived in order to support the empiricist preoccupations of thinkers like Boyle, Newton and others, and conversely, to enable these same empiricists to dismiss the rational approach of their critics not only on the grounds that it may be misconceived, but also on the grounds that it necessarily implies that God is not omnipotent, but is determined to operate in a particular way.[37]

THE THEOLOGY OF POST-LAPSARIAN ANTHROPOLOGY AND EMPIRICAL SCIENCE

More recently, another theological justification for empiricism has been recognized, namely the belief in the corrupt and deficient state of humankind, in both body and mind, after the Fall. According to this view, forcefully suggested by Peter Harrison, those who favoured the revival of Augustinianism over the Thomism of medieval scholasticism subscribed to assumptions about the post-lapsarian state of humanity which implied the inadequacy of human reasoning powers, and therefore the unreliability of rationalist natural philosophies. Adam had once known all things, was blessed with senses capable of discerning far more than we can, and with a mind which could unerringly interpret what his senses told him and enable him to achieve immediate knowledge of the essence of things. After the Fall, however, Adam and his progeny not only forgot what they once knew, but also the acuity of their senses was diminished, as were the powers of their minds. The scholastics of the Middle Ages had taken the Thomist line that Adam had originally been possessed of both natural and supernatural gifts and that at the Fall he had been deprived only of the supernatural gifts. Reason, according to the Thomist view, was a natural gift and had been unaffected by the Fall (which enabled scholastics to hold the view that, even though Aristotle was a pagan, he could still have a formidable capacity for reasoning).[38] This was counter to the Augustinian view, however, which took a much more pessimistic view of our abilities after we all became inheritors of original sin. The Augustinian view was vigorously revived by the leading reformers, Martin Luther and John Calvin, and embraced by the counter-reforming Catholics, the Jansenists, thereby introducing another important theological element into the mixture of science and religion in the early modern period. The response to this revived Augustinianism, of course, was to reject the Thomist approach which essentially favoured the use of reason, and to develop an empiricist approach, which was in itself rendered even less prone to dogmatic conclusions by scepticism about our ability correctly to interpret observations and other empirical results.[39] The emphasis, accordingly, was on painstaking work to slowly gather knowledge, either by observations or by the careful performance of many experiments, but this was accompanied not by assurances that certainty could be reached in this way, but by diffidence as to whether certain knowledge could ever be achieved.

Harrison's thesis is undeniably powerful, not only because it is backed by an impressive array of evidence from writers of the period, who all show a clear concern with the state of man after the Fall and its implications for what we can know, but also because it dovetails very neatly with many other aspects of current historiography. It stands alongside the work of Richard H. Popkin and others, for example, on the growth of scepticism from the Renaissance through the early modern period. Popkin has seen this in terms of a crisis of thought brought about by the dethroning of Aristotle and other ancient authorities, and the realization that scepticism was a popular standpoint among the ancients themselves, but it is possible that a more nuanced re-examination may reveal a theological dimension to this.[40]

Similarly, Harrison's claim goes hand-in-hand with the claims of Charles Webster and others about the importance of millenarian-inspired attempts to recover the lost wisdom of Adam for the development of modern science. While Webster has seen this as a feature of heightened millenarian expectations in the Reformation, chiefly by radical thinkers, Harrison argues that attempts to recover Adamic wisdom were a broader concern of Protestant natural philosophers.[41]

Harrison has even gone so far as to suggest that it is a concern with what can be known by fallen man that really lies behind voluntarist theology. Voluntarists reject the rationalism of the intellectualists not because they are concerned about the omnipotence of God, but because their Augustinianism persuades them that reliable rational thinking has not been possible since the expulsion from Eden. There is certainly something in this. There seem to be sufficient overlaps between the concerns of the supposed voluntarists and the post-lapsarian pessimists who form the focus of Harrison's study that it is impossible completely to separate them. It is worth pointing out, however, that to abandon the separate category of voluntarism would result in a diminishing of our understanding. The omnipotence of God certainly seems to be a pressing concern for those in the debates characterized heretofore as voluntarist versus intellectualist, and it is clear that this concern is bound up with attempts to prove God's existence to supposed atheists. The perceived threat of atheism is hardly likely to be dented by appeals to the inadequacy of our mental capacities based ultimately on what it says in the Bible. Indeed, it could even be argued that the appeal to the inadequacy of mental capacities after the Fall functions at a rhetorical level in the natural philosophical literature, showing the author's acceptance of Augustinian precepts to fellow Protestants, say, while the discussions of what God can and cannot do have a much more direct bearing on the content of their natural philosophies. It seems reasonable to conclude, anyway, that Harrison has exposed a rich part of the background to the development of the experimental method, especially in seventeenth-century England, but that this should be seen alongside the parallel and closely related voluntarist tradition, rather than substituted for it.[42]

DESCARTES, THEOLOGIAN, AND THE LAWS OF NATURE

It is evident from the depth and detail of theology into which the new philosophers descended that they were not simply paying lip-service to theology in order to avoid charges of impiety. On the contrary, it is evident that they really did see it as an essential aspect of their natural philosophies, often to the extent of underwriting their philosophical claims. A very clear example of this is provided by the first attempt to codify precise laws of nature as the basis for a new system of physics. The notion of laws of nature in a loose and vague sense (it is a law of nature that bees make honey, or that the sun always rises, and so forth) had been current since time immemorial, but Descartes introduced the modern concept of a restricted number of precise laws which could be used to explain or predict a vast array of physical phenomena. In essence, Descartes had to rely upon his laws to enable him to provide explanations of physical events in terms of causes. Causal explanations were the *sine qua non* of Aristotelian physics, but Descartes' new system disallowed explanation in terms of the traditional Aristotelian four causes. Descartes' three laws of nature, therefore, were offered as replacement explanatory principles in their own right. The second law, for example, 'that all movement is, of itself, along straight lines; and consequently, bodies which are moving in a circle always tend to move away from the centre of the circle', could be used to explain, among other things, why shot whirled in a sling will have a tendency to move away from the centre of rotation while constrained by the sling, but will fly off at a tangent to the rotation when released. These everyday phenomena in turn can then be used to explain, by analogy, the rotations of the planets, the behaviour of light rays, and other phenomena.[43]

But Descartes is supposed to be a physicist, not a law-maker, and besides, how can inanimate matter know the laws that Descartes has decreed, much less obey them? Descartes knew that he had to answer questions like this even before they were asked. Consequently, he had to introduce God into his physics. The laws were laid down not by Descartes but by God, and the laws were not so much imposed on inanimate matter as self-imposed upon God, who ensured that bodies always acted in accordance with the laws. Descartes' theology emphasized the immutability of God, not only to ensure the perpetuity of God's self-denying ordinance of always conforming to his own laws, but even to explain the second law (things left to themselves move in straight lines because this kind of movement does not require God continually to make new decisions as to which path a body should follow).[44] Here then we have a clear, and very profound, case of an innovator in natural philosophy introducing a carefully wrought theology into his natural philosophy, not on a whim owing to routine piety, but because he recognized that his physics would be completely unworkable without an immutable God to guarantee it.[45]

Descartes' theology, in its details, is effectively *sui generis*, tailor-made for his own purposes, although it certainly conforms in broad terms to standard Christian theologies. He was by no means the only one engaged on such an enterprise, however. Many of the leading natural philosophers took similar pains to show how their natural philosophies related to religion and theology. Perhaps the most prominent examples would be Johannes Kepler (1571–1630), Robert Boyle, Isaac Newton and G.W. Leibniz. Indeed, in view of the claims made about the importance of theology in early modern natural philosophy by Funkenstein and Gaukroger, we can now see why it is that the leading natural philosophers were the ones who seem in retrospect to be the most devout: they seem the most devout because they expended as much of their intellectual energy on theological matters as on scientific, and in so doing they became, *ipso facto*, the leading natural philosophers.

NATURAL THEOLOGY, DEISM AND BEYOND

Stephen Gaukroger's ambitious synthesis of much of the scholarship on science and religion in the early modern period takes due note of the undeniable importance of religion in the 'emergence of a scientific culture', but its main aim is to show 'the assimilation of all cognitive values to scientific ones and ... how this came about'.[46] In short it is a study of the rise of science, and ultimately, this is not a story in which science and religion remain equal partners, strolling hand-in-hand through subsequent ages. The secular theology developed by sixteenth- and seventeenth-century natural philosophers, as Funkenstein points out, emerged 'to a short career'.[47] Much of the scholarship on science and religion in the early modern period has been concerned with the decline of religion, as science moves into ascendancy. A major aspect of this story is, ironically, the development of so-called natural theology, which is fully discussed in the next chapter. Arguably, the earliest contributions to this particular manifestation of the coming together of science and religion were *The Darknes of atheism dispelled by the light of nature* (1652), by Walter Charleton (1620–1707), and Henry More's *Antidote against atheism* (1653). From these beginnings, natural theology went on from strength to strength. This was particularly true in England where Newtonian natural philosophy came to be used frequently in the annual series of lectures established by the terms of Robert Boyle's will 'for proving the Christian Religion'. Beginning with the series delivered in 1692 by Richard Bentley (1662–1742), the Boyle lectures ran until 1714 and helped to forge what has been seen as a holy alliance between Newtonian natural philosophy and Anglicanism which was characteristic of Enlightenment England.[48] The emphasis upon the intricacies of Newtonian natural philosophy to prove the existence of God meant that revelation was supplanted by reason, however, and the result was the growth of Deism at the expense of the traditional institutions of the church, and arguably (see John Hedley Brooke's discussion in chapter 5) the beginnings of secularization. For at least one commentator, this has been seen as the ultimate irony in relations between science and religion. R. S. Westfall has argued that the efforts of devout natural philosophers and even leading churchmen to use Newtonian natural philosophy to establish the existence of God, rather than relying on more traditional ways of asserting religious values, led many contemporaries into Deism. In seeking to overcome the threat of atheism, the Anglican Church's emphasis upon natural religion led to a deistic tendency to deny the validity of revelation and Scripture, and led to an irreversible weakening of the Church of England.[49]

Notes

1 J. Henry, *The Scientific Revolution and the Origins of Modern Science* (Basingstoke and New York: Palgrave Macmillan, 2008), pp. 1–11. On science and religion in the period, see, for example, ibid., ch. 6, pp. 85–98; R. Hooykaas, *Religion and the Rise of Modern Science* (Edinburgh: Scottish Academic Press, 1972); A. Funkenstein, *Theology and the Scientific Imagination from the Middle Ages to the Seventeenth Century* (Princeton University Press, 1986).

2 The biblical reference is Psalm 96:10.

3 See John Hedley Brooke, chapter 5 in this volume, and F.M. Turner, 'The Victorian Conflict between Science and Religion: a Professional Dimension', in F. M. Turner, *Contesting Cultural Authority* (Cambridge University Press, 1993), pp. 171–200.

4 The English mathematician and physicist Thomas Harriot (1560–1621) was accused of atheism but the truth of this is by no means certain, and besides, he hardly counts as a prominent figure in the historiography of science; R. Fox (ed.), *Thomas Harriot* (Aldershot: Ashgate, 2000). More prominent is Thomas Hobbes (1588–1679), who was also widely regarded as an atheist by his contemporaries, although from our perspective he looks more like a heterodox believer. Compare S.I. Mintz, *The Hunting of Leviathan* (Cambridge University Press, 1962), with A.P. Martinich, *The Two Gods of Leviathan* (Cambridge University Press, 1992).

5 For a detailed account, see A. Fantoli, 'The Disputed Injunction and its Role in Galileo's Trial', in E. McMullin (ed.), *The Church and Galileo* (University of Notre Dame Press, 2005), pp. 117–49. For a brief overview, see W.R. Shea, 'Galileo and the Church', in D.C. Lindberg and R.L. Numbers (eds.), *God and Nature* (Berkeley: University of California Press, 1986), pp. 114–35.

6 R. Bellarmino, *Disputationes de Controversiis* (Ingolstadt, 1586); R.J. Blackwell, *Galileo, Bellarmine, and the Bible* (University of Notre Dame Press, 1991).

7 N. Jolley, 'The Reception of Descartes' Philosophy', in John Cottingham (ed.), *The Cambridge Companion to Descartes* (Cambridge University Press, 1992), pp. 393–423.

8 M. Servetus, *Christianismi restitutio* (Geneva, 1553); J. Friedman, *Michael Servetus* (Geneva: Droz, 1978).

9 Jolley, 'The Reception of Descartes' Philosophy', pp. 394–7.

10 Funkenstein, *Theology and the Scientific Imagination*, p. 3.

11 On miracles, see, for example, P. Harrison, 'Newtonian Science, Miracles, and the Laws of Nature', *Journal of the History of Ideas* 56 (1995), 531–53.

12   A. Cunningham, 'Getting the Game Right: Some Plain Words on the Identity and Invention of Science', *Studies in History and Philosophy of Science* 19 (1988), 365–89, p. 384.

13   This has been spelt out in response to Cunningham by E. Grant, 'God, Science, and Natural Philosophy in the Late Middle Ages', in Lodi Nauta and Arjo Vanderjagt (eds.), *Between Demonstration and Imagination* (Leiden: Brill, 1999), pp. 243–67; Grant, 'God and Natural Philosophy: the Late Middle Ages and Sir Isaac Newton', *Early Science and Medicine* 5 (2000), 279–98.

14   Funkenstein, *Theology and the Scientific Imagination*, pp. 1, 4.

15   S. Gaukroger, *The Emergence of a Scientific Culture* (Oxford: Clarendon Press, 2006), pp. 506, 3.

16   F. Patrizi, *Nova de Universis Philosophia* (Ferrara, 1591); P. J. Forshaw, 'Vitriolic Reactions: Orthodox Responses to the Alchemical Exegesis of Genesis', in K. Killeen and P. J. Forshaw (eds.), *The Word and the World* (Basingstoke: Palgrave, 2007), pp. 111–36. Thomas Sprat, *History of the Royal Society* (London, 1667), pp. 371–2.

17   M. Hunter, 'Science and Heterodoxy: an Early Modern Problem Reconsidered', in D. C. Lindberg and R. S. Westman (eds.), *Reappraisals of the Scientific Revolution* (Cambridge University Press, 1990), pp. 437–60; M. Hunter and D. Wooton (eds.), *Atheism from the Reformation to the Enlightenment* (Oxford: Clarendon Press, 1992); R. H. Popkin, *The History of Scepticism from Savonarola to Bayle* (Oxford University Press, 2003).

18   G.D. Hadzsits, *Lucretius and his Influence* (London, 1935); W.B. Fleischmann, 'Lucretius Carus', *Catalogus Translationum et Commentariorum* 2 (1971), 349–65; C. Wilson, *Epicureanism at the Origins of Modernity* (Oxford: Clarendon Press, 2008).

19   A. Gabbey, '*Philosophia Cartesiana Triumphata*: Henry More (1646–1671)', in N. Davis and T. Lennon (eds.), *Problems of Cartesianism* (Toronto: McGill-Queens University Press, 1982), pp. 171–250. Newton's comment was recorded by John Craig, Cambridge University Library, Keynes MS 130.7, f. 1r.

20   Dorothy Stimson, 'Puritanism and the New Philosophy in 17th Century England', *Bulletin of the Institute of the History of Medicine* 3 (1935), 321–34, p. 321.

21   I. B. Cohen (ed.), *Puritanism and the Rise of Modern Science: the Merton Thesis* (New Brunswick: Rutgers University Press, 1990), pp. 145–58; Robert K. Merton, *Science, Technology and Society in Seventeenth-Century England* (New York: Fertig, 1970).

22   Max Weber, *The Protestant Ethic and the Spirit of Capitalism* (London: George Allen and Unwin, 1930). But see also S. Shapin, 'Understanding the Merton Thesis', *Isis* 79 (1988), 594–605.

23   Merton, *Science, Technology and Society*, p. 93.

24   Cohen, *Puritanism and the Rise of Modern Science*; Shapin, 'Understanding the Merton Thesis'.

25   C. Webster, *The Great Instauration* (London: Duckworth, 1975); F. Bacon, *Novum Organum* (London, 1620), Book II, Aphorism 52. On

Bacon's own religious position, see S. Matthews, *Theology and Science in the Thought of Francis Bacon* (Aldershot: Ashgate, 2008).

26 Webster effectively concedes this point, *Great Instauration*, pp. 517–20.

27 L. Mulligan, 'Civil War Politics, Religion and the Royal Society', and B.J. Shapiro, 'Latitudinarianism and Science in Seventeenth-Century England', both in C. Webster (ed.), *The Intellectual Revolution of the Seventeenth Century* (London: Routledge and Kegan Paul, 1974), pp. 317–39 and 286–316; J. Henry, 'England', in R. Porter and M. Teich (eds.), *The Scientific Revolution in National Context* (Cambridge University Press, 1992), pp. 178–210.

28 P. Redondi, *Galileo, Heretic* (London: Allen Lane, 1988); M. Artigas, R. Martinez and W.R. Shea, 'New Light on the Galileo Affair?', in McMullin, *Church and Galileo*, pp. 213–33.

29 P. Harrison, *The Bible, Protestantism, and the Rise of Natural Science* (Cambridge University Press, 1998), p. 266.

30 Gaukroger, *Emergence of a Scientific Culture*, p. 507.

31 First suggested in M. Foster, 'The Christian Doctrine of Creation and the Rise of Modern Natural Science', *Mind*, n.s. 43 (1934), 446–68; Foster, 'Christian Theology and Modern Science of Nature (I)', *Mind*, n.s. 44 (1935), 439–66; Foster, 'Christian Theology and Modern Science of Nature (II)', *Mind*, n.s. 45 (1936), 1–27. See also Hooykaas, *Religion and the Rise of Modern Science*; E.M. Klaaren, *Religious Origins of Modern Science* (Grand Rapids: Eerdmans, 1977); F. Oakley, *Omnipotence, Covenant and Order: an Excursion in the History of Ideas from Abelard to Leibniz* (Ithaca: Cornell University Press, 1984).

32 J. Henry, 'Henry More versus Robert Boyle: the Spirit of Nature and the Nature of Providence', in S. Hutton (ed.), *Henry More (1614–1687): Tercentenary Studies* (Dordrecht: Kluwer, 1990), pp. 55–75.

33 J. Henry, 'Medicine and Pneumatology: Henry More, Richard Baxter, and Francis Glisson's *Treatise on the Energetic Nature of Substance*', *Medical History* 31 (1987), 15–40.

34 D. Kubrin, 'Newton and the Cyclical Cosmos', *Journal of the History of Ideas* 29 (1967), 325–46.

35 G.W. Leibniz, 'First Paper' (November, 1715), in H.G. Alexander, *The Leibniz–Clarke Correspondence* (Manchester University Press, 1956), p. 11.

36 M.J. Osler, *Divine Will and the Mechanical Philosophy: Gassendi and Descartes on Contingency and Necessity in the Created World* (Cambridge University Press, 1994).

37 J. Henry, 'Voluntarist Theology at the Origins of Modern Science: a Response to Peter Harrison', *History of Science* 47 (2009), 79–113.

38 P. Harrison, *The Fall of Man and the Foundations of Modern Science* (Cambridge University Press, 2007), p. 43.

39 Harrison, *Fall of Man*. The sanction of empiricism as a result of revived Augustinianism is the main theme of Harrison's book.

40 Popkin, *The History of Scepticism*; H.G. van Leeuwen, *The Problem of Certainty in English Thought, 1630–1690* (Dordrecht: Kluwer, 1970);

L. Mulligan, '"Reason", "Right Reason", and "Revelation" in Mid-Seventeenth-Century England', in B. Vickers (ed.), *Occult and Scientific Mentalities in the Renaissance* (Cambridge University Press, 1984), pp. 375–401.

41 Webster, *Great Instauration;* Matthews, *Theology and Science in the Thought of Francis Bacon.*

42 P. Harrison, 'Voluntarism and Modern Science', *History of Science* 40 (2002), 63–89; Henry, 'Voluntarist Theology at the Origins of Modern Science'.

43 R. Descartes, *Principles of Philosophy* [1644], trans. by V.R. and R.P. Miller (Dordrecht: Reidel, 1983), Part II, § 39, p. 60.

44 J. Henry, 'Metaphysics and the Origins of Modern Science: Descartes and the Importance of Laws of Nature', *Early Science and Medicine* 9 (2004), 73–114.

45 Robert Boyle also discussed the theological implications of laws of nature. See, for example, R. Boyle, *A Free Enquiry into the Vulgarly Receiv'd Notion of Nature* (London, 1686).

46 Gaukroger, *Emergence of a Scientific Culture*, p. 3.

47 Funkenstein, *Theology and the Scientific Imagination*, p. 3.

48 M.C. Jacob, *The Newtonians and the English Revolution, 1689–1720* (Ithaca: Cornell University Press, 1976); J. Gascoigne, *Cambridge in the Age of the Enlightenment: Science, Religion and Politics from the Restoration to the French Revolution* (Cambridge University Press, 1989).

49 R.S. Westfall, *Science and Religion in Seventeenth-Century England* (New Haven: Yale University Press, 1958).

3 Natural theology and the sciences

JONATHAN R. TOPHAM

Historians of science have often emphasized the importance of natural theology in the development of modern science, invoking it in explanations of such diverse phenomena as the rapid spread of Newtonianism in Britain and the development of Charles Darwin's evolutionary theorizing. However, since the meaning of the term is not as transparent as might at first appear, it will be helpful to begin with some clarificatory remarks. A relatively stable definition of natural theology has prevailed among theologically informed writers, at least since the early modern era. This definition is nicely characterized in a British encyclopaedia of the 1840s, which describes natural theology as a theological system framed 'entirely out of the religious truths which may be learned from natural sources, that is, from the constitution of the human mind, and from the phenomena of the mental and material universe'.[1] Thus defined, natural theology is a type of theology which relies on reason (which is natural), unaided by any evidence derived from God's revelation through scriptures, miracles or prophecies (which is supernatural). On this basis, the appropriate contrast for natural theology is revealed theology; it is the source of the theological knowledge that is natural, not its object. Such a definition is in broad agreement both with that offered by Francis Bacon in 1605 and with that offered by philosopher of religion Richard Swinburne in 2005, and it is the one that will be viewed here as having been generally normative in the modern era.[2]

It is nevertheless important to note that changing perceptions of the realms of reason and revelation mean that significant changes have occurred over the centuries even in this narrow conception of natural theology.[3] Moreover, as we shall see, the arguments of natural theology have been used for a wide variety of purposes, which can easily be obscured by the imposition of an essentialist definition.[4] Partly in

I am grateful to Geoffrey Cantor, Peter Harrison, Chris Kenny, Robin Le Poidevin and Roberta Topham for helpful comments on earlier drafts of this chapter.

consequence, while theologians have generally agreed on the above definition of natural theology, the term has often been used with greater freedom in practice. Shortly before the publication of the definition quoted above, one Scottish writer complained:

> There are few subjects on which a wider variety of opinion has prevailed than natural theology. While some have held it up as all-sufficient, others have denied its existence, or pronounced it to be pernicious ... [T]his variety of opinion has been much increased by men differing as to what natural theology really is, so that what one man has condemned as natural theology, has often been a very different thing from that which another has defended under the same name.[5]

Sometimes, indeed, historical actors have used 'natural theology' to refer instead to theological doctrines pertaining to nature – what might more properly be called a theology of nature – though the source of such doctrines has often been revelation, at least in part. In this usage, it is the object of the theological knowledge that is natural, not its source.

It is perhaps this laxity of historical usage that has sometimes led historians themselves to be lax in their handling of natural theology. Certainly, references by scientific writers to design in nature have too often been supposed by historians to entail a commitment to one of the classic arguments of natural theology – the argument from design – in which the existence of a divine designer is inferred from the apparent design in natural objects. As we shall see, however, such references have often fallen far short of a natural theology, strictly defined. Far from being intended to provide a rational argument for the existence and attributes of God independent of the Christian revelation, they were often intended merely to offer exemplifications of divine design in illustration or confirmation of revealed theology. Indeed, many Christians have considered the project of a rationally constituted natural theology impossible; they have deemed the reasoning faculty of the sinful descendants of Adam to be too defective to perceive God without divine self-revelation. Yet, this has not stopped them from finding confirmations in nature of the doctrine of divine creation. It is thus important for the historian to approach such theological statements with due attention to their epistemological status – that is, to ask what claims (if any) are being made about the source of theological knowledge. As we shall see, this is not a hollow exercise in identifying proper natural theologies, but rather a way of clarifying the functions that such statements were intended to serve, or might actually have served.

THE NEW PHILOSOPHY AND THE RISE OF
NATURAL THEOLOGY

The idea that the existence and attributes of a divine being could be inferred using natural reason had its roots in classical antiquity, most notably in the works of Plato and the later Stoics. In addition, some Christians have used the Bible to justify the project of natural theology, citing passages such as that in the epistle to the Romans in which the ungodly are considered without excuse because 'the invisible things of [God] from the creation of the world are clearly seen, being understood by the things that are made' (Romans 1:20). Nevertheless, it was not until the medieval period that natural theology began to play any very significant role in Christian theology. Moreover, although modern philosophers readily identify the leading arguments of natural theology in medieval writings, such arguments were not at the time accorded the kind of significance, independent of revelation, that they later came to possess. Thus, for instance, modern philosophers recognize something like the ontological argument for the existence of God – one of the classic philosophical foundations of natural theology – in the writings of Anselm (1033–1109). However, for Anselm, a monk writing for other monks on the impossibility of rationally conceiving of God's non-existence, what was later taken as a philosophical argument was a manifestation of a 'mode of cloistered reflection that predates the birth of academic theology and philosophy in Latin Europe'.[6]

Even when taken as a rational argument, however, the *a priori* reasoning of the ontological argument makes no reference to the physical universe, reminding us again that nature (in the form of natural reason) is the source, rather than the object, of natural theology. By contrast, the phenomena of nature played a role (albeit a limited one) in the *a posteriori* arguments developed in the great theological system, the *Summa Theologiae*, of Thomas Aquinas (1225–74). Aquinas developed his famous five ways of establishing the rationality of belief in God as part of his project to render Aristotelianism consistent with Christianity. Whereas Aristotle had considered the universe to be eternal and purpose to be immanent within it, Aquinas sought to demonstrate that the universe must have been created by a first cause and that the order evident within it must have been the product of a divine creator. The first aspect of this – the argument that the chain of causes which accounts for the phenomena of the universe must ultimately be accounted for by an uncaused cause – found expression in four of Aquinas' five ways, and is now generally called the cosmological argument. The second

aspect – the argument that the purposiveness apparent in natural phenomena must be accounted for in terms of a divine designer – is now
generally called the teleological or design argument.[7]

It was during the early modern period that the belief that God's
existence and attributes could be established independently of divine
self-revelation came to prominence. As the previous chapter discussed,
this was not only the period in which a new and distinctive experimental
and mechanical natural philosophy emerged, but it was also the period in
which many of the leading natural philosophers for the first time articulated their own secular theologies (to use Amos Funkenstein's term), distinct from ecclesiastical authority and addressed to the laity.[8] The new
emphasis on natural theology, most especially on the design argument,
was to some extent expressive of this. Moreover, like other secular theologies devised by natural philosophers, the development of natural theology was clearly motivated in part by a desire to demonstrate that the
new philosophy was not at odds with Christian orthodoxy – despite any
appearances to the contrary – but rather offered original and valuable
means of support. Indeed, as we shall see, these intertwined concerns
with sanctifying and legitimating the scientific enterprise continued to
furnish significant motives for pursuing natural theology for much of
the subsequent two centuries during which it continued, at least in the
anglophone world, to be intimately connected with scientific practice.
The new prominence of natural theology was thus substantially expressive of the functions it fulfilled for those engaged in natural philosophy.
At the same time, however, it modified the character of Christianity,
placing a stronger emphasis on the role of reason in ways which some
religious commentators have subsequently regretted.[9]

Needless to say, the new natural theologies of the Scientific
Revolution were far from uniform, and the motivations of those who
developed them were not only diverse, but also mixed.[10] One prominent
concern actuating the development of natural theology in mid-
seventeenth-century England was the perception that immorality, scepticism, scoffing and other socially subversive activities to which the term
'atheism' was commonly applied had become a significant problem at the
time of the Interregnum and Restoration.[11] As natural philosopher and
Anglican bishop John Wilkins (1614–72) put it in his *Of the Principles
and Duties of Natural Religion* (1675), it was a 'degenerate Age', which
had been 'miserably over-run with *Scepticisme* and *Infidelity*'.[12] Of
course, this troubled the many genuinely pious natural philosophers on
religious grounds, but it did so all the more because natural philosophy
could readily be seen as supporting scepticism. For instance, natural

philosophers sought to account for phenomena in terms of secondary or natural causes, which might seem to sideline divine activity in the universe. Moreover, the new mechanical philosophy could easily be seen as a revival of ancient atomism, carrying with it the associated religious threat. This situation was exacerbated following the development by philosopher Thomas Hobbes (1588–1679) of a version of the mechanical philosophy which was widely perceived as being indistinguishable from materialist atheism. In such a context, it is not surprising that natural philosophers were quick to seek to demonstrate the religious tendency of their work. Nature's mechanisms, the natural philosopher Robert Boyle (1627–91) argued, provided clear evidence of divine design, and it was natural philosophers who could bring this evidence to light.

Such a concern with legitimating the philosophical enterprise by demonstrating its religious value in natural theology is evident in the highly rhetorical *History of the Royal Society* (1667). Written by the Anglican cleric Thomas Sprat (1635–1713), the work asserted that natural philosophers were best placed 'to advance that part of *Divinity*' which related to 'the *Power*, and *Wisdom*, and *Goodness* of the *Creator*' as 'display'd in the admirable order, and workman-ship of the *Creatures*'.[13] Similar concerns were also evident in the many theological works of Robert Boyle. His *Christian Virtuoso* (1690), for instance, was written with the intention of demonstrating that there was 'no Inconsistence between a Man's being an Industrious *Virtuoso*, and a Good *Christian*'.[14] Yet, like most natural philosophers, Boyle was sincere in making such claims, and his primary motivation for vindicating natural philosophy in this way lay in a deep-seated Christian piety. Indeed, his earliest involvement in experimental philosophy had been prompted by his perception that it provided a crucial means of confronting scepticism, and this persisted throughout his life. Similarly, the leading naturalist John Ray (1627–1705), who had forgone a clerical career rather than accept the terms of the Act of Uniformity in 1662, was actuated by a sense that the study of nature could be a religious vocation. His often reprinted *Wisdom of God Manifested in the Works of the Creation* (1691) was written in part to fulfil the sense of religious duty he felt as a naturalist, given that he was 'not permitted to serve the Church' in preaching.[15]

Thus, the rise of natural theology in seventeenth-century England was prompted not only by a desire to legitimate the new philosophy and defend it from imputations of an irreligious tendency, but by a range of religious motivations, including the desire to foster Christian belief in both sceptics and believers, to sanctify the practice of natural philosophy and natural history, and to explore the theological consequences of new scientific findings. In addition, some writers valued natural theology as a common core of rational belief on which people of differing theological views could agree. Thomas Sprat, for instance, argued that natural theology could assuage the fractious religious climate inherited from the Interregnum, providing a new route to social harmony through the calm empiricism of natural philosophy.[16] Such mediating functions continued to be important later in the century and, as we shall see, over succeeding centuries. Thus, when Robert Boyle left a bequest in 1691 to found an annual series of sermons in London 'for proving the Christian religion, against notorious Infidels, *viz.* Atheists, Theists, Pagans, Jews, and Mahometans', his will dictated that controversies 'among Christians themselves' were not to be discussed.[17] Indeed, it has been argued that the resultant Boyle lectures deployed a specifically Newtonian natural theology to shore up a latitudinarian commitment to a rational and anti-sectarian form of Christianity, as well as a providential reading of history that would justify the Whig defence of the Glorious Revolution of 1688.[18] However, while a few of the Boyle lectures examined the natural theological implications of Newtonianism at length – notably *A Confutation of Atheism* (1692) by Richard Bentley (1662–1742), *A Demonstration of the Being and Attributes of God* (1705) by Samuel Clarke (1675–1729) and *Physico-theology* (1713) by William Derham (1657–1735) – they were in the minority, and it would be easy to overplay such a 'Newtonian ideology'.[19]

REASON AND RELIGION IN THE AGE OF ENLIGHTENMENT

By the start of the eighteenth century, then, natural theology was a widely adopted practice by which natural philosophers and natural historians could explore and exploit the religious value of their work. This development was not merely British, but European, and works on natural theology were published in substantial numbers during the eighteenth century in Germany and the Netherlands.[20] Nevertheless, it was in Britain, and later in the anglophone world, that the natural theology tradition was strongest and longest lived. Several explanations have been offered for this. Following Margaret Jacob, John Gascoigne has suggested that the 'holy alliance' between Newtonianism and Anglican apologetics was fostered through much of the eighteenth century by political considerations deriving from the Glorious Revolution.[21] Another explanation is offered by John Brooke, who suggests that natural theology

prospered in eighteenth-century England as a manifestation of the inclu-
siveness of the English Enlightenment. It was an expression of the manner in which, in the peculiar socio-political conditions that prevailed
following the 1688 revolution, values of critical thought and progressiv-
ism were found to be consistent with the existing religious authorities.
Moreover, he suggests that the development of a market economy in
Britain may have contributed to breaking down divisions between people
of different religious affiliations. Once again, natural theology may have
served a mediating function, providing a common core of religious truth
about which all could agree.[22]

This view of natural theology seems to be implied by Anglican apologist Joseph Butler's observation, in his *Analogy of Religion, Natural and
Revealed, to the Constitution and Course of Nature* (1736), that 'natural religion' was 'the foundation and the principal part of Christianity'.
However, Butler's book was prompted by the desire to demonstrate that
it was 'not in any sense the whole' of Christianity.[23] This was a response
to the deist belief that all true religious doctrines could be known by
reason alone, and that reason disclosed a creator God whose agency
in the world was manifested in natural laws rather than supernatural
acts. Such views became increasingly prevalent in early eighteenth-
century Britain, finding expression in such works as *Christianity Not
Mysterious* ([1695]) by John Toland (1670–1722) and *Christianity as Old
as the Creation* (1731) by Matthew Tindal (1657–1733). In such circumstances, the challenge for Christian natural theologians – more pressing
now than it had been in the previous century – was to establish that the
God disclosed by natural theology was the God of the Bible and supernatural Christianity, rather than the God of Deism. Butler's approach
was to argue that the deist rejection of revealed religion was irrational,
since natural and revealed religion were subject to precisely analogous
difficulties, and that in each case the accumulation of probable evidence, while short of a logical demonstration, was capable of delivering
moral certainty. According to Butler, deists claimed too much certainty
for natural theology, and demanded too much certainty from revealed
theology. In religion, as more generally, he observed, it was probability
that was 'the very guide of life'.[24]

Butler's accusation that the natural theology of the deists was
over-reaching itself finds an echo in the devastating philosophical
assaults to which natural theology was subjected later in the eighteenth
century. In Britain, the most important of these appeared in the posthu-
mously published *Dialogues Concerning Natural Religion* (1779) of the
Scottish philosopher and sceptic David Hume (1711–76). (The equally

devastating, and in certain respects similar, critique of the German philosopher Immanuel Kant (1724–1804) was not at first widely known in Britain.[25]) For Hume, the foundations of religion – like those of morality – lay not in reason but in the affections or feelings, and his work provided a thoroughgoing critical examination of the arguments of natural theology. Hume argued that the central analogy between natural phenomena and human artefacts could not be used convincingly to infer the God of Christianity. The universe was so unlike human productions that the analogy between the two was extremely tenuous and the most that could be claimed was 'a guess, a conjecture, a presumption concerning a similar cause'.[26] This was doubly so, given that such analogies were based on so limited a knowledge of the universe; perhaps at other times and in other places nature was even less like a machine. Furthermore, this was the only universe of which anyone had experience, invalidating it as the basis of an inductive inference, and in any case, no one had had direct experience of the creation of a universe. Even if one allowed that the universe was the product of an intelligent designer, Hume suggested, that would only lead to an infinite regress, since the designer's intelligence would require explanation. Moreover, since the cause inferred must be proportionate to the effects, such a designer could not be the infinite being of Christian theology. Indeed, one could not be sure whether there were one designer or many, or, indeed, given the imperfections in nature, whether the designer(s) were incompetent or malevolent. There were, furthermore, other analogies that might be considered to be at least as satisfactory as that between the universe and a machine, such as that between the universe and a living organism. In this case, one might argue that, since all animals were actuated by a soul, God must be the soul of the world; or one might argue that, like a plant, the world had grown from a seed. Finally, with an eye to Epicureanism, Hume observed that the appearances of design in nature might reasonably be accounted for as the fortuitous consequences of a chaotic system of matter in motion.

It has sometimes seemed inexplicable to historians that natural theology, and particularly the argument from design, continued to be so prevalent in the anglophone world in the wake of Hume's assault. In particular, the clear and confident statement of the design argument in the immensely popular *Natural Theology* (1802) of Anglican theologian William Paley (1743–1805) might appear naïve when juxtaposed with Hume's objections. Paley retained a strong commitment to natural theology as the rational foundation for the entire scheme of Christian theology. Indeed, his *Natural Theology* was designed to provide the first part of a theological system which subsequently proceeded to the *Evidences of Christianity* (1794) and the *Principles of Moral and Political Philosophy* (1785). The work began with a memorable exposition, involving the example of a watch, of the analogy between natural phenomena and human mechanism. This was followed by an immense catalogue of examples of design in nature – mostly in living organisms, and particularly in animals – before the work returned briefly to consider the divine attributes in more detail at the end. However, while Paley responded only implicitly to Hume's critique, he nevertheless responded, as others had also done.[27] In his first two chapters, for instance, he considered several possible objections to his analogical argument and later in the work he confronted some alternative explanations of apparent design. Moreover, when Paley turned to the divine attributes he implicitly accepted certain of the limitations which Hume had insisted applied to the design analogy. Thus, for instance, he revealed an appreciation that the design argument was far from establishing the God of Christian theology when he admitted that terms such as 'omnipotence' were merely 'superlatives' and belief in the 'unity of the Deity' could go no further than 'unity of counsel'.[28]

Paley was not alone among writers on natural theology in being aware of certain of the epistemological limitations of the design argument. Indeed, as John Brooke and Geoffrey Cantor have emphasized, writers on natural theology generally appreciated that the design argument was not a proof in the strong, deductive sense of the term. Such writers nevertheless considered that, as the design argument was an inductive inference, the accumulation of evidence could increase the probability of the conclusion until it was sufficient to justify action (that is, until it reached 'moral certainty'). This was why William Paley informed his readers that the argument was cumulative and gave such a vast array of examples of design in his *Natural Theology*. Moreover, works of natural theology were generally rhetorical in character: they were designed to appeal not just to the reason, but also to the imagination and feelings of readers. The argument from design was not like a mathematical proof, and readers had to be persuaded of its truth by these tried and tested means. It would thus be a mistake to read such works as abstract specimens of philosophical theology, and to ridicule them for their failings as such.[29] Rather, the historian's task is to examine what purposes such works continued to fulfil as the logic of the argument came under increasing scrutiny – a point to which we will shortly return.

SCIENCE AND DESIGN IN THE AGE OF REVOLUTIONS

The theological rationalism of William Paley was, in any case, increasingly out of keeping with the religious tenor of England at the turn of the eighteenth century. John Gascoigne claims that the 'holy alliance' which he identifies as having united Newtonianism with Anglican apologetics throughout the eighteenth century, came increasingly under challenge in the last third of it from those who wished to reassert the relative importance of revelation.[30] In particular, the growing prominence in Anglicanism of the High Church and evangelical parties raised the status of revealed, as opposed to natural, theology. This was especially the case in the years after the French Revolution of 1789, when anxieties about the political radicalism of Unitarians and deists led High Church apologists to conclude that natural theology not only would fail to answer the church's opponents, but might even constitute part of the problem. Thomas Paine (1737–1809), whose widely read radical political and religious publications caused panic in the British establishment from the 1790s onwards, had, after all, endorsed the argument from design at length in his fiercely anti-Christian *Age of Reason* (1794–1807). As Pietro Corsi has shown, when the young High Church mathematician Baden Powell (1796–1860) wrote his *Rational Religion Examined* in 1826, he viewed natural theology as 'an insufficient and to some extent dangerous exercise'.[31]

The evangelicals – both in the established churches and among the dissenters – who came largely to dominate British culture in the nineteenth century, also often had significant doubts about natural theology. To many, it seemed that human reason, clouded by sin after Adam's fall from grace, was largely or totally incapable of discerning divine truth. In any case, they claimed, the route to salvation lay not in the mind, but in the heart convinced of its sinfulness and of its need of divine grace. Evangelicals were not, however, uniformly antagonistic towards natural theology. There were certainly many who found a limited but important role for it within their theological systems and apologetic practices, often tailoring it in distinctive ways.[32] Moreover, even those evangelicals (and others) who were dubious about, or antagonistic towards, the project of natural theology were quite prepared to engage in a discourse of design which resembled a natural theology, while falling far short of its epistemological claims. Nevertheless, looking back in 1874, Anglican Broad Churchman Charles Kingsley (1819–75) observed, with an eye to the nineteenth-century emphasis on personal religion, that for two or three generations the 'religious temper of England' had been 'unfavourable to a sound and scientific development of natural theology'.[33]

Given the extent to which the utility and even the validity of natural theology was now being questioned by Christian theologians and believers in Britain, it is striking how widespread references to design were in scientific pronouncements and publications. As John Brooke has established, the reasons for this were complex and multiform. One important consideration was certainly the continuing obligation felt by men of science to demonstrate the utility and safety of their work in both religious and social terms. In the decades following the French Revolution, it became important to demonstrate that new scientific findings would not lead to irreligion or revolutionary radicalism, as they were perceived to have done in France. In particular, British men of science exercised great care when handling important works by French natural philosophers and naturalists that were associated with atheism and Deism – most notably those of Pierre-Simon Laplace (1749–1827) and Jean-Baptiste Lamarck (1744–1829). By showing that the latest findings in the sciences could be rendered consistent with, or even enhance, the arguments of natural theology, they were able to fend off imputations of impiety and radicalism.[34]

This was all the more necessary since some of those involved in the new movements of working-class radicalism, like atheist agitator Richard Carlile (1790–1843), were keen to enlist 'the men of science' in a propaganda war against church and state.[35] In the social ferment of early nineteenth-century Britain, the commitment of men of science to natural theology thus acquired a political edge, often providing an implicit or explicit apology for the status quo. The politics of natural theology were played out in the 1820s and 1830s in the medical schools and new university colleges of London, where a commitment to design was sometimes identified with a resistance to reform.[36] However, it is important to recognize that political radicals, too, often used a discourse of design to further their ends. Whereas providential writers suggested that God's perfect design found in nature paralleled a similar perfection in the ordering of society, prophetic writers (like Thomas Paine) used the perfection of nature to highlight the failure of society to match up to God's plan. As anthropologist Clifford Geertz has noted of systems of religious symbols more generally, natural theology could thus provide a (reformist) model *for* social reality, as well as a (conservative) model *of* social reality.[37]

While natural theology was certainly valuable as a means of defending the practice of science in troubled times, it does not follow that the men of science who employed it were necessarily insincere. On the contrary, most of those who practised science were Christians, and many (especially those based at the Anglican universities of Oxford and Cambridge) were clergymen, for whom natural theology provided a means of productively combining religious and scientific concerns. Those in Oxford and Cambridge found natural theology especially useful in attempting to demonstrate the value of the sciences within the religiously based curriculum. For instance, in his 1819 inaugural lecture as Oxford's first Reader in Geology, William Buckland argued that his subject was of value to the university, because of the new evidences it provided of the truths of natural theology.[38] More generally, indeed, leading British scientists used natural theology to advertise the religious value of the sciences to the nation at large, as, for instance, through the British Association for the Advancement of Science, which was founded in 1831. Furthermore, it was precisely in such contexts as the British Association that natural theology came into its own in providing a common basis for those of differing denominational commitments to work together in harmony.[39]

While scientific practitioners in Britain thus continued to find natural theology valuable in a number of ways, they also reflected the growing ambiguity of Christians towards natural theology. A good measure of this is provided by the *Bridgewater Treatises* (1833–6), an important series of eight substantial works on the 'power, goodness, and wisdom of God as manifested in the creation' published by leading men of science in response to a bequest administered by the president of the Royal Society. The work was parcelled out so that subject specialists could expound the indications of divine design in their several disciplines, but while half the authors were ordained clergy, most made no attempt to provide a justification of the design argument. Moreover, the more theologically astute of the authors were distinctly circumspect about both its epistemological validity and its apologetic usefulness. In fact, the terms of the Bridgewater bequest themselves did not specify that the authors should develop a natural theology as such, since they implicitly allowed that the divine attributes could be made manifest in creation by the light of revelation as much as by reason. The Cambridge natural philosopher and polymath William Whewell (1794–1866) took his cue from this. What he had been asked to do, he observed, was 'to lead the friends of religion to look with confidence and pleasure on the progress of the physical sciences, by showing how admirably every advance in our knowledge of the universe harmonizes with the belief of a most wise and good God'.[40]

It was certainly this aspect of the *Bridgewater Treatises* that was particularly prized by most of those who read them, including many who were frankly dubious about or critical of the project of natural theology. Indeed, the commercial success of the series far outstripped the expectations of publishers, precisely because the treatises provided an up-to-date conspectus of the sciences, written by respected specialists, but combined with religious reflections in a way which was considered safe. This response reflected a growing concern among a wide range of Christians in the early nineteenth century about the effects that secular scientific reading might have in denuding religious sensibilities. Starting in the 1820s, the rapid expansion of the market for cheap literature on the sciences – often now for the first time conceived of as popular science – introduced scientific reading to a far wider population than ever before. Christian organizations and individuals of many hues were concerned by this development, since much of what was produced made no reference to God's agency in the natural world, and some of it was considered to be directly at odds with Christian doctrine. The arguments of natural theology might have been considered to be of limited epistemological or apologetic value, but works like the *Bridgewater Treatises*, which expounded the sciences in relation to divine design (or even in relation to the Bible), helped Christians to incorporate scientific reading within the daily practice of religion, eliciting feelings of religious devotion and confirming the validity of a faith based on other grounds entirely.[41]

NATURAL THEOLOGY AND NATURALISM IN THE AGE OF DARWIN

It is important, then, not to overestimate the extent to which men of science, and more especially the churches, were committed to natural theology, strictly so called, in early nineteenth-century Britain. One reason why historians have perhaps tended to do so is to be found in the manner in which Darwin's theory of evolution by natural selection is seen to have turned Paley's natural theology on its head. Darwin read Paley's *Natural Theology* as an undergraduate in Cambridge, where he was studying to become a clergyman, and he was profoundly impressed by its argument. Paley's fascination with the adaptation of structure to function in living organisms became Darwin's, too, and his work on a theory of species change in the 1830s was in part devoted to explaining such adaptation. Indeed, many years later, he told his publisher that his book on the adaptations by which orchids ensured cross-pollination was 'Like a Bridgewater Treatise'.[42] Yet, while Darwin accepted Paley's *explanandum*, he ultimately offered a different *explanans* – natural selection – which he felt undermined Paley's inference of a designer. However, this contrast between Paley's version of the design argument and Darwin's theory of natural selection not only tends to overemphasize the importance in Britain of the design argument as an argument in the years before Darwin's *Origin of Species* (1859), but also suggests too simplistic a view of the debate about design in the intervening half-century. In fact, as several historians have shown, natural theology had undergone considerable change in the interim, making the Paley–Darwin contrast distinctly anachronistic.

These developments in natural theology are nicely illustrated by the *Bridgewater Treatises*, whose authors, far from codifying a relatively homogeneous Paleyite natural theology, which Robert M. Young claimed was pervasive in British intellectual culture in the decades before 1859, departed from Paley's approach in a number of ways.[43] As we saw above, they were anxious for a variety of reasons to demonstrate that recent changes in the sciences only enhanced the impression of divine agency in the universe. One such scientific development was the historicization of the created order. Paley's *Natural Theology* had done nothing to disturb the standard view that the natural world had come into being relatively recently – within the six thousand years of established biblical chronology – as the result of a week of divine miraculous creation. Yet, in the decades that followed, the newly emerging science of geology provided an increasingly complex picture of an earth history that extended over millions of years. Thus, when William Buckland published his *Bridgewater Treatise* on geology in 1836, he provided an account of creation which charted the long history of the earth from a nebulous cloud of gas and dust through a progressive series of geological epochs to the present era. According to Buckland, these developments only added to the evidence of natural theology, showing that the same kind of adaptation was to be found in the extinct species of earlier eras as at the present time. Moreover, while Buckland believed that the progressive history of the earth was a consequence of the operation of natural laws, he thought the introduction of new species at the start of each geological epoch was a clear manifestation of God's immediate creative agency.[44]

Buckland's acceptance of a naturalistic account of the physical history of the earth points up a second development in early nineteenth-century natural theology. Paley's *Natural Theology* took as its paradigm the watchmaker analogy and was consequently dominated by instances of divine handiwork in the living world, each implicitly viewed as a singular production. Yet, as William Whewell pointed out in his *Bridgewater Treatise* on physics, the distinctive perspective of modern science was that 'nature, so far as it is an object of scientific research, is a collection of facts governed by *laws*'.[45] The object of Whewell's treatise was to demonstrate the consistency of this view with the Christian idea of God. Paley and Whewell were agreed that, when it came to the operation of physical laws such as that of gravity, the analogy with human contrivance was weak. However, Whewell developed an alternative analogy between God's agency in instituting and upholding physical laws and that of a human legislator in instituting and upholding the laws of a state. The existence of natural laws, he claimed, no less than the existence of human laws, implied a legislator, whose character was manifested in his legislation. This nomological conception of design provided Whewell with a means of demonstrating the religious safety of such naturalistic (not to say avowedly secular) theories as that of Laplace – dubbed the 'nebular hypothesis' by Whewell – which posited that the solar system had resulted from the condensation of nebulous matter under the influence of gravity. Such advances in naturalistic explanation, he explained, merely transferred our understanding of God's skill to a different part of the creative process.

In addition to the laws of matter, some of the Bridgewater authors also moved beyond Paley in embracing what they viewed as laws of organic structure, with a view to enhancing the argument from design. For Paley, it was the strict adaptation of the parts of living organisms to their function within the whole, and of the whole organism to its proper functioning within its environment, that provided evidence of design. By contrast, the physician Peter Mark Roget, in his *Bridgewater Treatise* on physiology, argued that such functional adaptation operated within limits prescribed by underlying morphological laws that provided further evidence of design. Groups of animals and plants did not merely resemble each other because they were adapted for similar purposes, he argued; their structure also reflected their conformity to general types. Thus, while adapted to radically different environments, whales, bats and horses were built on a common body plan. These underlying types in nature, he suggested, clearly implied a divine plan, and provided strong additional evidence for the existence of a creator.[46] This form of idealist argument was once again reactive to a perceived threat from developments in French science. In particular, the claims of French naturalist Etienne Geoffroy Saint-Hilaire (1772–1844) that animal morphology was determined by material laws of organization had been used in the 1820s by those seeking to challenge London's Anglican-dominated medical establishment. Roget, and those such as the leading naturalist Richard Owen (1804–92) who developed the idealist approach further, were thus able to render the new 'philosophical anatomy' religiously safe.[47]

While the Bridgewater authors and their contemporaries were generally more circumspect than Paley about the validity of natural theology, they nevertheless developed innovative ways of using the notion of divine design to demonstrate the religious compatibility of the rapidly changing sciences. Moreover, in so doing, these writers arguably smoothed the way for the public acceptance not only of progressivist geology and astronomy, but also of organic evolution. When the Edinburgh publisher Robert Chambers (1802–71) published his anonymous evolutionary blockbuster *Vestiges of the Natural History of Creation* in 1844, he followed the *Bridgewater Treatises* in justifying the notion of creation by natural law. Similarly, while Charles Darwin had by 1859 long since relinquished his earlier conviction that 'the Creator creates by laws',[48] he nevertheless placed a theological justification of that view, quoted from Whewell's *Bridgewater Treatise*, opposite the title page of *Origin of Species*. Moreover, the notion of creation by law continued to be invoked by many of the scientists and churchmen in Britain and North America who subsequently sought to construct a natural theology of evolution. In the formulation of Charles Kingsley, Darwin's theory manifested a God who was 'so wise, that he makes all things make themselves'.[49]

Such continuities undermine any facile assumption that, by turning Paley on his head, Darwin single-handedly gave the *coup de grâce* to natural theology. Nevertheless, attempts to represent natural selection as the divine law of organic creation presented particular difficulties. To begin with, Darwin's mechanism provided for an open-ended evolutionary process, instead of the unfolding of a predetermined divine plan. For many, like the leading American Darwinian Asa Gray (1810–88), a more obviously purposive process seemed called for, and Gray suggested that God directed the course of what Darwin took to be random variation.[50] Another serious concern lay with the problem of evil. How could one infer the existence of a creator from a natural law which required so much suffering and loss of life in order to produce new species? On the other hand, however, natural selection was sometimes seen as giving purpose to what might otherwise seem futile suffering. Nevertheless, for many of those seeking to develop a natural theology of evolution,

Darwin's theory was less appealing than the more directed alternatives which long and successfully competed with it in the late nineteenth and early twentieth centuries.[51]

EPILOGUE: NATURAL THEOLOGY IN THE PROFESSIONAL AGE

While Darwinian evolution did not sound the death knell of natural theology, the latter's role in the practice of the sciences in Britain and North America certainly diminished during the later decades of the nineteenth century. This was to a significant extent a consequence of developments in the social organization of the sciences. In Britain, in particular, the scientific young guard symbolized by Thomas Henry Huxley (1825–95) developed a professionalizing ethos of scientific naturalism, in which metaphysical questions were to be rigorously excluded from science. In order to secure professional status and social prestige, they believed, scientific practice and education alike had to be withdrawn from the sphere of religious, and especially clerical, influence, a development which was simultaneously fostered by the growing professionalization of the clergy.[52] The irenic function long played by natural theology was fundamentally at odds with a new rhetoric of conflict, carefully constructed by Huxley and his professionalizing peers, in which 'extinguished theologians' were to be found lying about the cradle of every science 'as the strangled snakes beside that of Hercules'.[53]

Yet, while the role of natural theology in scientific practice clearly declined in the late nineteenth century, historians have recently emphasized that the break was somewhat less dramatic than previously supposed. There were, for instance, numerous scientifically authoritative clergy in late Victorian Britain whose often staggeringly successful popular science books firmly embedded the sciences within Christian theologies of nature, maintaining a steady riposte to scientific naturalism.[54] Similarly, Peter Bowler has argued that a reaction against scientific naturalism in early twentieth-century Britain resulted in the development of a 'new natural theology' by theologically liberal scientists and churchmen wishing to reconcile science and religion.[55] However, as Bowler observes, the professional roles of scientists and clergy (as well as of scientific popularizers and journalists) were by this period even more markedly separate. Furthermore, it was orthodox Christians who were chiefly responsible for scuppering the new reconciliation, repudiating its theological modernism. In this, they echoed the 1934 negation of the entire project of natural theology by Karl Barth (1886–1968), whose reassertion of the primacy of divine self-revelation has had a lasting impact on Protestant theology. Moreover, while novel forms of natural theology such as intelligent design have been explored in more recent decades, they have generally been considered extraneous to the scientific project, a point amply illustrated by the heated reactions of scientists.

Notes

1   *Penny Cyclopædia of the Society for the Diffusion of Useful Knowledge*, 27 vols. (London: Charles Knight, 1833–43), s.v. 'Theology'.
2   Francis Bacon, *The Advancement of Learning*, ed. by Michael Kiernan (Oxford and New York: Clarendon Press, 2000), p. 78; Richard Swinburne, *Faith and Reason*, 2nd edn (Oxford University Press, 2005), pp. 91–2, 107.
3   John Brooke and Geoffrey Cantor, *Reconstructing Nature: the Engagement of Science and Religion* (Edinburgh: T. and T. Clark, 1998), pp. 143–8.
4   John Hedley Brooke, *Science and Religion: Some Historical Perspectives* (Cambridge University Press, 1991), esp. ch. 6; John Clayton, *Religions, Reasons, and Gods: Essays in Cross-Cultural Philosophy of Religion* (Cambridge University Press, 2006); Peter Harrison, 'Physico-Theology and the Mixed Sciences: the Role of Theology in Early Modern Natural Theology', in P. R. Anstey and J. A. Schuster (eds.), *The Science of Nature in the Seventeenth Century* (Dordrecht: Springer, 2005), pp. 165–83.
5   'Dr Chalmers' Bridgewater Treatise', *Edinburgh Christian Instructor*, 2nd ser. 2 (1833), 755–70, p. 767.
6   Clayton, *Religions*, pp. 162–3.
7   Anthony Kenny, *The Five Ways: Saint Thomas Aquinas' Proofs of God's Existence* (London: Routledge, 1969).
8   Amos Funkenstein, *Theology and the Scientific Imagination from the Middle Ages to the Seventeenth Century* (Princeton University Press, 1986), p. 3.
9   Brooke and Cantor, *Reconstructing Nature*, pp. 151–2; Peter Harrison, 'Miracles, Early Modern Science, and Rational Religion', *Church History* 75 (2006), 493–511.
10 Scott Mandelbrote, 'The Uses of Natural Theology in Seventeenth-Century England', *Science in Context* 20 (2007), 451–80.
11 Michael Hunter, 'Science and Heterodoxy: an Early Modern Problem Reconsidered', in David C. Lindberg and Robert S. Westman (eds.), *Reappraisals of the Scientific Revolution* (Cambridge University Press, 1990), pp. 437–60, esp. pp. 440–3.
12 John Wilkins, *Of the Principles and Duties of Natural Religion* (London: T. Basset, H. Brome, and R. Chiswell, 1675), p. [vi].

13 Thomas Sprat, *The History of the Royal Society of London for the Improving of Natural Knowledge* (London: J. Martyn and J. Allestry, 1667), p. 82.

14 Robert Boyle, *The Christian virtuoso shewing that by being addicted to experimental philosophy, a man is rather assisted than indisposed to be a good Christian* (London: John Taylor and John Wyat, 1690), p. [iii].

15 John Ray, *The Wisdom of God Manifested in the Works of Creation* (London: Samuel Smith, 1691), p. [xi].

16 Paul Wood, 'Methodology and Apologetics: Thomas Sprat's *History of the Royal Society*', *British Journal for the History of Science* 13 (1980), 1–26.

17 *The Works of the Honourable Robert Boyle*, 6 vols. (London: J. and F. Rivington [and sixteen others], 1772), vol. 1, p. clxvii.

18 Margaret C. Jacob, *The Newtonians and the English Revolution, 1689–1720* (Hassocks, Sussex: The Harvester Press, 1976).

19 Christopher J. Kenny, 'Theology and Natural Philosophy in Late Seventeenth and Early Eighteenth-Century Britain', unpublished PhD thesis, University of Leeds (1996).

20 William Clark, 'The Death of Metaphysics in Enlightened Prussia', in William Clark, Jan Golinski and Simon Schaffer (eds.), *The Sciences in Enlightened Europe* (University of Chicago Press, 1999), pp. 423–73, pp. 432–5; Ben Vermeulen, 'Theology and Science: the Case of Bernard Nieuwentijt's Theological Positivism', in S. Rossi (ed.), *Science and the Imagination in Eighteenth-Century British Culture* (Milan: Edizioni Unicopli, 1987), pp. 379–90.

21 John Gascoigne, *Cambridge in the Enlightenment: Science, Religion, and Politics from the Restoration to the French Revolution* (Cambridge University Press, 1989); Gascoigne, 'From Bentley to the Victorians: the Rise and Fall of British Newtonian Natural Theology', *Science in Context* 2 (1988), 219–56.

22 Brooke, *Science and Religion*, pp. 198–203; John Hedley Brooke, 'Why Did the English Mix their Science and Religion?', in Rossi (ed.), *Science and the Imagination*, pp. 57–78.

23 Joseph Butler, *The Analogy of Religion, Natural and Revealed, to the Constitution and Course of Nature* (London: James, John and Paul Knapton, 1736), p. 144.

24 Butler, *Analogy*, p. iii.

25 For a good introduction to Kant's critique, see Brooke, *Science and Religion*, pp. 203–9.

26 David Hume, *Dialogues Concerning Natural Religion* ([London?: n.p.], 1779), p. 27.

27 M. A. Stewart, 'Arguments for the Existence of God: the British Debate', in Knud Haakonssen (ed.), *The Cambridge History of Eighteenth-Century Philosophy*, 2 vols. (Cambridge University Press, 2006), vol. II, pp. 710–30, esp. pp. 725–6.

28 William Paley, *Natural Theology; or, Evidences of the existence and attributes of the deity, collected from the appearances of nature* (London: R. Faulder, 1802), pp. 476, 487.

29   Brooke and Cantor, *Reconstructing Nature*, ch. 6. See also Matthew Eddy, 'The Science and Rhetoric of Paley's *Natural Theology*', *Literature and Theology* 18 (2004), 1–22.

30   Gascoigne, *Cambridge in the Enlightenment*, esp. ch. 8; Gascoigne, 'From Bentley to the Victorians'.

31   Pietro Corsi, *Science and Religion: Baden Powell and the Anglican Debate, 1800–1860* (Cambridge University Press, 1988), p. 192.

32   Boyd Hilton, *The Age of Atonement: the Influence of Evangelicalism on Social and Economic Thought, 1795–1865* (Oxford: Clarendon Press, 1988); Jonathan R. Topham, 'Evangelicals, Science, and Natural Theology in Early Nineteenth-Century Britain: Thomas Chalmers and the *Evidence* Controversy', in David N. Livingstone, Daryl Hart and Mark A. Noll (eds.), *Evangelicals and Science in Historical Perspective* (New York: Oxford University Press, 1998), pp. 142–74.

33   Charles Kingsley, 'The Natural Theology of the Future', in *Scientific Lectures and Essays* (London: Macmillan, 1880), pp. 313–36, p. 316.

34   John Brooke, 'Scientific Thought and its Meaning for Religion: the Impact of French Science on British Natural Theology, 1827–1859', *Revue de synthèse*, 4th series, 1 (1989), 33–59.

35   Richard Carlile, *An Address to the Men of Science* (London: Richard Carlile, 1821).

36   Adrian Desmond, *The Politics of Evolution: Morphology, Medicine, and Reform in Radical London* (Chicago and London: University of Chicago Press, 1989).

37   Clifford Geertz, 'Religion as a Cultural System', in Michael Banton (ed.), *Anthropological Approaches to the Study of Religion* (London: Tavistock, 1966), pp. 1–46, esp. pp. 6–7; Jonathan Topham, '"An Infinite Variety of Arguments": the *Bridgewater Treatises* and British Natural Theology in the 1830s', unpublished PhD thesis, University of Lancaster (1993), ch. 7.

38   Nicolaas A. Rupke, *The Great Chain of History: William Buckland and the English School of Geology, 1814–1849* (Oxford: Clarendon Press, 1983), pp. 237–8.

39   Jack Morrell and Arnold Thackray, *Gentlemen of Science: Early Years of the British Association for the Advancement of Science* (Oxford: Clarendon Press, 1981), pp. 225–9.

40   John Hedley Brooke, 'Indications of a Creator: Whewell as Apologist and Priest', in *William Whewell: a Composite Portrait* (Oxford: Clarendon Press, 1991), pp. 149–73; William Whewell, *Astronomy and General Physics Considered with Reference to Natural Theology* (London: William Pickering, 1833), p. vi.

41   Jonathan R. Topham, 'Science and Popular Education in the 1830s: the Role of the *Bridgewater Treatises*', *British Journal for the History of Science* 25 (1992), 397–430; Topham, 'Beyond the "Common Context": the Production and Reading of the *Bridgewater Treatises*', *Isis* 89 (1998), 233–62; Topham, 'Science, Natural Theology, and the Practice of Christian Piety in Early Nineteenth-Century Religious Magazines', in Geoffrey Cantor and Sally Shuttleworth (eds.), *Science*

Serialized: Representations of the Sciences in Nineteenth-Century Periodicals (Cambridge, MA: MIT Press, 2004), pp. 37–66.

42 Frederick Burkhardt *et al.* (eds.), *Correspondence of Charles Darwin*, vol. IX (Cambridge University Press, 1994), p. 273.

43 Robert M. Young, *Darwin's Metaphor: Nature's Place in Victorian Culture* (Cambridge University Press, 1985), pp. 127–8.

44 William Buckland, *Geology and Mineralogy, Considered with Reference to Natural Theology*, 2 vols. (London: William Pickering, 1836).

45 Whewell, *Astronomy*, p. 3.

46 Peter Mark Roget, *Animal and Vegetable Physiology, Considered with Reference to Natural Theology*, 2 vols. (London: William Pickering, 1834).

47 Desmond, *Politics of Evolution*.

48 Quoted in John H. Brooke, 'Darwin and Victorian Christianity', in Jonathan Hodge and Gregory Radick (eds.), *The Cambridge Companion to Darwin* (Cambridge University Press, 2003), pp. 192–213, p. 197.

49 Frederick Burkhardt *et al.* (eds.), *Correspondence of Charles Darwin*, vol. X (Cambridge University Press, 1997), p. 634.

50 Richard England (ed.), *Design after Darwin, 1860–1900*, 4 vols. (Bristol: Thoemmes Press, 2003), vol. I, p. xiii.

51 James R. Moore, *The Post-Darwinian Controversies: a Study of the Protestant Struggle to Come to Terms with Darwin in Great Britain and America, 1870–1900* (Cambridge University Press, 1979).

52 Frank M. Turner, 'The Victorian Conflict between Science and Religion: a Professional Dimension', *Isis* 69 (1978), 356–76.

53 [T. H. Huxley], 'Darwin on the Origin of Species', *Westminster Review*, 2nd ser. 17 (1860), 541–70, p. 556.

54 Bernard Lightman, *Victorian Popularizers of Science: Designing Nature for New Audiences* (Chicago and London: University of Chicago Press, 2007), esp. ch. 2.

55 Peter J. Bowler, *Reconciling Science and Religion: the Debate in Early-Twentieth-Century Britain* (Chicago and London: University of Chicago Press, 2001).

4 Religious reactions to Darwin

JON H. ROBERTS

In 1896 Andrew Dickson White (1832–1918), author of the influential *A History of the Warfare of Science with Theology in Christendom* (1896), suggested that Charles Darwin's *Origin of Species* had entered the theological arena 'like a plough into an ant-hill'. As was so often the case when he assessed the impact of science on theology, White exaggerated when he alleged that Darwin's theory 'rudely awakened' believers from a lethargic state of 'comfort and repose'. Still, it is unquestionably true that from the outset of its publication in November 1859, Darwin's work elicited much attention and generated more than a little hostility. Religious thinkers in Great Britain and the United States, who serve as the subjects of this chapter, initially charged that in rejecting the interpretation of the history of life as a succession of independent creations of species in favour of a theory predicated on 'random' variation and natural selection, the Darwinian hypothesis challenged the idea that natural history was the realization of a plan initiated and sustained by a providential deity and undermined the veracity of the scriptural depiction of the scheme of redemption. Although some of those thinkers felt compelled to alter their views after it became apparent that most natural historians had embraced the transmutation hypothesis, others continued to regard that hypothesis as a fundamental assault on both natural theology and biblical revelation. By 1920, the chronological endpoint of this chapter, the theory of evolution had become the most theologically controversial scientific hypothesis since the time of Galileo.

INITIAL RESPONSES

Religious thinkers in the United States and Great Britain were members of a transatlantic intellectual community in which the methods and results of scientific inquiry had long played an important role in shaping theological discourse. By the time Darwin's book appeared, numerous clergy, theologians and scientists alike took it for granted that scientific investigation fostered a pious appreciation of the benevolence and wisdom that pervaded the creation and served as 'an indispensable concomitant of the Bible' in illustrating the glory of the creator. Perhaps even more significantly, they valued scientific knowledge as 'the great storehouse of facts on which is based the whole system of natural religion'.[1]

Most of the numerous apologists in Great Britain and the United States who invoked scientific data in defending their belief in the existence and providence of a divine creator placed special emphasis on an argument from design that drew on the organic world for its most vivid and compelling examples. During the nineteenth century two versions of that argument became popular. One focused on the usefulness of plant and animal structures in fostering the adaptation of those organisms to their environment. The other called attention to the pervasiveness of intelligible patterns within the organic world. It was inconceivable, apologists maintained, that these data were the result of chance; it made far more sense to ascribe them to the activity of a divine designer. The research of palaeontologists served to reinforce the credibility of these arguments by disclosing data that seemed both to reveal 'the steady march of one vast and comprehensive plan' and to demonstrate that the myriad plants and animals that had appeared and then disappeared during the course of the history of life had been just as well adapted to the conditions of their existence as the organisms currently in existence. Convinced that the fossil record contained life forms too intricately designed to 'be slid in and out by the simple operations of material law', defenders of the faith concluded that those now-extinct organisms bore witness instead to the legitimacy of the biblical idea of God's continual 'superintending Providence'.[2]

Because they held that the origin of living things 'touches upon beliefs which are the very foundation of all religion', Christian thinkers, who constituted the overwhelming majority of religionists in Great Britain and the United States interested in the relationship between science and religion in the period prior to 1875, commonly denounced the *Origin of Species* as an assault on 'the fundamental principles both of natural and revealed religion'. In spite of the fact that Darwin had been careful to avoid discussion of the origin of life and to credit God with having 'impressed on matter' the laws governing the universe, his theory attributed the appearance of the multitude of species that had arisen during the course of the history of the planet to a capricious, wasteful and sometimes cruel process, a process that required neither divine intervention nor seemingly even a divine plan. In addition, in assailing the commonly held belief in the fixity of species, Darwin's work challenged the veracity of the biblical account of the creation of each organism 'after its kind'.[3]

Not all religious thinkers shared this early hostility to Darwin's views. The prominent English Catholic intellectual John Henry Newman (1801–90), for example, professed to see nothing in Darwin's work that conflicted with either divine revelation or the idea of 'an Almighty God and Protector'. The Anglican clergyman Charles Kingsley (1819–75) informed Darwin that he had 'gradually learnt to see that it is just as noble a conception of Deity, to believe that He created primal forms capable of self-development into all forms needful ... as to believe that He required a fresh act of intervention to supply the lacunas which He Himself had made'. Asa Gray (1810–88), the Fisher Professor of Natural History at Harvard and a Reformed Protestant, attempted to persuade readers of the *Atlantic Monthly* that Darwin's theory permitted believers to continue to ascribe the 'orderly arrangements and admirable adaptations pervading the organic world' to the activity of 'an ordaining and directing intelligence'.[4]

Unfortunately, public opinion polling did not begin until after 1920, and because our knowledge of people's ideas in the late nineteenth and early twentieth centuries is dependent on the written sources that have survived, we know very little about what views, if any, the vast majority of people held about Darwinism. We do know that most commentators in the United States and Great Britain who published assessments of the religious implications of Darwin's work were less charitable in their appraisal than people like Newman and Gray. One of the considerations that doubtless contributed to their animosity was the fact that the *Origin of Species* appeared at a time when intelligent spokespersons within the Anglo-American intellectual community were convinced that the scientific arena had become 'the Armageddon – the final battle-field – in the conflict with infidelity'. Religious apologists warned that this provided the forces of unbelief with a strong incentive to try to lend credibility to ideas that eliminated the role of divine activity within the created order by conferring on those ideas the name and prestige of science. Many defenders of the faith regarded promotion of the transmutation hypothesis in this light. Accordingly, most religious thinkers who evaluated Darwin's work in the period between 1859 and about 1875 concluded that the most effective strategy they could employ in destroying the credibility of that hypothesis was to impeach its scientific credentials. A careful examination of the data of natural history, they believed, would disclose the weaknesses of evolutionary theory and thus render a sustained examination of its theological implications unnecessary.[5]

DARWINISM AS UNSCIENTIFIC

One of the considerations giving religious thinkers confidence that Darwin's theory lacked scientific credibility was the fact that previous expositions of the transmutation hypothesis had been widely condemned by natural historians. Whether espoused by reputable scientists such as Jean-Baptiste Lamarck (1744–1829) or by writers aiming at a more popular audience such as Robert Chambers (1802–71), the author of *Vestiges of the Natural History of Creation* (1844), the development hypothesis had received rough treatment at the hands of the scientific community. That prompted many religious thinkers to dismiss Darwin's work as an 'old exploded theory' and to predict that his ideas would soon be consigned to the 'museum of curious and fanciful speculations'.[6]

The initial response of natural historians to the *Origin of Species* seemed to confirm that assessment. Although Darwin had earned a reputation as a reputable investigator and had amassed a vast array of observations and facts in disciplines ranging from embryology and morphology to biogeography and palaeontology in an effort to lend credibility to his theory, few naturalists were quick to endorse his theory enthusiastically. Some, most notably Louis Agassiz (1807–73), the most eminent natural historian in the United States, adamantly opposed the Darwinian hypothesis as 'a scientific mistake, untrue in its facts, unscientific in its method, and mischievous in its tendency'.[7]

Doubtless heartened by the lukewarm response that Darwin's work initially received from members of the scientific community, Roman Catholic and Protestant opinion leaders became eager participants in calling attention to deficiencies in the theory of 'descent with modification'. Catholics, still smarting from criticism attending the Galileo affair, did not wish to be perceived as assailing science with the cudgel of theology. Hence, many of them reasoned that in those instances when theories put forward in the name of science seemed to be intimately connected with the fortunes of materialism and agnosticism, the ideal response was to deny the scientific merit of those theories. For their part, Protestants assumed that anything they could do to demonstrate the fallacious character of theologically suspect views of nature lent credibility to their claim that the natural world attested to the existence of a providential creator. Accordingly, they made concerted efforts to show that Darwin's work was little more than a tissue of specious conjectures. Some of the arguments that Christian clergy and theologians advanced in an effort to undermine the credibility of Darwin's theory were strained, garbled, uninformed, even silly. Most of them, however, echoed the criticisms that were being made by tough-minded critics of Darwin's work within the scientific community.[8]

DARWINISM AND THE ORIGIN OF
THE HUMAN SPECIES

At the same time that many natural historians, clergy and theologians were subjecting the theory of evolution by natural selection to careful scrutiny, a number of Darwin's supporters were extending the logic of that theory to include the human species. Darwin had conspicuously avoided explicit discussion of human origins in the *Origin of Species*. Other transmutationists were less reticent. In 1863 both the geologist Charles Lyell (1797–1875) and 'Darwin's bulldog', the zoologist Thomas Henry Huxley (1825–95), published books placing the origin of humanity within an evolutionary conceptual framework. Although Lyell ascribed the appearance of humanity's intellectual and moral faculties to the creative activity of God, he made it clear that most human attributes had arisen through evolution. Huxley went even farther, contending that the same 'process of physical causation' that Darwin had employed in accounting for the 'genera and families of ordinary animals' was 'amply sufficient to account for the origin of Man'. Then in the later 1860s and 1870s several important treatises in archaeology and anthropology appeared that described civilization in the dawn of human history as quite primitive and held that subsequent development was the result of a process of gradual cultural evolution.[9]

These works did little more than confirm a suspicion that religious thinkers had harboured since the very outset of the Darwinian controversy: that supporters of the theory of evolution were determined to show that 'Bacon, Newton, Plato, the orang-ou-tang [*sic*] and the ape' possessed common ancestors. As the taunt that the Anglican bishop Samuel Wilberforce (1805–73) allegedly made about Huxley's simian ancestors during the meeting of the British Association in Oxford in 1860 suggests, much of the rancour and repugnance that Darwinism evoked among religious thinkers sprang from their conviction that there was nothing in the logic of transmutation that would preclude its advocates from extending the scheme to human beings.[10]

By the time Darwin opted to break his self-imposed silence on the subject of human origins in 1871 with his two-volume *The Descent of Man, and Selection in Relation to Sex*, he found himself in the midst of a controversy that was already well along. Although Darwin described the human species as 'the wonder and glory of the Universe', he maintained that it had descended – though 'ascended' might have been a more felicitous term – from progenitors that had been 'covered with hair, both sexes having beards; their ears were pointed and capable of movement; and their bodies were provided with a tail, having the proper muscles'. If this were not sufficient to shock Victorian sensibilities, he speculated that humanity's ancestors 'apparently consisted of a group of marine animals resembling the larvae of existing Ascidians'. Darwin maintained that if the human species were not the product of evolution, then the similarities of human beings to other animals with regard to general bodily structure, rudimentary organs and embryological development would all be 'mere empty deceptions'.[11]

In attempting to demonstrate that even human intellectual, spiritual and moral attributes could be understood within an evolutionary context, Darwin employed two interwoven strategies. First, he sought to persuade his readers that the mental differences between the human species and the higher animals were differences of degree rather than kind by showing that those higher animals possessed in incipient form numerous mental endowments – powers and aptitudes such as the capacity for improvement, the ability to use tools, and even religious impulses – that had frequently been thought of as uniquely human. Second, through a process of imaginative historical reconstruction, Darwin sought to show that even humanity's possession of a moral sense, which he regarded as 'the best and highest distinction between man and the lower animals', could be explained 'exclusively from the side of natural history'. Darwin located the 'prime principle' of human morality in the 'social instincts' of love and sympathy for others. Those instincts, which human beings had inherited from their non-human progenitors through natural selection, had prompted humans in the early stages of their existence to band together in discrete social groups and to act in accordance with 'what is best in the long run for all the members'. Conscience then emerged once members of the human species acquired sufficient intelligence to permit reflection on the consequences of their actions and to feel regret when they subordinated impulses associated with the social instincts to other, more primitive and more transient impulses such as vengeance and lust.[12]

Darwin's work did not fundamentally change the structure of the debate over human evolution. It did, however, serve as a pointed reminder that the theological implications of the transmutation hypothesis extended well beyond issues relating to natural theology. In challenging the idea that an immense intellectual, moral and spiritual chasm separated the human species from all other creatures, the *Descent of Man* seemed to question the claim that humans enjoyed a privileged status as beings created in God's image.

Although religious thinkers frequently resorted to sarcasm in their discussions of human evolution, they invested most of their energies in efforts to show that the idea was scientifically untenable. Towards that end, they called attention not only to such structural attributes as the size and structure of the human brain and the human capacity for speech, but even more profoundly, to humanity's impressive array of intellectual, moral and spiritual powers. Those attributes, they maintained, provided a warrant for affirming the existence of an 'immense interval between even savage man and the highest brute' that natural agencies were incapable of bridging.[13]

FROM NATURALISTIC METAPHYSICS TO SCIENTIFIC RESPECTABILITY

In the fifteen years after publication of the *Origin of Species* most religious thinkers in Great Britain and America who participated in the Darwinian controversy had associated Darwin with Thomas Huxley, the philosopher Herbert Spencer (1820–1903), the physicist John Tyndall (1820–93) and a growing number of other individuals in the third quarter of the nineteenth century who seemed to be working assiduously to establish the naturalistic philosophical principle that matter and the laws describing its operation were sufficient to account for the activities of all natural phenomena. It was in pursuit of that goal, they believed, that Darwin had sought to claim scientific status for his unfounded speculations. As long as outspoken support for the transmutation hypothesis appeared to be largely restricted to proponents of scientific naturalism with ulterior philosophical motives, the claim that Darwin's theory should be seen as irreligious metaphysical legerdemain rather than tough-minded science remained plausible. During the decade after 1865, however, virtually all natural historians endorsed the theory of organic evolution.[14]

The factor that proved most decisive in accounting for the conversion of those scientists was neither their belief that Darwin succeeded in providing a mechanism that could plausibly account for transmutation nor a dramatic influx of data favourable to an evolutionary interpretation of the history of life. Rather, the paramount consideration was meta-empirical: a conviction that transmutation was more consistent with the norms of scientific discourse than was the 'dogma of special creations'. Long before the *Origin of Species* appeared, scientists in discipline after discipline had succeeded in dispensing with supernatural intervention in describing the behaviour of nature. By the third quarter of the nineteenth century even the most pious members of the scientific community were coming to assume that efforts 'to narrow the domain of the supernatural, by bringing all phenomena within the scope of natural laws and secondary causes' were among the most important goals of scientific investigation. From that perspective, they reasoned that it was 'clearly the duty of science to seek for some other explanation' for the origin of species than 'half a million distinct miracles'. Darwin's theory provided natural historians with a working hypothesis that succeeded in opening to scientific investigation the question of how species related to one another through time.[15]

During the late nineteenth and early twentieth century most natural historians believed that Darwin had exaggerated the efficacy of natural selection. Although they did not reach a consensus as to which mechanisms were most salient in accounting for evolution, most tended to envision the process as somewhat more progressive and less fortuitous than Darwin had originally suggested. Nevertheless, natural historians credited Darwin for leading the revolution in scientific opinion that culminated in acceptance of evolution and showed little hesitation in equating Darwinism with the theory of organic evolution in common parlance.[16]

The conversion of natural historians to the transmutation hypothesis led clergy, theologians and other religious believers in Great Britain and the United States to make significant changes in their analysis of that hypothesis. Discussion of its scientific merits increasingly gave way to consideration of its theological implications. Christians and Jews alike found themselves engaged in an often animated dialogue concerning the terms of relationship that should be established between the theory of evolution and their religious traditions. Although most religious thinkers recognized that the theory challenged the credibility of prevailing ways of formulating their beliefs, they failed to reach agreement as to how to deal with this problem. Some took the position that the scientific community's endorsement of the evolutionary hypothesis required believers to reconstruct their religious beliefs to bring them into accord with the precepts of evolution. Others concluded that acceptance of the transmutation hypothesis would necessitate the abandonment of doctrines essential to their worldview and therefore rejected the hypothesis.

EVOLUTIONISM AND THE BREAKDOWN
OF CONSENSUS

For much of the nineteenth century Jews had expressed little interest in science or its religious implications. It was only after the origin of the human species had become a topic of sustained discussion that Jewish commentators entered into the Darwinian controversy. Reform Jews devoted greater attention to the theory of evolution than did Jews of a more traditionalist persuasion, who typically refused to discuss scientific issues from the pulpit. Some Reform Jews, such as the rabbi David Einhorn (1809–79) and Isaac Mayer Wise (1819–1900), his principal rival for the intellectual leadership of Reform Judaism in the United States, opposed the transmutation hypothesis on the grounds that it was irreconcilable with the idea that humans had been created in the image of God, inimical to morality, and too closely associated with materialistic and atheistic philosophies. A growing number of others, however, held that the scientific community's conversion to the hypothesis meant that it was now appropriate to view organic evolution as the method God had employed in creating the world. Few of the conciliators appear to have believed that acceptance of evolutionary theory necessitated a fundamental reformulation of religious beliefs or practices.[17]

The controversy over human origins also brought additional Catholic commentators into the fray. In his review of the *Descent of Man* Orestes Brownson (1803–76), an American Catholic convert who tirelessly opposed ideas that he interpreted as theologically suspect, denounced Darwin as one of 'Satan's most efficient ministers'. For the most part, however, Roman Catholics in Great Britain and the United States proceeded cautiously in responding to the transmutation hypothesis. Although they agreed that no theory of evolution that denied the immediate divine creation of the soul was acceptable, the Vatican's failure to take a position on the larger theory of evolution led to a great deal of uncertainty. A few Catholics suggested that some versions of the theory could be reconciled with church doctrine. More commonly, however, Catholic thinkers expressed hostility to ideas of human evolution, the close association between evolutionary ideas and the doctrines of materialism and atheism, and the allegiance of many evolutionists to ideas promoting human fitness such as eugenics and birth control that they deemed to be hostile to the interests of the Catholic working class. Even some who championed the idea of a rapprochement with modernity, such as James Cardinal Gibbons, the archbishop of Baltimore, expressed little sympathy with evolution.[18]

Beginning in the last decade of the nineteenth century the fortunes of the transmutation hypothesis became bound up with the Catholic hierarchy's growing hostility to modernism. A particularly graphic illustration of this can be seen in the fortunes of John Zahm, a professor and eventual chair of the natural sciences at the University of Notre Dame. In his *Evolution and Dogma*, published in 1896, Zahm made a concerted effort to show not only that there was 'nothing in Evolution, when properly understood, which is contrary to Scripture or Catholic teaching', but also that there was 'much in Evolution to admire, much that is ennobling and inspiring, much that illustrates and corroborates the truths of faith'. Notwithstanding his exemption of the human soul from the evolutionary process and his claim that the intellectual roots of evolutionary ideas could be found in the declarations of Augustine and Thomas Aquinas, Zahm's work was condemned by the Vatican's Congregation of the Index. The fate of Zahm and several other zealous proponents of the evolutionary hypothesis doubtless had a chilling effect, deterring Catholics who found merit in the idea of organic evolution from committing themselves wholeheartedly to the theory.[19]

During the period after 1875 Protestants continued to dominate discussions of the religious implications of the transmutation hypothesis in Great Britain and the United States alike. This is hardly surprising, given both their larger numbers and the prominence that scientific ideas had long enjoyed in their approach to theology. What may be somewhat more surprising is that demographic variables are generally not terribly useful as predictors of the way in which individuals within mainline Protestantism would respond to evolution. Moreover, the differences in the way that Protestant thinkers responded to the transmutation hypothesis cut across the divisions that had been most prominent in determining the course of theological discussion during the first three quarters of the nineteenth century. On occasion local differences in cultural environment led Protestants with otherwise quite similar theological outlooks to respond to the theory of evolution quite differently.

Even more important than local cultural idiosyncrasies in shaping their responses, however, were the differing judgements that clergy and theologians rendered with regard to the relative authority of experts in the natural and human sciences and the biblical narrative with regard to matters relating to the history of the created order. Those judgements, in turn, rested on presuppositions concerning human nature and the nature of God's relationship to the world.[20]

A majority of commentators on transmutation within the Anglo-American Protestant intellectual community took the position that natural scientists were the most able expositors of God's revelation within nature. Accordingly, they reasoned, natural historians' endorsement of the theory of organic evolution indicated that it was time for proponents of the Christian worldview to give their assent to the theory. Failure to do so, these Protestant evolutionists warned, would give aid and comfort to sceptics bent on equating Christian thought with obscurantism and drive the literate masses to abandon their faith.

Protestant evolutionists recognized that it was imperative that they allay concerns that the transmutation hypothesis undermined the credibility of arguments for the existence of a divine designer. Dedicating themselves to that task, some apologists maintained that it made more sense to ascribe a process characterized by ever 'higher variations and more perfect organization' to the oversight of a 'directing mind' than to attribute it to 'trial and error in all directions'. Others emphasized that the most credible explanation for the emergence of 'more highly organized species' during the course of the history of life was not the operation of 'blind, automatic nature' but the guidance of a divine 'coordinating power'. Still others moved beyond the organic world to the universe as a whole and argued that the very fact that the cosmos was sufficiently pervaded by order to be understood constituted the strongest conceivable evidence for the existence of a divine mind. Whatever realms of the natural world they chose to emphasize, Protestant evolutionists confidently concluded that Darwinism 'does not touch the great truths of natural theology nor can it touch them, except as it gives us new materials with which to prove them'.[21]

Protestant evolutionists could agree that establishing the existence of God constituted only a first step in demonstrating that the transmutation hypothesis could be reconciled with the precepts of Christianity. Their assessment of the subsequent measures that should be taken to effect the necessary reconciliation, however, differed in significant ways. One sizeable group of Protestant evolutionists was convinced that harmony could be established with rather minimal revisions in Christian doctrine. Although those thinkers regarded themselves as committed evolutionists, they made it clear that they were willing to counten-ance the idea of periodic infusions of 'fresh creative energy' from God in accounting for the emergence of such fundamentally new elements of being as matter, life and mind. Clearly, this retention of the concept of supernaturalism existed in uneasy tension with the transmutation hypothesis as understood by most natural historians. Its primary value from the vantage point of the 'progressive creationists' was that it ena-bled them to believe that they could endorse the principle of organic evolution without needing to accept fundamental revisions in Christian doctrine.[22]

Progressive creationists' acceptance of supernaturalist concep-tions of providential activity also enabled them to remain committed to strong views of biblical authority. Those thinkers typically coupled the claim that God had condescended to an unsophisticated audience by employing non-scientific language in describing natural processes with the assertion that when properly interpreted, the Scriptures would prove to be consistent with the insights of modern science. Appealing to the 'remarkable flexibility of the language of Scripture', they held that just as Christians in the past had altered their interpretation of biblical passages in response to new disclosures from the scientific community, so in their own day it would be possible to reinterpret the scriptural nar-rative of creation to bring it into accord with the transmutation hypoth-esis without undermining the doctrine of biblical inspiration. Given their willingness to countenance the notion of supernatural interven-tion, proponents of this view did not feel compelled to engage in much alteration of their interpretation of other scriptural passages involving the special redemptive acts within the history of the divine–human encounter.[23]

In the period after 1875 an ever-increasing number of other Protestant evolutionists maintained that a more fundamental reconstruction of Christian theology would be necessary in order to bring doctrinal pre-cepts into accord with the implications of the evolutionary hypothesis. One of the most important outgrowths of that conviction was their use of the scientific community's conversion to the transmutation hypothesis as the occasion for dramatically altering their conception of the nature of God's relationship with the world. The Anglican cleric Aubrey Lackington Moore (1848–90) praised Darwinism, which 'under the disguise of a foe' had actually done 'the work of a friend by impelling people to choose between two alternatives: either God is everywhere in nature, or He is nowhere'. Many like-minded religious thinkers in Great

Britain and the United States repudiated the idea of limiting the scope of divine activity to events not yet described in terms of natural laws and processes in favour of belief in a doctrine of divine immanence that identified God as 'the efficient cause and constant mover of all things'. In thus ascribing the source of all causal activity to 'energy' provided by a providential deity in constant and intimate contact with the creation, immanentists found it possible freely to concede to science the task of describing all interactions among natural phenomena in the confidence that 'the agency of God in creation can never be negatived or obscured, but only more clearly revealed by the unveiling of the processes by which He works'.[24]

Most Protestants who regarded scientists' endorsement of the evolutionary hypothesis as an opportunity to place greater emphasis on the biblical idea of God as a father in whom all things live and move and have their being used an evolutionary model to describe God's interaction with humanity. Speciation, they asserted, was not the only process that could be described in terms of a process of gradual, continual and progressive development. Rather, 'because God is wise as he is loving, and has no reason to change a method he has once adopted', evolution should be regarded more generally as 'God's way of doing things'. Accordingly, during the late nineteenth century many of the most influential proponents of the New Theology and other versions of liberal Protestantism in the late nineteenth century employed an evolutionary perspective and vocabulary in reformulating and discussing many Christian doctrines, and in the process sought to make a plausible case for the idea that evolution could be Christianized.[25]

Those Protestants recognized that certain doctrines were so central to the Christian worldview that they simply could not be abandoned. The idea that human beings had been created in God's image was a particularly important example of such a doctrine, for it provided the foundation on which the entire Christian scheme of redemption rested. Few proponents of evolution within the Anglo-American Protestant intellectual community baulked at accepting the notion that humans had acquired their physical frame through evolution. Most of their discussion centred instead on the origin of the attributes of personality. Whereas more cautious Protestant evolutionists ascribed the origin of humanity's intelligence, emotions, will and religious sentiments to special infusions of supernatural power, evolutionists who championed more radically immanentist notions of divine activity emphasized that the manner by which human beings had been created was not relevant to either their nature or their status within the created order. From this perspective they ascribed the emergence of the sacred elements of human personality to the work of an immanent God working through an evolutionary process.[26]

Protestants who employed an evolutionary model in describing divine activity found themselves reformulating many important Christian ideas in developmental terms. In discussing Christian morality, for example, many of them suggested that God had in effect embedded Christian standards of morality within the process of transmutation itself, thereby ensuring that 'that society is most fit which is most Christlike'. Others took a different view, acknowledging that Christian ethical norms were essentially different from the fierce competitive impulses that were decisive in shaping the behaviour of other organisms, but then citing the emergence of those norms as another indication of human superiority. Many Protestant evolutionists cheerfully abandoned belief in the historicity of Adam's fall while retaining the idea that sinfulness was endemic to the human condition. Human beings, they asserted, consistently and perversely chose not to realize their full potential as beings created in God's image. Protestants who conceived of divine activity in evolutionary terms reformulated redemption as 'a steady process by which God accomplishes the uplift of the race'. As both God incarnate and the 'consummate flower' of humanity, Jesus was an essentially 'new type' within 'the chain of evolution'. His life served as a model to emulate, and his teachings provided human beings with both a more adequate understanding of God's nature and will and a standard by which Christians could evaluate their spiritual condition. Some Protestants even employed evolutionary language in describing the everlasting life that attended salvation: it was, they asserted, a particularly spectacular instance of 'the great law of the survival of the fit'.[27]

In discussing the sources, function and finality of religious knowledge, Protestants who regarded evolution as the means that God typically used in accomplishing his purposes eschewed the strategy of reinterpreting scriptural passages in an effort to reconcile them with the implications of the transmutation hypothesis. Instead, they repudiated the notion that the author of Genesis 'had the science of the nineteenth century in his brain' and insisted on viewing the Bible as 'a book purely of religious teaching, not of scientific, historical or philosophical information'. Some even regarded Scripture as a 'historical growth' that instantiated the 'same powers of development, the same law of evolution' as that which was displayed in nature. Although they insisted that this view left the value of the Bible intact, the idea that the 'messengers of revelation were of the people, limited by their conditions, and bound under the burdens of their own generation' simply could not be squared with the doctrine of biblical infallibility. Many Protestant evolutionists came to think of the books of the Bible as mere chapters, albeit 'uniquely precious' chapters, of a larger, more comprehensive story of God's disclosures to humanity 'in the constitution and course of nature, in the constitution and history of man, and pre-eminently in Christ'. From this perspective, revelation itself became 'a continuous process, adjusted to the developing reason of man', and the appropriate subject for theological reflection became the entirety of human experience. While the Bible remained an invaluable repository of humanity's experience of God's redeeming activity, it could no longer serve as final arbiter in formulating theology.[28]

During the period between about 1875 and 1920 a significant minority of theologians and clergy within mainline Protestantism, as well as numerous religious leaders within the holiness and Pentecostal movements, rejected the theory of organic evolution, especially its extension to human beings. While the issues that concerned opponents of the theory of organic evolution were essentially the same on both sides of the Atlantic, even before 1920 Americans were somewhat more aggressive in contesting the theory than were their counterparts in Great Britain. The difference in approach was partly a function of the fact that the number and the percentage of religious thinkers who rejected Darwinism were greater in the United States. But it also reflected variations in cultural and religious traditions and styles of argumentation. The strong tradition of theological latitudinarianism that existed in Great Britain, as well as the pervasive tendency of thinkers in that nation to take developmental views of historical process seriously, served to mitigate the harshness of the anti-evolutionist invective there. By contrast, in the United States, the long dominance of a Scottish Common-Sense realist tradition that instinctively favoured fixed rather than dynamic conceptions of reality, coupled with the existence of a fluid religious marketplace that encouraged less temperate rhetorical strategies, tended to encourage greater militance.[29]

Although some Protestants continued even after 1875 to raise objections to evolution based on scientific considerations, most made it clear that the primary source of their animus towards that theory was theological or moral. Anti-evolutionists typically embraced views of human nature and divine activity that differed significantly from those embraced by Protestant evolutionists. From their vantage point, the sinfulness and fallibility of human nature were among the paramount lessons of human experience. Mitigating that bleak assessment of the human condition, however, was their conviction that a gracious and merciful deity had not simply cast human beings adrift but had provided them in the Bible with a divinely inspired, 'ultimately authoritative standard' of religious truth that was clear, complete and infallible. When they compared that unique guide to Christian faith and practice with the results of scientific investigation, with its legacy of error and vacillation, they found it reasonable to conclude that in cases where the conclusions of scientists conflicted with the teachings of the Scriptures the most appropriate course of action was to remain committed to the 'faith once delivered to the saints' and refuse to give 'that infallibility to secular science which alone belongs to the theology of the Bible'.[30]

When Protestants who adhered to that way of thinking examined the transmutation hypothesis, they typically concluded that in contrast to several previous scientific disclosures, which had prompted changes in biblical interpretation with regard to inessentials, the theory of organic evolution was irreconcilable 'with the whole system of truth, for the revelation of which the Scriptures were given to men'. Reinterpretation was thus not an option. The idea of human evolution evoked particular concern, for it challenged not only the biblical account of God's creation of the human species but also the historicity of the Fall, the consequent meaning of Christ's atonement and other doctrines central to the traditional understanding of Christian theology. Most Protestant anti-evolutionists were convinced that 'the doctrine of a first man made man by the fiat of God' played such a central role in the biblical narrative that if the human species had actually originated by means of evolution, 'then the Scriptures are in fatal error, not simply with regard to man's advent on the globe, but in all their doctrines concerning his original and present spiritual condition, the method of his recovery and his future destiny – that is, their entire system of spiritual teaching, for which they were confessedly given, is at fault'. From that perspective, they repudiated the transmutation hypothesis and with it the views of those timid apologists who in the name of harmony with science seemed willing to eviscerate Christian theology.[31]

EMERGENT NEW PATTERNS IN THE TWENTIETH CENTURY

During the period between 1900 and 1920, although important changes occurred within genetics and other fields relevant to evolutionary thought, clergy and theologians who embraced the transmutation hypothesis in the United States and Great Britain did not fundamentally alter their views of the relationship between that hypothesis and Christian theology. In Great Britain partisans of the New Theology, such as R. J. Campbell (1867–1956), continued to emphasize the importance of an immanentist conception of divine activity as a way of reconciling evolution with a recognizably Christian view of deity. In the United States, liberal Protestants also continued to embrace evolution, but as a group they devoted far less attention to describing its theological implications than had their predecessors in the last quarter of the nineteenth century. In some cases, this lessened attention may have sprung from a conviction that the controversy was essentially over. That conviction prompted Newell Dwight Hillis, the pastor of the Plymouth Church in Brooklyn, to declare in 1900 that 'already the time has come when almost everybody exclaims, "evolution – certainly; why, I always believed in theistic evolution"'. More often, though, liberals gave less sustained attention to evolution because they were looking to realms other than nature for insights into the foundations and impulses underlying religion. After 1900 a growing number of them found themselves drawing on the work of the German theologian Albrecht Ritschl, who emphasized that religion and the natural sciences appealed to different elements of human experience: whereas the sciences were essentially cognitive enterprises devoted to discovering facts and formulating theories based on those facts, religion involved augmenting cognition with the feelings and the will in fostering the formation of independent value judgements that differed fundamentally from the products of scientific inquiry.[32]

The first two decades of the twentieth century also witnessed little change in the nature of the arguments that anti-evolutionists advanced in attacking the transmutation hypothesis. In contrast to the liberals, however, religious thinkers who rejected the transmutation hypothesis remained quite active in discussing their position. Although they typically regarded the higher criticism of the Bible as their most dangerous adversary, many recognized that the theory of organic evolution supplemented biblical criticism in challenging the veracity of the plain sense of the Bible, and some even came to believe that the 'theory of evolution underlies and is the inspiration of the Higher Criticism'. Anti-evolutionists also emphasized the existence of a close connection between commitment to transmutation and both unbelief and unacceptable theological formulations. The Baptist clergyman and ardent fundamentalist William Bell Riley, for example, declared in 1909 that 'the theory of evolution and false theology are indissolubly linked together'. The common denominator, he asserted, was the rejection of biblical authority.[33]

In the period after the First World War some critics of the transmutation hypothesis, most notably William Jennings Bryan, began to emphasize that evolution was associated with a 'might makes right' social philosophy most clearly and tragically manifested in German war-mongering. No less important, Bryan and others pointed to both anecdotal evidence and the results of social science research that suggested that the teaching of evolution had been instrumental in leading to a growing incidence of loss of faith among the nation's youth. Such views played an instrumental role in making anti-evolutionism an increasingly prominent issue among conservative Christians, especially in the United States.[34]

By 1920 members of the Anglo-American religious community were quite sharply divided in their assessment of the theory of organic evolution. Many, probably even most, religious commentators assumed that it was a truth to be reckoned with. Those commentators warned that if religion was to retain its credibility and cultural influence, it would be necessary to reconstruct the tenets of religious thought to bring them into accordance with the implications of the transmutation hypothesis. Many other religious commentators, however, insisted that it was simply not possible to endorse evolutionary theory without abandoning ideas that were of central importance within the Judeo-Christian tradition. Allowing science to dictate the terms of faith, they insisted, would destroy the substance of religious faith. Because proponents of each of these positions were convinced that the stance taken by believers towards evolution would play a crucial role in determining the status of religion within the modern world, their discussions were characterized by a good deal of self-righteous indignation and on occasion even vitriol. In the period since 1920 discussions between religious believers who have embraced evolution and those who have not have often continued to generate as much heat as light.

Notes

In preparing this article I have drawn freely on several previous works that I have written on the subject. These works include *Darwinism and the Divine in America: Protestant Intellectuals and Organic Evolution, 1859–1900* (Madison: University of Wisconsin Press, 1988); 'Darwinism, American Protestant Thinkers, and the Puzzle of Motivation', in Ronald L. Numbers and John Stenhouse (eds.), *Disseminating Darwinism: the*

Role of Place, Race, Religion, and Gender (Cambridge University Press, 1999), pp. 145–72; and 'Conservative Evangelicals and Science Education in American Colleges and Universities, 1890–1940', *Journal of the Historical Society* (2005), 297–329.

1   Andrew Dickson White, *A History of the Warfare of Science with Theology in Christendom*, 2 vols. (New York: D. Appleton, 1896), vol. I, p. 70; James A. Lyon, 'The New Theological Professorship of Natural Science in Connection with Revealed Religion', *Southern Presbyterian Review* 12 (1859), 181–95, p. 191; Edward Hitchcock, 'The Relations and Consequent Mutual Duties between the Philosopher and the Theologian', *Bibliotheca Sacra and American Biblical Repository* 10 (1853), 166–94, p. 177. See also Alvar Ellegard, *Darwin and the General Reader: the Reception of Darwin's Theory of Evolution in the British Periodical Press, 1859–1872* (1958; University of Chicago Press, 1990), p. 102.

2   L. W. Green, 'The Harmony of Revelation and Natural Science: With Especial Reference to Geology', in *Lectures on the Evidences of Christianity Delivered at the University of Virginia, during the Session of 1850–1* (New York: Robert Carter and Brothers, 1851), pp. 459–90, p. 463; Anonymous, 'Review of *The Course of Creation*, by John Anderson', *Biblical Repertory and Princeton Review* 24 (1852), 148; Edward Hitchcock, *Elementary Geology*, 8th edn (New York: M. H. Newman, 1852), p. 284. See also Ellegard, *Darwin*, 114–15.

3   H. Alleyne Nicholson, 'Life and its Origin', *Presbyterian Quarterly and Princeton Review*, n.s., 2 (1873), 689; Edward Hitchcock, 'The Law of Nature's Constancy Subordinate to the Higher Law of Change', *Bibliotheca Sacra* 20 (1863), 522; Charles Darwin, *On the Origin of Species by Means of Natural Section, or the Preservation of Favoured Races in the Struggle for Life* (1859; facsimile edn, Cambridge, MA: Harvard University Press, 1964), p. 488.

4   John Henry Newman to E. B. Pusey, 5 June 1870, Vol. xxv of *The Letters and Diaries of John Henry Newman*, ed. by Charles Stephen Dessain and Thomas Gornall (Oxford: Clarendon Press, 1973), pp. 137–8; John Henry Newman [1874], quoted in A. Dwight Culler, *The Imperial Intellect: a Study of Newman's Educational Ideal* (New Haven: Yale University Press, 1955), p. 267 ('Protector'); C. Kingsley to C. Darwin, 18 November 1859, in Francis Darwin (ed.), *The Life and Letters of Charles Darwin, Including an Autobiographical Chapter*, 3 vols. (London: John Murray, 1887), vol. II, p. 288; Asa Gray, 'Natural Selection not Inconsistent with Natural Theology' [1860], in *Darwiniana: Essays and Reviews Pertaining to Darwinism*, ed. by A. Hunter Dupree (1876; Cambridge, MA: Harvard University Press, 1963), pp. 119–20.

5   Andrew P. Peabody, 'The Bearing of Modern Scientific Theories on the Fundamental Truths of Religion', *Bibliotheca Sacra* 21 (1864), 711.

6   Edward A. Walker, 'The Present Attitude of the Church toward Critical and Scientific Inquiry', *New Englander* 19 (1861), 345; W. C. Wilson, 'Darwin on the Origin of Species', *Methodist Quarterly Review*, 4th series, 13 (1861), 627.

7 [Louis Agassiz], 'Prof. Agassiz on the Origin of Species', *American Journal of Science and Arts*, 2nd series, 30 (1860), 154.

8 Mariano Artigas, Thomas F. Glick and Rafael A. Martinez, *Negotiating Darwin: the Vatican Confronts Evolution, 1877–1902* (Baltimore: Johns Hopkins University Press, 2006), p. 281; John Henry Newman, 'Christianity and Physical Science. Lecture in the School of Medicine' [1855], in John Henry Newman, *The Idea of a University*, ed. by Frank M. Turner (New Haven: Yale University Press, 1996), p. 201. For more on the objections that were made to Darwin's theory on scientific grounds, see Roberts, *Darwinism and the Divine*, pp. 41–9; Ellegard, *Darwin*, p. 95.

9 Charles Lyell, *The Geological Evidences of the Antiquity of Man* (Philadelphia: G.W. Childs, 1863), pp. 469–506; Thomas H. Huxley, *[Evidence as to] Man's Place in Nature* (1863; Ann Arbor: University of Michigan Press, 1959), p. 125; J. W. Burrow, *Evolution and Society: a Study in Victorian Social Theory* (1966; Cambridge University Press, 1974), pp. 80–1.

10 [Albert Barnes], 'Readjustments of Christianity', *Presbyterian Quarterly Review* 11 (1862), 69; Ellegard, *Darwin*, pp. 42–3. A useful discussion of the Wilberforce–Huxley exchange can be found in David N. Livingstone, 'Re-placing Darwinism and Christianity', in David C. Lindberg and Ronald L. Numbers (eds.), *When Science and Christianity Meet* (University of Chicago Press, 2003), pp. 189–91.

11 Charles Darwin, *The Descent of Man, and Selection in Relation to Sex*, 2 vols. (1871; Princeton University Press, 1981), vol. 1, pp. 213, 206, 212, 185–6, 10–33.

12 Ibid., vol. 1, pp. 105, 106, 71, 85, 99, 89–90. For a brief summary of Darwin's treatment of humanity's mental powers and moral sense, see ibid., 1, pp. 103–6.

13 R. T. Brumby, 'Gradualness Characteristic of All God's Operations', *Southern Presbyterian Review* 25 (1874), p. 525. See also Ellegard, *Darwin*, pp. 311–29; Marc Swetlitz, 'American Jewish Responses to Darwin and Evolutionary Theory, 1860–1890', in Numbers and Stenhouse (eds.), *Disseminating Darwinism*, pp. 216–17.

14 Peter J. Bowler, 'Scientific Attitudes to Darwinism in Britain and America', in David Kohn (ed.), *The Darwinian Heritage* (Princeton University Press, 1985), pp. 654–5; Ronald L. Numbers, 'Darwinism and the Dogma of Separate Creations: the Responses of American Naturalists to Evolution', in *Darwinism Comes to America* (Cambridge, MA: Harvard University Press, 1998), pp. 29–30.

15 Numbers, 'Darwinism and the Dogma', pp. 43–4; Darwin, *Descent of Man*, vol. 1, p. 153; W.N. Rice, 'The Darwinian Theory of the Origin of Species', *New Englander* 26 (1867), 608–9. For a broader discussion of the history of methodological naturalism, see Ronald L. Numbers, 'Science without God: Natural Laws and Christian Beliefs', in Lindberg and Numbers (eds.), *When Science and Christianity Meet*, pp. 265–85.

16 Peter J. Bowler, *The Eclipse of Darwinism: Anti-Darwinian Evolution Theories in the Decades around 1900* (Baltimore: Johns Hopkins

University Press, 1983). Non-scientists also tended to conflate Darwinism and organic evolution. Ellegard, *Darwin*, p. 58; Roberts, *Darwinism and the Divine*, pp. 121–2.

17   Swetlitz, 'American Jewish Responses', pp. 213–17, 219–21, 223, 231, 233–4; Naomi W. Cohen, 'The Challenges of Darwinism and Biblical Criticism to American Judaism', *Modern Judaism* 4 (1984), 121–57, pp. 122–3; Marc Swetlitz, 'Responses of American Reform Rabbis to Evolutionary Theory, 1864–1888', in Yakov Rabkin and Ira Robinson (eds.), *The Interaction of Scientific and Jewish Cultures in Modern Times* (Lewiston, NY: Mellen Press, 1995), p. 106; Geoffrey Cantor, 'Anglo-Jewish Responses to Evolution', in Geoffrey Cantor and Marc Swetlitz (eds.), *Jewish Tradition and the Challenge of Darwinism* (University of Chicago Press, 2006), pp. 26, 29–31, 34–5.

18   Orestes A. Brownson, 'Darwin's Descent of Man' [1873], in *The Works of Orestes A. Brownson, Collected and Arranged by Henry F. Brownson*, 20 vols. (1882–7; New York: AMS Press, 1966), vol. IX, p. 496; Artigas *et al., Negotiating Darwin*, pp. 4, 277, 279–80 (quotation on p. 279); R. Scott Appleby, 'Exposing Darwin's "Hidden Agenda": Roman Catholic Responses to Evolution, 1875–1925', in Numbers and Stenhouse (eds.), *Disseminating Darwinism*, pp. 182–5, 178–80, 194–7; James Cardinal Gibbons, *Our Christian Heritage* (Baltimore: John Murphy, 1889), p. 281; John Rickards Betts, 'Darwinism, Evolution, and American Catholic Thought, 1860–1909', *Catholic Historical Review* 45 (1959), 161–85, pp. 172–3.

19   J.A. Zahm, *Evolution and Dogma* (1896; Hicksville, NY: Regina Press, 1975), xxx, pp. 345, 312–13; Artigas *et al., Negotiating Darwin*, pp. 124–202. See also Barry Brundell, 'Catholic Church Politics and Evolution Theory, 1894–1902', *British Journal for the History of Science* 34 (2001), 81–95; Appleby, 'Exposing Darwin's "Hidden Agenda"', pp. 175–6, 192–200; Michael V. Gannon, 'Before and After Modernism: the Intellectual Isolation of the American Priest', in John Tracy Ellis (ed.), *The Catholic Priest in the United States: Historical Investigations* (Collegeville, MN: Saint John's University Press, 1971), pp. 313–14.

20   Jon H. Roberts, 'Darwinism, American Protestant Thinkers, and the Puzzle of Motivation', in Numbers and Stenhouse (eds.), *Disseminating Darwinism*, pp. 145–72; David N. Livingstone, 'Science, Region, and Religion: the Reception of Darwinism in Princeton, Belfast, and Edinburgh', in Numbers and Stenhouse (eds.), *Disseminating Darwinism*, pp. 7–38. Unfortunately, no one has chosen to follow up Livingstone's provocative study with a more extensive examination of the role that local factors may have played in shaping responses.

Denominational affiliation has greater value in predicting the attitude of groups outside the Protestant mainline. See, for example, Ronald L. Numbers, '"Sciences of Satanic Origin": Adventist Attitudes toward Evolutionary Biology and Geology'; Numbers, 'Creation, Evolution, and Holy Ghost Religion: Holiness and Pentecostal Responses to Darwinism', in *Darwinism Comes to America*, pp. 92–135.

21 James T. Bixby, 'The Argument from Design in the Light of Modern Science', *Unitarian Review and Religious Magazine* 7 (1877), 21–3; F.A. Mansfield, 'Teleology, Old and New', *New Englander*, n.s., 7 (1884), 220; Andrew P. Peabody, 'Science and Revelation', *Princeton Review*, 4th series, 54th yr (1878), 766; William Newton Clarke, *An Outline of Christian Theology* (1898; New York: Charles Scribner's Sons, 1922), p. 107; Lewis F. Stearns, 'Reconstruction in Theology', *New Englander*, n.s., 5 (1882), 86.

22 M.H. Valentine, 'The Influence of the Theory of Evolution on the Theory of Ethics', *Lutheran Quarterly Review* 28 (1898), 218; Peter J. Bowler, *Reconciling Science and Religion: the Debate in Early-Twentieth-Century Britain* (University of Chicago Press, 2001), pp. 219–20.

23 G[eorge] F. W[right], 'Adjustments between the Bible and Science', *Bibliotheca Sacra* 49 (1892), 154. See also Bowler, *Reconciling Science and Religion*, pp. 221–2.

24 Aubrey Moore, 'The Christian Doctrine of God', in Charles Gore (ed.), *Lux Mundi: a Series of Studies in the Philosophy of the Incarnation* (1889; London: John Murray, 1890), p. 99; F.H. Johnson, 'Theistic Evolution', *Andover Review* 1 (1884), 372, 365 [originally the statement on 365 was in italics]. See also Owen Chadwick, *The Victorian Church*, 2 vols. (New York: Oxford University Press, 1966–70), vol. II, p. 31.

25 Henry A. Stimson, 'The Bible in the Conditions Created by Modern Scholarship', *Bibliotheca Sacra* 57 (1900), 370; Lyman Abbott, *The Theology of an Evolutionist* (Cambridge, MA: Riverside Press, 1897), p. 76. See also Henry Drummond, *The Lowell Lectures on The Ascent of Man*, 3rd edn (New York: James Pott, 1894), p. 342.

26 For a more extensive discussion of this theme, see Roberts, *Darwinism and the Divine*, pp. 176–9.

27 Myron Adams, *The Continuous Creation: an Application of the Evolutionary Philosophy to the Christian Religion* (Boston: Houghton, Mifflin and Company, 1889), pp. 193, 114, 87; Newman Smyth, *Old Faiths in New Light*, 2nd edn (New York: Charles Scribner's Sons, 1879), p. 265; John Coleman Adams, 'The Christ and the Creation', *Andover Review* 17 (1892), 233, 228–9.

28 S.R. Calthrop, 'The Great Synthesis, or the Foundation on Which All Things Rest', *Unitarian Review and Religious Magazine* 16 (1881), 1; William Rupp, 'The Theory of Evolution and the Christian Faith', *Reformed Quarterly Review* 35 (1888), 162–3, 165 (quotation on 162); Smyth, *Old Faiths*, pp. 38, 119, 76; William Newton Clarke, *Sixty Years with the Bible* (New York: Charles Scribner's Sons, 1912), p. 149; Samuel Harris, 'Have We a Theology?', *New Englander and Yale Review*, n.s., 9 [45] (1886), 123; F.H. Johnson, 'Coöperative Creation', *Andover Review* 3 (1885), 438.

29 Chadwick, *The Victorian Church*, vol. II, pp. 23–35; Bernard M.G. Reardon, *Religious Thought in the Victorian Age: a Survey from Coleridge to Gore* (London: Longman, 1980), p. 293; Ian S. Rennie, 'Fundamentalism and the Varieties of North Atlantic Evangelicalism', in Mark A. Noll, D. Bebbington and George A. Rawlyk (eds.),

Evangelicalism: Comparative Studies of Popular Protestantism in North America, the British Isles, and Beyond, 1700–1990 (New York: Oxford University Press, 1994), p. 337; George Marsden, 'Fundamentalism as an American Phenomenon: a Comparison with English Evangelicalism', *Church History* 46 (1977), 215–32.

30   John L. Girardeau, 'The Signs of the Times – In the Church' [1892], in George A. Blackburn (ed.), *Sermons* (Columbia, SC: The State Company, 1907), p. 116; Henry Darling, 'Preaching and Modern Skepticism', *Presbyterian Review* 2 (1881), 763–4.

31   John T. Duffield, 'Evolutionism, Respecting Man and the Bible', *Princeton Review*, 4th series, 54th yr (1878), 173, 174–5; M.E. Dwight, 'The Contest as it is To-day', *New Englander*, n.s., 7 (1884), p. 586; Roberts, *Darwinism and the Divine*, p. 212; Ronald Numbers, 'Creation, Evolution, and Holy Ghost Religion', *Religion and American Culture* 2 (1992), 127–58. Christian anti-evolutionism has received relatively little attention from historians of British religion. See, however, James R. Moore, *The Post-Darwinian Controversies: a Study of the Protestant Struggle to Come to Terms with Darwin in Great Britain and America, 1870–1900* (Cambridge University Press, 1979), pp. 201–2; Ellegard, *Darwin*, pp. 155–73, 203, 332–3.

32   Bowler, *Reconciling Science and Religion*, pp. 208–9, 224–9, 236–8, 246–52, 263–5, 270–3; Gary Dorrien, *The Making of American Liberal Theology: Idealism, Realism, and Modernity, 1900–1950* (Louisville, KY: Westminster John Knox Press, 2003), pp. 9, 25, 523; Newell Dwight Hillis, *The Influence of Christ in Modern Life: Being a Study of the New Problems of the Church in American Society* (New York: Macmillan, 1900), p. 211; Albrecht Ritschl, *The Christian Doctrine of Justification and Reconciliation: the Positive Development of the Doctrine*, ed. by H.R. Mackintosh and A.B. Macaulay, 3 vols., 3rd edn (New York: Charles Scribner's Sons, 1900), vol. III, pp. 16, 398, 205, 225.

33   Ronald L. Numbers, *The Creationists: From Scientific Creationism to Intelligent Design*, expanded edn (Cambridge, MA: Harvard University Press, 2006), pp. 52–3; J.J. Reeve, 'My Personal Experience with the Higher Criticism', in *The Fundamentals: a Testimony to the Truth* (Chicago: Testimony, n.d.), vol. III, p. 99; William B. Riley, *The Finality of Higher Criticism; Or, The Theory of Evolution and False Theology* (n.p.: n.p., 1909), pp. 72–3, 86–8.

    Higher critics insisted on bringing historical and philological expertise to bear in determining the dates and authorship of the biblical texts and on reading those texts, like any other book, as the product of the times and places in which they had been written. Many theologically conservative believers regarded that approach as an assault on the claim that the Scriptures had been divinely inspired.

34   Numbers, *Creationists*, pp. 55–6; Roberts, 'Conservative Evangelicals', 308–9.

5 Science and secularization

JOHN HEDLEY BROOKE

In August 2008, anticipating the 200th anniversary of the birth of Charles Darwin, and the 150th anniversary of the publication of his *Origin of Species* (1859), Richard Dawkins presented on British television three programmes designed to celebrate Darwin's genius. By contrasting Darwin's theory with ideas of creation that he ascribed to religion, Dawkins stressed the originality of Darwin's naturalistic account of how species developed from pre-existing forms. The invocation of a contrasting religious position had a didactic function – to reinforce the viewer's understanding of Darwin's science and its naturalistic presuppositions. A second goal, having many antecedents in the history of science, was to use the theory's supposed implications for religion as a technique for exciting public interest in, and appreciation of, Darwin's achievement. However brilliant the exposition of a scientific theory, without claims that the theory has major implications for something else there has always been the risk of indifference in a general audience. Because of their prevalence, religious beliefs have often, conveniently, constituted that something else. There can be a temptation in such contexts to exaggerate the cultural implications of scientific innovations for the purpose of promoting the science. Dawkins' anti-religious juxtaposition of science and religion does, however, serve a third and explicitly avowed goal – that of persuading those who live in religious darkness that there is a great light. For Dawkins, the need to convert creationists to neo-Darwinian evolution is a truly serious matter because of their tendency to demean the very science that means most to him and to other evolutionary biologists.[1]

It is hard not to sympathize with that concern. It does, however, raise a question of great interest to historians and sociologists of religion. What precisely is the relationship between scientific progress and the secularization of society? My purpose in this chapter is to offer reasons why there is no simple or general answer. Much depends on how the concept of secularization is understood and applied. Indeed problems arise immediately when the mutual bearings of science and religion are considered. This is because the word 'secularization' has been used to describe two processes that pull in contrary directions: the separation of science from religion, supposedly achieved in seventeenth-century Europe, and the fusion of science and religion whenever theological doctrines have been reinterpreted in the light of innovative science – as when Isaac Newton saw God's providence at work in the maintenance of the solar system.[2] Definitions of secularization usually refer to the displacement of religious authority and control by civic powers that usurp the functions formerly undertaken by religious institutions. The word also connotes a loss of plausibility and credibility affecting beliefs held within religious traditions. There is no simple relationship between these two processes. It has proved perfectly possible for religious institutions having political power to retain their control and influence, despite vigorous assaults on the credibility of their doctrine. The established Church in England in the late eighteenth century may have been ruffled by the onslaught of rationalist dissenters such as the Unitarian Joseph Priestley, but the disestablishment for which he campaigned was hardly a realistic possibility, especially during the conservative reaction following the French Revolution. Conversely, religious authorities may cede power to secular institutions in circumstances of irresistible political pressure (as in twentieth-century totalitarian regimes) when questions about the credibility of the religious teaching could be completely irrelevant.

Despite these immediate complications, it has seemed reasonable to suppose that secularization in the second sense – meaning a loss of plausibility in conventional religious teaching – might expedite secularization in the first sense – the loss of church involvement in the major events of a person's life. Is there not then a direct relation between the advance of science and a retreat of religion? This view is certainly favoured by many natural scientists and, from the mid-nineteenth to the mid-twentieth century, was often taken for granted by social scientists who, echoing one of the founders of their discipline, Auguste Comte, detected a sense of direction in human history. There had once been a theological phase, in which natural phenomena were ascribed to the actions of deities. This had been followed by a metaphysical age, in which nature was understood through deductive reasoning from abstract concepts. Finally, triumphantly, a new age had dawned – that of positive science, in which, for the understanding of nature, all that was required was an empirical method leading to the establishment of facts and laws.[3] There have been many variants of this scenario, having in common the view that the religious beliefs of antiquity irreversibly lost their credibility as scientific cosmologies progressively embarrassed them.

The difficulty, highlighted by Dawkins' encounter with American creationists, is that 150 years of Darwinian evolution have not yet eroded ultra-conservative religious positions. Moreover, recent decades have witnessed a resurgence of religious fundamentalism, even in societies permeated by science-based technologies. Consequently many social scientists have had to reconsider the formula that science has been the primary cause of an irreversible secularization. In the words of one, this formula belongs to a category of obviously true propositions, which on closer examination turn out to be largely false.[4] In those of another, 'the world today is massively religious, is anything but the secularised world that had been predicted (whether joyfully or despondently) by so many analysts of modernity'.[5]

The possibility of a divergence of perception between natural and social scientists could be illustrated in other ways. In November 2006 a new Center for Inquiry held its inaugural press conference in Washington, DC. Its aim was to 'promote and defend reason, science, and freedom of inquiry in all areas of human endeavor'. It stood for the belief that public policies should be shaped by secular values and it declared that science and secularism are 'inextricably linked'. From the standpoint of scientists worried by oppressive features of the Bush administration, it was imperative that new avenues of enquiry, such as stem cell technologies, should not be blocked by what appeared to be religiously informed scruples. But the reasons given for the urgency of their message included circumstances perhaps more consonant with the revised perspectives of the social sciences. For the annoyance sprang from 'the resurgence of fundamentalist religions across the nation, and their alliance with political-ideological movements to block science', from the 'persistence of paranormal and occult beliefs', and from a 'retreat into mysticism'.[6] If these were accurate perceptions, then one conclusion might be that the expanding scientific culture of the past three hundred years has not been so decisive (certainly not uniformly decisive) as an agent of secularization. In this chapter, I shall therefore consider several reasons why the issues are not as straightforward as they may seem. Is there perhaps an element of mythology in the proposition that science is a primary cause of secularization and in claims for inextricable linkage?

THE PLAUSIBILITY OF A PARADIGMATIC VIEW

Confidence in the power of the sciences to dissolve religious commitment has often been expressed. A typical prophecy would be that of the anthropologist Anthony Wallace: 'belief in supernatural powers is doomed to die out, all over the world, as a result of the increasing adequacy and diffusion of scientific knowledge'.[7] For Daniel Dennett the process of evaporation needs only a few more years to approach completion: 'in about 25 years almost all religions will have evolved into very different phenomena, so much so that in most quarters religion will no longer command the awe that it does today'. One reason for his confidence lies in the 'worldwide spread of information technology (not just the internet, but cell phones and portable radios and television)'.[8] An eyebrow might be raised when one reflects on the use of mobile phones among the Taliban, or the emergence of a virtual al-Qaida on the web; but Dennett's confidence is underpinned by the belief that religions can best be understood as sets of antiquated beliefs – beliefs about the supernatural – a characterization convenient for polemical purposes but scarcely adequate.[9]

It is not difficult to appreciate why correlations have been made between scientific progress and secularization. For the atomists of antiquity, one of the attractions of explaining the world through the categories of matter and motion was that one could then show, in the words of Lucretius, that nature had no need of gods. For Thomas Hobbes, writing in the seventeenth century when Epicurean atomism was enjoying a revival, the origins of religious belief lay in the fear and incomprehensibility of nature's forces. As scientific knowledge replaced ignorance, superstition (and with it religious credulity) would surely recede? It is a simple idea with a long pedigree. Where scientific explanation remained incomplete, religious thinkers might still plug the gaps with their gods, but further scientific advance would repeatedly shrink the jurisdiction of such gods-of-the-gaps. Whether it is always correct to identify the Christian God, for example, with a god-of-the-gaps is a question that advocates of the secularization thesis have not always asked. A transcendent God conceived as the source and ground of all being (and therefore of all natural processes) need not be the same as one invoked to explain specific natural phenomena. But a correlation between science and secularization retains its plausibility because of the manner in which scientific theories have clashed with conventional readings of sacred texts. The motion of the earth in Galileo's day and evolutionary accounts of human origins in Darwin's have been iconic examples, which in popular, simplified accounts have encouraged the view that science and religion are inherently incompatible. In this respect the conflict thesis, as it has become known, and the secularization thesis can be mutually reinforcing. Indeed, it was in the context of planning a secular curriculum for what became Cornell University that Andrew Dickson White experienced a clerical odium that motivated him to write his influential *History of the Warfare of Science with Theology in Christendom* (1896).[10]

The association of science with secularity does have deep roots. At their foundation in the 1660s, both the Royal Society of London and the Academy of Sciences in Paris had prohibited the discussion of religion at their meetings. Members of the clergy in seventeenth-century England who became absorbed by the study of nature sometimes expressed discomfort while managing their twin allegiances.[11] At different times new forms of science have provided solace for materialists and atheists, as they did in France in the middle years of the eighteenth century when several exciting discoveries (including the spectacular ability of a freshwater polyp to regenerate itself from dismembered parts) seemed to show that matter could organize itself.[12] Crucially, it would be difficult to deny that advances in medicine and technology have helped to dispel a reliance on Providence alone in the pursuit of human health and prosperity.

Although it is impossible to generalize, it is easy to find examples of eminent scientists renouncing their religious heritage. The description godless or non-Jewish applies to prominent Jewish scientists of the twentieth century.[13] Since professed and vociferous atheists are more likely to catch the public ear than scientists who quietly combine their scientific and spiritual lives, a correlation between science and antireligious sentiment tends to endure. The atheism of Francis Crick, for example, was highly newsworthy in the early 1960s when he resigned his Fellowship at Churchill College Cambridge at the prospect of the building of a college chapel. The atheism of scientists today such as Richard Dawkins, Daniel Dennett and Steven Weinberg attracts public attention because of its forceful expression. Nevertheless, the question still remains whether it is science that has driven the processes of secularization. Reflecting on the heated debates within Churchill College in the 1960s, a historian of the college has recently written:

> It is now harder to assert that secularisation is a one-way process
> to be equated with modernity. The atheist's conception of
> religion as a primitive stage in the evolution of humankind and

hence a branch of anthropology – the view of ... Crick in 1961 – involves an Enlightenment teleology, which heralds a hopeful secular millennium, an end of history, in which a benign and rational Age of Science arrives. That story (what postmodernists would call the 'grand narrative' of modernity) now seems a little threadbare. In a post-positivist age there is greater acceptance of the radical incommensurability of diverse modes of understanding, and less readiness to reduce all knowing to a single, reductive epistemology.[14]

For good measure he adds that within the Fellowship at Churchill College two Nobel Prize winners out of three had been churchgoers.

TOWARDS A CRITIQUE OF THE PARADIGM

Is there something essential to both science and religion that necessarily places them in opposition? Detailed historical investigations suggest otherwise.[15] Does respect for scientific methods necessarily lead to corrosion of religious belief? It may do so, but it is difficult to see a necessary connection when those remaining loyal to their spiritual formations have included eminent scientists.[16] Is it even appropriate to reduce the major religions to sets of beliefs (ostensibly primitive explanatory hypotheses) when what has mattered most to their adherents has been forms of practice and the transformative experiences accompanying them? In addition, most scientific knowledge has no, or very little, bearing on beliefs held within religious communities. Conversely, religious affiliation, and the sense of self-identity it may confer, can be completely unaffected by advances in the sciences. Taking such complications seriously, critics of the secularization thesis have observed that 'publicized scientific claims about the world seem largely inconsequential to belief and practice in contemporary American religion' while 'most of the truth claims of religion are not publicly contested by science'.[17] In the only partial coalescence of their respective spheres lies one reason why the paradigm that science causes secularization should be questioned.

Another reason stems from the difference between secularization of science and secularization by science. It is true that in Europe and North America religious language had almost completely disappeared from technical scientific literature by the end of the nineteenth century. This might be called the endpoint of a secularization of science. Contrary to a common assumption, scientific achievement at the highest level had not been prevented by earlier deference to divine power and its expression in the world. Newton, for example, had been able to articulate his laws of motion and construct his theory of gravitation while still believing that it was possible for the deity to vary the laws of nature in different parts of the universe and even to initiate processes designed to protect the long-term stability of the solar system.[18] Nevertheless, to explain observable phenomena only by reference to natural causes proved so successful in succeeding centuries that this principle (sometimes described today as methodological naturalism) was firmly consolidated as part of the culture of science. The fact that an active deity was no longer required for scientific purposes does not, however, mean that it was rendered redundant for others, such as the construction of a theology reflective of and relevant to moral and spiritual refinement. The establishment of a methodological naturalism did not entail the ontological conclusion that there is nothing but nature; nor did it prevent distinguished scientists in the twentieth century from holding fast to their faith. A striking example would be the British Quaker Arthur Eddington, whose pacifism during and immediately following the First World War found expression in his determination to re-establish collaboration with German scientists and to honour Einstein in particular.[19]

Even in iconic forms of secular science, such as Darwin's theory of evolution by natural selection, it was possible to speak, as Darwin had, of a creator who created by laws.[20] The limit questions, such as why anything should exist at all, could still attract theistic answers from those whose lives were confessedly enriched by their religious commitment. Even the figure most commonly associated with science-based agnosticism, Thomas Henry Huxley, insisted that those who wished to see design in a Darwinian universe could continue to do so, since there was nothing to prevent the positing of design in a rudimentary configuration of the universe that contained the potential for subsequent evolution. Darwin's theory, in that respect, had no implications for theism.[21] Huxley even contested one of the main supports of the paradigm we are examining – that science necessarily conflicted with religion. Huxley's anti-clericalism, anti-Catholicism and opposition to a powerful Anglican establishment was sometimes expressed in ways suggesting that it did; but his considered view was otherwise.[22] As he put it in 1885, 'the antagonism between science and religion, about which we hear so much, appears to me to be purely factitious – fabricated, on the one hand, by short-sighted religious people who confound a certain branch of science, theology, with religion; and, on the other, by equally short-sighted scientific people who forget that science takes for its province only that which is susceptible of clear intellectual comprehension'.[23] The dogmatic theologian might be threatened by science but the experiential and emotional aspects of the religious life were not.

Huxley's discrimination reminds us that the wider cultural significance given to scientific theories has depended on values specific to particular times and places and on the preconceptions of those who presume to act as interpreters. There are many examples of scientists with religious convictions having found confirmation of their faith in the beauty and elegance of the mechanisms their research uncovers.[24] For the seventeenth-century astronomer Johannes Kepler the mathematical elegance of the laws describing planetary motion was such that he had been carried away by 'unutterable rapture at the divine spectacle of heavenly harmony'.[25] A contemporary example would be the former director of the Human Genome Project, Francis Collins, who, as an evangelical Christian, sees his work not as corrosive of faith but as the unravelling of a God-given code.[26]

Instead of regarding science as the agent of an inexorable secularization, it is surely more accurate to say that scientific theories have been susceptible of both theistic and atheistic readings. Historically they have provided resources for both. Sometimes the same scientific concept, in different hands, has been manipulated to generate a sense of the sacred or of the profane. For Richard Dawkins, Darwin's theory of evolution by natural selection first made it possible to be an intellectually fulfilled atheist. But it is easy to forget that among Darwin's earliest sympathizers in Britain were Christian clergymen such as Charles Kingsley, and Frederick Temple.[27] Kingsley delighted Darwin by suggesting that the idea of a God who could make things make themselves was nobler than the idea of one who had to intervene to conjure new species into existence. Temple, who welcomed the discovery of natural laws because they gave analogical support for belief in the provenance of moral laws, was later to become archbishop of Canterbury. Although an agnostic late in life, Darwin denied he had ever been an atheist.[28] Instead of seeing science as intrinsically and inextricably secular, it is the cultural meanings attached to it, and invested in it, that require analysis. With respect to the existence of a transcendent deity it would be difficult to claim that science has ever settled the issue. This is not to deny that Darwin's theory has been used to justify unbelief. It has, many times. But the ulterior question is whether its use as justification might not conceal other, more potent, reasons for unbelief.

THE SPRING OF UNBELIEF

If one facet of secularization is a reduction in the plausibility of the truth-claims by which religious traditions authenticate themselves, it becomes important to discover the reasons given by honest doubters for their doubts. How prominent is science as a determinant? Although it is impossible to generalize, it is striking how, even among scientists themselves, an antipathy to organized religion has sprung from other roots. Darwin's rejection of Christianity hardly derived from the role he gave to natural causes in explaining the origin of species. Like other Victorian thinkers, Darwin reacted strongly against evangelical Christian preaching on heaven and hell. Members of his family, including his father and his brother Erasmus, were freethinkers. The doctrine that after death they would suffer eternal damnation was, for Charles, a 'damnable doctrine'.[29] He was also deeply sensitive to the extent of pain and suffering in the world, which he described as one of the strongest arguments against belief in a beneficent deity. Each of these concerns was intensified by deaths in his family – that of his father in the late 1840s and of his ten-year-old daughter, Annie, early in 1851.[30] Darwin also found the concept of divine revelation unacceptable, citing the ignorance of the gospel writers and the peculiar relationship between Old and New Testaments. Independently of any scientific considerations, he confessed to the Harvard botanist Asa Gray that he was simply unable to ascribe the contingencies affecting every human life to a designing and watchful Providence.[31] It would be false to say of Darwin that science, more than any other factor, was responsible for his unbelief.

Examining the trajectory of one individual, even one as illustrious as Darwin, can of course only be suggestive. Surveys have, however, been conducted on larger samples of secularists to ascertain the reasons for their unbelief. The results only confirm that to give primacy to science is a mistake. From the direct testimony of one hundred and fifty unbelievers in the period 1850 to 1960, and drawing on related evidence from two hundred additional biographies, it has been found that science barely featured at all.[32] Conversions to unbelief were often associated with a change from conservative to more radical politics, with religion being rejected as part of established, privileged society. The reading of radical texts, such as Thomas Paine's *Age of Reason*, was another prominent influence.[33] Ironically, another frequently mentioned book was the Bible itself, close study of which revealed what were seen as inconsistencies, absurdities or (particularly in the Old Testament) depictions of a vengeful and anthropomorphic deity. In 1912 the president of the National Secular Society in Britain protested that biblical stories of 'lust, adultery, incest and unnatural vice' were 'enough to raise blushes in a brothel'.[34] The fact that every Christian sect, indeed every religion, claimed its own hotline to the truth was a prevalent consideration having nothing to do with science. Perceptions of immorality in some religious doctrines, particularly those concerning an afterlife, and the perceived immoral behaviour of some priests fuelled a rejection of religious authority. The realization that atheists could be as morally upright as believers also took its toll, as it did for Darwin when, in his London years, he encountered the circle of radical dissenters that gathered around his brother's friend Harriet Martineau. The high moral stand they took on subjects such as the abolition of slavery showed him that orthodox Christians did not have a monopoly on moral sensibility.[35] It was Martineau who translated Comte's *Positive Philosophy* into English, spreading the word that the universe ran according to fixed laws not to divine caprice.

This drive towards a more secular view of nature relied, however, as much on historical as scientific research. In particular the efforts of German biblical scholars to recover the context in which the gospel writers had interpreted the life and death of Jesus Christ proved unsettling as the biblical authors came to be seen not as timeless authorities but as fallible products of their own culture. The notion that the Bible should be read like any other book featured prominently in a collection of *Essays and Reviews* (1860) published in England hard on the heels of Darwin's *Origin of Species* (1859). Because Oxford clergy were among the contributors, this book caused more of a stir within the English church than that of Darwin. Samuel Wilberforce, bishop of Oxford, is associated with clerical attacks on Darwin's theory because of his notorious wrangle with Huxley, but his response to *Essays and Reviews* was more vituperative than his indictment of Darwin.[36] Internecine disputes within religious bodies have arguably been more damaging to their authority than attacks from outside.

RELIGION IN SOCIETY

Changing concepts of nature have certainly changed the terms of debate on such questions as the origin, age and autonomy of the universe, on issues such as whether there is evidence for design in the structure of living things, and whether humankind may still be said to be unique in a post-Darwinian world. However, as Mary Douglas observed, those who imagine science the principal cause of secularization forget that religious activity is grounded in social relations, not primarily in concepts of nature.[37] Membership of a religious group, in addition to providing emotional support, may contribute to a shared sense of purpose, reinforce a sense of self-identity and provide an orientation that scientific knowledge alone, at least for many, is unable to provide. Observers of the large (by European standards) congregations in the churches of many American cities cannot but be struck by the fact that these are institutions that also provide generous opportunities to engage in many socially cohesive sporting and cultural pursuits. Consequently it seems wise to look to changes in social structure and to changes in organized religion itself if one wishes to understand the momentum of secularity. There are detailed case studies that support this emphasis on the social. An investigation into the reduction of religious activity on a Danish island led to the conclusion that it was not due to an encounter with scientific knowledge or methods but rather to a transformation of social relations, associated with the mechanization of agriculture. This had depleted village populations and weakened social bonds. For the author of this study the problem with the conventional secularization paradigm is its definition of religion as a method of explaining the physical world through the supernatural. On the contrary, 'it is explaining the social world, giving it meaning and moral value, which is religion's primary concern'.[38]

In modern times, the expansion of secularism can be correlated with social, political and economic transformations having little direct connection with science but having much to do with the weakening of the social ties that religious affiliation has provided. Historians point to increases in social and geographical mobility that have fractured communities once bound by common religious values. In many contexts, the growth of capitalism, commerce and consumerism has fostered a pervasive hedonism that threatens commitment to religious institutions and their long-term goals. Competing attractions have encouraged the marginalizing of religious worship. Secular values have been heavily promoted in the sphere of education and by the media. In some countries religious solidarity has been displaced by national solidarity or by the ideology of political parties. The fact that such transformations have taken place at different rates and to different degrees in different cultures means there is 'no consistent relation between the degree of scientific advance and a reduced profile of religious influence, belief and practice'.[39]

Because different societies have experienced the tension between secular and sacred values in contrasting ways, there is no one, universal process of secularization that can be ascribed to science or to any other factor. The freedom in the United States to believe more or less anything from a smorgasbord of ideas, ideals and therapies contrasts sharply with the repressive constraints at work in societies such as the former East Germany, where, under a communist regime, such freedom of expression was denied. Where nations with a long religious tradition have been oppressed by a foreign power, religion has often reinforced a sense of national identity that breaks out of its chains with a new vitality once freedom has been gained. The strength of Catholicism in Poland supplies a modern example. The collapse of communist ideology within Russia itself allowed an old union of faith and nation to be reignited. A history of secularization in France would be very different from its history in the United States, where centralizing tendencies of all kinds have been resisted.[40] As a very broad generalization, it has been the mainly Catholic societies in Europe that have experienced the more militant forms of secular activism, as resistance to the imposition of religious conformity has, at different times, inspired an oppositional culture. Provocation can, however, cut both ways. Aggressive anti-religious remarks made by vociferous scientists frequently elicit strong reactions and reinforced resolve from those who find in their social and religious identity a meaning and value they are unwilling to renounce.

SECULARIZATION – A THIRD DIMENSION

Of the two primary meanings of secularization so far considered – a diminution in the scope and power of religious institutions and a loss of plausibility in their doctrines – it is the second on which the sciences are usually assumed to have the most impact. Epitomizing a common view would be Darwin's remark that the more we know of the fixed laws of nature, the more incredible do miracles become.[41] There are, however, significant problems with a formula as simple as this, not least because a sharp distinction between nature and supernature is not a timeless one, but in its modern form is itself a product of secularization. What has been meant by nature (and therefore by supernature) has itself changed with time. For Robert Boyle, as a Christian natural philosopher writing in the second half of the seventeenth century, it was a mistake to ascribe any causal agency to nature. To speak of nature abhorring a vacuum or initiating effects was simply vulgar talk. Physical phenomena were not caused by a personified nature, or by laws of nature. Causal efficacy was ultimately grounded in the will and power of God.[42] As Newton's advocate Samuel Clarke explained, the laws uncovered by scientific research were summaries of the rules by which God normally chose to work in the world. This image of a deity working through nature differs from a modern secular understanding in which natural and supernatural explanations are (often unquestioningly) assumed to be in competition. More fundamental changes in religious sensibility were therefore necessary before the dichotomy could assume its modern secular form.[43] Only when it had done so would it begin to appear self-evident that, where scientists could explain phenomena naturalistically, appeals to divine activity would lose credibility.

Here it is helpful to introduce a third dimension of secularization – one to which the sciences could be relevant but only in conjunction with other transformations. This additional dimension has received masterly analysis in Charles Taylor's *A Secular Age* (2007), which examines the change 'from a society in which it was virtually impossible not to believe in God, to one in which faith, even for the staunchest believer, is one human possibility among others'.[44] What makes secularization in this sense possible is the multiplication of admissible, alternative options. On the basis of this understanding, Taylor suggests a significant contrast between contemporary Christian and Muslim societies: 'there are big differences between these societies in *what it is to believe*, stemming in part from the fact that belief is an option, and in some sense an embattled option in the Christian (or "post-Christian") society, and not (or not yet) in the Muslim ones'.[45] In other words, in Western democracies the presence of serious alternatives to Christian monotheism has subtly changed the conditions of belief:

> Belief in God is no longer axiomatic. There are alternatives.
> And this will also likely mean that at least in certain milieux,
> it may be hard to sustain one's faith. There will be people who
> feel bound to give it up, even though they mourn its loss. This
> has been a recognizable experience in our societies, at least since
> the mid-nineteenth century. There will be many others to whom
> faith never even seems an eligible possibility. There are certainly
> millions today of whom this is true.[46]

At first glance, Taylor's emphasis on the opening up of new possibilities and their secularizing role would seem to leave plenty of room for scientific input. During the past three hundred and fifty years scientific innovations have graduated into worldviews that have surely constituted alternatives to worldviews informed by religious values? The mechanistic worldview of seventeenth-century cosmology, worldviews constructed on the basis of evolutionary biology or informed by influential schools of psychoanalysis surely challenged sacred understandings of what was once our more central place in the universe?

Sigmund Freud for one certainly believed so and it could hardly be disputed that crusading secularists have beaten the drum of science when seeking to undermine the authority and power of religious institutions. There is a well-documented example in the success of popular Darwinism in nineteenth-century Germany.[47] Of the major European countries, Germany had seen the greatest surge in mass literacy, creating the conditions for Darwinism to engage a wider public. It did so through the efforts of scientific rationalists and materialists such as Ernst Haeckel, Carl Vogt, Ludwig Büchner and Wilhelm Bölsche, each peddling the notion that evolution was now victorious over a defunct Christianity. Typically, a primordial creation of matter was ridiculed and rejected on the ground that it violated the scientific principle of energy conservation. Darwin's account of human evolution was the perfect scientific resource for advancing monistic views in opposition to the body/soul dualism that, in different forms, had dominated theological understanding. A high degree of receptivity to Darwinism in Germany owed much to the influence of earlier dissident philosophies such as that of Ludwig Feuerbach, for whom images of God were essentially human projections that the churches had too readily objectified, and to a materialism in which the relation of mind to brain was simply that of urine to kidneys. The idea that a worldview constructed on the basis of scientific rationality was opposed to the worldview of conventional religion took such a hold among a receptive proportion of the German working classes that popular Darwinism almost became a surrogate religion. In its proclamation of an evolving, self-improving universe it proved more seductive to many than Marxism, which itself added to the range of alternative worldviews.[48]

Despite the manner in which forms of popular science might reflect and reinforce secular attitudes, Taylor gives cogent reasons for rejecting the thesis that science has crowded out religion. Despite the protestations of anti-religious crusaders, arguments for disbelief in the existence of God based on scientific knowledge are not in themselves particularly binding. When scientists do invoke their science to legitimate unbelief, they may easily overlook the real reasons for their stance and the hidden assumptions concealed in them. Taylor does not deny that once one has taken the step into unbelief, there are overwhelming reasons why one will be induced to buy into the official, science-driven story. But the crucial question is why, if science-based arguments are inconclusive, do they seem so convincing? Taylor's answer is that the power of materialism today comes not from the scientific facts, but from the power of a larger package uniting materialism with a moral outlook. This package he calls atheist humanism, or exclusive humanism. To make scientific progress the driving force of secularism is to conflate religious beliefs with explanatory hypotheses and to miss the most important items in the larger package. It is in the development of an exclusive humanism in Western cultures that Taylor locates the deeper springs of secularization.

By an exclusive or self-sufficient humanism Taylor means 'a humanism accepting no final goals beyond human flourishing, nor any allegiance to anything else beyond this flourishing'.[49] Although in Christianity human flourishing was seen as a good, single-mindedly to seek it was never an ultimate goal. The quality of one's earthly life was not an end in itself. A more pressing goal was to live according to the will of God in the hope of finding an acceptance that would be of greater significance beyond the grave. Taylor's claim is that the coming of modern secularity has been 'coterminous with the rise of a society in which for the first time in history a purely self-sufficient humanism came to be a widely available option'.[50]

To understand how that came about it is more instructive to examine changes in moral sensibility than changes in scientific theory. Taylor himself notes the emergence of a polite sociability increasingly evident in much of eighteenth-century Europe, which put a strain on strong forms of sacral authority.[51] This sidelining of the sacred is visible in the writings of David Hume, for example, which for Taylor exemplify the main characteristics of a new moral order. What Hume decried as sterile monkish virtues had to be replaced by a civic morality in which human actions were for the benefit and improvement of society: 'Celibacy, fasting, penance, mortification, self-denial, humility, silence, solitude, and the whole train of monkish virtues; for what reason are they everywhere rejected by men of sense, but because they serve no manner of purpose; neither advance a man's fortune in the world, nor render him a more valuable member of society.'[52]

Fundamental to the construction of the newer, alternative morality was an emphasis on personal liberty, a respect for the interests and opinions of others, an understanding that social intercourse is for mutual benefit, and the ascription of high value to commerce and productive activities.[53]

How is such a major shift to be explained? Taylor's study is important because it gives added substance to the claim that we should not look to progress in the natural sciences for an easy answer. Rather the new moral order was associated with what he describes as a providential deism, a philosophy in which the world ran according to laws that had been set up by a benevolent creator who had not, however, made any special revelation to humankind. This was a philosophy that in Matthew Tindal's *Christianity as Old as the Creation* (1730) reduced the Christian faith to what could be believed on the basis of natural reason. The concomitant secularization shone in Tindal's affirmation that the duties of a truly religious person and of a good citizen are one and the same.

It is undeniable that science had a place in the writings of the deists. The brilliance of Newton's synthesis, for example, enshrined in his *Principia Mathematica* (1687), showed what human reason could achieve in the interpretation of nature. A new tone of thought, as well as an incipient new morality, made common religious practices seem more superstitious than ever before. Nevertheless, there is ample evidence to show that awareness of an emerging scientific culture played at most a subordinate role. Tindal, whose book was described as the bible of the deists, laid far greater stress on cultural relativism. Ever since the great voyages of discovery there had been problems concerning the exclusivity of the Christian dispensation. What redemption would be available to those who had never heard of Jesus Christ? If a culture as civilized as that of the Chinese had prospered without the Christian gospel, the implications could be serious and disturbing. Especially disturbing to Tindal was the thought that, if the primacy of reason were denied, one would succumb to the religious mores of one's native society. When he attacked the biblical miracles, it was not their incompatibility with scientific laws that he stressed, but rather the presence of miracle stories in every religious tradition. This was a point on which Hume would capitalize in his critique of reported miracles, claiming that those of one religion effectively cancelled out those of any other. Far from being the mainspring of Tindal's secular theology, scientific progress was a resource actually used against him by orthodox divines. In his subtle work of Christian apologetics, *The Analogy of Religion* (1736), Joseph Butler observed that obscurities in the meaning of Scripture, in which the deists revelled, might with further research be clarified – just as obscurities in the book of nature had yielded to scientific research.[54]

A PERVASIVE IRONIC PATTERN

If it is correct to regard the providential deism of the eighteenth century as the pivotal development that paved the way for a respectable self-sufficient humanism, there is irony in the fact that this deistic philosophy was itself an outcome of the Christian culture that it eventually subverted. Since the Reformation, Protestant Christians had been attacking many features of Catholic beliefs and practices. The belief that, during the Eucharist, the bread and wine were miraculously turned into the body and blood of Christ had been a common target, as had the higher profile in general given to miracles by the Catholic Church. In many respects the de-mystification of Christianity by the deists was an extension of continuing Protestant attacks on papal authority. Tindal's abhorrence of Catholic practices illustrates the continuity: 'the Popish priests claiming a power by divine right to absolve people upon confession, have been led into the secrets of all persons, and by virtue of it have governed all things'.[55]

The irony here is an aspect of a recurring ironic pattern that must be recognized if the complex relations between science and secularization are to be understood. The vision of a science-based utopia that had emerged during the seventeenth century, particularly in the writings of Francis Bacon, involved a translation of Christian ideas concerning a future millennium when Christ would return to earth to reign for a thousand years.[56] Discussions of scientific method in seventeenth-century England were often grounded in the doctrine of the Fall and the degree to which a pristine Adamic knowledge could be restored.[57] A mechanistic worldview, which did eventually challenge Christian ideas of a deity involved in the minutiae of human lives, had earlier featured as a defence of Christian theism through its support for arguments from design.[58] Machines did not, could not, design or make themselves. The concept of laws of nature that was eventually placed in opposition to notions of divine intervention originated, at least in part, in the theological concept of a divine legislator.[59] The ironic pattern is, however, most deeply etched in a dialectical relationship between the use of science to defend Christianity and its unintended consequences. This is one of several respects in which scientists could be destructive despite themselves.[60] In sophisticated accounts of the origins of modern atheism it is recognized that where Christian apologists relied on a science-based natural theology to secure the rationality of belief, their efforts often backfired either by inviting an atheistic response or by depending, damagingly, on obsolescent theories.[61] The adage that nobody doubted the existence of God until the Boyle lecturers undertook to prove it is certainly an exaggeration. It does, however, capture an ironic aspect of secularization and of scientific progress in relation to it. Tempting though it may be to see in the sciences the driving force of secularization, this ironic pattern, in conjunction with the other considerations reviewed in this chapter, indicates that it was rarely that simple.

Notes

1   Richard Dawkins, *The Genius of Charles Darwin*, Channel 4 television series, August 2008.
2   For this and other problems in the application of the term 'secularization', see John Hedley Brooke, 'Science and Secularisation', in Linda Woodhead (ed.), *Reinventing Christianity* (Aldershot: Ashgate, 2001), pp. 229–38.
3   John Hedley Brooke and Geoffrey Cantor, *Reconstructing Nature: the Engagement of Science and Religion* (Edinburgh: T. and T. Clark, 1998), pp. 47–57; Richard G. Olson, *Science and Scientism in Nineteenth-Century Europe* (Urbana: University of Illinois Press, 2008), pp. 62–84.
4   David Martin, 'Does the Advance of Science mean Secularisation?', *Science and Christian Belief* 19 (2007), 3–14.
5   Peter L. Berger, 'The Desecularization of the World: a Global Overview', in Peter L. Berger (ed.), *The Desecularization of the World: Resurgent Religion and World Politics* (Grand Rapids, MI: Eerdmans, 1999), pp. 1–18, p. 9.
6   Center for Inquiry, 'Declaration in Defense of Science and Secularism', at www.cfidc.org/declaration.html, accessed 9 May 2007.
7   Anthony F. C. Wallace, *Religion: an Anthropological View* (New York: Random House, 1966), pp. 264–5. Cited in Ronald L. Numbers, *Science and Christianity in Pulpit and Pew* (New York: Oxford University Press, 2007), p. 129.
8   Daniel Dennett, from an interview entitled 'The Evaporation of the Powerful Mystique of Religion' on the website of the Edge Foundation, www.edge.org, cited by John Gray, 'The Atheist Delusion', *The Guardian*, review section, 15 March 2008.
9   John H. Evans and Michael S. Evans, 'Religion and Science: Beyond the Epistemological Conflict Narrative', *Annual Review of Sociology* 34 no. 5 (2008), 87–105.
10   James R. Moore, *The Post-Darwinian Controversies* (Cambridge University Press, 1979), pp. 29–49.
11   Mordechai Feingold, 'Science as a Calling? The Early Modern Dilemma', *Science in Context* 15 (2002), 79–119.
12   John Hedley Brooke, *Science and Religion: Some Historical Perspectives* (Cambridge University Press, 1991), pp. 171–80.
13   Noah Efron, *Judaism and Science: a Historical Introduction* (Westport, CT: Greenwood Press, 2007), p. 205.

14 Mark Goldie, *God's Bordello: Storm over a Chapel. A History of the Chapel at Churchill College Cambridge* (Cambridge: Churchill College, 2007), p. 30.

15 For an introduction to a large revisionist and anti-essentialist historical literature, see David C. Lindberg and Ronald L. Numbers (eds.), *God and Nature: Historical Essays on the Encounter between Christianity and Science* (Berkeley: University of California Press, 1986); Brooke, *Science and Religion*; Brooke and Cantor, *Reconstructing Nature*.

16 Nicolaas A. Rupke (ed.), *Eminent Lives in Twentieth-Century Science and Religion* (Frankfurt: Peter Lang, 2007).

17 Evans and Evans, 'Religion and Science', p. 100.

18 Isaac Newton, Query 31 of *Opticks*, reprint edn (New York: Dover, 1952), pp. 400–4.

19 Matthew Stanley, *Practical Mystic: Religion, Science, and A. S. Eddington* (University of Chicago Press, 2007).

20 John Hedley Brooke, '"Laws Impressed on Matter by the Deity"?: The *Origin* and the Question of Religion', in Michael Ruse and Robert J. Richards (eds.), *The Cambridge Companion to the Origin of Species* (Cambridge University Press, 2008), pp. 256–74.

21 T.H. Huxley, 'On the Reception of the "Origin of Species"', in Francis Darwin (ed.), *The Life and Letters of Charles Darwin*, 3 vols. (London: Murray, 1887), vol. II, pp. 179–204.

22 Bernard Lightman, 'Victorian Sciences and Religions: Discordant Harmonies', *Osiris* 16 (2001), 343–66.

23 T.H. Huxley, *Science and Hebrew Tradition* (London: Macmillan, 1904), pp. 160–1.

24 Brooke and Cantor, *Reconstructing Nature*, pp. 207–43.

25 Max Caspar, *Kepler* (London and New York: Abelard-Schuman, 1959), p. 267.

26 Francis Collins, *The Language of God* (London: Simon and Schuster, 2007).

27 John Hedley Brooke, 'Darwin and Victorian Christianity', in Jonathan Hodge and Gregory Radick (eds.), *The Cambridge Companion to Darwin* (Cambridge University Press, 2003), pp. 192–213.

28 Francis Darwin (ed.), *Life and Letters of Darwin*, vol. I, p. 304.

29 Charles Darwin, *The Autobiography of Charles Darwin, 1809–1882, with Original Omissions Restored*, ed. by Nora Barlow (London: Collins, 1958), p. 87.

30 Adrian Desmond and James Moore, *Darwin* (London: Michael Joseph, 1991), pp. 375–87.

31 Francis Darwin (ed.), *Life and Letters of Darwin*, vol. I, p. 315.

32 Susan Budd, *Varieties of Unbelief: Atheists and Agnostics in English Society, 1850–1960* (London: Heinemann, 1977).

33 Ibid., pp. 107–9.

34 Ibid., p. 109.

35 Fiona Erskine, 'Darwin in Context: the London Years', PhD dissertation, Open University (1987).

36 Samuel Wilberforce, *Essays Contributed to the Quarterly Review*, 2 vols. (London: Murray, 1874), vol. I, pp. 52–103, 104–83.

37   Mary Douglas, 'The Effects of Modernization on Religious Change', *Proceedings of the American Academy of Arts and Sciences* 111 (1982), 1–19.

38   A. Buckser, 'Religion, Science, and Secularisation Theory on a Danish Island', *Journal of the Scientific Study of Religion* 35 (1996), 432–41; Evans and Evans, 'Religion and Science', p. 90.

39   Martin, 'Advance of Science', p. 9.

40   I have drawn these remarks from John Hedley Brooke, 'The Myth that Modern Science has Secularized Western Culture', in Ronald L. Numbers (ed.), *Galileo Goes to Jail and Other Myths in Science and Religion* (Cambridge, MA: Harvard University Press, 2009), ch. 25.

41   Darwin, *Autobiography*, p. 86.

42   Robert Boyle, *A Free Enquiry into the Vulgarly Received Notion of Nature* (1686), sections II and IV, in M. A. Stewart (ed.), *Selected Philosophical Papers of Robert Boyle* (Manchester University Press, 1979), pp. 176–91. For the full text of this essay, see Michael Hunter and Edward B. Davis (eds.), *The Works of Robert Boyle*, 14 vols. (London: Pickering and Chatto, 1999–2000), vol. x.

43   Brooke, *Science and Religion*, p. 36.

44   Charles Taylor, *A Secular Age* (Cambridge, MA: Harvard University Press, 2007), p. 3.

45   Ibid., p. 3.

46   Ibid., p. 3.

47   Alfred Kelly, *The Descent of Darwin: the Popularization of Darwinism in Germany, 1860–1914* (Chapel Hill: University of North Carolina Press, 1981); Frederick Gregory, *Scientific Materialism in Nineteenth-Century Germany* (Dordrecht: Reidel, 1977).

48   Brooke, *Science and Religion*, pp. 296–303.

49   Taylor, *Secular Age*, p. 18.

50   Ibid., p. 18.

51   Ibid., p. 238.

52   David Hume, *Enquiry Concerning the Principles of Morals*, Section IX, para. 219, in A. Selby-Bigge (ed.), *David Hume, Enquiries* (Oxford University Press, 1902), pp. 269–70; Brooke, *Science and Religion*, pp. 180–9.

53   Taylor, *Secular Age*, pp. 236–7.

54   In this paragraph I have followed Brooke, *Science and Religion*, pp. 168–71.

55   Matthew Tindal, *Christianity as Old as the Creation* (London, 1732), p. 102.

56   Charles Webster, *The Great Instauration: Science, Medicine and Reform, 1626–1660* (London: Duckworth, 1975), pp. 15–31; E. L. Tuveson, *Millennium and Utopia* (New York: Harper, 1964).

57   Peter Harrison, *The Fall of Man and the Foundations of Science* (Cambridge University Press, 2007).

58   Brooke, *Science and Religion*, pp. 13, 118, 130–44.

59 John R. Milton, 'The Origin and Development of the Concept of the "Laws of Nature"', *European Journal of Sociology* 22 (1981), 173–95; Francis Oakley, 'Christian Theology and the Newtonian Science: the Rise of the Concept of the Laws of Nature', *Church History* 30 (1961), 433–57; Lydia Jaeger, *Lois de la nature et raisons du coeur: les convictions religieuses dans le débat épistémologique contemporain* (Bern: Peter Lang, 2007).

60 Peter Burke, 'Religion and Secularisation', in Peter Burke (ed.), *The New Cambridge Modern History*, vol. xiii (Cambridge University Press, 1979), pp. 293–317, p. 303.

61 Michael J. Buckley, *At the Origins of Modern Atheism* (New Haven: Yale University Press, 1987).

Part II

Religion and contemporary science

6 Scientific creationism and intelligent design

RONALD L. NUMBERS

For the past century and a half no issue has dominated discussions of science and religion more than evolution. Indeed, many people see the creation–evolution debates as the central issue in the continuing controversy. And for good reason. More than a century after the scientific community had embraced organic evolution, many laypersons continued to scorn the notion of common descent. In the United States, where polls since the early 1980s have shown a steady 44–47 per cent of Americans subscribing to the statement that 'God created human beings pretty much in their present form at one time within the last 10,000 years or so', nearly two-thirds (65.5 per cent), including 63 per cent of college graduates, according to a 2005 Gallup poll, regarded creationism as definitely or probably true.[1] As we shall see, such ideas have been spreading around the world.

CREATION AND CREATIONISM

In 1929 an obscure biology teacher at a small church college in northern California self-published a book entitled *Back to Creationism*. This brief work, appearing just as the American anti-evolution movement of the 1920s was winding down, attracted little attention. And it would deserve scant mention today except for the fact that it was one of the first books to use the term 'creationism' in its title. Until well into the twentieth century critics of evolution tended to identify themselves as anti-evolutionists rather than creationists.[2]

Three factors help to explain this practice. First, the word already possessed a well-known meaning unrelated to the creation–evolution debate. Since early Christianity theologians had attached 'creationism' to the doctrine that God had specially created each human soul – as opposed to the traducianist teaching that God had created only Adam's soul and that children inherited their souls from their parents. Second, even the most prominent scientific opponents of organic evolution differed widely in their views of origins. Some adopted the biblical view that all organisms had descended from the kinds divinely created in the Garden of Eden and preserved on Noah's ark. Others, such as the British geologist Charles Lyell (1797–1875), advocated the spontaneous but non-supernatural appearance of species in regional centres or foci of creation. Still others followed the leading American anti-evolutionist, the Harvard zoologist Louis Agassiz (1807–73), in arguing for repeated plenary creations, during which 'species did not originate in single pairs, but were created in large numbers'.[3] Third, even Bible-believing fundamentalists could not agree on the correct interpretation of the first chapter of Genesis. A majority probably adopted the ruin-and-restoration view endorsed by the immensely popular *Scofield Reference Bible* (1909), which identified two creations (the first 'in the beginning', the second associated with the Garden of Eden) and slipped the fossil record into the vast gap between the two events. Another popular reading of Genesis 1, advocated by William Jennings Bryan (1860–1925), the leading anti-evolutionist of the time, held that the days mentioned in Genesis 1 represented immense ages, each corresponding to a section of the geological column or perhaps to a period in the history of the cosmos. Only a handful of those writing against evolution insisted on what later came to be known as young-earth creationism but was then called flood geology: a recent special creation of all kinds in six twenty-four-hour periods and a geologically significant flood at the time of Noah that buried most of the fossils.[4]

Flood geology was the brainchild of the scientifically self-educated George McCready Price (1870–1963). A Canadian by birth, Price converted to Seventh-Day Adventism as a youth and accepted the writings of the Adventist prophetess Ellen G. White (1827–1915) as divinely inspired. Throughout her life White had experienced religious dreams and trance-like visions, which she and her followers saw as divine. During one episode she claimed to have been 'carried back to the creation and ... shown that the first week, in which God performed the work of creation in six days and rested on the seventh day, was just like every other week'.[5] She also endorsed a 6,000-year-old earth and a worldwide catastrophe at the time of Noah that had buried the fossils and reshaped the earth's surface.[6] There was nothing novel about White's history, except its timing. By the middle of the nineteenth century, when she began writing, almost all evangelical expositors on Genesis and geology had conceded the antiquity of life on earth and the geological insignificance of Noah's flood.[7]

As a young man full of religious zeal, Price dedicated himself to providing a scientific defence of White's outline of earth history. Although he could scarcely tell one rock from another, he read the scientific literature voraciously – and critically. Early on it struck him that the argument for evolution all turned 'on its view of geology', which provided the strongest evidence for both the antiquity of life and its progressive development. But the more he read, the more he became convinced that the vaunted geological evidence for evolution was 'a most gigantic hoax'. Guided by Mrs White's 'revealing word pictures of the Edenic beginning of the world, of the fall and the world apostasy, and of the flood', he concluded that 'the actual facts of the rocks and fossils, stripped of mere theories, splendidly refute this evolutionary theory of the invariable order of the fossils, which is the very backbone of the evolution doctrine'.[8]

In 1906 Price published a booklet entitled *Illogical Geology: the Weakest Point in the Evolution Theory*, in which he offered a thousand-dollar reward 'to any who will, in the face of the facts here presented, show me how to prove that one kind of fossil is older than another'. Before his death in 1963 he would author some two dozen books, the most systematic and comprehensive being *The New Geology* (1923). In it, he restated his 'great "law of conformable stratigraphic sequences"', which he modestly described as 'by all odds the most important law ever formulated with reference to the order in which the strata occur'. According to this law, 'Any kind of fossiliferous beds whatever, "young" or "old," may be found occurring conformably on any other fossiliferous beds, "older" or "younger".' To Price, so-called deceptive conformaties (where strata seem to be missing) and thrust faults (where the strata are apparently in the wrong order) proved that there was no natural order to the fossil-bearing rocks, all of which he attributed to Noah's flood.[9]

Despite repeated attacks from the scientific establishment, Price's influence among non-Adventist fundamentalists grew rapidly. By the mid-1920s the editor of *Science* could accurately describe Price as 'the principal scientific authority of the Fundamentalists', and Price's byline was appearing with increasing frequency in a broad spectrum of religious periodicals.[10] Nevertheless, few fundamentalist leaders, despite their appreciation for Price's critique of evolution and defence of a biblical flood, gave up their allegiance to the gap and day–age theories for his flood geology.

In *Back to Creationism*, the book with which we began this chapter, one of Price's former students, Harold W. Clark (1891–1986), tried to establish Price's Bible-based theory as the science of creationism. This new science, he wrote optimistically,

> will interpret the records of the rocks, the lives of plants and animals, and human history, in the light of the creation story ... As men go deeper into the science of creationism, the inmost secrets of the cell and the atom will display the power of the Creator in ways that have never been understood; and in the degeneracy and evil that biology and sociology bring to light will be seen the activity of the counter-power [i.e. Satan] that has been trying to mar the beautiful creation ... The time is ripe for a rebellion against the domination of evolution, and for a return to the fundamentals of true science, BACK TO CREATIONISM.[11]

ORGANIZED CREATIONISM

As the American anti-evolution movement petered out in the late 1920s, a few diehards tried to keep the protest alive by organizing a new society. Their efforts, however, immediately ran into two obstacles: a paucity of trained scientists and the continuing disagreement over the meaning of Genesis 1. Price had never finished college nor even taken an advanced course in science, though Clark in the early 1930s would earn a master's degree in biology at the University of California, Berkeley. Other anti-evolution activists with some exposure to science were Harry Rimmer (1890–1952), a Presbyterian evangelist and self-described research scientist who had briefly attended a homeopathic medical school; Arthur I. Brown (1875–1947), a Canadian surgeon whose handbills described him as 'one of the best informed scientists on the American continent'; S. James Bole (1875–1956), a professor of biology at Wheaton College, who had earned a master's degree in education and would in 1934 receive a PhD in horticulture from Iowa State College; and Bole's colleague on the Wheaton faculty, L. Allen Higley (1871–1955), a chemist.[12]

In 1935 Price, Clark, Rimmer and Higley joined with a few others to create 'a united front against the theory of evolution'. The resulting society, the Religion and Science Association, quickly dissolved, however, when the members fell to squabbling about the age of the earth, with Price and Clark supporting flood geology, Rimmer and Higley pushing for the gap theory, and still others arguing for the day–age interpretation. As one frustrated anti-evolutionist observed in the 1930s, fundamentalists were 'all mixed up between geological ages, Flood geology and ruin, believing all at once, endorsing all at once'. How, he wondered, could evangelical Christians possibly turn the world against evolution if they themselves could not even agree on the meaning of Genesis 1?[13]

A few years after the demise of the Religion and Science Association Price and a small number of mostly Adventist colleagues in southern California, where he had retired, organized a Deluge Geology Society, which for several years in the early 1940s published a *Bulletin of Deluge Geology and Related Science*. The group consisted of 'a very eminent set of men', bragged Price. 'In no other part of this round globe could anything like the number of scientifically educated believers in Creation and opponents of evolution be assembled, as here in Southern California.' By far the best-trained scientist in the society was a Missouri Synod Lutheran, Walter E. Lammerts (1904–96), who had earned a PhD in genetics at the University of California, Berkeley, and was teaching horticulture at its southern branch in Los Angeles. The society's most exciting moment came in the early 1940s, when it announced the discovery of giant fossil footprints, believed to be human, in geologically ancient rocks. This find, one member predicted, would demolish the theory of evolution 'at a single stroke' and 'astound the scientific world!' But even this group of flood geologists, who all agreed on the recent appearance of life on earth, divided bitterly over the issue of 'pre-Genesis time for the earth', that is, whether the inorganic matter of the earth antedated the Edenic creation. About 1947 the society died.[14]

By this time a more ecumenical society of evangelical scientists had appeared on the scene: the American Scientific Affiliation (ASA). Created in 1941 by associates of the Moody Bible Institute, the association at first took a dim view of evolution. By the end of the decade, however, the presence of a number of well-trained young scientists who embraced theistic evolution (or its intellectual sibling, progressive creationism) was dividing the association. The most influential of the insurgents were J. Laurence Kulp (1921–2006) and Russell L. Mixter (1906–2007). Kulp, a Wheaton alumnus who had earned a doctorate in physical chemistry from Princeton University and then completed the course work for a second PhD in geology, had established himself at Columbia University as an early authority on radioisotope dating. As one of the first evangelicals with advanced training in geology, he spoke with unique authority. Worried that Price's flood geology had 'infiltrated the greater portion of fundamental Christianity in America primarily due to the absence of trained Christian geologists', he set about exposing its abundant scientific flaws. In an influential paper first read to ASA members in 1949, he concluded that the 'major propositions of the theory are contraindicated by established physical and chemical laws'. Mixter, meanwhile, was pushing for greater acceptance of the evidence for limited organic evolution. While teaching biology at Wheaton College, he earned a doctorate in anatomy from the University of Illinois School of Medicine in Chicago in 1939. Before long he was nudging creationists to accept evolution 'within the order' and assuring them that they could 'believe in the origin of species at different times, separated by millions of years, and in places continents apart'.[15]

THE CREATIONIST REVIVAL

In 1954 Bernard Ramm (1916–92), a theologian-philosopher associated with the leadership of the ASA, brought out a book audaciously called *The Christian View of Science and Scripture*. Damning hyperorthodox Christians for their 'narrow bibliolatry' and 'ignoble' attitude towards science, this avatar of neo-evangelicalism urged Christians to stop obtaining their science from Genesis and adopt the progressive creationism so popular within the ASA. He dedicated his book to one of the founders of the ASA and thanked Kulp for vetting the book for 'technical accuracy'. Ramm aimed his harshest rhetoric at the flood geology of Price, whose growing influence among fundamentalists he regarded as 'one of the strangest developments of the early part of the twentieth century'. Despite Price's manifest ignorance, his brand of creationism had come, at least in Ramm's imagination, to form 'the backbone of much of Fundamentalist thought about geology, creation, and the flood'.[16]

Many evangelicals, including Billy Graham (b. 1918), hailed Ramm's book, but fundamentalists tended to respond angrily to what they regarded as an arrogant and heterodox attempt to equate progressive creationism with the Christian view. Ramm's attack provoked one young fundamentalist, John C. Whitcomb, Jr. (b. 1924), a Princeton-educated Old Testament scholar teaching (and working on a doctorate) at the fundamentalist Grace Theological Seminary, into turning his dissertation into a spirited response to Ramm and a defence of 'the position of George M. Price'. When Whitcomb approached the Moody Press about publishing his study, the editor recommended that the biblical scholar recruit a trained scientist as co-author. He eventually found an acceptable, if not perfect, partner: Henry M. Morris (1918–2006), a fundamentalist Baptist who had earned a PhD in hydraulics from the University of Minnesota and had just taken over as head of the large civil-engineering programme at Virginia Polytechnic Institute.[17]

As defenders of Price's flood geology, Whitcomb and Morris faced the difficult – perhaps impossible – task of not being dismissed as 'crackpots' for trying to promulgate his theory. Early on Morris suggested to Whitcomb that it might be best 'simply to point out Price's arguments as a matter of historical record, and then leave your main emphasis on the Scriptural framework and the geological implications thereof'.[18] Later, as he and Morris neared the end of their project, Whitcomb shared his own concerns about being identified with the disreputable Price and his strange church:

> I am becoming more and more persuaded that my chapter on 'Flood Geology in the Twentieth Century' will hinder rather than help our book, at least in its present form. Here is what I mean. For many people, our position would be somewhat discredited by the fact that 'Price and Seventh-Day Adventism' (the title of one of the sections in that chapter) play such a prominent role in its support. My suggestion would be to supply for the book a fairly complete annotated bibliography of twentieth-century works advocating Flood-geology, without so much as a mention of the denominational affiliation of the various authors. After all, what real difference does the denominational aspect make?[19]

In the end the authors camouflaged their intellectual debt to Price by deleting all but a few incidental references to him and all mention of his Adventist connections.

In 1961, after Moody declined to publish their book, the Orthodox Presbyterian Rousas J. Rushdoony (1916–2001), founder of the ultra-right-wing Christian Reconstruction movement, guided them to a small fundamentalist press in Philadelphia, which finally brought out *The Genesis Flood*. Although one critic accurately described the book as 'a reissue of G. M. Price's views brought up to date', it created a sensation within the evangelical community.

Two years after the appearance of *The Genesis Flood* a small group of Christian scientists energized by Whitcomb and Morris' book – and increasingly annoyed by the ASA's drift towards evolution – walked out of the ASA and founded their own hyperorthodox society, the Creation Research Society (CRS). Leading this effort, both administratively and financially, was the Lutheran geneticist Lammerts, who until this time had maintained a low creationist profile. The initial eighteen-man CRS steering committee imprecisely reflected the theological composition of the emerging young-earth creationism movement: six Missouri Synod Lutherans, six Baptists (four Southern, one Regular, and one independent), two Seventh-Day Adventists, and one each from the Reformed Presbyterian church, the Christian Reformed church, the Methodist church, and the Church of the Brethren. The committee included five biologists with PhDs earned at major universities, two more biologists with master's degrees, and one biochemist with a doctorate in that field. There were no physicians in the group and only one engineer, Morris. Twelve of the eighteen lived in the Midwest, four in the Southwest, one in California and one in Virginia.[20]

The CRS claimed to be a 'research society', but it conducted few investigations outside of libraries. The chairman of the committee on research, Larry G. Butler (1933–97), a Baptist biochemist at Purdue University and one of the few active members of the CRS with a major academic appointment, grew increasingly frustrated with the proposals he received. Hoping to 'present an image of scientific respectability as much as possible without Biblical compromise', he diligently tried 'to exclude authentic psychopaths, cranks, and kooks' looking for a forum for their farfetched ideas. As he quickly discovered, too many fellow creationists suffered from a fondness for the sensational: 'We make astonishing observations (human footprints contemporary with dinosaurs); we postulate dramatic upheavals (sudden deposits of masses of ice from a planetary visitor); we propose sweeping scientific generalizations (negation of the entire system of 14C dating).' Although some colleagues in the society pushed him for the presidency, he found himself increasingly impatient with what he called 'the lunatic fringe' of creationism. Discouraged by the failure of his efforts to raise the scientific standards of creationist research, he resigned from the board of directors in 1975 and later allowed his membership (in both the CRS and his church) to lapse.[21]

Despite a common commitment to young-earth creationism, disagreements soon arose. One of the most significant was over the issue of speciation. As biologists discovered more and more species, it became clear to creationists that Noah's ark could not have accommodated representatives of each one. Thus many of them adopted the solution of a former student of Price's, Frank Lewis Marsh (1899–1992), who argued that the Genesis kinds should be not equated with species but with families or what he called baramins. This solved the problem of space on the ark but created another one: how had the kinds preserved on the ark produced so many genera and species, and in only 4,300 years? It seemed likely, for example, that the *Canidae* family – including domestic and wild dogs, wolves, foxes, coyotes, jackals and dingoes – had descended from a single kind. Morris and most of his colleagues embraced rapid microevolution.

However, as a geneticist, Lammerts knew that that was scientifically impossible, that there must have been a second creation to repopulate the earth after the deluge. Unfortunately for him, the Bible never mentioned such an event, so his supernatural solution never caught on.[22]

For a young-earth creationist organization, the CRS grew rapidly. On the occasion of its tenth anniversary it boasted a membership of 1,999, with 412 of them holding advanced degrees in science. By this time society leaders were switching from flood geology as the name of choice for their model of earth history and substituting the labels 'creation science' and 'scientific creationism'. In truth, there was little difference between the old and the new, except that scientific creationism made no mention of biblical events and persons, such as the Garden of Eden, Adam and Eve, and Noah's flood. However, the focus on the flood remained the same. Morris made this clear in a book entitled *Scientific Creationism* (1974):

> The Genesis Flood is the real crux of the conflict between the evolutionist and creationist cosmologies. If the system of flood geology can be established on a sound scientific basis, and be effectively promoted and publicized, then the entire evolutionary cosmology, at least in its present neo-Darwinian form, will collapse.
>
> This, in turn, would mean that every anti-Christian system and movement (communism, racism, humanism, libertinism, behaviorism, and all the rest) would be deprived of their pseudo-intellectual foundation.[23]

Driving the switch in labels was a desire to have a product acceptable for use in public schools, especially in California, which was revising its guidelines for teaching science. Tellingly, *Scientific Creationism* appeared in two almost identical versions: one for public schools, stripped of all references to the Bible, and another for church schools, which retained biblical references and added a chapter on 'Creation according to Scripture'.[24]

Scientific creationists liked to contrast the creation model of origins with the evolution model – and to insist that the former was just as scientific as the latter. In their own minds – and as revealed in their published writings – they loved science and simply wanted to protect its good name. In selling their two-model approach to school boards and state legislatures, they repeatedly appealed not only to their scientific credentials but to their desire to promote science. 'Stress that creationists are not proposing to teach the "creation story of Genesis" in the schools,' advised Morris, 'but only to show that the facts of science can be explained in terms of the scientific model of creation.'[25]

In 1968 the US Supreme Court struck down as unconstitutional the last of the laws from the 1920s outlawing the teaching of evolution. This forced creationists to abandon any thought of making the teaching of evolution illegal and turned their attention to writing legislation that would allow the teaching of creation science alongside that of evolution science. The creationists sought scientific status for their views in order to circumvent the constitutional separation of church and state, which had implications for the teaching of religion in schools. The Bill of Rights in the US Constitution forbade Congress from passing any 'laws respecting an establishment of religion, or prohibiting the free exercise thereof'. Before the Second World War the Supreme Court had interpreted this narrowly in its literal sense; in the late 1940s, however, it held that the Constitution had erected 'a wall of separation' between church and state. At a time when public opinion polls were revealing that 'half of the adults in the US believe God created Adam and Eve to start the human race', the movement for 'balanced treatment' enjoyed a large reservoir of popular support.[26] In the end only two states, Arkansas and Louisiana, adopted the two-model approach. In 1982 a federal judge in Arkansas, having been tutored by the philosopher Michael Ruse (b. 1940) on the demarcation criteria that allegedly distinguished science from non-science, declared the Arkansas law to be an infringement of the constitutional requirement to keep church and state separate; three years later a court in Louisiana reached a similar decision. The US Supreme Court ratified these judgments in 1987, while allowing, in the words of one justice, that 'teaching a variety of scientific theories about the origins of humankind to schoolchildren might be validly done with the clear secular intent of enhancing the effectiveness of science instruction'.[27]

INTELLIGENT DESIGN

The Supreme Court's decision dashed the hopes of creation scientists who had expected their stripped-down version of creationism to pass constitutional muster, but it did little to dampen the widespread antipathy towards evolution in America. Few found the decision more disappointing than two creationist authors, Dean H. Kenyon and Percival Davis, who had drafted a manuscript tentatively entitled *Biology and*

Creation in anticipation of the demand for a high-school textbook when the court ruled for creationism. Their optimistic publisher calculated a financial bonanza of 'over 6.5 million in five years'. When the court virtually wiped out the market for creationist texts, Kenyon and Davis quickly sanitized their manuscript by substituting *Of Pandas and People* for the original title and replacing the words 'creation' and 'creationists' with the euphemisms 'intelligent design' and 'design proponents'. As they defined it, intelligent design (ID) provided a frame of reference that 'locates the origin of new organisms in an immaterial cause: in a blueprint, a plan, a pattern, devised by an intelligent agent'.[28]

Of Pandas and People may have begun as a conventional creationist work, but it put into play a new slogan in the ongoing campaign against evolution: intelligent design. The intelligent design movement began in the early 1990s with the publication of an anti-evolution tract, *Darwin on Trial* (1991), by a Berkeley law professor, Phillip E. Johnson (b. 1940). Upset by the anti-Christian stridency of some Darwinists – such as Richard Dawkins – the Presbyterian layman set out to expose what he saw as the logical weaknesses of the case for evolution, particularly the assumption made by its advocates that naturalism is the only legitimate way of doing science. Ever since investigators of nature in the early nineteenth century had shifted from natural philosophy (which allowed for appeals to the supernatural) to science (which did not), practitioners, regardless of religious persuasion, had refrained from invoking divine or diabolical forces when explaining the workings of nature. In short order, explaining nature naturally became the defining characteristic of science, for Christians as well as for atheists. In contrast to metaphysical naturalism, which denied the existence of a transcendent God, this methodological naturalism supposedly implied nothing about God's existence. Johnson vehemently disagreed. Professing to see little difference between methodological naturalism and scientific materialism, he set out to resacralize science or, as one admirer put it, 'to reclaim science in the name of God'. If the evidence warranted a supernatural explanation, Johnson argued, then invoking intelligent design should count as a legitimate scientific response. Intelligent design, as one insider conceded, was simply a politically correct way to refer to God.[29]

Johnson aspired to pitch a tent big enough to accommodate all anti-evolutionists who were willing to set Genesis aside (at least temporarily) and focus on the purported scientific evidence against evolution. Although a few young-earth creationists sought shelter in the tent, Morris and other Bible-based creationists resented the effort of the intelligent designers to marginalize their views and to avoid 'having to confront the Genesis record of a young earth and global flood'. In the mid-1990s the founder of the right-of-centre Discovery Institute in Seattle invited ID theorists to establish an institutional home within the institute called the Center for the Renewal of Science and Culture. Within a year or so they had raised 'nearly a million dollars in grants'. The most generous donor was Howard Fieldstead Ahmanson, Jr. (b. 1950), heir to a fortune made in the savings-and-loan business. An intimate of Rousas J. Rushdoony, the theocrat who had found a publisher for Whitcomb and Morris' *Genesis Flood*, Ahmanson, like his mentor, sought 'the total integration of biblical law into our lives'.[30]

By this time several younger men had joined Johnson as the public face of the movement, among them Michael J. Behe (b. 1952), a Catholic biochemist at Lehigh University. In 1996 the Free Press of New York released Behe's *Darwin's Black Box: the Biochemical Challenge to Evolution*, the first anti-evolution book in seven decades published by a mainstream publisher.[31] In his book Behe argued that biochemistry had 'pushed Darwin's theory to the limit ... by opening the ultimate black box, the cell, thereby making possible our understanding of how life works'. The 'astonishing complexity of subcellular organic structure' – its 'irreducible complexity' – led him to conclude that intelligent design had been at work. 'The result is so unambiguous and so significant that it must be ranked as one of the greatest achievements in the history of science,' he concluded grandiosely. 'The discovery of [intelligent design] rivals those of Newton and Einstein, Lavoisier and Schroedinger, Pasteur and Darwin.'[32] The tip of the hat to Darwin was no slip. In contrast to most of his colleagues in the movement, Behe did not rule out the possibility of divinely guided evolution.

More typical of attitudes towards theistic evolution within the ID camp was that of another rising star, the mathematician-philosopher William A. Dembski (b. 1960). 'Design theorists are no friends of theistic evolution,' he declared:

> As far as design theorists are concerned, theistic evolution is American evangelicalism's ill-conceived accommodation to Darwinism. What theistic evolution does is take the Darwinian picture of the biological world and baptize it, identifying this picture with the way God created life. When boiled down to its scientific content, theistic evolution is no different from atheistic evolution.[33]

On the origin of organic forms his position did not vary much from that of the scientific creationists. While acknowledging that organisms had 'undergone some change in the course of natural history', he believed that such changes had 'occurred within strict limits and that human beings were specially created'. As an expert in probability theory, Dembski focused on the unlikelihood of organisms arising by accident, and especially on a method for detecting intelligence, his much-maligned 'explanatory filter'. Like Johnson, Dembski attacked evolution as part of a much larger strategy to revolutionize the way science was practised. 'The ground rules of science have to be changed,' he declared quixotically. 'We need to realize that methodological naturalism is the functional equivalent of a full blown metaphysical naturalism.'[34] For a brief period at the turn of the millennium the prolific Dembski headed an ID centre at Baylor University, described as the 'first intelligent design think-tank at a research university'.

Intelligent design emerged as front-page news in 2005, after a group of parents in Dover, Pennsylvania, filed suit against the school board for promoting ID in ninth-grade biology classes. The religiously conservative board had instructed teachers to tell their students about the weaknesses in Darwin's theory and direct them to *Of Pandas and People*. The case, like the creation–science trials of the 1980s, hinged on whether the recommendation of ID theory constituted the teaching of religion and therefore violated the US Constitution. Behe appeared as the star witness for the defence but scarcely helped his side when he lamely, but honestly, conceded that ID 'does not propose a mechanism in the sense of a step by step description of how these structures arose'. In the end the judge condemned the school board for its actions – memorably declaring it a 'breathtaking inanity' – and ruled that ID was 'not science' because it invoked 'supernatural causation' and failed 'to meet the essential ground rules that limit science to testable, natural explanations'. A conservative Christian himself, the judge rejected as 'utterly false' the assumption 'that evolutionary theory is antithetical to a belief in the existence of a supreme being and to religion in general'.[35]

INTO ALL THE WORLD

Although scattered critics of evolution could be found around the globe throughout the twentieth century, organized anti-evolutionism rarely appeared outside the United States before the late twentieth century. When Price lived in England for four years in the mid-1920s he found little interest in fighting evolution, even among conservative Christians. In the early 1930s, however, a band of British anti-evolutionists, led by the barrister and amateur ornithologist Douglas Dewar (1875–1957), formed the Evolution Protest Movement (EPM) – after the Zoological Society of London had rejected a paper of his on mammalian fossils, leading him to conclude that evolution had become 'a scientific creed'. During its first quarter-century the EPM reached a membership of about two hundred and established tiny outposts in Australia, New Zealand, Canada and South Africa.[36]

The creationist awakening in the United States in the 1960s sparked a number of brush fires around the world. The head of the somnolent EPM predicted that Whitcomb and Morris' 'revolutionary re-interpretation' of earth history would usher in 'a new era'. Indeed, it did. 'More than any other single factor', explained one British creationist, 'this scholarly but highly controversial volume lifted creationism from the Gospel Hall tract-rack to the College seminar room.' By 1980 young-earthers had largely captured the EPM; that year they changed its name to the Creation Science Movement. Just as American creationists dreamed of getting into the public school curriculum, British creationists aspired to air time on the BBC.[37] In the wake of visits from Morris and his irrepressible sidekick Duane Gish (b. 1921), sometimes joined by other colleagues at the Institute for Creation Research (founded in 1972), anti-evolutionists around the world began rallying around young-earth creationism. Still, as late as 2000, the American palaeontologist Stephen Jay Gould (1941–2002) confidently assured non-Americans that they had nothing to fear. 'As insidious as it may seem, at least it's not a worldwide movement,' he said. 'I hope everyone realizes the extent to which this is a local, indigenous, American bizarrity.'[38]

Gould, a great scientist, proved to be a false prophet. Even as he spoke, creationism was becoming a truly global phenomenon, successfully overcoming its 'Made in America' label and flourishing not only among conservative Protestants but also among pockets of Catholics, Eastern Orthodox believers, Muslims and Jews. Conservative Protestants, however, continued to lead. In Australia, for example, young-earth creationists in 1980 established an energetic Creation Science Foundation.[39] After seven years one of its co-founders, the charismatic former high-school biology teacher Kenneth A. Ham (b. 1951), moved to the United States to work with Morris at the Institute for Creation Research. In 1994 he launched his own creationist ministry, Answers in Genesis (AiG), headquartered in northern Kentucky, just south of Cincinnati. Within a decade AiG had emerged as the most dynamic creationist organization worldwide, with Ham alone speaking to more than 100,000 people a year. In 2007, to great fanfare, AiG opened an impressive $27 million Creation Museum, which attracted hundreds of thousands of visitors annually. South Korea became another major centre of Christian creationism. Since its founding in the winter of 1980/1 the Korea Association of Creation Research has established branches throughout the land, published a successful bimonthly magazine and held thousands of seminars. In 2000 it began a programme of sending creationist missionaries to other countries, the first going to Indonesia, a predominantly Muslim country.

The spread of organized creationism from Christianity to Islam began in the mid-1980s, when the Muslim minister of education in Turkey contacted the Institute for Creation Research with a request to help promote a two-model curriculum that would teach both creation and evolution. In 1990 a small group of young Turks in Istanbul formed the Science Research Foundation (BAV in Turkish), headed by the shadowy Adnan Oktar (b. 1956), who had adopted the pen name Harun Yahya. A student first of interior design and then of philosophy, young Oktar had grown increasingly distressed with the materialism that flourished in Turkish universities, a philosophy he linked to Darwinism and Zionism. The activities of the cult-like BAV repeatedly brought him to the attention of the police, and earned him a jail sentence on at least three occasions. As part of their 'great intellectual campaign against Darwinism', Oktar and his circle produced scores of books, including *The Evolution Deceit: the Collapse of Darwinism and its Ideological Background* (1997), millions of copies of which circulated in many languages. Although the Qur'an did not require belief in a young earth, twenty-four-hour creation days or a global flood, Oktar for years drew heavily on the writings of young-earth creationists for his critique of evolution. By the early twenty-first century, however, he seemed to be moving into the more intellectually compatible ID camp – so much so that the Discovery Institute listed Harun Yahya's website as 'An Islamic Intelligent Design Site'. But in a pique over the ascendancy of a former disciple in the ID world, Oktar dismissed ID as just 'another of Satan's snares' because of its failure to recognize Allah. However branded, his anti-evolutionist crusade prompted a widespread debate among conservative Muslims.

On a much smaller scale creationism also acquired a foothold among Orthodox Jews, who, despite believing that God had created the world no more than 6,000 years ago, had typically paid little attention to Christian efforts to stop the spread of evolution. Occasionally an individual Jew had spoken up, but it was not until 2000 that Jewish creationists organized the Torah Science Foundation, a largely Israeli-American group inspired by the Lubavitcher rebbe Menachem Mendel Schneerson (1902–94). Eager to maintain an identity separate from Christian fundamentalists, these Jewish anti-evolutionists meshed the teachings of the Torah and the Kabbalah with off-the-rack creationism to create a uniquely Jewish product.

Continental Europe, perhaps the most secular region on earth, at first proved resistant to American-style creationism. But conditions changed rapidly. With the demise of the Soviet Union in 1991, evangelical Christianity boomed in Russia, and along with it creationism. Before long bureaucrats in the Russian ministry of education were co-sponsoring creationist conferences, collaborating with American creationists on the writing of textbooks, and urging that creationism be taught to help restore academic freedom in Russia after years of state-enforced scientific orthodoxy. As one academician put it, 'no theory should be discounted after the long Communist censure'. Other former Soviet bloc countries – Poland, Hungary, Romania and Serbia – also witnessed the spread of creationism. In 2004 the Serbian minister of education, an Orthodox Christian, instructed primary school teachers that they should no longer have students read a dogmatic chapter on Darwinism in the commonly used eighth-grade biology textbook, and the following year the Romanian ministry of education granted permission for teachers in both public and Christian schools to elect to use a creationist alternative to the standard biology textbook.

Sporadic outbreaks of anti-evolutionism also occurred in western Europe. In 2004, for instance, the Italian minister of education announced her intention to eliminate the teaching of evolution for students aged eleven to fourteen, which prompted mass protests and a quick retreat. The following year the Dutch science and education minister triggered a fierce debate in the Netherlands by suggesting that the teaching of intelligent design might help to heal religious rifts because Christians, Jews and Muslims all believe in creation. The furore prompted one alarmed observer to ask 'Is Holland becoming the Kansas of Europe?'[40]

Assessments of the depth of anti-evolution sentiment in Europe in the early twenty-first century must rely on public opinion surveys. One of the earliest polls of European attitudes towards creation and evolution, in 2002, found that 40 per cent favoured naturalistic evolution, 21 per cent endorsed theistic evolution, 20 per cent (with the Swiss leading the way) believed that 'God created all organisms at one time within the last 10,000 years', and 19 per cent remained undecided.[41] Four years later the BBC shocked many when it announced the results of a poll showing that 'four out of 10 people in the UK think that religious alternatives to Darwin's theory of evolution should be taught as science in schools'. The survey indicated that only 48 per cent of Britons believed that the theory of evolution 'best described their view of the origin and development of life': 22 per cent said that 'creationism' best described their views, 17 per cent favoured 'intelligent design', while 13 per cent were undecided.[42]

According to a Gallup poll in 2005 almost twice as many Americans preferred 'creationism' to 'intelligent design', with 58 per cent of the respondents regarding creationism as definitely or probably true compared with 31 per cent for intelligent design and 55 per cent for evolution. (Such figures hint at a lack of clarity on the issues.) More than a quarter (28 per cent) reported being unfamiliar with intelligent design; 11 per cent, with creationism; 8 per cent, with evolution.[43]

Well into the new century creationism and ID continued to roil American politics at the local, state and federal levels. The 2008 US presidential election was no exception. The Republican nominee for president, Senator John McCain, a Southern Baptist, advocated teaching students 'all points of view' about the origins of humans, as did his Pentecostal running mate, Governor Sarah Palin of Alaska. 'Teach both,' she said. 'You know, don't be afraid of information. Healthy debate is so important, and it's so valuable in our schools. I am a proponent of teaching both.' The Democratic candidates, though also religious, unequivocally supported science. Senator Barack Obama, a member of the United Church of Christ, dismissed ID as 'not science'. As he explained to the York, Pennsylvania, newspaper:

> I'm a Christian . . . I believe in evolution, and I believe there's a difference between science and faith. That doesn't make faith any less important than science. It just means they're two different things. And I think it's a mistake to try to cloud the teaching of science with theories that frankly don't hold up to scientific inquiry.

His pick for the vice-presidency, Senator Joe Biden, a Catholic, dismissed ID as 'malarkey'.[44]

The big question looming over this entire discussion is why so many people reject evolution. Unfortunately, there is no simple answer, such as lack of education or hatred of science. Most anti-evolutionists profess a love of science; they refer to young-earth creationism as creation science and regard intelligent design as a scientific theory. Some, such as the Seventh-Day Adventists, reject evolution largely because their founding prophet told them that evolution was Satanic. Others, such as the Christian fundamentalists, believe that evolution contradicts the plain meaning of God's word in Genesis. Some critics have linked Darwinism with unsavoury social and political movements, such as German militarism after the First World War, to communism after the Second World War, to atheism and materialism today. Virtually all take the view, promoted by anti-evolutionists and scientific materialists alike, that evolutionary thought is incompatible with genuine religious belief. Faced with an apparently stark choice, they elect to maintain their religious faith. All of this suggests that these movements will not succumb to evolutionary orthodoxy any time soon.

Notes

1 Jeffrey M. Jones, 'Most Americans Engaged in Debate about Evolution, Creation', 13 October 2005, and David W. Moore, 'Most Americans Tentative about Origin-of-Life Explanations', 23 September 2005, both available at http://poll.gallup.com. The figure of 65.5 per cent appears in the profile for Question 30c, surveyed 5–7 August 2005.

2 Harold W. Clark, *Back to Creationism: a Defense of the Scientific Accuracy of the Doctrine of Special Creation, and a Plea for a Return to Faith in the Literal Interpretation of the Genesis Record of Creation as Opposed to the Theory of Evolution* (Angwin, CA: Pacific Union College Press, 1929). The only earlier book with which I am familiar is Judson D. Burns, *What is Man? or, Creationism vs. Evolutionism* (New York: Cochrane, 1908). Burns, a small-town physician in Iowa, defended the special creation of the first humans but ignored the meaning of 'creationism'.

3 Ronald L. Numbers, *Darwinism Comes to America* (Cambridge, MA: Harvard University Press, 1998), ch. 2, 'Creating Creationism: Meanings and Uses since the Age of Agassiz'. See also Nicolaas A. Rupke, 'Neither Creation nor Evolution: the Third Way in mid-Nineteenth Century Thinking about the Origin of Species', *Annals of the History and Philosophy of Biology* 10 (2005), 143–72.

4 Numbers, *Darwinism Comes to America*, pp. 52–3.

5 Ellen G. White, *Spiritual Gifts: Important Facts of Faith, in Connection with the History of Holy Men of Old* (Battle Creek, MI: Seventh-Day Adventist Publishing Association, 1864), pp. 90–1.

6 Much of this chapter is based on Ronald L. Numbers, *The Creationists: From Scientific Creationism to Intelligent Design*, expanded edn (Cambridge, MA: Harvard University Press, 2006); on White's views, see p. 90. See also Ronald L. Numbers, *Prophetess of Health: a Study of Ellen G. White*, 3rd edn (Grand Rapids, MI: Eerdmans, 2008).

7 Rodney Lee Stiling, 'The Diminishing Deluge: Noah's Flood in Nineteenth-Century American Thought,' unpublished PhD thesis, University of Wisconsin-Madison (1991).

8 Numbers, *Creationists*, pp. 91–2.

9 Ibid., pp. 95–7; George McCready Price, *The New Geology* (Mountain View, CA: Pacific Press, 1923), pp. 637–8.

10 *Science*, 5 March 1926, p. 259.

11 Clark, *Back to Creationism*, pp. 138–9. Regarding Clark, see Numbers, *Creationists*, pp. 142–8.

12 Numbers, *Creationists*, ch. 4, 'Scientific Creationists in the Age of Bryan'.

13 Ibid., ch. 6, 'The Religion and Science Association'.

14 Ibid., ch. 7, 'The Deluge Geology Society'.

15 Ibid., ch. 9, 'Evangelicals and Evolution in North America'.

16 Ibid., pp. 208–11.

17 This and the following two paragraphs are based on ibid., ch. 10, 'John C. Whitcomb, Jr., Henry M. Morris, and *The Genesis Flood*'.

18 Henry M. Morris to J. C. Whitcomb, 7 October 1957, Whitcomb Papers.

19 J. C. Whitcomb to H. M. Morris, 24 January 1959, Whitcomb Papers.

20 Ibid., ch. 11, 'The Creation Research Society'.

21 Ibid., pp. 283–5.

22 Ronald L. Numbers, 'Ironic Heresy: How Young-Earth Creationists came to Embrace Rapid Microevolution by Means of Natural Selection', in Abigail J. Lustig, Robert J. Richards and Michael Ruse (eds.), *Darwinian Heresies* (Cambridge University Press, 2004), pp. 84–100.

23 H. M. Morris (ed.), *Scientific Creationism*, general ed. (San Diego: Creation-Life Publishers, 1974), p. 252.

24 Numbers, *Creationists*, ch. 12, 'Creation Science and Scientific Creationism'. On changing interpretations of the Constitution, see Edward J. Larson, *Trial and Error: the American Controversy over Creation and Evolution*, 3rd edn (New York: Oxford University Press, 2003), pp. 93–4.

25 Ibid., pp. 276–7.

26 'The Christianity Today–Gallup Poll: an Overview', *Christianity Today*, 21 December 1979, pp. 12–15, p. 14. Beginning in 1982 Gallup began assessing what percentage of Americans subscribed to 'Creationism, that is, the idea that God created human beings pretty much in their present form at one time within the last 10,000 years.' Between 1982 and 2008 the number varied between 43 and 47 percent. See www.gallup.com/poll/21814/Evolution-Creationism-Intelligent-Design.aspx.

27 The best introduction to the legal debates over creationism is Larson, *Trial and Error*.

28 This section is based on Numbers, *Creationists*, ch. 17, 'Intelligent Design'.

29 On methodological naturalism, see Ronald L. Numbers, 'Science without God: Natural Laws and Christian Beliefs', in David C. Lindberg

and Ronald L. Numbers (eds.), *When Science and Christianity Meet* (University of Chicago Press, 2003), pp. 265–85. The evangelical philosopher-theologian Paul de Vries coined the term in 'Naturalism in the Natural Sciences', *Christian Scholar's Review* 15 (1986), 388–96.

30 For a scholarly appraisal of Reconstructionism, see Molly Worthen, 'The Chalcedon Problem: Rousas John Rushdoony and the Origins of Christian Reconstructionism', *Church History* 77 (2008), 399–437.

31 In 1925 Macmillan of New York published George Barry O'Toole, *The Case against Evolution*.

32 Michael J. Behe, *Darwin's Black Box: the Biochemical Challenge to Evolution* (New York: Free Press, 1996), pp. 15 (ultimate black box), 232–3 (greatest achievements).

33 William A. Dembski, 'What Every Theologian Should Know about Creation, Evolution, and Design', *Transaction* 3 (May/June 1995), 1–8, p. 3.

34 Ibid., pp. 7–8.

35 John E. Jones III, 'Memorandum Opinion', 20 December 2005, found on the NCSE's web site.

36 Numbers, *Creationists*, ch. 8, 'Evangelicals and Evolution in Great Britain'.

37 Ibid., pp. 355–62.

38 This section is based largely on ibid., ch. 18, 'Creationism Goes Global'.

39 On creationism in Australasia, see Ronald L. Numbers, 'Creationists and their Critics in Australia: an Autonomous Culture or "the USA with Kangaroos?"', *Historical Records of Australian Science* 14 (June 2002), 1–12, and Ronald L. Numbers and John Stenhouse, 'Antievolutionism in the Antipodes: From Protesting Evolution to Promoting Creationism in New Zealand', *British Journal for the History of Science* 33 (2000), 335–50, both of which are reprinted in Simon Coleman and Leslie Carlin (eds.), *The Cultures of Creationism: Anti-Evolutionism in English-Speaking Countries* (Aldershot: Ashgate, 2004).

40 Martin Enserink, 'Is Holland Becoming the Kansas of Europe?', *Science* 308 (2005), 1394.

41 Ulrich Kutschera, 'Darwinism and Intelligent Design: the New Anti-Evolutionism Spreads in Europe', *NCSE Reports* 25 (September–December 2003), 17–18.

42 Numbers, *Creationists*, p. 408; www.Mori.com/polls/2006/bbc-horizon. shtml. See also Joachim Allgaier and Richard Holliman, 'The Emergence of the Controversy around the Theory of Evolution and Creationism in UK Newspaper Reports', *Curriculum Journal* 17 (2006), 263–79.

43 See www.gallup.com/poll/21814/Evolution-Creationism-Intelligent-Design.aspx; Moore, 'Most Americans Tentative'.

44 C.J. Karamartin, 'McCain Sounds like Presidential Hopeful', *Arizona Daily Star*, 24 August 2005, at www.azstarnet.com/sn/politics/90069; Tom Kizzia, '"Creation Science" Enters the Race', *Anchorage Daily News*, 27 October 2006, at dwb.adn.com/news/politics/elections/ v-printer/story/8347904p-8243554c.html; Flynn Murphy, 'Obama

Townhall: Math, Science Add Up', *Naperville Sun*, 18 January 2006, obama.senate.gov/news/060118-obama_townhall/ (not science); Tom Joyce, 'Obama Talks about York', *York Sunday News*, 30 March 2008, pp. 1, 7; 'Real Time with Bill Maher', Episode 74, 7 April 2006, interviewing Joe Biden.

7 Evolution and the inevitability of intelligent life

SIMON CONWAY MORRIS

Near the end of his epochal book *On the Origin of Species* Charles Darwin (1860) famously remarked that 'light will be thrown on the origin of man and his history'.[1] Indeed it has. If Darwin were with us today we can be sure that he would be fascinated by the remarkable progress made over the past 150 years, but one suspects that he would not be over-surprised at the achievements to date. Molecular biology has confirmed our close relationships to the great apes while palaeontology has documented a series of dramatic changes, most obviously in brain size and tool cultures. In little more than a geological instant, a population of apes scattered thinly across Africa transmogrified into extremely complex societies numbered in billions, representatives of which have sent probes beyond the solar system and (at somewhat less expense) can determine the molecular profile of any living organism. These are two of many examples, and nobody needs to be reminded that whatever else humans have achieved, and however much we may take it for granted, the capacity to arrive at scientific understandings which are underpinned by the rational discourse of mathematics is not only astonishing, it is actually very odd indeed. But whilst our *zeitgeist* is dominated by science, many humans also purposefully engage in a series of what might appear, at least to that fictional construct the disinterested observer, as even more bizarre: via the construction of specific buildings, the consulting and analysis of dedicated texts and the employment of precise ritual, a substantial part of the world's population insists that the universe we perceive has more to it than meets the eye. That is, it is populated by, and using such routes as prayer and numinous revelations access may be granted to, one or more invisible agencies that amongst other things can define, or indeed in some traditions distort, ethical imperatives. So too, although certainly not

My warm thanks to Vivien Brown for expert preparation of this manuscript. Critical comments by Peter Harrison are greatly appreciated.

universally held, convictions exist about survival after death and the inevitability of some sort of post-mortem judgement.

We seem to be binaries: *Homo scientificus* walks hand in hand with *Homo religiosus*. Clearly we are products of evolution, but we are also endowed with a religious sensibility. In certain circles the latter is regarded as at best a category error or, more pungently, a massive delusion, a colossal wish-fulfilment. We will gently pass by the paradox that as often as not these pronouncements are delivered with a fervour and conviction, not to mention self-righteousness, that would do credit to the most extreme literary creations of, say, Flannery O'Connor. Even so, not surprisingly, and sometimes more generously, evolutionary explanations are proffered as to why religions not only have emerged and been maintained for thousands of years, but have done so in very different societies embedded in wildly disparate environments. Writing as an evolutionary biologist it would seem inevitable that I would take just such a naturalistic path. Thus by customary procrustean procedures, special pleading, rhetorical sleight of hand, philosophical naïveté, employment of absurd synecdoche, wilful historical ignorance and sheer belligerence, should I not construct a Darwinian narrative as to why we are religious, why we know the numinous, why we can be stricken in awe and realize we stand in a holy place? As perhaps my language will indicate I will do no such thing.

What then does Athens, home of rational enquiry and scepticism, have to do with Jerusalem, a place where by reliable report the world was intersected by the one who simply said 'I am'? It seems an impossible conjunction. First, as has been repeatedly pointed out, we are merely a twig on the tree of life, a tree that is not only immense, but for the most part dead, in that practically all species that have ever lived are now extinct. To some it might seem peculiar that our species alone (with perhaps the Neanderthals[2]) developed a religious sensibility, but it is a Darwinian commonplace to regard humans 'as just another species', which like any other species has its little oddities (like religion). This view, moreover, also meshes with the very widely accepted view that other than at the coarsest level there is effectively no predictability to the evolutionary process. This was perhaps most famously articulated by Stephen Jay Gould's conceit that if we were to re-run the tape of life from the time of the Cambrian explosion, presumably we would have animals of a sort, but nothing remotely like a human.[3] This view, however, has also been put forward as forcibly by such neo-Darwinian luminaries as George Gaylord Simpson[4] and Jared Diamond.[5] Not only that, but it is also widely held that many of the major transitions in life, amongst which arguably the most important (other than the origin of life itself) are the evolution of the eukaryotic cell and the nervous system, are equally fortuitous. That is, they may well arise by an accidental series of events which depended on mutual concatenations that were themselves exceedingly improbable. Paradoxically, the very origin of life usually escapes these sceptical strictures. That is, life itself is widely assumed to be universal, but almost as universally is thought to be quite unlike anything planet Earth has spawned. In a nutshell, praying humans here but out there gelatinous blobs and who knows what else? This is hardly an encouraging prospect for those with a religious outlook. One can almost see the smug grins of the committed materialists: 'Well, if the nervous system is a fluke of circumstance, needn't spend much time worrying about God, eh?'

WHAT IS INHERENT IN EVOLUTION?

As I argue below this view of life actually turns out to be difficult to sustain. Major transitions in evolution there certainly are, but in each and every case it appears that a great deal of the groundwork was achieved beforehand. Thus, even if developments such as the eukaryotic cell or nervous system transformed the world, it seems that much of their complexity was inherent in the earlier stages of the history of life. Indeed, although surprisingly neglected, this question of inherency, or some similar innate property, is surely central to evolution. Moreover, so far as it is addressed at all, it is usually cast in the context of constraints – the notion that ultimately all species find themselves in dead-ends or, at best, with a limited choice for further elaboration. There is certainly some truth in this. What I suggest, however, is the much more interesting possibility, usually half-articulated, that certain groups have an innate tendency to evolve in a specific direction. But in any case, there is also the sheer ubiquity of evolutionary convergence – that is, the propensity for biological forms (and examples extend from molecular to social systems) to navigate repeatedly to the same solution. This, too, also strongly suggests that, however many times we re-run the tape, we will still end up with much the same result. This, as the title of this chapter indicates, must include intelligence.

More detailed arguments to support these views follow below. In the context of our evolutionary origins and our propensity to religion there is, however, an aspect of this inherency that at first sight would seem very much to support a naturalistic, if not materialist, view. Put simply, whatever escalator we clambered aboard some millions of years ago, a great deal of what defines our human-ness is identifiable in a nascent form amongst other animals, and notably in groups that extend well beyond the mammals. Indeed the differences that serve to separate us from the rest of animal creation are in one sense utterly profound (when did you last see a chimpanzee go to the library?), but in nearly all other respects seem less than a hair's-breadth away. And that, of course, is entirely consistent with the Darwinian formulation: evolution by ceaseless and gradual change. To be sure, one or other invention may transform some or even most of the world, but if we want to understand who we are we need to know where we came from.

EVOLUTION AS A SEARCH ENGINE

At this juncture, according to received wisdom, the matter seems to be closed. We live in a Darwinian world, and if we happen to be the only species that has ever understood the mechanism of evolution, that particular manifestation of a general intellectual capacity is an entirely fortuitous by-product of our nervous system. We can at least be sure that it is of no wider significance. Here I will suggest not only that this view is incorrect but that it leads to metaphysical suppositions that are incoherent. As argued below, the understandable emphasis on the diversity of life, and the concomitant range of taxonomic specializations, is misleading because, notwithstanding the wonderful diversity of life (in itself consistent with a theology of creative self-fructification), both the transformations that are central to the evolutionary process and the end-products are far more predictable than is often supposed. In brief, ultimately divergence is always local, convergences are global. If this analysis is correct, then evolution can be more readily seen as a sort of search engine, driven to be sure by a Darwinian motor, but one that effectively discovers the inevitable. That I argue is the central importance of evolutionary convergence. But there is more. First in other sciences, most obviously physics, we see no obvious termination of inquiry. Classical mechanical physics had to accommodate itself to quantum mechanics and general relativity, and these too evidently need to depend on yet deeper levels of explanation, which some hope will one day be found in string theory. Nor is it obvious that even if a workable hypothesis that employs multiple collapsed dimensions is ever arrived at, this will not immediately open further avenues of still deeper inquiry. The idea that there is a theory of everything is a statement of faith.

Biology and evolution appear to be different. Indeed Ernst Mayr[6] insists evolutionary theory somehow is autonomous, divorced from physics and chemistry. In a somewhat different vein, Daniel Dennett[7] argues that Darwinism is a 'universal acid' that effectively explains everything. When it is pointed out that it is not obvious how evolution itself avoids this corrosive process then Dennett simply proclaims that 'the theory of evolution is itself a product of evolutionary processes'[8] which can hardly be described as helpful – how, for example, are we to know evolution is actually true? – and more importantly this outlook seems to offer no possibility of discovering whether evolution might depend on deeper principles. In one sense this is already obvious because, Mayr's exclusion clauses notwithstanding, it has long been evident that thermodynamically life is a very distinctive state that is poised between systems that are either frozen into crystalline immobility, or entirely diffuse and unable to form any sort of ordered structures.[9] In this context it is obvious why in the past vitalistic thinking has been so attractive, even though it provides no workable scientific framework. Yet if in some sense life is envisaged as something like a quick-silver, capable of change but with a rather mysterious coherence, metaphorically hovering between immutable solids and chaotic gases (and this analogy to a phase system is, of course, very approximate), so too we can also see that if evolutionary convergences are ubiquitous, then the lines of vitality will be forced to navigate across a precipitous landscape defined by the narrowest of roads that thread their way through regions that, although potentially open to biological occupation, in reality are entirely uninhabitable. Put bluntly, so far as life is concerned, rather than most things being able to work, in reality almost nothing does. The metaphor of a landscape is, of course, a familiar biological trope, especially when employed in adaptive or epigenetic contexts. However, in combination with evolutionary convergence, it may provide a starting point to identifying how evolution must respond to a deeper structure that imparts a predictability to the process.

One might complain that this formulation is distressingly vague. So it is, but the very fact of evolutionary convergence suggests it must reflect some deeper reality. Perhaps an imperfect analogy from physics may help. Experimental evidence exists for things we call photons and so too we infer their given physical properties such as having zero mass and an invariant speed *in vacuo*. Yet photons must obey the deeper landscape imparted by, amongst other things, gravitationally massive structures. This is not to deny that any notion of an evolutionary landscape is largely metaphorical. But recall that Einstein's first insights often came from just such an approach: what, he asked himself, is it like to be a photon? So too, although we inevitably think of landscapes in a three-dimensional context, this is much too simplistic. Rather we need to look to a hyper-dimensional landscape that governs how evolution navigates to increasing levels of complexity, including the discovery of consciousness. This is obviously a very heterodox view. I would suggest, however, that the concept of an effectively pre-existent landscape – a reasonable hypothesis given that evolution is no more self-explanatory (*contra* Dennett) than anything else – has a number of unexpected advantages. First, it may explain why so much of what we regard as part of the human condition is nascently present in other organisms. If evolution is a search engine but is constrained by deeper structures (if you like, something akin to prior organizational templates), then we can hardly be surprised if the same solutions are repeatedly discovered. But even more importantly this view of life also serves to free us from the rigid and stifling insistence that material factors alone will explain mind and consciousness. So too a religious identity can be regarded not as some sort of bizarre neural aberration (and as likely a catastrophic delusion), but as an inevitable outcome of an evolutionary process that is intended to allow matter not only to become self-aware but first to intuit, then know, and finally love the Maker. In this way we see the basis of our existence is natural, and thereby open to scientific investigation, but also points to deeper matters that ironically a sizeable fraction of Western intellectual life believes cannot exist. It is surely paradoxical that the very success of science, with its guiding assumptions of a rational world that is open to unlimited exploration, has been hijacked by the materialists to enforce a closure against whole areas of inquiry. If, however, religious investigations are not only a valid outcome of the evolution of the nervous system, but a sure pointer to sources that lie beyond the known cosmos, then we can have some confidence that, to echo T. S. Eliot, our starting place is our destination, but we will only know this when we return to the garden with new eyes. So it is that only the evolutionary process is capable of making us first *Homo sapiens* and then *Homo religiosus*. It is, however, essential to understand that evolution is the mere mechanism and emphatically not the entity itself. This surely provides a much richer view of life, opening the world not only to re-enchantment but also to a genuine dialogue between religion and science. All this presupposes, however, that the evolution of nervous systems, brains and sentience are inevitabilities. But where is the evidence?

THE ROAD TO HUMAN-NESS

To achieve human-ness a great deal of prior work is necessary. First, life itself must emerge. It is widely assumed, and possibly correctly, that the appearance of life is inevitable. Despite the fact that no detailed path for this event has been formulated, the supposition that life *must* emerge revolves around the well-known observation that all the major building blocks necessary for life, such as the amino acids that are employed in proteins, can be built as part of the routine processes of organic chemistry and in some cases in a remarkable range of environments. The diversity of such compounds far exceeds those actually employed by life, and one might speculate that on remote biospheres similar but not identical repertoires are to be found. So too, an abundance of energy sources and possible templates for either primitive molecular ordering and/or catalysis can be invoked as essential prerequisites for the isolation of biochemistry in primitive cells and the capacity for replication in what ultimately emerged as the classic DNA-RNA system. Nevertheless, the immense gulf between the medley of building blocks and even the most primitive of living organisms has to date proved practically impossible to bridge. It may well be that the range of experiments is far too narrow and the recent recognition, for example, of the importance of borate in the stabilization of ribose (a notoriously unstable sugar that is of key importance in the construction of the deoxyribonucleic acid (DNA))[10] could suggest that the problem is difficult, but will ultimately yield to the patient application of the experimental method. Others are less sure, and Francis Crick's remark that the origin of life remains 'almost a miracle'[11] carries as much force as ever. Crick, I suspect, would have stressed the word 'almost', and there is certainly no intention here to invoke a gaps argument whereby the deity temporarily dons a white coat to stir the Darwinian warm, little pond and engage in some off-the-record chemistry. But we might wish to consider the possibility that the origin of life was completely natural, but also literally a complete fluke, an exceedingly improbable event. Given, however, enough earth-like planets (presumed to run into the trillions) and enough time (perhaps 8 billion years), it will happen. This is the position adopted by David Bartholomew, who argues that the universe has to be at least the size it is for the fantastically unlikely to occur and that, given this, it is unlikely that it only happened once.[12] Such is quite consistent with a theistic stance, and indeed Bartholomew writes as a Christian. The world is so arranged that certain things are inevitable, but they always occur by natural processes and some will choose to accept this explanation at face value. Others, however, will not, and as scientists, will inquire what deeper organizational principles might exist. Note also, in passing, that this has nothing to do with so-called intelligent design, which not only falls far beyond any recognizable scientific method but makes theological assumptions that are perversely heterodox.

Such evidence as we have suggests life was established on the earth at least 3.5 billion years ago. Today, to the first approximation, we identify three fundamental divisions of life: archaea, eubacteria and eukaryotes, and in the last assemblage five major groupings (protistans, fungi, algae, plants and animals). These, in turn, comprise more than a hundred principal divisions (which in animals are known as the phyla).[13] Evolutionary biologists are naturally fascinated by these repeated divergences and, as already indicated, will severely admonish non-specialists who seek a more linear depiction of the evolution of life: monad to man. Nevertheless if my thesis, that the emergence of intelligence must be an evolutionary inevitability, is to remain credible it will be necessary to focus on a few of the key steps. In parenthesis, however, we might observe that as a biological property, intelligence per se, is no different from many others. Thus, whilst it is of peculiar interest, much the same arguments apply to evolutionary end-products ranging from the molecular (for example, the convergent evolution of such enzymes as carbonic anhydrase) to societies (as, for example, the intriguing similarities in social organization of bacteria when compared with higher organisms).[14]

Accordingly in pursuit of my general thesis I will examine very briefly the transitions and associated innovations that involve the origins of (a) eukaryotes, (b) animals, (c) the nervous system and (d) intelligence. Even with a list of only four we face a vast field, and also one where many aspects are still shrouded in ignorance.

(a) The eukaryotes. Eukaryotes probably evolved approximately 2 billion years ago, although both older and younger estimates can be readily found. It is now quite widely agreed that they are chimaeric – that is, that at least in their genome they have significant components of both archael and eubacterial ancestry.[15] Nevertheless, the details of the origin of the eukaryotic cell are largely obscure. It is clear, however, that this progenitor was itself a complex entity.[16] In passing, it is worth mentioning that this type of occurrence is one of the better kept secrets of evolution. The intuitive belief that things start simple and become more complex may be true in the broadest sense, but frequently (possibly invariably?) the earliest forms of a given biological state are highly organized. It would be a mistake, moreover, to assume

these complex forms necessarily imply vast periods of geological time over which they were assembled. This might be the case, but the many examples of explosions of diversity indicate that new forms can be put together with remarkable speed and efficiency and it is quite likely that self-assembly plays an important role. This too is yet another pointer to what may be deeper organizational principles operating throughout the history of life.

Notwithstanding the inferred complexity of even the earliest eukaryotes it is important to emphasize that a number of features that were long thought to be hallmarks of this stage of evolutionary complexity had evolved in their prokaryotic antecedents. Perhaps most striking in this regard are proteins, notably the actins and tubulins, that are central to the cytoskeleton of eukaryotes but which also occur in bacteria.[17] They are generally assumed to have a common evolutionary origin, but in bacterial cells are employed in widely diverse roles. This observation represents another more open secret amongst evolutionary biologists, to the effect that the tool-kit of life is astonishingly versatile in its different applications. In part this will be because very different functions actually employ similar if not identical molecular decisions. But here too if one is seeking deeper organizational principles in evolution, then what to us in their various contexts look like tweezers, backhoes, sledgehammers and feather dusters, but actually turn out to be the same tool, may point to both unexpected commonalities and quite possibly predictabilities.

Other aspects of prokaryotes that are instructive are the many examples of convergence, including those in the various extremophiles,[18] and complex organizational states that include both organelle-like structures (notably the magnetosomes that house the magnetic grains employed by the aptly named magnetotactic bacteria, an arrangement that is convergent)[19] and multicellular states (again in the magnetotactic bacteria)[20] with very much the same arrangement as a number of colonial algae. Thus both arrive at the obvious solution: a ball of cells propelled through the water by either bacterial flagellar motors (again convergent)[21] or eukaryotic cilia (or an equivalent flagellum).

Certainly in the case of the eukaryotic cilia their precise origin is not yet established, although they represent one of the fundamental ingredients for eukaryotic success. Even humans are so dependent: think of the motile sperm or pulmonary passages densely lined with masses of cilia essential to the proper function of the lungs. There are, however, two other hallmarks of the eukaryotes. In each case their origin is now beyond dispute: respectively, the ancient incorporation of once free-living chloroplasts (from cyanobacteria), and mitochondria (from α-proteobacteria). The consensus is that these organelles were acquired only once, but some caution is required. First, whilst their origins amongst the bacteria are established, we know very little of the ancestral forms which ultimately lost their freedom and became the organelles. Indeed arguments have been put forward for multiple origins of the chloroplasts.[22] As striking is the case of an amoeba known as *Paulinella* in which an ongoing symbiosis with a cyanobacteria (and one quite different from the group associated with the chloroplasts) has been documented.[23] Nor is this the only example of a latter-day symbiosis to echo the Precambrian evolution of cyanobacteria and mitochondria. We can certainly insist the acquisition of these organelles was amongst the most important steps in eukaryotic evolution, but as an evolutionary step neither seems inherently improbable.

(b) Steps to animals. The classification of eukaryotes has improved remarkably in recent years, and at present approximately five major groups are identified. Of these we need to concentrate on the so-called opisthokonts because they include both ourselves, the animals, and the sister group of the fungi. A third fact of evolution, widely acknowledged in principle, but in reality difficult to conceptualize with any ease, is that the common ancestor of a mushroom and a human looked quite unlike either. Indeed it requires a major feat of imagination to envisage the nature of this ancestral form, and in many cases the exercise is one of almost pure speculation, given that the intermediate forms are all likely to be extinct and for the most part too delicate to fossilize readily. There are, however, potentially vital insights from molecular biology which can point towards at least some of the biological capacities that must have evolved at the very dawn of the evolution of the opisthokonts. That, at least, is the principle. Unfortunately, the sorts of organism that serve to connect the fungi and animals not only rejoice in unfamiliar names (e.g. corallochytids and ichthyosporeans), but they do not seem to be especially informative about what key steps ultimately led to the emergence of these two major and successful groups.

But there are a few straws in the wind that might be instructive. Thus, whilst in the wider framework of opisthokont phylogeny the most important fact is the relationship between fungi and animals, at a more local level the closest relatives of the animals are a group of protistans known as choanoflagellates. At first sight these tiny organisms hardly appear promising in terms of explaining either how the first animals emerged (although the common possession of so-called collar cells in the choanoflagellates and sponges is presumably important) or, more importantly in the context of this review, what the probability of such an emergence might be. However, in part, our problem may be that we can be over-impressed by manifest morphological differences, whereas the reality could be that moving to a new body-plan might actually involve a relatively modest molecular reorganization.

The first point to stress is that while on the scale of morphological complexity the choanoflagellates rank relatively low, so far as certain signalling pathways (involving tyrosine kinases) are concerned, to the surprise of the investigators they show an unexpected richness that far outstrips that of any known animal.[24] Even more importantly, various molecular systems that involve cell signalling and cell adhesion, and are involved with multicellularity in animals, are also found in choanoflagellates. Moreover, whilst some choanoflagellates are colonial (but not otherwise differentiated), the data relevant to these particular molecules actually come from a single-celled choanoflagellate.[25] Nor is this feature the only part of a metazoan-in-waiting repertoire. This is because the molecular arsenal of choanoflagellates also includes genes connected to immunoglobin (and thus a link to immunology) and collagen (a key structural protein in animals).[26] But as these workers point out, whilst a significant part of metazoan molecular architecture is already available in the choanoflagellates, much is not, including crucial homeodomain proteins. Perhaps most notable are those connected to *Hox* genes which are instrumental in the basic developmental patterning of the embryo. Not only that, but with no obvious intermediates (at least yet discovered) the origins of these key molecules that usher in a metazoan organization are, as they say, mysterious.[27]

(c) Evolution of the nervous system. Of all the metazoan innovations, arguably the most important is the evolution of a nervous system. However, as we shall see below it may be a mistake to equate the biological property of intelligence with a nervous system, although arguably consciousness itself does require the mediation of neural tissue (also see below). But the antecedents of the nervous system go much deeper than the animals. Here are three striking examples. The first involves acetylcholine, one of the key molecules involved with transmission of nervous signals across the synapses. Far from being an invention of animals and concomitant with the evolution of neural tissue, acetylcholine not only evolved much earlier but has a very wide distribution.[28] Here, of course, it has non-neuronal functions and can occur in much larger concentrations than are found in the brain: in the rapidly proliferating tips of bamboo, measured amounts of acetylcholine are some eighty times higher than in the rat brain.[29] Another key aspect of

nervous conduction are the ion channels, notably the sodium voltage-gated channels. These are sometimes assumed to be unique to the animals and their nervous systems. This is not so. In fact these channels have evolved independently in a group of protistans that are themselves capable of very fast contraction.[30] More significant is the independent evolution of a sodium voltage-gated channel in bacteria associated with high alkalinity.[31] The third example involves the molecular commonplace that if genetically we are 99 per cent chimpanzee, so we are about 50 per cent banana. Moreover in an analysis of the model organisms *Arabidopsis* (a plant) and yeast (a fungus) it transpires that about a third of the genes associated with the animal nervous system are found in green plants and fungi, both of course quite lacking neuronal tissue.[32] In subdividing these genes into five categories of function within the nervous system, counterparts of each are also found in *Arabidopsis* and yeast. Clearly important components of the nervous system are inherent in the eukaryotes. Nerve cells themselves are unique to animals (and their exact origin remains undetermined), but key components are the connecting synapses – junctions between adjacent nerves. Of particular importance, therefore, are those genes associated with the transport of vesicles in the synapses, and these find a direct counterpart in the sponges. The importance of this with respect to evolutionary inherency is that whilst the sponges are widely regarded as amongst the most primitive of animals, and indeed exhibit such features as co-ordinated activity, they do not possess any sort of nervous system. Nevertheless in sponge larvae, proteins associated with the so-called flask cells are those otherwise involved with post-synaptic activities.[33] This has led to the interesting speculation that these flask cells may in some way be the precursor of the nervous system. But what is more important in the context of this chapter is the observation that a significant part of the molecular scaffolding of the nervous system is available for recruitment by the animals.

Given that features such as ion channels, vesicle formation and transfer of information are all central to the currency of the cell, and given also that whilst electrical currents serve to accelerate neural signals greatly, it remains the case that the nervous system (including the brain) is effectively a chemical system.[34] Seen from these perspectives, it is difficult to argue that the evolution of a nervous system is *a priori* a wildly improbable proposition. So too, it is not unexpected that within the nervous system of animals we see not only successive elaborations, but ones that are convergent. Most obvious in this context are brains, and to many biologists the convergences between those of cephalopods and vertebrates are the most striking. Indeed it is clear that, at least to some extent, specific regions, such as the cerebellum, find direct equivalents.[35] Again, apparent differences may turn out to be relatively superficial and it will be interesting to see the extent to which phylogenetically remote brains, and here one would also include the insects,[36] have fundamental similarities. Another recurrent innovation is to arrange the more efficient transmission of nervous impulses. One approach is via what are known as giant axons, and these are convergent.[37] The alternative, as found in the vertebrates, is to wrap the axons in fatty layers (known as myelin) that serve as an insulating layer. This layer needs to be interrupted in places and these Nodes of Ranvier see a particular concentration of ion channels. But this myelinization is convergent, with parallel examples being found in the crustaceans (where it has almost certainly evolved several times)[38] and the annelids (such as earthworms),[39] with correspondingly very fast speeds of nervous conduction. Not only do these respective axons demonstrate a variety of myelin sheaths, but they also characteristically show so-called fenestrae that are directly analogous to the Nodes of Ranvier.

We can similarly argue that not only is the evolution of a nervous system very probable, but so too are complex brains. And it might be thought that the argument has now reached the appropriate stage to address the likelihood of intelligence. And so it has, but it is first necessary to step back and consider what the most primitive manifestations of intelligence might be. This is important because along with other concepts, notably numerosity (see below), it seems that the distinction between a sensory interpretation of the world (and this can easily be chemical), and what we believe to be conscious perception, is far less clear cut than might be thought. This fundamental ambiguity has, I will argue, profound implications for the extent to which a purely naturalistic account of evolution is credible. Or rather, if it is, then we would be forced to conclude that what we experience as consciousness (and here I am emphatically including sleep (including dreams) and other matters such as moments of intuition) is a fiction, a massive delusion. If so, then our warrant for believing that we inhabit an interpretable world – one that is rationally organized but, as importantly, appears to be open to indefinite interrogation – has no basis. In fact, as has often been observed, any materialist agenda must stumble on the fundamental contradiction. Here is why.

(d) Primitive intelligence. The chemical basis for neural organization, and by implication sentience, was stressed above. From this perspective we should not be surprised that some sort of primitive

intelligence extends far below the animal kingdom. Two examples must suffice. During unguarded moments I have heard more than one investigator of protistan behaviour remark that their subject organisms, notably the ciliates, exhibit something that looks to be purposeful. In this context what are we to make, for example, of observations of co-operative hunting in another group of the protists, the amoeba?[40] At least as striking is the employment of maze experiments, a familiar enough gambit of animal behaviourists. But here, instead of the laboratory rat, the experimenter employs the slime-mould. This is a social amoeba that can form a branching structure known as a plasmodium. The maze, or labyrinth, is effectively two-dimensional so that the walls consist of dry plastic strips which the plasmodium is disinclined to cross. The experiment aims to discover how adept this amoeboid organism is at both navigating the maze and finding the best path to earn a reward, in the form not of the traditional peanut but irresistible porridge flakes. The results are impressive. The plasmodium readily explores the maze, finding the shortest path without difficulty.[41] As the principal investigator Toshiyuki Nakagaki notes, the behaviour of this amoeboid organism 'is somewhat akin to primitive intelligence'.[42] Evidently the plasmodium is employing a form of cellular computation, but its basis remains unknown. Nor is the intelligence of this organism restricted to solving maze problems: additional experiments have demonstrated its capacity to construct efficient networks for transport,[43] the adoption of a minimum-risk path when under threat[44] and, perhaps most remarkably, the ability to anticipate future events on the basis of past periodic experiences.[45] That an amoeboid is capable of a sort of primitive learning is disconcerting. Not only is the amoeboid primitive but, as is also stressed, there cannot be any central processing. Nevertheless, the Japanese team are not embarrassed to use the word 'smart'. We know, of course, that this behaviour must be unconscious.

One needs, however, not to be over-dismissive. As already indicated, the sponges lack a nervous system, but show behaviours that must involve transmission of information. Even more interesting are the group known as the cnidarians, probably most familiar in the form of the sea-anemone and jellyfish. Amongst the most remarkable of the latter are the so-called box-jellies (Cubozoa). In a number of respects these are honorary fish, being effective swimming predators that also engage in courtship and even copulate. Most extraordinarily they are equipped with a complex visual system that includes not only camera-eyes (thus convergent on better-known examples such as those of the octopus and fish), but shows further levels of sophistication that include an iris as well as a lens that corrects for spherical aberration.[46] What, however, does the box-jelly actually see? This is a pertinent question because, although like all cnidarians they have a nervous system, they lack any sort of brain. There is some evidence that at least some of the visual processing takes part in the nerves adjacent to the eyes, and intriguingly this system is bilaterally symmetrical.[47] Again our instinct is that the jellyfish may see but they are unconscious, chemical machines that lack any awareness. This too may be premature because there is evidence that at least some cubozoans sleep.[48] Now sleep is evidently convergent at various levels, both in its general state as amongst insects and vertebrates,[49] but also in more specific similarities as between birds and mammals.[50] Why sleep matters is controversial, although one function appears to be the processing of prior experience. Brainless they may be, but evidently box-jellies have just such a requirement.

(e) Evolution by numbers. Invoking any sort of intelligence in slime-moulds and jellyfish might appear to be consistent with an emergentist programme whereby the roots of consciousness could lie deep in the phylogenetic tree, but only reach self-awareness at a given point. The difficulty in identifying that 'given point' will be self-evident. In this context it will be clear why some might wish to sign up to one or other of the pantheist agendas, that is the notion that consciousness permeates the universe and is latent in even in-animate [*sic*] objects. That this might be premature, however, comes from very different sorts of experiments involving monkeys (which few now would doubt are conscious) and a capacity known as numerosity, that is the capacity to distinguish numbers. This too has deep, and most probably convergent, evolutionary origins, with an elementary ability to count to four (determined by the capacity to discriminate between integers) in fish,[51] and also honey bees.[52]

In the monkeys, however, the capacity for numerosity is not in doubt. Not only are the areas of the brain responsible for this capacity well identified,[53] but unsurprisingly they are equivalent to those in humans.[54] What is under investigation here, however, is what is known as numerical judgement.[55] Specifically, the question is whether the monkeys are capable of discriminating what are called magnitude effects. Typically these are divided into numerical distance and magnitude, and it would seem reasonable to suppose that both draw on a cognitive capacity. Experimental studies demonstrated that indeed monkeys were perfectly capable of exercising numerical judgements, but crucially the accuracy was not uniform. In fact, the powers of discrimination obeyed the well-known psychophysical Weber–Fechner law. This effectively states that the greater the stimulus, and a typical experiment will employ weights rather than numbers, the larger the weight must be if one is to detect a barely noticeable difference. In other words a very small weight requires a metaphorical feather to be added for the observer to realize that the sensation of the weight has increased. However, a massive weight requires not only a larger addition for a corresponding stimulus, but importantly a disproportionately larger addition. In other words the Weber–Fechner law follows an exponential distribution, not a linear one.

In the case of the numerosity of monkeys, we assume that the numerical judgements must, as in us, have a cognitive basis. Crucially, however, sensitivity of the numerical judgements follows the same psychophysical Weber–Fechner process that we associated with sensory processes. As Andreas Nieder and Earl Miller remark: 'These results suggest that certain cognitive and perceptual/sensory representations share the same fundamental mechanisms and neural coding schemes.'[56] This indicates, and what from an evolutionary perspective should be unsurprising, that our cognitive capacities (which we usually align with language) not only have deep roots, but look to the same constructional principles that are employed in sensory processes.

(f) The problem of qualia. But this, to my mind [*sic*], merely reinforces the difficulties in explaining our cognitive capacities: we could hardly survive if we did not know the world – in the case of numerosity the identification of five lions as against five antelopes is a case in point – but how we do so from a naturalistic perspective is actually opaque. A telling parallel to this can be found in looking at the evolution and function of sensory systems, and thus the question of qualia. Invocation of qualia, of course, leads into areas of philosophical inquiry that are vexed and controversial. Given their notorious intangibility at first sight the relevance of evolutionary biology to this discussion might seem equally tangential. Nevertheless, and space only allows the briefest of comments, it might be worth making two observations. First, the convergence of all sensory modalities, including to us arcane areas like echolocation, infra-red vision and electroreception, may indicate that the respective qualia of perception in phylogenetically remote animals are identical. Second, and related to the first point, Frank Jackson's invocation of Fred and his capacity to enjoy separate qualia of redness that are denied to the rest of us would find a parallel, for example, in the convergent capacity for ultra-violet vision.[57] My own view is that qualia are not illusions, nor even epiphenomena, but the crucial interface – however problematic this may be – between our

materiality and our mental capacities. This too might accord with evolution being the universe's way of discovering itself (see also below). In other words, far from being epiphenomena qualia represent realities of the world, even though they must be through the lens (as in the eye) of interpretation. Traditionally it is the employment of vision and the perception of redness – sunsets, blood, ochre – that is the reference point for qualia. I suggest, however, that at least as strong a case can be made by looking at a capacity that is notoriously non-verbal, that is olfaction. That is, whilst our visual capacity carries with it a rich repertoire of descriptors, in the case say of a wine-tasting note the vocabulary seems hopelessly imprecise even though the nose of the wine may not only be instantly recognizable but readily unlock cascades of memories or other associations.

To the first approximation, olfactory processes depend on hair-like receptors, enclosed in a fluid-filled cavity. The receptors activate neurons when specific molecules impinge on the receptor surface having been transported there from the external milieu by dedicated olfactory proteins. It is a remarkable system, not only on account of its sensitivity, but also because this basic arrangement is strikingly convergent.[58] Not only are there some truly remarkable convergences at the molecular level,[59] but olfaction is fascinating because of its specificity.[60] This extends, for example, to mirror-image molecules (known as enantiomers) that may smell entirely different.[61] Although humans have, in comparison to many animals, a depleted olfactory repertoire (with a significant proportion of our olfactory genes now converted into pseudogenes), the connoisseurship (not to mention financial implications) of perfume, tea or wine is a reminder of the subtlety of our perceptions. Yet not only are the olfactory descriptors notoriously vague, even though a specific scent or smell may instantly unlock deeply buried memories, but, as a number of researchers have stressed, the increasingly sophisticated understanding of the neurobiology of the olfactory processes, from binding protein to bipolar neuron, hits a brick-wall when it comes to the qualia of experience. As A. Keller and L. Vosshall write, how we know, discriminate and remember smells 'is still completely mysterious'.[62] Once again, we reach an impasse where the mind insists there is a reality that is simply not reducible to any conceivable naturalistic programme.

To some readers I fear that the arguments presented may have seemed very circuitous. I would suggest, however, that if we are to argue convincingly that the evolution of intelligence is indeed inevitable, we need to achieve two things before we can move on to any metaphysical or theological conclusions. These are to establish, first, that a great deal of the nervous system is inherent in more primitive organisms which are a-neuronal, and second, that none of the major transitions in the history of life is inherently improbable. It is also evident that our entire cognitive world has a naturalistic base, as is evident from the study of animal numerosity. And that seems to be exactly as far as we can go, because beyond that the questions of qualia and consciousness remain as elusive as ever. One can almost sympathize with those materialists who would explain them away as mere illusions, but the metaphysics of mathematics and rational discourse provide an immediate reality check. As will be clear, I hope, my view is that not only is intelligence an evolutionary inevitability, but evolution itself is not self-explanatory. Rather it can be likened to a search engine, and the discovery of consciousness is when neural matter (and quite possibly other sorts of biological organization[63]) encounters mind. The convergence we see in the cognitive worlds of corvids (crows, ravens and magpies)[64] and dolphins[65] with the great apes suggests that equivalent search engines are only a few million years behind ourselves. Indeed, as already stressed, the paradox is the hair's-breadth that separates us from the rest of creation. Think, for example, of the interest elephants display in their own mortal remains,[66] not to mention their response to death itself.[67] So too elephants are also capable of mirror self-recognition[68] and tool use,[69] although when it comes to animal tools the New Caledonian crows are little short of extraordinary.[70]

SO HOW NATURAL ARE WE?

Curiously from a Darwinian perspective not only is any answer elusive, but any formulation seems to be hedged in by paradoxes. It is entirely unsurprising that our bodies bear the cipher of our evolutionary origins ranging from the skin-deep differences from the great apes to the deep imprint of our bacterial ancestors. It is no more peculiar that many of the features we associate with the human condition, notably tool making, cultures and emotion, are recognizable in a nascent form amongst other animals. Yet the chasm that now separates us from the rest of the biosphere psychically is virtually unbridgeable. If, moreover, my thesis that intelligence and cognitive complexity are convergent is correct, then this makes the isolation of humans all the stranger.

Thus humans are of the world, and a product of evolution. Nevertheless for all intents and purposes we are now beyond the world. The explanations proffered seem strangely unconvincing. Simple extrapolation, a steady process of emergence? Quite possibly, especially as the hominid fossil record is difficult to interrogate in this respect. Yet such evidence as we have suggests that a good half of our history (as *Homo sapiens*) had elapsed before the cognitive explosion began. Even more puzzling, perhaps, is the fact that the ingredients necessary for language are found amongst other animals yet it still fails to crystallize. Think, for example, of lingual articulation in a parakeet[71] or the ability of dolphins to recognize semantic and syntactical distinctions.[72] Alternatively, maybe it was just a fluke, a freak mutation that ushered in the human adventure, and had it occurred in parakeets or dolphins it would have endowed them with language: Again, possible, but when biologists invoke freak mutations one should be sceptical. A third suggestion: maybe our exceptionalism is a category error, simply an illusion based on false data. We think we are different, but we are just telling ourselves fairy stories. This might appeal to the most world-weary of postmodernists, but is hardly credible.

So why are we different? In a sense the answer is obvious: notwithstanding those animals like parakeets and dolphins seemingly hovering on the very threshold, it is our possession of language, through which we can not only explore a potential infinity of meaning, but amongst them articulate truths that are discovered, not made, and apply as much to morals as to science. And there is no reason to regard this as some sort of fluke. Rather taking my proposal that evolution can be seen as a mechanism that ultimately allows at least one part of the universe to become self-aware, so we may find fertile new ground for a dialogue between science and religion.

Thus the Darwinian mechanism is entirely unexceptional, but I would argue it possesses a hitherto unrecognized predictability as is evident from the ubiquity of evolutionary convergence. But if evolution can discover mundane solutions repeatedly, so too we might suggest that it has the capacity to discover deeper realities, not least consciousness and language. It is easy to see why this process looks like emergence given the nascent manifestations in lower animals, but it is important to insist that cognitive capacity and grammar are as likely to be pre-existent realities that evolution effectively discovers. It would take me too far afield, but recall that it was Owen Barfield who insisted that language could not have emerged from a series of grunts and howls, but rather was inextricably linked to our discovery of myth. Not fiction, but realities that are too deep to be simply articulated. Our struggle to encompass these leads in many intriguing directions. Consider in particular how Barfield's co-inkling J. R. R. Tolkien insisted that the Christian myth was unique because it was actually true. I would suggest that if we reconsider what evolution has achieved, rather than unproblematically what it is, then we may be able to move on.

Notes

1   C. Darwin, *On the Origin of Species, etc.*, 2nd edn (London: John Murray, 1860), p. 484.

2   For example, R. S. Solecki, 'Shanidar-4, a Neanderthal Flower Burial in Northern Iraq', *Science* 190 (1975), 880–1.

3   S. J. Gould, *Wonderful Life: the Burgess Shale and the Nature of History* (New York: Norton, 1989).

4   G. G. Simpson, 'The Nonprevalence of Humanoids', *Science* 143 (1964), 769–75.

5   J. Diamond, 'Alone in a Crowded Universe', in B. Zuckermann and M. H. Hart (eds.), *Extraterrestrials: Where are They?* (Cambridge University Press, 1995), pp. 157–64.

6   E. Mayr, *What Makes Biology Unique: Considerations on the Autonomy of a Scientific Discipline* (Cambridge University Press, 2004).

7   D. C. Dennett, *Darwin's Dangerous Idea: Evolution and the Meanings of Life* (London: Allen Lane and The Penguin Press, 1995).

8   D. C. Dennett, 'An Unlovable Puddle', *Times Literary Supplement* 5418 (2 February 2007), p. 17.

9   P. Macklem, 'Emergent Phenomena and the Secrets of Life', *Journal of Applied Physiology* 104 (2008), 1844–6.

10   A. Ricardo, M. A. Carrigan, A. N. Olcott and S. A. Benner, 'Borate Minerals Stabilize Ribose', *Science* 303 (2004), 196.

11   F. Crick, *Life Itself: Its Origin and Nature* (London: Macdonald, 1982), p. 38.

12   D. J. Bartholomew, *God, Chance and Purpose: Can God Have it Both Ways?* (Cambridge University Press, 2008), pp. 180–2.

13   S. M. Adl *et al.*, 'The New Higher Level Classification of Eukaryotes with Emphasis on the Taxonomy of Protists', *Journal of Eukaryotic Microbiology* 52 (2005), 399–451.

14   B. J. Crespi, 'The Evolution of Social Behaviour in Microorganisms', *Trends in Ecology and Evolution* 16 (2001), 178–83.

15   See N. Yutin, K. S. Makarova, S. L. Mekhedov, Y. I. Wolf and E. V. Koonin, 'The Deep Archaeal Roots of Eukaryotes', *Molecular Biology and Evolution* 25 (2008), 1619–30.

16 See, for example, R. Derelle, P. Lopez, H. Le Guyader and M. Manuel, 'Homeodomain Proteins Belong to the Ancestral Molecular Toolkit of Eukaryotes', *Evolution & Development* 9 (2007), 212–19; T.H. Kloepper, C.N. Kienle and D. Fasshauer, 'SNAREing the Basis of Multicellularity: Consequences of Protein Family Expansion During Evolution', *Molecular Biology and Evolution* 25 (2008), 2055–68.

17 See P.L. Graumann, 'Cytoskeletal Elements in Bacteria', *Annual Review of Microbiology* 61 (2007), 589–618; J. Pogliano, 'The Bacterial Cytoskeleton', *Current Opinion in Cell Biology* 20 (2008), 19–27.

18 See E.F. Mongodin *et al.*, 'The Genome of *Salinibacter ruber*: Convergence and Gene Exchange among Hyperhalophilic Bacteria and Archaea', *Proceedings of the National Academy of Sciences, USA* 102 (2005), 18147–52; P. Puigbò, A. Pasamontes and S. Garcia-Vallve, 'Gaining and Losing the Thermophilic Adaptation in Prokaryotes', *Trends in Genetics* 24 (2008), 10–14.

19 See E.F. DeLong, R.B. Frankel and D.A. Bazylinski, 'Multiple Evolutionary Origins of Magnetotaxis in Bacteria', *Science* 259 (1993), 803–6.

20 See C.N. Keim, F. Abreu, U. Lins, H. Lins de Barros and M. Farina, 'Cell Organization and Ultrastructure of a Magnetotactic Multicellular Organism', *Journal of Structural Biology* 145 (2004), 254–62.

21 See, for example, S. Trachtenberg and S. Cohen-Krausz, 'The Archaeabacterial Flagellar Filament: a Bacterial Propeller with a Pilus-like Structure', *Journal of Molecular Microbiology and Biotechnology* 11 (2006), 208–20.

22 J.W. Stiller, D.C. Reel and J.C. Johnson, 'A Single Origin of Plastids Revisited: Convergent Evolution in Organellar Genome Content', *Journal of Phycology* 39 (2003), 95–105.

23 For example, B. Marin, E.C.M. Nowack and M. Melkonian, 'A Plastid in the Making: Evidence for a Second Primary Endosymbiosis', *Protist* 156 (2005), 425–32.

24 G. Manning, S.L. Young, W.D. Miller and Y.-F. Zhai, 'The Protist, *Monosiga brevicollis*, has a Tyrosine Kinase Signaling Network more Elaborate and Diverse than Found in any Known Metazoan', *Proceedings of the National Academy of Sciences, USA* 105 (2008), 9674–9.

25 I. Ruiz-Trillo, A.J. Roger, G. Burger, M.W. Gray and B.F. Lang, 'A Phylogenomic Investigation into the Origin of Metazoa', *Molecular Biology and Evolution* 25 (2008), 664–72.

26 N. King and JGI Sequencing Group, 'The Genome of the Choanoflagellate *Monosiga brevicollis* and the Origin of Metazoans', *Nature* 451 (2008), 783–8.

27 Ibid., p. 787.

28 For example, I. Wessler, H. Kilbinger, F. Bittinger and C.J. Kirkpatrick, 'The Biological Role of Non-neuronal Acetylcholine in Plants and Animals', *Japanese Journal of Pharmacology* 85 (2001), 2–10.

29 K. Kawashima, H. Misawa, Y. Moriwaki, Y.X. Fujii, T. Fugii, Y. Horiuchi, T. Yamada, T. Imanaka and M. Kamekura, 'Ubiquitous Expression

of Acetylcholine and its Biological Functions in Life Forms without Nervous Systems', *Life Sciences* 80 (2007), 2206–9.

30 C. Febvre-Chevalier, A. Bilbaut, Q. Bone and J. Febvre, 'Sodium-Calcium Action Potential Associated with Contraction in the Heliozoan *Actinocoryne contractilis*', *Journal of Experimental Biology* 122 (1986), 177–92.

31 For example, M. Ito, H.-X. Xu, A.A. Guffanti, Y. Wei, L. Zvi, D.E. Clapham and T.A. Krulwich, 'The Voltage-gated Na+ Channel Na$_v$BP has a Role in Motility, Chemotaxis, and pH Homeostasis of an Alkaliphilic *Bacillus*', *Proceedings of the National Academy of Sciences, USA* 101 (2004), 10566–71; R. Koishi, H.-X. Xu, D.-J. Ren, B. Navarro, B.W. Spiller, Q. Shi and D.E. Clapham, 'A Superfamily of Voltage-gated Sodium Channels in Bacteria', *Journal of Biological Chemistry* 279 (2004), 9532–8.

32 K. Mineta, M. Nakazawa, F. Cebrià, K. Ikeo, K. Agata and T. Gojobori, 'Origin and Evolutionary Process of the CNS Elucidated by Comparative Genomics Analysis of Planarian ESTs', *Proceedings of the National Academy of Sciences, USA* 100 (2003), 7666–71.

33 O. Sakarya, K.A. Armstrong, M. Adamska, M. Adamski, I.-F. Wang, B. Tidor, B.M. Degnan, T.H. Oakley and K.S. Kosik, 'A Post-synaptic Scaffold at the Origin of the Animal Kingdom', *PLoS One* 2(6) (2007), e506.

34 P. Thagard, 'How Molecules Matter to Mental Computation', *Philosophy of Science* 69 (2002), 497–518.

35 J.Z. Young, 'The "Cerebellum" and the Control of Eye Movements in Cephalopods', *Nature* 264 (1976), 572–4.

36 For example, C. Helfrich-Förster, 'The Circadian Clock in the Brain: a Structural and Functional Comparison between Mammals and Insects', *Journal of Comparative Physiology, A* 190 (2004), 601–13.

37 D.K. Hartline and D.R. Colman, 'Rapid Conduction and the Evolution of Giant Axons and Myelinated Fibers', *Current Biology* 17 (2007), R29–R35.

38 For example, A.D. Davis, T.M. Weatherby, D.K. Hartline and P.H. Lenz, 'Myelin-like Sheaths in Copepod Axons', *Nature* 398 (1999), 571.

39 For example, P.M. Pereyra and B.I. Roots, 'Isolation and Initial Characterization of Myelin-like Membrane Fractions from the Nerve Cord of Earthworms (*Lumbricus terrestris* L.)', *Neurochemical Research* 13 (1988), 893–901.

40 See I. Walker, 'Rede de alimentacao de invertebrados das aguas pretas do sistema rio Negro. 1. Observacoes sobre a predacao de uma ameba do tipo *Ameba discoides*', *Acta Amazonica* 8 (1978), 423–38.

41 T. Nakagaki, H. Yamada and A. Tóth, 'Maze Solving by an Amoeboid Organism', *Nature* 407 (2000), 470.

42 T. Nakagaki, 'Smart Behavior of True Slime Mold in a Labyrinth', *Research in Microbiology* 152 (2001), 767–70 (p. 767).

43 T. Nakagaki, H. Yamada and M. Hara, 'Smart Network Solutions in an Amoeboid Organism', *Biophysical Chemistry* 107 (2004), 1–5.

44 T. Nakagaki, M. Iima, T. Ueda, Y. Nishiura, T. Saigusa, A. Tero, R. Kobayashi and K. Showalter, 'Minimum-risk Path Finding by an Adaptive Amoebal Network', *Physical Review Letters* 99 (2007), art. 068104.

45 T. Saigusa, A. Tero, T. Nakagaki and Y. Kuramoto, 'Amoeba Anticipate Periodic Events', *Physical Review Letters* 100 (2008), art. 018101.

46 D. E. Nilsson, L. Gislén, M. M. Coates, C. Skogh and A. Garm, 'Advanced Optics in a Jellyfish Eye', *Nature* 435 (2005), 201–5.

47 C. Skogh, A. Garm, D. E. Nilsson and P. Ekström, 'Bilaterally Symmetrical Rhopalial Nervous System of the Box Jellyfish *Tripedalia cystophora*', *Journal of Morphology* 267 (2006), 1391–405.

48 J. E. Seymour, T. S. Carrette and P. A. Sutherland, 'Do Box Jellyfish Sleep at Night?', *Medical Journal of Australia* 181 (2004), 707.

49 For example, A. D. Eban-Rothschild and G. Block, 'Differences in the Sleep Architecture of Forager and Young Honeybees (*Apis mellifera*)', *Journal of Experimental Biology* 211 (2008), 2408–16.

50 P. S. Low, S. S. Shank, T. J. Sejnowski and D. Margoliash, 'Mammalian-like Features of Sleep Structure in Zebra Finches', *Proceedings of the National Academy of Sciences, USA* 105 (2008), 9081–6.

51 C. Agrillo, M. Dadda, G. Serena and A. Bisazza, 'Do Fish Count? Spontaneous Discrimination of Quantity in Female Mosquitofish', *Animal Cognition* 11 (2008), 495–503.

52 M. Dacke and M. V. Srinivasan, 'Evidence for Counting in Insects', *Animal Cognition* 11 (2008), 683–9.

53 For example, A. Nieder, 'The Number Domain – Can We Count on Parietal Cortex?', *Neuron* 44 (2004), 407–9.

54 For example, A. Nieder and E. K. Miller, 'A Parieto-frontal Network for Visual Numerical Information in the Monkey', *Proceedings of the National Academy of Sciences, USA* 101 (2004), 7457–62.

55 A. Nieder and E. K. Miller, 'Coding of Cognitive Magnitude: Compressed Scaling of Numerical Information in the Primate Prefrontal Cortex', *Neuron* 37 (2003), 149–57.

56 Ibid., p. 149.

57 F. Jackson, 'Epiphenomenal Qualia', *The Philosophical Quarterly* 32 (1982), 127–36.

58 For example, H. L. Eisthen, 'Why are Olfactory Systems of Different Animals so Similar?', *Brain, Behavior and Evolution* 59 (2002), 273–93; B. W. Ache and J. M. Young, 'Olfaction: Diverse Species, Conserved Principles', *Neuron* 48 (2005), 417–30; R. Benton, S. Sachs, S. W. Michnick and L. B. Vosshall, 'Atypical Membrane Topology and Heteromeric Function of *Drosophila* Odorant Receptors In Vivo', *PLoS Biology* 4(2) (2006), art. e20.

59 For example, C. Lundin, L. Käll, S. A. Kreher, K. Kapp, E. L. Sonnhammer, J. R. Carlson, G. von Heijne and I.-M. Nilsson, 'Membrane Topology of the *Drosophila* OR83b Odorant receptor', *FEBS Letters* 581 (2007), 5601–4; P. Pelosi, J.-J. Zhou, L. P. Ban and M. Calvello, 'Soluble Proteins in Insect Chemical Communication', *Cellular and Molecular Life Sciences* 63 (2006), 1658–76; R. Smart, A. Kiely, M. Beale, E. Vargas,

C. Carraher, A.V. Kralicek, D.L. Christie, C. Chen, R.D. Newcomb and C.G. Weir, 'Drosophila Odorant Receptors are Novel Seven Transmembrane Domain Proteins that Can Signal Independently of Heterotrimeric G Proteins', *Insect Biochemistry and Molecular Biology* 38 (2008), 770–80.

60 For example, I. Gaillard, S. Rouquier and D. Giogi, 'Olfactory Receptors', *Cellular and Molecular Life Sciences* 61 (2004), 456–69.

61 For example, R. Bentley, 'The Nose as a Stereochemist: Enantiomers and Odor', *Chemical Reviews* 106 (2006), 4099–112.

62 A. Keller and L.B. Vosshall, 'Human Olfactory Psychophysics', *Current Biology* 14 (2004), R875–R878 (p. R875).

63 For example, F. Baluška, S. Mancuso and D. Volkmann (eds.), *Communication in Plants: Neuronal Aspects of Plant Life* (Berlin: Springer, 2006).

64 For example, N.J. Emery and N.S. Clayton, 'The Mentality of Crows: Convergent Evolution of Intelligence in Corvids and Apes', *Science* 306 (2004), 1903–7.

65 For example, D. Reiss and L. Marino, 'Mirror Self-recognition in the Bottlenose Dolphin: a Case of Cognitive Convergence', *Proceedings of the National Academy of Sciences, USA* 98 (2001), 5937–42.

66 K. McComb, L. Baker and C. Moss, 'African Elephants Show High Levels of Interest in the Skulls and Ivory of Their Own Species', *Biology Letters* 2 (2006), 26–8.

67 For example, I. Douglas-Hamilton, S. Bhalla, G. Wittemyer and F. Vollrath, 'Behavioural Reactions of Elephants Towards a Dying and Deceased Matriarch', *Applied Animal and Behaviour Science* 199 (2006), 87–102. See also F. Ritter, 'Behavioral Responses of Rough-toothed Dolphins to a Dead Newborn Calf', *Marine Mammal Science* 23 (2007), 429–33 for a comparable example in a dolphin.

68 J.M. Plotnik, F.B.M. de Waal and D. Reiss, 'Self-recognition in an Asian Elephant', *Proceedings of the National Academy of Sciences, USA* 103 (2006), 17053–7.

69 B.L. Hart, L.A. Hart, M. McCoy and C.R. Sarath, 'Cognitive Behaviour in Asian Elephants: Use and Modification of Branches for Fly Switching', *Animal Behaviour* 62 (2001), 839–47.

70 For example, G.R. Hunt and R.D. Gray, 'Direct Observations of Pandanus-tool Manufacture and Use by a New Caledonian Crow (*Corvus moneduloides*)', *Animal Cognition* 7 (2004), 114–20; G.R. Hunt and R.D. Gray, 'Parallel Tool Industries in New Caledonian Crows', *Biology Letters* 3 (2007), 173–5; G.R. Hunt, J. Abdelkrim, M.G. Anderson, J.C. Holzhaider, A.J. Marshall, N.J. Gemmel and R.D. Gray, 'Innovative Pandanus-tool Folding by New Caledonian Crows', *Australian Journal of Zoology* 55 (2007), 291–8; A.H. Taylor, G.R. Hunt, J.C. Holzhaider and R.D. Gray, 'Spontaneous Metatool Use by New Caledonian Crows', *Current Biology* 17 (2007), 1504–7; A.A.A. Weir and A. Kaczelnik, 'A New Caledonian Crow (*Corvus moneduloides*) Creatively Re-designs Tools by Bending or Unbending Aluminium Strips', *Animal Cognition* 9 (2006), 317–34.

71 G. J. L. Beckers, B. S. Nelson and R. A. Suthers, 'Vocal-tract Filtering by Lingual Articulation in a Parrot', *Current Biology* 14 (2004), 1592–7.
72 L. M. Herman, S. A. Kuczay II and M. D. Holder, 'Responses to Anomalous Gestural Sequences by a Language-trained Dolphin: Evidence for Processing of Semantic Relations and Syntactic Information', *Journal of Experimental Psychology, General* 122 (1993), 184–94.

8 God, physics and the Big Bang

WILLIAM R. STOEGER, SJ

Over the past ninety years we have come to understand and appreciate the world, the universe which embraces it, and their emergence and development in completely new ways. Thanks to astronomy and physics – particularly to the speciality known as cosmology – we now know that the universe we inhabit began expanding and cooling from an extremely hot and dense, homogeneous, simple state about 13.7 billion years ago. That initial state, often now referred to as the Planck era, was so extreme that our current physics is completely unable to describe it. Space and time as we know them had not yet emerged, and the fundamental forces of gravity, electromagnetism, and the strong and weak nuclear interactions were undoubtedly unified, and thus indistinguishable from one another. Only a thorough and complete quantum description of reality, including space-time and gravity – a quantum cosmology – would be adequate. That is something we do not yet possess, although many people are expending tremendous efforts to develop the components of such a description by exploring superstrings, loop-quantum gravity and non-commutative geometry, as well as exploiting semi-classical approaches to quantizing space-time, gravity and the universe itself.[1]

However, great progress is being made in this area, and there are strong reasons to expect that the process or processes by which our universe began its expansion, cooling and complexification will eventually be adequately modelled and understood. In fact, over the past twenty-five years, educated preliminary proposals for such processes have been made. These include the no-boundary proposal of Hartle and Hawking, and the chaotic inflationary scenario of Andrei Linde.[2] Such proposals have led to the realization that our universe may be just one of an enormous number of other universes or universe domains. We shall briefly describe and discuss these and other tantalizing, imaginative and informed scenarios later in this chapter.

Well before this focus on quantum cosmology, the strong evidence that the universe was much different in the distant past – hotter, denser and simpler, and produced by a physical process in the Big Bang – raised many philosophical and theological questions. Did God as creator trigger the Big Bang? Was it the moment of creation? With the prospect that physics and cosmology might be able to provide a detailed account of the origin of the universe, is there really any need for God – for a creator? Is not physics perfectly able to supply all that is needed for the origin of the universe, and in a much more compelling and well-substantiated way than either philosophy or theology can? There are also more subtle queries: What can the discoveries of cosmology and physics contribute to philosophy and theology? What can a careful theology of creation contribute to physics and cosmology? These are the questions we shall explore in this chapter. In doing so, we shall critically accept the primary conclusions which contemporary cosmologists have reached about the character and history of our universe. At the same time we shall argue that physics and cosmology as sciences are incapable of exploring or directly accounting for the ultimate source of existence and order which philosophy and theology, properly understood, provide. By the same token, philosophy and theology are not equipped to investigate and describe the processes and relationships which contributed to the expansion, cooling and subsequent structuring of the universe on macroscopic and on microscopic scales. Thus, philosophy and theology seek to provide an understanding of the origin and evolution of the universe which is complementary to that which physics and cosmology contribute – that is, a basic but unadorned ontological account which cannot legitimately displace or compete with the findings of cosmology. They probe and attempt to render intelligible the ultimate existence and ordering of the dynamisms, relationships and entities which are the primary concern of the natural sciences.

In pursuing this discussion, we shall first briefly summarize the central findings of contemporary cosmology, including an analysis of the concept of the Big Bang. As part of that process we shall explore some of the current scenarios for initiating that expansion from the Planck era. Next, we shall indicate some of the basic limitations of these scenarios – or indeed of any account of the origin of the universe couched in terms of physics alone. This will lead us to a brief exposition of what divine creation is and what it is not. Together these considerations will reveal the possibility of a deep consonance between any adequate physics of the Big Bang, quantum or otherwise, and a creator God, properly understood. A brief treatment of the anthropic principle and the apparent fine-tuned character of the universe will follow. This will be followed by an exploration of multiverses as objects of scientific investigation and explanation, and of some of the limitations and cautions we need to apply when invoking them. Again, we will return to the question of whether some account needs to be offered of the ultimate source of existence and order of any really existing multiverse. Here, too, the potential complementarity of the sciences, and philosophy and theology, will be evident. Finally, we shall briefly summarize what physics and cosmology contribute to theology, particularly a theology of creation and, similarly, consider what contributions theology might make to physics and cosmology.

THE BIG BANG, QUANTUM COSMOLOGY AND EMERGENCE FROM THE PLANCK ERA

From a vast amount of independent evidence, provided by extra-galactic astronomy and precision measurements of the cosmic microwave background radiation (CMWBR), we know that the universe is expanding and cooling, and has been doing so for almost 14 billion years. This means, obviously, that at earlier times the universe was much hotter and denser than it is now, and that the farther we go back into its history, the hotter and denser it was. We also know that on the very largest scales – scales of at least 600 million light years – the universe is almost spatially homogeneous and isotropic. Its average density over scales larger than that is almost constant at any given time. Using a simple physical-mathematical model of such a universe, the Friedmann–Lemaître–Robertson–Walker (FLRW) model, we find that at a finite time in the past, such a universe had to be infinitely hot and infinitely dense. This is often referred to as the initial singularity or the Big Bang.

However, we have already stressed that the physics of space-time that we know – and which is assumed in the FLRW model – breaks down at extremely high temperatures, at about 10^{32} K (the so-called Planck temperature). Above that temperature the universe was enjoying the Planck era. Accordingly, this Big Bang initial singularity given by the FLRW model does not represent what really occurred, and is not the beginning of the universe. It is only the beginning in time according to the FLRW model – but precisely in the region where that model fails. The Big Bang as this initial singularity, then, is an artefact of a model which is very reliable at lower temperatures but far from correct for temperatures above the Planck temperature. Thus, it should be considered only as the past limit of the hotter denser phases of the universe as one goes back into the past – a limit falling outside the reliability of the model, as does the Planck era itself. A new physics is needed, which, as we have already indicated, requires a quantum treatment of space-time and gravity. This is the realm of quantum cosmology. Although we do not yet have an adequate quantum cosmology, we do have a number of well-founded provisional indications of the processes which may have been important in the Planck era, and in triggering the expansion and cooling of the universe into its FLRW or classical phase. That occupies its entire history – all but the very first tiniest part of a second after the Big Bang – from the point of view of the FLRW model.

Before discussing some of these preliminary conclusions of quantum cosmology, we should briefly describe what we know of the history of the universe after the Planck era.[3] Immediately upon exiting the Planck era – in fact this may have caused the universe to exit the Planck era – most cosmologists believe that there was a very brief period (much, much less than a second) of extraordinarily rapid expansion called inflation. At the same time, of course, the universe would have super-cooled. This inflation would have been driven by a large amount of vacuum energy (Einstein's cosmological constant) which possesses a large negative pressure and thus induces a gravitational repulsion. It is this inflationary process which we believe generated the density fluctuations which were the seeds of future galaxy formation. It is very difficult to see any other way, so far at least, that such seeds could have been generated. Another very strong reason for invoking inflation is the extraordinary smoothness of the CMWBR, the afterglow of the Big Bang. That means that the universe we see at that time, about 300,000 years after the Big Bang, must have been causally connected on length scales much larger than the light-travel time since the Big Bang. (Remember, the Big Bang was 13.7 billion years ago!) The only sure way we know of doing that is by inflating an extremely small, causally connected patch immediately after the Planck era to a size encompassing our entire observable universe.

Very quickly inflation was brought to halt, and the universe was reheated to a very high temperature. This was effected by the rapid transformation of vacuum energy into radiation and particles. This transformation required a very special type of inflationary potential – a hypothetical field which cosmologists call the inflaton. Because of the requirements that such an inflaton must fulfil, there is as yet no fully adequate model of the inflationary era and the subsequent reheating of the universe. The fine-tuning needed for such a model is one of the unsettling aspects of the inflationary paradigm.

Once the inflationary era had passed, the universe expanded and cooled much more gently, with the density fluctuations generated by inflation frozen into the cosmic plasma. For at least 100,000 years, the temperature of the gas was high enough that the gas was ionized, and therefore interacted strongly with radiation. That prevented the fluctuations from growing. However, this was not true of the dark matter fluctuations, which were not affected by radiation and were able to begin growing in density earlier than those composed of protons and neutrons (baryons). Once the temperature of the universe fell below about 4,000 K, however, the dominant hydrogen was no longer ionized, and the baryonic matter could begin to clump on its own, also falling into the clumps of dark matter which had already formed. The increasing density in the fluctuations generated higher local gravitational fields, enabling them to separate from the cosmic expansion. Eventually they stopped expanding – although the universe around them continued to do so – and they collapsed under their own weight to form galaxies and clusters of galaxies. Within the galaxies, stars eventually formed.

The advent of stars was extremely important for our universe. Without them, the universe would have remained chemically impoverished – and therefore biologically sterile. Up until the formation of stars, the only elements present were hydrogen, helium and a little lithium, the lightest metal. All the other elements – including carbon, oxygen, iron, etc. – were formed in stars or as the result of stellar explosions.

We must now return to discuss some of the important preliminary quantum cosmology scenarios for the initial stages of our universe. Our reason for delving into this is to appreciate what physics and cosmology may eventually be able to say about the Planck era, what led to it, and what triggered the expansion of our universe in its emergence from the Planck era – the Big Bang. We further want to determine, from a more philosophical or theological perspective, whether physics and cosmology are able to provide an ultimate ontological explanation for the universe and its principal characteristics. If so, then they would be able to compete with philosophical-theological concepts of divine creation as an account of the ultimate ground of existence and order. If not, then physics and cosmology provide an understanding of the universe and reality which is complementary to the contributions of philosophy and theology. After this, we shall go on to delineate the differences between the two forms of intelligibility, their limitations, and how they are indeed complementary, if properly understood.

First, we shall look at Hartle and Hawking's no-boundary proposal.[4] In the 1960s, John A. Wheeler and Bryce DeWitt had formulated the elegant and well-known Wheeler–DeWitt equation, which describes the quantum wave function of the universe.[5] This essentially represents the probability of different universes emerging from the initial cosmic quantum state. Under certain conditions on the Wheeler–DeWitt equation, there will be a definite probability that our particular universe will emerge and begin to expand and cool as the FLRW model prescribes. It is important to realize that the Wheeler–DeWitt equation itself does not explicitly contain time. In the quantum regime it describes, the wave function of the universe in some definite sense just is. Time can emerge from the equation with the fulfilment of appropriate boundary conditions. Then in the 1980s, Hartle and Hawking showed, using the Wheeler–DeWitt equation, that with no initial three-dimensional spatial boundary for the cosmic wave function, we can obtain a universe like ours. In fact the resulting universe also has a very early inflationary phase, which we have seen seems to be required on other grounds. Several years later Alex Vilenkin proposed a rather different scenario which leads to a similar result.[6]

Some have interpreted the Hartle–Hawking result as demonstrating that physics and cosmology are now able to explain how the universe emerges from nothing, since there is no initial boundary, nor any classical time that can be defined at a boundary. However, this is an illusion. At the very least, one needs the existence of the wave function of the universe, and its ordered behaviour – its physics – as described by the Wheeler–DeWitt equation. Thus there remain the questions of where these came from, and why they were that way, rather than some other way. In an important sense, then, neither the Hartle–Hawking nor the Vilenkin scenario describes the process – or much more correctly, the relationship – by which the universe was created, in the radical philosophical sense.[7] There are also technical problems with the proposal, which render it inadequate. Despite these shortcomings, it certainly is and continues to be an important landmark and stimulus in the continuing pursuit of a more adequate quantum cosmology.

String theory recently stimulated two other well-recognized and popular scenarios for modelling the emergence of the universe from the Planck era.[8] In neither of them is the Big Bang in any way conceived as the origin of the universe. One of these is the pre-Big-Bang scenario in which, because of symmetries allowed by string theory, there is the possibility of an earlier phase of the universe (before the Big Bang).[9] During this phase, the universe collapses from an almost empty state an infinite time ago to become very dense and very hot, leading to the Planck era. But the volume of the universe has a minimum, and the temperature has a maximum. When these are reached the universe bounces and enters the post-Big-Bang phase. As yet, however, there is not a satisfactory account of how the transition from one phase to the other might be effected.

The second proposal is the ekpyrotic scenario.[10] According to this picture, our universe is simply one of many large three-dimensional membranes (D-branes) floating in a higher dimensional space. Because of the gravitational attraction between these branes, they collide now and then, triggering a Big-Bang-like event, which leads to the expansion and cooling of each of the three-dimensional branes. However, not just any pair of colliding branes would yield the Big Bang and our universe. The collision would have to be finely tuned – for instance, the branes would have to be almost exactly parallel.[11]

Among the intriguing consequences of research in early-universe and quantum cosmology is the strong suggestion that our universe is not the only one. In fact, some of the scenarios for the emergence of our universe imply that there are extraordinarily large numbers of others. Processes which could have triggered the birth of our universe have a tendency to produce many others along with it. It is very likely that these other universes would be very different from one another in terms of the parameters which characterize them – their coupling constants, geometry and history. An ensemble of many really existing universes, a multiverse, is often used to explain the apparent fine-tuning of our own universe for complexity and life (the anthropic principle). Since these issues are often included in discussions of divine creation and the Big Bang, we shall explore them more fully later. Of course, such a multiverse cannot itself be an ultimate explanation, even from a scientific perspective. Its existence and character will require a more fundamental physical explanation – some generating process, which in turn will require a physical underpinning.[12]

This brief overview of quantum cosmology has revealed a number of important points about our understanding of the processes which led to our universe. First, the Big Bang cannot be considered the beginning of the universe, even from the point of view of physics and cosmology, and certainly not its ultimate origin or explanation. In fact, at present, although we have some preliminary ideas of how the Planck era may have come about, this very early stage of cosmic history falls outside the region of our relatively secure standard FLRW model of the universe. Second, any reliable physical account or scenario for the Big Bang, or for the origin of the Planck era itself, requires more fundamental detailed physics describing the fields and states which underlie the processes and features of the Planck era. Any such account will always demand some further explanation or physical foundation and, ultimately, a metaphysical foundation or ground that physics itself is incapable of supplying. What spurs the physics and fundamental structures into existence? What explains why there is something rather than nothing? And why this particular order rather than some other particular order? There is no physics of absolutely nothing – or, more exactly, a physics describing how existence is realized from non-existence – which there would have to be if physics were able to give an ultimate explanation for the existence of the universe. This leads us to philosophical questions about ultimate origins, and to religious questions about creation.

GOD AND PHYSICS: THE COMPATIBILITY OF CREATION WITH THE BIG BANG

Now the time has come to explore what creation, properly speaking, means. We have just begun to see that physics and cosmology seem to be incapable in principle of supplying an adequate account of the ultimate ground of existence and order. They have been extraordinarily successful in uncovering and modelling in great qualitative and quantitative detail the structures and dynamisms of nature. They can tell us how any system evolves: given a particular state, physics and cosmology can help us find the range of states which led to that state, and the range of states which will follow. But they cannot tell us ultimately why the whole system exists or why it is endowed with the particular order it manifests.

In a definitive sense, philosophy and theology cannot answer these questions either, at least not adequately. But they can and do propose accounts which provide consistent and intelligent preliminary answers to the question which are less inadequate than their competitors. Here I shall briefly synthesize the insights on divine creation which are the fruit of late medieval Judaic, Christian and Muslim philosophical thinking by such influential scholars as Maimonides, Thomas Aquinas, Averroes and Avicenna.[13] My argument will be that the idea of divine creation, as developed in these religious traditions, is complementary to scientific explanation (and therefore to whatever quantum cosmology and physics may reveal about the earliest stages of our universe), because it simply provides an explanation or ground for the existence and basic order of whatever the sciences propose and discover. It does not provide an alternative to scientific explanation. According to these theological accounts, the creator grounds, empowers and enables the physical processes – including those which are primordial – to be what they are. As we have just seen, what quantum cosmology discovers cannot substitute for what divine creation accomplishes, for it is unable to provide an ultimate ground for existence and order.[14] Theological accounts of creation accomplish this by proposing a self-subsisting, self-explanatory cause – the creator – which is the fundamental source of being and order, and in which all existing things participate. As such, this creator is not another entity or process in the universe which can be detected and isolated from other physical causes or entities. It is causally distinct from them because without it nothing would exist. And yet, as we have just emphasized, it is not a substitute for created causes: instead, it endows them with being, efficacy and autonomy. This is the classical distinction between the complementary categories of primary and secondary causality. The central point is that the primary cause is unlike any other cause, both because it gives existence and order, and because it does not act in place of or in parallel to any other cause. In fact, in this instance we are using the concept 'cause' in a deeply analogous or metaphorical way, to point to something we cannot fully comprehend – the mystery of existence and ordered activity. God is radically transcendent and beyond all adequate concepts. But we can point to that reality, and we can filter out less inadequate ways of speaking about God and God's creative activity from the completely inadequate ways.

There are a number of aspects to this concept of divine creation which are worth pointing out. The first is that creation is not a temporal event, but a relationship – a relationship of ultimate dependence. Thus, 'cause' as applied to God should be conceived not as a physical force or an interaction, as it is in physics, but rather in terms of a relationship of dependence which is always present.[15] Thus, the creator is always sustaining, or conserving, all that is in its existence. This is the *creatio continua* side of *creatio ex nihilo*, the metaphorical term which refers to this particular idea of 'creation' which has dominated the monotheistic theological traditions. It follows from this that creation is not about a temporal beginning of physical reality – although we cannot completely rule that out – but about an ontological origin, the ultimate source of being and order. Thus, also, the relationship of creation does not effect change, as do other physical causes. God, as primary cause, is a necessary condition, or cause, for all that happens. But God is never a sufficient condition and does not bring about changes in the world in isolation from secondary causes. All of these specifications are simply to clarify what is meant in these theistic traditions by intelligent talk about God's creative action.

Second, it has been helpful to conceive the relationship of creation as a participation in the being and activity of the creator.[16] In this regard, too, many have argued that it is better to conceive this creator as a verb, rather than as a noun (an entity). Thus we might say that creation is the limited participation of whatever exists in the pure, self-subsisting being, activity, and creativity of the creator. Traditionally, some philosophers and theologians have referred to God as Pure Act.

Third, this concept of divine creation discourages us from conceiving the creator as controlling nature or the universe, or intervening in its dynamisms. Instead, God, as we have already stressed, endows all the processes, regularities and relationships in nature with their being and their capacities for autonomous activity. They possess their own integrity and adequacy. We can say, in a somewhat metaphorical way, that God as creator is working in and through these dynamisms, regularities and relationships of nature (including those which are statistical, such as quantum mechanics) by empowering them to operate. But we should not understand that action as micromanagement or control – as constraints beyond those which are inherent to nature itself. God gives natural causes full freedom to function as they are.

Finally, this creative relationship of ultimate dependence is not uniform, but rather highly differentiated. Although God sustains everything in being and activity, that creative support is different in every case, since God is sustaining different things in being, with particular individualities, properties and capabilities, and through different relationships with the environment in which they thrive. And each responds to that environment, and to those relationships – and therefore to God – in different ways.[17]

This overview provides the essence of what many philosophers and theologians regard as the least inadequate approach to divine creation that has been developed, and one which has deep roots in the best philosophical theology of the monotheistic religions.

It clearly helps us understand why divine creation, if properly understood, is deeply compatible with physics, cosmology or any other natural science in explaining the origin of the universe, or of any system emerging within it. The theology of creation provides explanation and intelligibility on a level different from, but complementary to, that of physics, cosmology and the other natural sciences. Deep misunderstandings have resulted from confusing these levels.

Having established in very general terms what is meant by ideas of creation in the Western religious traditions, we now turn to an important set of specific issues to which we have already made brief reference: the apparent fine-tuned character of the universe, the possibility of God's creative role in effecting that fine-tuning, and the scope for explaining such fine-tuning by considering our universe to be one member of a multiverse.

AN UNLIKELY UNIVERSE: FINE-TUNING, GOD AND MULTIVERSES

Since about 1961 there has been a growing realization that our universe is very special.[18] If any of the four fundamental physical forces (gravity, electromagnetism, and the strong and weak nuclear interactions) had even slightly different strengths, as given by their coupling constants, or if the parameters giving the basic geometry and dynamics of the universe (for instance, its rate of expansion after the inflationary era) had been slightly different from what they are, the universe would be so different that there would be no complexity, and no life.[19] It would have been completely sterile. If no stars had formed, for example, then there would have been no elements heavier than helium and lithium, and therefore no chemistry or biology, no rocky planets. From many different considerations, then, it appears that our universe has been fine-tuned for complexity and for life – and perhaps for consciousness. The discovery of these characteristics of our universe has given rise to what is known as the anthropic principle (AP).[20]

From the earliest discussions of the AP, particularly by Brandon Carter,[21] cosmologists have spoken of its weak versions (WAP) and its strong versions (SAP).[22] The weak versions state that since complexity, life and consciousness are present in the universe, the fundamental constants of nature and the initial conditions for the universe itself must be such as to allow and support their existence. The conditions of possibility for complexity have been fulfilled – their realization acts *a posteriori* to constrain the possible values of the fundamental parameters. The strong versions of the AP go much further. They assert that our universe had to be such that complexity, life and consciousness would eventually emerge within it. This implies that somehow the specific characteristics of the universe were chosen ahead of time – that the universe was indeed fine-tuned – so that complexity, life and consciousness would emerge. Thus, the strong versions involve an *a priori* constraint on the fundamental cosmic parameters.[23]

Clearly the SAP, which is the primary focus of our concern here, requires definite evidence or justification for why complexity, life and consciousness must emerge. This obviously implies a finality or purposiveness in the universe, which goes considerably beyond where the natural sciences, including physics and quantum cosmology, can go. It clearly invites philosophical and theological solutions, most of which have essentially proposed that God as creator selected the specific characteristics of the universe, so that complexity, life, consciousness and freely choosing beings would be assured. In other words, God set the initial conditions for the universe.

A dominant second proposed resolution to the SAP, which attempts to keep the entire discussion within the competencies of the natural sciences and avoid theological considerations, is the multiverse scenario. Our universe is one of an extremely large number of other really existing universes, or universe domains, representing a range of different laws, fundamental constants and initial conditions. There is then within this multiverse a definite probability that any one of them will allow the emergence of complexity, life and consciousness. This, of course, presumes that we can define a probability measure on the ensemble of universes. This would not be possible, for instance, if the multiverse contained an infinite number of universes, or all possible universes, as some have suggested.[24]

The multiverse scenario does in some sense explain why our universe is biofriendly, if evidence for it can be found. But this explanation is obviously incomplete scientifically. It immediately demands further understanding of the process by which the multiverse was generated, and why it contains universes which allow for the emergence of complexity. This strongly suggests that the generation of such a multiverse itself would require fine-tuning. Certainly it would also require an ultimate explanation for its existence, for the existence of the cosmic process producing it, and for the particular order and properties it possesses. It would require a creator. Thus, the multiverse hypothesis really does not resolve, or constitute an equivalent version of, the SAP, compared with the philosophical/theological approach. In some sense, it is a retreat back to the WAP.[25] However, we can certainly continue to treat it as a strong intermediate explanation for the fine-tuned character of our universe. Our universe may in fact be one of a large number of other universes!

There are scientific, though not directly observational, grounds for taking this possibility seriously. From all the theoretical work that has been done in early-universe cosmology, including quantum cosmology, we now know that there are a number of very natural ways in which a multiverse could have been generated. In fact, it seems that almost any well-motivated proposal for explaining the Big Bang, or the emergence of our universe from the Planck era, leads to the production of not just one universe, but many. For instance, there is Andrei Linde's chaotic or eternal inflation scenario,[26] as well as more recent proposals, such as those of Weinberg[27] and Garriga and Vilenkin,[28] who have speculated that the quantum fluctuations generated during inflation led to a large number of separate cosmic regions, each with a different vacuum-energy density. Each of these would evolve as separate universes, or universe domains. Superstring theory has also provided landscapes possessing extremely large numbers of vacua, each of which would be a separate universe domain.[29]

While multiverses might be attractive theoretical possibilities, it seems reasonable to ask whether the hypothesis of their existence is scientifically testable. Would it ever be possible to demonstrate, even if only in principle, that our universe is likely to be a part of an ensemble of many other universes? If not, then it is impossible for these universes to be scientifically legitimate objects. Certainly, we shall never be able to observe other universes directly. Are there other ways in which evidence for them can be obtained?

A compelling approach to this question is provided by retroductive or abductive inference as an important component of scientific method.[30] This was developed by C. S. Peirce,[31] and much more recently by E. McMullin.[32] 'Retroduction' is an inference from observed consequences of a hypothesis to its explanatory antecedents – that is, it is based on the success of a hypothesis in accounting for a set of phenomena or rendering them more intelligible. As scientists modify and adjust their hypotheses in light of ongoing experiment and careful observation, these hypotheses become more and more fruitful and precise in what they predict, reveal and explain. As McMullin emphasizes, they often postulate the existence of hidden entities (like multiverses) or properties which are basic to their explanatory power. As they become more and more central and reliable within the fabric of scientific theory, accounting for all the relevant data, connecting previously considered unrelated phenomena, contributing deeper understanding to the field and stimulating new fruitful lines of inquiry, this success leads us to affirm the existence of these hidden entities or properties – or something very much like them – even though we never directly detect them.[33]

Thus, if a multiverse becomes a central component of a quantum cosmological theory and establishes its importance for understanding our universe more deeply, then on the basis of retroductive inference we have scientific evidence for its existence and its properties. We are presently a very long way from that situation, but it is possible that one of the multiverse hypotheses will achieve that status in the future. Even if it does, however, it is certainly clear, as we have emphasized, that it would not provide anything more than an intermediate answer to the SAP. It would require a deeper explanation for its own existence and bio-friendly character, including an ultimate ground for its being and order – a creative relationship.

COSMOLOGY AND THEOLOGY IN INTERACTION

From our discussion of these issues what can we conclude about the present and potential contributions of scientific cosmology to the theology of creation? And, reciprocally, what about the potential contributions of a critical theology of creation to cosmology?

Because theology of creation is primarily concerned with the ultimate source of the existence, dynamism and order of whatever physics and cosmology reveal about the primordial processes in the very early universe – something which is necessarily beyond the scope of physics and cosmology – their influence on one another will be indirect, but very important. First, cosmology really strongly constrains theology of creation to that particular role, discouraging it from entering into competition with physics to provide alternative agents of change. In doing so, it essentially acts to purify theology by filtering out inadequate and anthropomorphic representations of divine creative action. In short, it is consistent with the sort of theology of creation we have presented here. Second, a critical theology of creation supports whatever cosmology as a science legitimately concludes. At the same time it acts to remind physics and cosmology of the larger and deeper search for understanding and meaning in which it participates, and of the limitations of its own mode of inquiry.

A corollary to this approach is that what physics and cosmology discover and what theology legitimately asserts can never be in essential conflict. If conflict or incompatibility appear then that is a sure sign that there has been misinterpretation or the transgression of disciplinary limitations on one side or the other. In sum, fruitful interactions between cosmology and the theology of creation will reinforce their complementarity and prove to be mutually beneficial and enriching.

Notes

1 For basic background in this area, see Lee Smolin, *Three Roads to Quantum Gravity* (New York: Basic Books, 2001).

2 J.B. Hartle and S.W. Hawking, 'Wave Function of the Universe', *Physical Review* D28 (1983), 2960–75; A.D. Linde, 'Chaotic Inflation', *Physics Letters B* 129 (1983), 177–81. For an updated, more readable account, see A.D. Linde, *Particle Physics and Inflationary Cosmology* (Chur: Harwood, 1990).

3 There is a vast popular and semi-popular literature giving more details of this account, as well as the observational evidence for it. See, for instance, Martin J. Rees, *Just Six Numbers: the Deep Forces that Shape the Universe* (New York: Basic Books, 2001), and George F.R. Ellis, *Before the Beginning: Cosmology Explained* (London: Boyars/Bowerdean, 1993). For more technical introductory references, see Edward W. Kolb and Michael S. Turner, *The Early Universe* (Reading, MA: Addison-Wesley, 1990); Andrew R. Liddle and David H. Lyth, *Cosmological Inflation and Large-Scale Structure* (Cambridge University Press, 2000).

4 Hartle and Hawking, 'Wave Function'. For a more accessible, non-technical presentation, see C.J. Isham, 'Creation of the Universe as a Quantum Process', in Robert John Russell, William R. Stoeger, SJ and George V. Coyne, SJ (eds.), *Physics, Philosophy and Theology: a Common Quest for Understanding* (Vatican City State: Vatican Observatory Publications, 1988), pp. 375–408.

5 See B.S. DeWitt, 'Quantum Theory of Gravity I: the Canonical Theory', *Physical Review* 160 (1967), 1113–48. For a more recent and simple presentation, see Carlo Rovelli, *Quantum Gravity* (Cambridge University Press, 2004).

6 A. Vilenkin, 'Quantum Cosmology and the Initial State of the Universe', *Physical Review* D37 (1988), 888; for a non-technical but detailed presentation, see C.J. Isham, 'Quantum Theories of the Creation of the Universe', in Robert John Russell, Nancey Murphy and C.J. Isham (eds.), *Quantum Cosmology and the Laws of Nature: Scientific Perspectives on Divine Action* (Vatican City State and Berkeley, CA: Vatican Observatory Publications, and the Center for Theology and the Natural Sciences, 1993), pp. 49–89.

7 Isham, 'Creation of the Universe'.

8 Gabriele Veneziano, 'The Myth of the Beginning of Time', *Scientific American* 290, no. 5 (May 2004), 54–65.

9 See also Maurizio Gasparini and Gabriele Veneziano, 'The Pre-Big-Bang Scenario in String Cosmology', *Physics Reports* 373, nos. 1–2 (2003), 1–212.

10 Veneziano, 'The Myth of the Beginning'; Justin Khoury, Burt A. Ovrut, Nathan Seiberg, Paul J. Steinhardt and Neil Turok, 'From Big Crunch to Big Bang', *Physical Review* D65 (2003), 086007.

11 I am indebted to George Ellis for this qualification, via a private communication.

12 See G. F. R. Ellis, U. Kirchner and W. R. Stoeger, 'Multiverses and Physical Cosmology', *Monthly Notes of the Royal Astronomical Society* 347 (2003), 921, and W. R. Stoeger, G. F. R. Ellis and U. Kirchner, 'Multiverses and Cosmology: Philosophical Issues', *arXiv: astro-ph/0407329*, and references therein, for a detailed treatment of these issues.

13 For brief summary treatments of divine creation, see Catherine Mowry LaCugna, *God for Us: the Trinity and Christian Life* (San Francisco: Harper-San Francisco, 1993), pp. 158–67; Langdon Gilkey, 'Creation, Being and Nonbeing', in David B. Burrell and Bernard McGinn (eds.), *God and Creation: an Ecumenical Symposium* (Notre Dame, IN: University of Notre Dame Press, 1990), pp. 226–41; William E. Carroll, 'Divine Agency, Contemporary Physics, and the Autonomy of Nature', *The Heythrop Journal* 49, no. 4 (2008), 582–602 (I am grateful to Charles L. Harper for this reference); William R. Stoeger, 'The Origin of the Universe in Science and Religion', in Henry Margenau and Roy A. Varghese (eds.), *Cosmos, Bios, Theos: Scientists' Reflection on Science, God, and the Origins of the Universe, Life and Homo Sapiens* (La Salle, IL: Open Court, 1992), pp. 254–69; William R. Stoeger, 'Conceiving Divine Action in a Dynamic Universe', in Robert John Russell, Nancey Murphy and William R. Stoeger, SJ (eds.), *Scientific Perspectives on Divine Action* (Vatican City State and Berkeley, CA: Vatican Observatory Publications and the Center for Theology and the Natural Sciences, 2008), 225–48.

14 For a more detailed presentation of these ideas, see William R. Stoeger, 'The Big Bang, Quantum Cosmology and *Creatio ex Nihilo*', in Janet M. Soskice, David B. Burrell, Carlo Cogliati and William R. Stoeger (eds.), *Creation and the God of Abraham* (Cambridge University Press), forthcoming.

15 On this point, see Carroll, 'Divine Agency, Contemporary Physics', pp. 592–3.

16 See, for instance, David B. Burrell, in Soskice *et al.* (eds.), *Creation and the God of Abraham*.

17 Stoeger, 'The Big Bang, Quantum Cosmology'.

18 R. H. Dicke, 'Dirac's Cosmology and Mach's Principle', *Nature* 192 (1961), 440–1.

19 There are many examples of such sensitive dependence – for an earlier exhaustive compendium, see J. D. Barrow and F. J. Tipler, *The Cosmological Anthropic Principle* (Oxford University Press, 1986).

20 For a more detailed presentation of the material in this section, see William R. Stoeger, 'Are Anthropic Arguments, Involving Multiverses and Beyond, Legitimate?', in Bernard Carr (ed.), *Universe or Multiverse?* (Cambridge University Press, 2007), pp. 445–57.

21 B. Carter, 'The Anthropic Principle and its Implications for Biological Evolution', *Philosophical Transactions of the Royal Society of London* A 310 (1983), 347–63.

22 For a careful, scientifically sensitive philosophical treatment of weak and strong versions of the AP, and other related issues, see E. McMullin, 'Indifference Principle and Anthropic Principle in Cosmology', *Studies in History and Philosophy of Science* Part A, 24 (1993), 359–89.

23 Ibid., p. 376.

24 On these issues, see Ellis *et al.*, 'Multiverses and Physical Cosmology', pp. 921–2; and Stoeger *et al.*, 'Multiverses and Cosmology: Philosophical Issues'.

25 See Stoeger, 'Are Anthropic Arguments Legitimate?', pp. 447–8.

26 Linde, 'Chaotic Inflation', 177–81; Linde, *Particle Physics and Inflationary Cosmology*.

27 S. Weinberg, 'The Cosmological Constant Problem', in D. Cline (ed.), *Sources and Detection of Dark Matter and Dark Energy in the Universe* (Berlin: Springer-Verlag, 2001), pp. 18–26.

28 J. Garriga and A. Vilenkin, 'Many Worlds in One', *Physical Review* D64 (2001), 043511.

29 S. Kachru, R. Kallosh, A. Linde and S.P. Trevedi, 'de Sitter Vacua in String Theory', *Physical Review* D68 (2003), 046005; L. Susskind, 'The Anthropic Landscape of String Theory', in Carr (ed.), *Universe or Multiverse*, pp. 247–66.

30 See Stoeger *et al.*, 'Multiverses and Cosmology'; Stoeger, 'Are Anthropic Arguments Legitimate?', pp. 450–1.

31 C.S. Peirce, in *Collected Papers, Vols. 1–6*, ed. by C. Hartshorne and P. Weiss (Cambridge, MA: Harvard University Press, 1931–5), vol. I, para. 65; vol. v, para. 188; in *Collected Papers, Vols. 7 and 8*, ed. by A. Burks (Cambridge, MA: Harvard University Press, 1958), vol. vii, paras. 202–7; 218–22.

32 E. McMullin, *The Inference that Makes Science* (Milwaukee, WI: Marquette University Press, 1992); E. McMullin, 'Truth and Explanatory Success', *Proceedings, American Catholic Philosophical Association* 59 (1985), 206–31.

33 Paul L. Allen, *Ernan McMullin and Critical Realism in the Science–Theology Dialogue* (Aldershot: Ashgate, 2006), pp. 70–3; Stoeger, 'Are Anthropic Arguments Legitimate?', p. 451.

9 Psychology and theology

FRASER WATTS

This chapter is about the dialogue between psychology and theology. I will first briefly distinguish this specific topic from others to do more generally with the interface of psychology and religion. One of those is the practical application of psychology to the work of faith communities. Here the primary focus has been the area of pastoral care (although in *Psychology for Christian Ministry*[1] I showed that the potential practical application of psychology to religion is much broader). In contrast, the dialogue between theology and psychology is focused more on truth questions and less on practical ones. Another intersection between psychology and religion is the psychology of religion – one of several human sciences, including sociology and social anthropology, which are concerned with religious belief and practice. The psychology of religion generally takes as detached a view as possible of religious phenomena. This observational approach to religion is not my central focus in this chapter, although I will return later to those aspects of the dialogue between theology and psychology which deal with the nature of religion itself.

The dialogue between theology and science is notoriously one-sided, as will have been apparent from other chapters in this volume. Theology has been much more interested in science than science has been in theology. Individual scientists may be interested in theology, but it is difficult to argue that theology has much contribution to make to science as such. In contrast, I suggest that the dialogue between theology and psychology can be a more two-way one. Admittedly, it is not a fully mutual relationship, and psychology probably does not recognize what it might have to learn from theology. However, it is at least possible to argue that theology has a substantial contribution to make to psychology.

The theological contribution to psychology takes two forms. The negative side is a theological critique of psychology, or at least of the reductionist tendencies to be found in some branches of psychology.

The positive side is the contribution that theology can make to the enrichment of psychology. Theology has reasons for objecting to that narrowness, and is able to suggest particular ways in which psychology can be broadened and enriched.

THEOLOGICAL CHALLENGES TO REDUCTIONISM IN PSYCHOLOGY

There are four main forms of reductionism currently running in psychology. In neuroscience, there is a tendency to argue, as Francis Crick put it, that we are nothing but a 'bundle of neurones'.[2] In evolutionary psychology, there is a tendency to argue that we are just survival machines for our genes.[3] In artificial intelligence there is a proposal that the mind is, in effect, just a computer program.[4] In some branches of social psychology, there is a proposal that human realities are just 'social constructs'.

There are complex and subtle issues here that it is not possible to explore fully. However, one key point to note is that there is nothing in these areas of scientific investigation that makes them inherently reductionist, and that not all psychologists working in these areas are reductionist in their approach. The problem arises, not with scientific evidence itself, but with how that evidence is sometimes interpreted. It is also worth noting that strong reductionist positions are more likely to be advocated in popularizations of scientific work than in careful, detailed scientific inquiry itself.

For example, recent neuropsychology has provided increasingly strong evidence for a tight connection between particular areas of the brain and specific mental functions.[5] That is uncontroversial, even though there are complications, such as those arising from the fact that the mapping of mind onto brain is not exactly the same in detail in any two individuals. Problems arise with two assumptions that become intertwined with the scientific evidence.

One is that mind–brain linkages are often explained utilizing an entirely one-way model of causation, that is, the effect of the physical brain on mental functioning. It is equally possible that there is a two-way causal interaction between them. It is also arguable that mind and brain cannot be separated sufficiently to speak of causal relations between them at all. The other problematic assumption is that mental functioning can be explained entirely (that is, without remainder) in terms of brain processes. In fact, it is difficult to rule out other possible influences, and difficult to provide scientific evidence that the brain is the only possible influence on mental processes. Indeed this sort of claim is unlikely to be the kind of thing that science could substantiate.

However, the real problem arises when people go beyond the claim that the brain explains mental processes completely, and draw the inference that mental (or spiritual) functions are somehow not real, that they have not only been explained, but explained away. That is a completely unjustified conclusion, for which there is no evidence or sound argument; explaining something does not show that it is not real. However, this position is so attractive to people with materialist assumptions that it continues to be widely asserted. Religious people, in contrast, will want to assert that people really have mental capacities and spiritual qualities, and that these are not illusory.

Similar issues arise about the other reductionisms. For most religious people, there is no problem with the idea that human beings have evolved from other forms of life. So, evolution provides at least a partial explanation of human moral and religious attributes. However, it is a big jump from there to say that evolution explains everything, or that the higher aspects of humans, such as the capacity to be moral, are not what they seem, and are really nothing but a product of evolution.

In artificial intelligence, there is no doubt that the analogy between the human mind and a computer program has been very fruitful theoretically, and that computers can perform a wide range of intelligent functions pretty well. However, that does not show that the human mind can be reduced to a set of computational processes, or that it really is just a computer program.

Equally, there is no doubt that all human concepts, about humans themselves and about everything else, are social constructs in the sense that they are influenced by language and culture. However, it is a huge and unjustified step from there to say that things are just social constructs. God, for example, is undoubtedly a social construct (that is, ideas about God arise in a linguistic and cultural context), but it does not follow from that that God is nothing but a social construct.

The slide from legitimate to illegitimate claims in each of these areas can be subtle and insidious, and constant vigilance is needed to monitor the slide from reasonable points that present no theological problems to unjustified conclusions that are theologically objectionable. The critical contribution that theology can make here is to challenge reductionist interpretations of psychological research, though there is no direct challenge to detailed research work itself. Theology will want to urge much greater caution in the interpretation of research findings than is often the case. It can aspire to clean up the reduction ideology that often distorts the way in which scientific research is presented.

THEOLOGICAL ENRICHMENT OF PSYCHOLOGY

In addition to the theological critique of illegitimate reductionism, there are psychological topics that can be enriched by a theological perspective. For example, there are perspectives from both theology and psychology on many human emotions.[6] Guilt is thus an important topic in both theology and psychology, though handled rather differently. Although emotions are now regarded as psychological categories, it is interesting to note that there was a prior religious discourse about passions and affections before a psychology of the emotions developed.[7]

However, I will take forgiveness as my main example of how there can be a theological enrichment of psychology, drawing on the recent book *Forgiveness in Context*.[8] Forgiveness has always been a central topic in religious thought, but recently there has been a significant development of psychological theory, research and practice about it. It is a topic that has, in a sense, migrated across from theology to psychology. That raises interesting issues about the different emphases of theological and psychological approaches to forgiveness. Some aspects of the theological approach to forgiveness are more relevant to psychology than are others, and the focus here will be largely on the human experience and practice of forgiveness.

Psychology has developed quite full and elaborate procedures for helping people with forgiveness where they find that difficult, and there is encouraging evidence of the practical value of forgiveness therapy.[9] Though there is a faith-based pastoral literature on forgiveness, it is not anything like as fully developed as the psychological approach. Religious communities have much to learn, at a practical level, from forgiveness therapy. However, there are things to be learned in the other direction as well. At several significant points, theology has a broader approach to forgiveness than does psychology, though there is nothing in the discipline of psychology that prevents it from adopting that broader perspective. Indeed, it could profitably learn from theology at a number of points.

First, theology has a better grasp of the fact that forgiveness is often costly, and there may be situations in which it is almost impossible. Psychology is right to emphasize the practical benefits of forgiveness, but it may sometimes be guilty of implying that it is more straightforward than it really is. L. G. Jones, in *Embodying Forgiveness*,[10] has accused it of peddling a kind of 'cheap grace'. Forgiveness that is not costly may be pseudo-forgiveness. However, the development of forgiveness therapy within psychology arises from an implicit recognition of how difficult forgiveness can be, and there is no reason why a psychology cannot be more explicit about that.

Second, psychology tends to imply that forgiveness is a human initiative, and forgiveness therapy is largely focused on how people can be helped to forgive others. Theology has a broader sense that forgiveness is something that we receive from God and from others. It can make a great difference to how forgiveness proceeds psychologically to regard this as a gift rather than a human initiative. Psychology needs to focus on receiving forgiveness, not just on giving it. So far the receiving of forgiveness has simply been neglected by psychology, but that is something that can be rectified.

Third, the psychological approach to forgiveness is pragmatic in that it proposes that people should be engaged in forgiveness because it will make them feel better. Theology does not deny that, but also has a sense of the moral imperative to forgive. It is an open question whether the practical benefits of forgiveness can be fully delivered if people approach it in a purely pragmatic spirit. It is possible that you need a sense of the moral rightness of forgiveness for its benefits to become fully apparent. It may be a specific case of 'first seeking the kingdom of God', before other benefits are added.

Finally, psychology tends to see forgiveness as episodic, in the sense that it focuses on a particular act of forgiveness that needs to be undertaken at a particular time with a particular person. Theology, by contrast, tends to see forgiveness as a virtue that needs long-term cultivation, and which will then manifest itself in a variety of contexts. Psychodynamic psychology is potentially well able to understand the personality development that may be necessary before episodic forgiveness becomes possible.

The general point is that theology and psychology offer complementary perspectives and elucidate different aspects of phenomena such as forgiveness. They each have something to contribute to the other, so that there is value in bringing them into creative dialogue.

PSYCHOLOGICAL CONTRIBUTIONS TO THEOLOGY

So far I have argued that theology has a critique to make of reductionist trends in psychology, and also that the theological approach to topics of mutual interest such as forgiveness can enrich the psychological approach. I now want to turn to how psychology can contribute to theology.

Psychology has a distinctive intersection with Christian theology; indeed each science interfaces with theology at slightly different points. Psychology is concerned with human beings and how they function, so its point of intersection with theology concerns the theology of human beings, 'theological anthropology' as it is called. That prompts some comments about the current state of theological anthropology, and its place within Christian doctrine.

Some people might see 'theological anthropology' as a misnomer. If you define theology as the science of God, as some people do, then theological anthropology sounds like a contradiction in terms. However, there are good reasons for not defining theology in that way. Because God is, in large measure, beyond human comprehension, the idea that human beings are capable of developing a science to study him is preposterous. The very idea seems to arise from an inappropriate transplantation of the methods of natural science to theology. As Hegel remarked, 'God does not offer himself for observation.'[11]

Whatever theology is, I submit that it clearly cannot be the study of God by human beings. Theology should be taken, not as indicating a distinctive object of study, that is, God, but rather as a discipline in which things are studied from a distinctive perspective. Whatever theology studies, it does it from the point of view of religious faith. Seen like that, theological anthropology (i.e. the theological perspective on human beings) makes perfectly good sense.

It really is central to theology to have a perspective on human nature. The vast majority of religious doctrine, at least in the monotheisms, is about the interaction between God and humanity. The two exceptions are the pure doctrine of God and the doctrine of human nature (i.e. theological anthropology). It is indispensable in theology to have a good way of conceptualizing the interaction between God and humanity, and that depends on having a considered and defensible account of human nature.

It has to be admitted that this is not currently the most vigorous area of theology. In the Christian tradition, for example, there is currently much less work being undertaken in theological anthropology than in, say, Trinitarian theology. Also, there is a widespread feeling that theological anthropology has got into a rut, and that fresh approaches are needed to revive it. Making it more explicitly interdisciplinary seems the best way forward.[12] There is much more such work to be done on interdisciplinary theological anthropology, and psychology makes an excellent dialogue partner for theology in that task.[13]

Another problem with theological anthropology is that claims are often made that seem highly determined by other areas of doctrine. For example, if, in the Christian tradition, you have a theology of the cross that focuses on removing guilt, then it is tempting to assume that human beings feel guilty, and to make that a central claim in your theological anthropology. Equally, if you have a doctrine of the church as a salvific community, it is tempting to make strong claims about what church membership does for people, and about what un-churched people are deprived of. If you believe religion provides people with meaning, it is tempting to claim that people are afflicted by a sense of meaninglessness.

The real problem here is that the claims are often made in theological anthropology just because they fit in with other theological positions, and without theologians feeling any need to check empirically whether their claims are correct. Moreover, there is a tendency to make exaggerated claims, whether of idealization or denigration. There is also too much theological generalization about human nature, and neglect of differences between people. If theological anthropology were more interdisciplinary, and conducted in dialogue with an empirical discipline like psychology, the result would be much more satisfactory.

It is helpful for the interface between psychology and theological anthropology to include general conceptual frameworks as well as specific claims about human beings. Both disciplines often need to grapple with the problem of reconciling different aspects of human nature, though they tend to have different emphases, and there can be a fruitful dialogue about those.

For example, both disciplines need to recognize that human beings are physical, personal and social beings, and to find a way of understanding how those aspects intersect with one another. Christian theology currently tends to overemphasize relationality, and some areas of psychology overemphasize the biological aspects of human nature. Dialogue between them might help to correct each other's imbalances.

Equally, both disciplines need to reconcile continuity of personality across different situations with change from one context to another. Theology tends to see unity of personality as normative, and diversity as breakdown of the norm. Psychology is more likely to start from the diversity of how people function in different situations, and to see integration as an achievement rather than a norm.[14]

Another rather different area of theology to which psychology can make a useful contribution is hermeneutics (that is, the process of interpretation). The study and interpretation of texts is central to theology. The main focus is on scriptural texts, but the study and interpretation of other theological texts is also important. There are similar contributions to be made to religious history; there is, for example, a psychological literature on the life and work of Augustine.

In recent years, there has been much interest in the contribution of the human sciences to the interpretation of religious texts, and there is a substantial literature on the contribution of social science. More recently, there has been a rapid development of work on the psychological interpretation of the Hebrew Bible and the New Testament.[15] It has to be admitted that not all psychological hermeneutics has been of good quality. Indeed much has been so bad that it has nearly brought the whole enterprise into disrepute. However, it is now possible to set some guidelines for good work in this area.

First, it should build on what is already known about the background and meaning of the texts concerned. It should be cautious about presumed historical facts, and not overinterpret them. Too much psychological work has been naïve in its reading of the texts; Gerd Theissen's work is a model of good practice in this regard. Second, it should be critical about the psychology it uses, recognizing that psychology is a diverse discipline, that there are many different psychologies available, and they may lead to different interpretations of the texts concerned; again Theissen's work serves as a model. Third, psychology should be used not in an exclusive or reductionist way, but in dialogue with other more theological interpretations of the texts concerned.

THEOLOGICAL AND PSYCHOLOGICAL PERSPECTIVES ON RELIGION

One of the important ways in which the dialogue of theology with human sciences such as psychology differs from its dialogue with the natural sciences is that the human sciences study religion. Because there is also a psychology of religious beliefs and practices, there can be a dialogue between theology and psychology about religion itself.

It is here that the reductionist tendency in psychology often comes to the surface. However, I believe that there is nothing necessarily reductionist about the psychology of religion. On the contrary, the reductionist tendencies in psychology are something that can and should be challenged, for scientific as much as for theological reasons. It is the job of the psychology of religion to develop an understanding of how religious phenomena and practices such as conversion, religious experience or speaking in tongues come about. There is also, of course, a theological perspective on such phenomena. Unfortunately, neither theology nor psychology generally welcomes a dialogue with the other about religion; both are inclined to assume that their own approach is sufficient in itself.

As far as psychology is concerned, that arises in part from the principle that scientific explanations should be parsimonious, and that simple explanations are to be preferred to complex ones. The rule of thumb that simple explanations are preferable works well in the natural sciences, especially in theoretical physics, as the work of Einstein illustrates. However, I have become increasingly convinced that preferring simple explanations is a bad principle in psychology. Human phenomena are inherently complex and multifaceted, so that emphasizing a single strand of explanation is usually overly simplistic.

Psychology can potentially draw on quite a broad range of factors in framing accounts of religion, including brain processes, social processes, cognitive processes, personal development and individual differences. The psychology of religion has already been forced to recognize the relevance of a variety of factors. For example, it is hard to avoid admitting that both brain processes and social processes are involved in religious experience. In a similar way, there is no reason why theological and psychological accounts of religious phenomena and practices should not co-exist fruitfully.

However, one can go further than simply claiming that theological and psychological perspectives do not contradict one another. That is a conclusion that can be reached by the apartheid approach that keeps theology and science in separate categories that never interact. I propose, rather, that psychology is, in principle, never capable of ruling theological explanations in or out. For example, it can study religious experience, but can never determine whether or not that experience arises from God.

However, psychology can perhaps influence the details of how a theological account is best framed. I suggest that is true of most areas of interchange in science and religion. For example, cosmological work on the origin of the universe can never adjudicate on the religious doctrine of creation, though it can affect how the doctrine is explicated in detail. (See William Stoeger's chapter in this volume.) Equally, psychological theory and research on religious practices and experiences cannot adjudicate on whether a theological interpretation of them is right or wrong, but it can influence the details of how a theological account is cast.

To illustrate that, let me turn to the dialogue between theology and psychology about prayer. There is no need, for this purpose, to say anything very distinctive about the theology of prayer, though I assume that a satisfactory theological account of prayer will make realist assumptions about God. It will see prayer as a deliberate psycho-spiritual activity in which there is a communion between God and the person praying, and that prayer will be seen as enabling that person to see things increasingly from a God's-eye perspective, and open themselves to God's grace.

Alongside that theological perspective, I suggest that psychology can help us to understand the human side of prayer.[16] The theology of prayer can be of surprisingly little help to people who want to learn how to do it. The psychology of prayer, in contrast, is much more practical. The focus here will be on the benefits of prayer for the person who prays, because that is where there is the richest engagement between theology and psychology, not because it is assumed there are no other benefits of prayer.

Petitionary prayer can be seen as a kind of education of our desires. People's desires can influence prayer in various ways. At one extreme, there are things we would rather like, but which we sense are in no way relevant to God's purposes. At the other extreme, there are things that we know we ought to pray for, but for which we have no real desire. The personal benefits of petitionary prayer probably lie in working towards the integration of those two; it is an activity in which people rework their desires so that they grow increasingly close to what they believe are God's purposes.

In a similar way, the benefits of thanksgiving can be seen as lying in a retraining of attributions. Over the past two decades, psychology has become increasingly aware of the very important consequences of causal attributions. Whether you put successes and failures down to yourself or to chance, external factors make a huge difference. Thanksgiving involves learning a pattern of attributions to God, alongside other attributions. Attributions to God defy the usual distinction between internal and external attributions, and I suspect that there is something psychologically very helpful about that.

Confession involves a sifting of what is a proper subject of confession. Guilt feelings do not serve as a very good marker of that, though they are a good starting point. As Freud realized, much guilt is neurotic rather than realistic. The regular practice of confession can help people to recognize that, and making confession to a priest can be useful in discriminating between what does and does not need to be confessed. Hearing forgiveness proclaimed by a priest can help people to move on from guilt that is proving troublesome, and encourage them to make whatever life-changes are needed if guilt is not to recur.

Psychology can thus give an account of how prayer is helpful to the person who prays. Such an account is neutral about whether prayer involves communion with God. It could be taken either as an account of how prayer can be helpful even if there is no God, or as an account of how some of the benefits of prayerful communion with God are mediated at the human level.

Another interesting topic in the psychology of religion, from the point of view of the dialogue with theology, is glossolalia, or speaking in tongues. This is the most studied of the charismatic phenomena, and we now know a good deal about it. One key question is whether explanations of charismatic phenomena from the human sciences are compatible with religious interpretations, such as seeing it as the work of the Holy Spirit. Many people (both social scientists and charismatics) assume not, but in contrast, I want to suggest that the two approaches are not necessarily incompatible.

A key assumption of many charismatics is that speaking in tongues defies natural explanation, because people are speaking languages that they do not know. However, there are good research reasons for rejecting that claim. Glossolalic speech just does not have the syntactical structure of language; there is too much repetition of sounds, etc.[17] Also, there are severe constraints on what you can say in glossolalic utterance. For example, you cannot conduct an argument in a glossolalic language.

However, accepting that it is not language does not necessarily mean that it is not inspired by the Holy Spirit, or that it has no spiritual value. It can be seen as 'ecstatic utterance', rather than a human language. It seems to be an unusually fervent and disinhibited way of praising God. Whether glossolalia is language or not may be less important than is sometimes thought. Note that the conclusions that follow are asymmetrical. If glossolalics were speaking languages they did not know, it would require a supernatural explanation, but the fact that they are not speaking such languages still leaves open the possibility that their utterance is, in some sense, inspired by the Holy Spirit.

Psychologically speaking, it seems likely that people are in an unusual cognitive state when they speak in tongues, but it has not proved easy to specify exactly what that is. One suggestion is that it is a trance-like state, but research does not support that. Others have speculated that it may be a regressive state in which people become more open to unconscious processes. There may be some truth in that, but it is not a hypothesis that it is easy to test empirically. However, it is clear that the cognitive architecture of the mind is being employed in an unusual way in glossolalia. People who speak in tongues seem to know the gist of what they are saying (praising God), but that gist seems to feed through into speech, without being recoded into more defin-ite linguistic meanings on the way. In the terminology of Interacting Cognitive Subsystems, there seem to be general, tacit (implicational) meanings which get through to speech, while the propositional system seems to be virtually switched off.[18]

Whatever state people are in when they are speaking in tongues, it seems to have personal as well as religious benefits.[19] There is evidence of positive personality changes, such as being more open to feelings, more spontaneous, less depressed and anxious. There is also decrease in addictive behaviour. These changes are not specific to glossolalia; they are similar, for example, to those produced by transcendental medita-tion. Again, they are neutral as to whether or not they are combined with a theological interpretation. Psychology can be seen as giving a complete account of why and how glossolalia is of personal benefit, or it might just be used in conjunction with a theological account, expli-cating at a human level how the effects of religious inspiration are mediated.

Another interesting question is whether speaking in tongues is the result of social learning. There are a number of facts that fit this idea. People who speak in tongues are often introduced to the practice by friends. There is often encouragement and suggestion about how to do it. People become better at it with practice. That suggests that a role theory of glossolalia might be appropriate. Most charismatics would be resistant to such a theory, though it is not clear why that should be so. The claim that glossolalia is a valuable spiritual practice, and one that results from religious inspiration, is perfectly consistent with people learning to open themselves to this way of praising God through the example and encouragement of other religious people.

So, research on glossolalia is by no means incompatible with a theological account that sees it as a valuable and inspired form of spir-itual practice. However, it does suggest some detailed refinements of the usual charismatic view of it. In particular, it suggests that it is an ecstatic form of religious praise, but not a language.

OBJECTIVITY AND SUBJECTIVITY

One of the enduring issues with which theology has had to grapple is the relationship between the objective and the subjective, and the dialogue between theology and psychology nearly always raises issues about this. The initial suspicion is often that the subjectivization of doctrine will be the inevitable outcome of a dialogue between theology and psychology. I argue that that is not necessarily the case.

It will be helpful briefly to put this general issue in context.[20] There was a sea-change in the relationship between science and religion in the nineteenth century. In some sense it can be traced back to Kant's division between pure and practical reason. On the back of that, the nineteenth century saw a growing distinction between two uses of language, literal and symbolic. Literal uses of language were associated with objective truth, whereas symbolic uses of language were associated with subjective experience.

Religion became caught up in this bifurcation, and found itself largely cast on the symbolic side, along with art and poetry. Much subsequent theology has been a protest against this assignment, and an attempt to reassert the objectivity of Christian belief against programmes of demythologization and subjectivization. Forced to choose between these alternatives, it is understandable that theology should want to defend the objectivity of Christian belief, or at least to say that there is more at stake than subjective experience. However, some might want to decline to start from this distinction at all; there are many good reasons for refusing to accept the distinction between literal and symbolic uses of language, and between objectivism and subjectivism.

It may be helpful to note that psychology has made its own protest against being cast on the symbolic/subjective side of this distinction. For more than a century, there has been an attempt to develop a scientific psychology that can claim to be on the objective side of this divide. However, psychology is, methodologically, a hybrid, one that stands between the objective and the subjective. For example, it is a long way, methodologically, from experimental psychology to psychoanalysis. The ability of psychology to hold its diverse strands together illustrates how the divide between objective and subjective can be healed.

Owen Barfield, in a beautiful paper on language and discovery, talks about how the objectivity that is claimed for science needs to recognize more clearly the personal journey that is involved in developing a commitment to truth. Equally, those concerned with personal significance of language need to hold on to a concern with knowledge and discovery. Barfield concludes, perhaps each needs the clasp and support of the other in his half-blinded staggering towards the light. Perhaps there is not one prison cell, but two: the non-objectifying subjectivity in which the humanities are immured, and the adjoining cell of subjectless objectivity, where science is locked and bolted, and may be the first step towards escape for the two prisoners of language is to establish communication with one another.[21]

Work on the interface of theology and psychology can elucidate the personal significance of religious beliefs, and help to heal this divorce between the objective and subjective aspects of religious belief. Christian theology may have been right to want to hold on to the object-ivity of religious belief, but the cost of largely neglecting its subject-ive significance has been very high. There are exceptions of course, the most notable among major theologians being Paul Tillich, whose method of correlation in theology involves a mapping of theology on to psychology.[22] We now have a situation in which it is widely recognized that religious people believe that they are making objective claims. Nevertheless, many people probably fail to see what difference those claims might make to them personally.

Harry Williams, one of the pioneers in work on the interface between theology and psychology, put it like this: 'In my view, strict academic scholarship has already given to theological thinking all that for the time being it has to give ... Our present task is of a different kind ... We must discover and try to tell how God's redemption of us has made itself known to the most secret places of our being.'[23] The dialogue between theology and psychology can help with that important task.

One example of this concerns eschatological hope.[24] In the Christian tradition, for example, hope rests on the belief that it is God's purpose to redeem his creation and bring everything to fullness in Christ. There has been an interesting discussion about how that squares with the rather gloomy predictions of cosmologists about the heat death of the universe. It would be a digression for me to discuss how the two can be reconciled. My point here is that Christian hope for the future, and cosmological predictions about the end of the universe, have different concerns.

Cosmology is trying to make objective predictions about the future. Theology is operating at a level that integrates the objective and the subjective. So, the dialogue between eschatology and cosmology needs to be complemented by a dialogue between eschatology and psychology that is more concerned with the human phenomena of hope. If eschato-logy gets into dialogue only with cosmology or only with psychology, it will fail to hold together the objective and subjective aspects of Christian thinking.

Incidentally, there is an interesting dialogue about hope to be had between theology and psychology. There has recently been a good deal of psychological research on hope, but this has in fact largely focused on optimism and pessimism – that is, on whether people are making good or bad predictions about the future. What religious people mean by hope is not mere optimism, but a constructive commitment to a good future.[25] Psychological research on hope, in this religious sense, would be very fruitful and interesting, and something that has not yet really been broached. It would be a theological contribution to psychology.

In this chapter, I have tried to give something of the flavour of the dialogue between theology and psychology, drawing attention to some of the distinctive features of that dialogue and to how it differs from the dialogue between theology and other sciences. I have also tried to give an indication of the range of topics that can be tackled on the interface between theology and psychology. It is currently a very neglected aspect of theology and science, but I hope I have shown that there is much of interest here, and that it deserves to be given higher priority than it usually receives.

Notes

1   Fraser N. Watts, Rebecca Nye and Sara Savage, *Psychology for Christian Ministry* (London: Routledge, 2002).
2   Francis Crick, *The Astonishing Hypothesis: the Scientific Search for the Soul* (London: Touchstone, 1995), p. 3.
3   Richard Dawkins, *The Selfish Gene* (Oxford University Press, 2006).
4   Hans Moravec, *Mind Children: the Future of Robot and Human Intelligence* (Cambridge, MA: Harvard University Press, 1988).
5   Malcolm A. Jeeves, *Human Nature at the Millennium: Reflections on the Integration of Psychology and Christianity* (Grand Rapids, MI: Baker Books, 1997).
6   On shame and guilt, see Fraser N. Watts, 'Shame, Sin and Guilt', in A. McFadyen and M. Sarot (eds.), *Forgiveness and Trust* (Edinburgh: T. and T. Clark, 2001), pp. 53–69; on anger, see Fraser N. Watts, 'Emotion Regulation and Religion', in J.J. Gross (ed.), *Handbook of Emotion Regulation* (New York: Guilford Press, 2001), pp. 504–20.
7   Thomas Dixon, *From Passions to Emotions: the Creation of a Secular Psychological Category* (Cambridge University Press, 2003).
8   Fraser N. Watts and Liz Gulliford (eds.), *Forgiveness in Context: Theology and Psychology in Creative Dialogue* (London: T. and T. Clark, 2004).
9   Everett L. Worthington, *Forgiving and Reconciling: Bridges to Wholeness and Hope* (Downers Grove, IL: InterVarsity Press, 2003).

10 Gregory L. Jones, *Embodying Forgiveness: a Theological Analysis* (Grand Rapids, MI: Eerdmans, 1995).

11 Georg Friedrich Wilhelm Hegel, *Lectures on the Philosophy of Religion*, ed. by Peter C. Hodgson, trans. R. F. Brown (Oxford: Clarendon Press, 2007), vol. 1, p. 258.

12 One example emerged from a European Society for the Study of Science and Theology meeting – Niels Henrik Gregersen, Willem B. Drees and Ulf Görman (eds.), *The Human Person in Science and Theology* (Edinburgh: T. and T. Clark, 2000); another emerged from the Center of Theological Inquiry in Princeton – R. Kendall Soulen and Linda Woodhead, *God and Human Dignity* (Grand Rapids, MI and Cambridge: Eerdmans, 2006); Wentzel van Huyssteen has made a significant contribution to interdisciplinary theological anthropology. See *Alone in the World? Human Uniqueness in Science and Theology* (Grand Rapids, MI and Cambridge: Eerdmans, 2006).

13 An early path-breaking effort in this area was Paul Meehl and Richard Klann (eds.), *What, Then, Is Man? A Symposium of Theology, Psychology, and Psychiatry* (Saint Louis, MO: Concordia Publishing House, 1971). It brought together a rigorous and conservative Lutheran theology with a rigorously scientific approach to empirical psychology.

14 Léon Turner has argued for the importance of narrative methods for both disciplines in reconciling unity and diversity. See Léon P. Turner, *Psychology, Theology and the Plural Self* (Farnham: Ashgate, 2008).

15 Wayne G. Rollins, *The Soul and Psyche: the Bible in Psychological Perspective* (Minneapolis: Fortress Press, 1999) provided an initial survey. J. Harold Ellens and Wayne G. Rollins, *Psychology and the Bible: a New Way to Read the Scriptures*, 4 vols. (Westport, CT: Greenwood-Praeger, 2004), followed that up with work bringing together many of the best studies done so far. Rollins and D. Andrew Kille edited a volume of texts and readings, *Psychological Insight into the Bible: Texts and Readings* (Grand Rapids, MI: Eerdmans, 2007). Together they provide a good overview of the field. Gerd Theissen's psychological study of Pauline theology remains one of the best individual examples of this type of work: *Psychological Aspects of Pauline Theology* (Edinburgh: T. and T. Clark, 1987). I have myself also recently edited a book on *Jesus and Psychology* (London: Darton Longman and Todd, 2007) that includes chapters on the contribution of psychology to understanding the mindset of Jesus himself, chapters elucidating the psychological significance of his teaching and chapters on the psychology of how the gospels are read.

16 See, for example, Laurence B. Brown (ed.), *The Human Side of Prayer: the Psychology of Praying* (Birmingham, AL: Charles Creegan, 1994); Fraser N. Watts, 'Prayer and Psychology', in Fraser N. Watts (ed.), *Perspectives on Prayer* (London: SPCK, 2001), pp. 39–52.

17 See William J. Samarin, *Tongues of Men and Angels: Religious Languages of Pentecostalism* (New York: Macmillan, 1972).

18 See Fraser N. Watts, *Theology and Psychology* (Aldershot: Ashgate, 2002).

19 Newton H. Malony and A. Adams Lovekin, *Glossolalia: Behavioral Science Perspectives on Speaking in Tongues* (New York and Oxford: Oxford University Press, 1985).

20 There is a guide to the background issues in an excellent chapter by John Bowker, 'Science and Religion: Contest or Confirmation?', in Fraser N. Watts (ed.), *Science Meets Faith: Theology and Science in Conversation* (London: SPCK, 1988), pp. 95–119.

21 Owen Barfield, *The Rediscovery of Meaning and Other Essays* (Middletown, CI: Wesleyan University Press, 1977), pp. 148–60, quotation from p. 160.

22 See, for example, Terry D. Cooper, *Paul Tillich and Psychology: Historic and Contemporary Explorations in Theology, Psychotherapy, and Ethics* (Macon, GA: Mercer University Press, 2005).

23 Harry A. Williams, *The True Wilderness* (London: Constable, 1965), p. 138.

24 See, for example, Fraser N. Watts, *Theology and Psychology*, ch. 9.

25 Fraser N. Watts, Kevin Dutton and Liz Gulliford, 'Human Spiritual Qualities: Integrating Psychology and Religion', *Mental Health, Religion and Culture* 9 (2006), 277–89.

10 Science, bioethics and religion

JOHN H. EVANS

In this chapter I will examine the relationship between religion and science in debates over issues having to do with the human body from the 1960s to the present. These are now generally called bioethical debates, and these debates have been a primary location of interaction between religion and science from the mid-twentieth century forward.

While the ability of scientists to intervene in the human body has obviously been increasing for centuries, in the 1960s this ability was perceived to have taken a quantum leap. In 1953 the structure of DNA had been discovered, suggesting to many in the 1960s that scientists would soon be able to control the genetic constitution of the human species through human genetic engineering. While kidneys had been transplanted for a number of years, 1967 saw the first heart transplant, which in turn led to more organs being transplanted. Whereas historically a person was considered dead when their heart and breathing stopped, the invention of artificial respiration, coupled with the need for transplantable organs, led in the 1960s to novel questions about who was really dead and therefore could be taken off life-support. While abortion had been practised for millennia, by the mid-1960s women could, for the first time, find out the genetic characteristics of the foetus through amniocentesis and decide, to a limited extent, what kind of child they would have. In 1969 scientists in England created the first embryo in a test-tube, which would later lead to the first 'test-tube baby' in the late 1970s.[1] There were also concerns about mind control – that the emerging field of psychopharmacology and advanced behaviouralist training techniques would allow one human to control the behaviour of others. The response from one participant in this debate typifies the response to all of these emergent technologies: 'Man's existence now, and for the first time, is threatened.'[2]

These debates originally included a great deal of interaction between scientists and religious leaders. In this chapter I will first examine the subsequent marginalization of religious voices in these debates by looking at the sociological context of these debates – who obtained power from whom and how they used this power to marginalize particular types of inputs to the debate. I will then turn to even more recent history where religious contributors to these debates have returned in two distinct venues to continue the religion and science debate begun in the 1960s.

This chapter will focus upon the USA because the involvement of religion in bioethical debates is so much more extensive than in Europe. The general reason for this difference is probably the massive difference in religiosity of the citizens. For example, while 46 per cent of Americans report weekly religious service attendance, less than 20 per cent of British, Dutch, Belgians and (West) Germans attend at this rate, and less than 10 per cent of French and Scandinavians.[3] Furthermore, while there are religiously oriented social movement organizations in Europe surrounding embryonic life and end of life issues, such as the Society for the Protection of Unborn Children in the UK, their influence seems far less than that of analogous groups in America. Finally, while religious elites do have an influence on elite debates in some European countries by serving in institutions such as government commissions, there are almost no academic studies of their influence on these debates for me to summarize.[4] This contrasts with an extensive literature on the more religious American situation. So, while I focus on the USA, I will bring in European comparisons when appropriate.

I will also refer to elites and ordinary citizens. Elites are people who have the resources to influence the views of others. The primary resource in this case is the ability to publish one's views. Elites would include professors, bioethicists, newspaper editors, authors, clergy and others. Ordinary citizens are those who lack these resources.

When scholars use the term bioethics they are referring to (at least) three separate elite debates: foundational bioethics, clinical bioethics and public bioethics. Foundational bioethical debate concerns how the ethics of particular issues – such as organ transplants – are related to broader ethical systems, democratic practices and so forth. An example is the debate about whether professional bioethicists should be utilitarians or deontologists. I will not be describing this type of bioethics in this chapter (although this chapter itself could be considered a contribution to foundational bioethics). Clinical bioethics concern ethical decisions in medical or research settings, such as whether a mechanical ventilator should be turned off in a particular situation. I will also not discuss this further. In contrast, most of the interaction between religion and science is in public bioethics, the focus of this chapter, which I define as societal elites debating what society should do about a particular issue (such as organ transplantation).[5] For example, should the British government allow scientists to create hybrid animal–human embryos? I will also discuss the efforts of ordinary religious citizens to influence policies regarding scientific developments independent of the elite public bioethical debate.

EMERGENCE OF PUBLIC BIOETHICAL DEBATE

The technological possibilities that beckoned in the 1960s alarmed many practising scientists, and resulted in these elites having a debate about what should be done with the new technological possibilities. This created the first public bioethical debate as I have defined it above, which most prominently took place at a number of conferences in the USA and the UK, with occasional participation from western Europeans.

Consider a conference in the early 1960s in London which brought together many leading scientists of the day such as Sir Julian Huxley, Hermann Muller, Joshua Lederberg and J. B. S. Haldane to discuss the genetic modification of humans, population control, the elimination of disease and mind control. The conference proceedings, published under the apt title *Man and his Future*, noted in the preface that 'the world was unprepared socially, politically and ethically for the advent of nuclear power. Now, biological research is in a ferment, creating and promising methods of interference with "natural processes" which could destroy or could transform nearly every aspect of human life which we value. Urgently it is necessary for men and women ... to consider the present and imminent possibilities.'[6]

Before the ordinary citizens considered the possibilities, as the scientists in this era ostensibly desired, theologians did. This was primarily because issues such as the meaning of life and death touched on deeper issues that theologians had considered to be their area of exclusive expertise, and the scientists were perceived to be encroaching upon this area. Indeed, many of the elite scientists in these debates thought that science should produce a sense of meaning and source of ethics for society, given that Darwin had utterly discredited religion, in their view.[7] For example, one analyst concludes that C. H. Waddington and Peter Medawar, along with other biologists, implied that 'the "direction" of evolution, both biological and cultural, is the "scientific" foundation upon which to reestablish our system of ethics and to rest "our most cherished hopes"'.[8]

Similarly, scientist Jacob Bronowski would pronounce at the London conference in 1962: 'I am, therefore, not in the least ashamed to be told by somebody else that my values, because they are grounded in my science, are relative, and his are given by God. My values, in my opinion, come from as objective and definitive a source as any god, namely the nature of the human being ... That makes my values richer, I think; and it makes them no less objective, no less real, than any values that can be read in the Testaments.'[9] In case the challenge was not clear, the first pull-quote on the back cover of *Man and his Future* was from Francis Crick, co-discoverer of the structure of DNA, who wrote 'I think that in time the facts of science are going to make us become less Christian. There is eventually bound to be a conflict of values.'

This was prescient, in that a conflict of values would soon emerge as theologians challenged the scientists' encroachment into what they perceived to be their jurisdiction. For instance, Methodist theologian and Princeton University religion professor Paul Ramsey stated that he was opposed to the surrogate theology of the scientists. At a 1965 conference, he said that the scientists have

> a distinctive attitude toward the world, 'a program for utterly
> transforming it,' an 'unshakable,' nay even a 'fanatical,'
> confidence in a 'worldview,' a 'faith' no less than a 'program'
> for the reconstruction of mankind. These expressions rather
> exactly describe a religious cult, if there ever was one – a cult
> of men-gods, however otherwise humble. These are not the
> findings, or the projections, of an exact science as such, but a
> religious view of where and how ultimate human significance
> is to be found.[10]

Theologians became increasingly involved in these elite debates. This is illustrated by a conference held in Houston, Texas, in reaction to the first heart transplant in 1967, where four of the six speakers were theologians or identifiably religious. Moreover, many in these early years provided an explicitly theological alternative to the ethical views of the scientists. German theologian Helmut Thielicke's argument about who should receive a transplant concluded that evaluating patients by their social utility was wrong because 'the basis of human dignity is seen to reside not in any immanent quality of man whatsoever, but in the fact that God created him. Man is the apple of God's eye. He is "dear" because he has been bought with a price: Christ died for him.'[11]

THE MARGINALIZATION OF THEOLOGY
IN PUBLIC BIOETHICS

Scientists began these debates, and theologians followed them in, challenged by the threat to their traditional jurisdiction of determining the ethics of these big questions. Shortly after the theologians' entry came philosophers, lawyers, social scientists and others, resulting in a fairly interdisciplinary discussion. Scholars all agreed that the religious presence would quickly fade. Typical is M. Therese Lysaught, who speaks of the 'standard narrative of the genesis of bioethics' in these terms: 'its earliest origins lay among theologians, but substantive theological discourse was quickly replaced by the more advanced discourse of philosophy'.[12]

The primary scholarly debate is whether these religiously-identified elites ever spoke theologically at all, or whether they simply were theologians making secular philosophical arguments.[13] I have argued elsewhere that a short-lived era did exist when theologians did use explicitly religious arguments in these debates, although it was so short that some analysts have not noticed it, but that this quickly turned to an era when theologians made secular arguments.[14] Regardless, it is important to note that these secular contributions from the religiously-identified were not the same as those of the non-religious participants, who were typically philosophers and scientists.[15] The religiously-identified made secular translations of theological ideas, and therefore the debates were different when the theologians participated.[16]

Theologians were also more likely to make secular yet thick arguments. Others, especially those in the emerging profession of bioethics that used analytic philosophical reasoning, made thin arguments. For our purposes, a thick argument is about which ends or goals we should uphold as a society. A thick argument asks: should we try to perfect the human species, or should we try to maximize human health? A thin argument starts with assumed, undebatable ends, and argues about the most efficacious means to achieve those ends. A thin argument asks: given the unquestioned goal of promoting health and relieving suffering, is human genetic engineering an efficacious way to proceed? These distinctions are important for understanding why even the theologians who either changed to (or always used) secular yet thick arguments disappeared from the field, resulting in the decline of religious involvement in the elite public bioethical debate.[17]

What happened is that the theologians and their allies were essentially victims of their own success. They had started a movement that questioned the ends scientists were pursuing with their technologies, and the public began to pay attention. In fact, the public was paying so much attention that these issues soon caught the eye of elected officials, who began to suggest various legislative remedies to force scientists and physicians to adhere to the basic ethical insights that were being generated by theologians and others.

It was not the ethical debates about new developments in bioscience described above that made some sort of collective oversight of scientists inevitable, but the long-running issue of unethical experimentation on human beings.[18] In 1972 it was revealed that the US Public Health Service had been conducting a forty-year-long experiment in which the syphilis of a group of about six hundred poor and uneducated black men in Tuskegee, Alabama was left untreated. When combined with other revelations that physicians in hospitals had been experimenting on regular patients without their knowledge, Congress felt compelled to create the National Commission for the Protection of Human Subjects of Biomedical and Behavioral Research, which first met in 1974.

One of the mandated tasks of the commission was to 'conduct a comprehensive investigation and study to identify the basic ethical principles which should underlie the conduct of biomedical and behavioral research involving human subjects' and 'develop guidelines which should be followed in such research to assure that it is conducted in accord with such principles'.[19] The commission reduced the debate about principles to three that were 'among those generally accepted in our cultural tradition': autonomy, beneficence and justice. These ends would be applied to ethical decisions made by the members of Institutional Review Boards throughout the country who, by accepting government money, were implicitly making decisions for the government.

I consider these articulated principles to be like ends or goals for society. They are a statement about what is of value, and research must be consistent with or maximize these values (depending on one's perspective). While principles have different meanings in philosophical and bioethical theory, in practical use by ordinary bioethics professionals they take on a simplified meaning,[20] becoming a list of societal goals that should be satisfied through medical research. By my terminology above, the National Commission engaged in a thick debate when it decided that these three should be the universal values, goals or ends of Western civilization. By setting these ends as unquestionable (and part of public law), it created a subsequent thin debate about whether various scientific technologies would maximize these ends.

In and of itself, this setting of universal ends with which human research must be consistent was not threatening to the theologians. Their own method had evolved to this point: one could search the Protestant and Catholic traditions and determine that human experimentation should be consistent with these ends. While each tradition could have come up with more than three ends, this was not a path that was inherently destructive to the theologians.

The problem for theology came from a different angle. At the same time as the commission was trying to create its principles, ends or goals for the government to use for human experimentation, the commission's consultant for this project – philosopher Tom L. Beauchamp – was co-authoring a textbook with theologian James Childress which would also use a principle-based approach to ethical problems that could be applied to public policy.[21] First published in 1979, the *Principles of Biomedical Ethics*, now in its sixth edition,[22] is by far the most influential textbook (and ethical system) in bioethics.[23] This principle-based approach came to be called the Georgetown model after the university where the authors were based while writing the book, and also because the ethicists at that university made great efforts to further the spread of the approach. The principles in the textbook were the same as those of the National Commission, except that they split beneficence into beneficence and non-maleficence, with their new list being: autonomy, beneficence, non-maleficence and justice.

Principlism assumes that the principles are drawn from the common morality. This aspiration for a universal ethics was not only central to the philosophical tradition that Beauchamp was embedded in, but an aspiration among the most liberal of theologians in this era, some of whom were involved in creating this non-religious ethical system. Creating a secular and universalistic ethical system fit not only with the Catholic natural law theory, and the death of God theology of some liberal Protestants at the time, but also with the Quakerism of co-author James Childress.[24]

The religious identity of the theologians involved with inventing and promoting principlism became more difficult to see as they were more likely to become simply bioethicists. The threat to the remaining theologians in public bioethics came from another universal claim in principlism that harkens more from its philosophical rather than theological origins. It was argued not only that the principles were universally held by all the citizens of the USA, and were the ends to pursue for human experimentation, but that they were the ends for all issues in science and medicine, including the issues discussed in the first paragraph of this chapter. The form of argument preferred by theologians had been to examine each technology in its particularity, and discuss how it was or was not consistent with the myriad ends found in their traditions. They were interested in the technologies and the ends as a package, not only in the technologies themselves. Once means and ends are split by not allowing debate about the ends because they have been set, debate becomes thin because the only remaining question is whether the technology maximizes these predetermined ends. If we cannot debate ends, what use are the theologians? It turns out there would be no use for them, which was the beginning of the end of their influence. How had this ethical system become dominant so as to marginalize the theologians?

With principlism enshrined into public law for human experimentation, and the embodiment of the form of argumentation available in a popular textbook, the form of argumentation began to spread rapidly. According to observers of the profession, this one book has more than anything else 'shaped the teaching and practice of biomedical ethics in this country. . . . [becoming] a standard text in courses and a virtual bible to some practitioners'. The ethical framework provided by the book 'shapes much of the discussion and debate about particular bioethical issues and policy, whether in the academy, the literature, the public forum or the clinic'.[25] The institutionalization of this form of argumentation for human experimentation and increasingly for other problems was so strong that one set of critics would go so far as to begin their essay with the mocking claim that 'throughout the land, arising from the throngs of converts to bioethics awareness, there can be heard a mantra ". . . beneficence . . . autonomy . . . justice . . ."'.[26] Fox and Swazey claim that the approach in the book 'has been so widely disseminated across national boundaries that it has become a kind of bioethical lingua franca'.[27]

Key to the institutionalization of principlism is that the government had become the ultimate consumer of ethical arguments about science. Reflecting on the birth of the bioethics profession, Warren Reich states that 'there was a political urgency to many of the biomedical issues' at the time. 'The media craved the biomedical controversies and federal and state policy makers wanted answers.'[28] The medical research components of the government had already made principlism the central ethical system, enshrining it as ethics in every medical school and research university in the USA. Less immediately applied parts of the government research apparatus also preferred thin forms of ethical argument like principlism. In this the American and European cases diverge.

In historian Ted Porter's rendering, in other countries government officials are 'trusted to exercise judgment wisely and fairly. In the United
States, they are expected to follow rules.'[29] This is because, put simply,
it is part of US political culture not to trust authority, especially government authority, and particularly the authority of bureaucrats. The
thin ethics are therefore perfect for government agencies, because government bureaucrats are not using their judgement to determine what
the ends or principles should be, but are rather engaged in rule-like
following of the common morality, the ends or goals that thin bioethics
theories claimed that all reasonable persons already held. Principlism
was the perfect bioethical morality for government action in America,
and it excluded those like the theologians who wanted to debate ends
(principles) and means (technologies) as a piece.

In Europe, the pressure for a calculable ethical system was not
nearly as strong, and the elite debate could remain more 'thick'. In contrast to the USA, 'in some societies the right of government officials
to make decisions is taken for granted. People may disagree about the
substance of the decision but they do not question the authority behind
it.'[30] Another study finds that, compared with the distrust of experts in
the USA, the 'more insulated regulatory processes of both Britain and
Germany historically depended on greater trust in expertise'. In the UK,
objective knowledge is pursued 'through consultation among persons
whose capacity to discern the truth is regarded as privileged'.[31]

Therefore, compared with the USA, unelected government officials
and members of government agencies in Europe are more likely to be
able to have a thick debate and debate the goals or ends of society with
discussions of scientific technology. Consider, for example, the UK's
Human Fertilization and Embryology Authority which, among other
tasks, determines which genetic diseases are serious enough to warrant
genetic intervention. This sort of setting of societal values or purposes
about what a serious disease is by an unelected government body would
be unlikely to happen in the USA, where 'policies would be set by those
bureaucrats in Washington' is considered to be a convincing argument
against universal health care. However, while theologians who are more
likely to want a thick debate would in principle be more welcome in
Europe, their particular expertise has less credibility than in the USA,
probably because of the lesser degree of religiosity, and therefore their
participation in this elite bioethical debate remains more limited than
in the USA. To sum up, in the USA, the rise of government consump-
tion of bioethical arguments provided an exceptionally good environment for the growth of this thin form of argumentation used by the

profession of bioethics, and the marginalization of those who wanted a thick debate, like the theologians.

THE SHIFT TO PUBLIC INFLUENCE

Even the religious participants in elite debates who were willing to translate their explicitly theological concerns into a thick secular language were subtly excluded because they were not willing to speak the thin language now required to be a legitimate participant in these debates. However, this was not the end of religious involvement in bioethical debates. Public bioethics is focused on influencing government policy through elite channels – serving on government commissions, forming public opinion through media appearances, and advising scientific societies and the medical/scientific industry. But ordinary religious citizens could still have influence through their roles as citizens, using social movements and political activism. This is what occurred in at least the USA and the UK.

The early public bioethical debate had largely remained on the elite level, never working its way down to the attention of ordinary citizens. For example, while theologians had been discussing human genetic engineering for decades, a recent study shows that most ordinary religious citizens remain unaware of this technology.[32] However, on other issues, ordinary religious conservatives began to take notice. By the year 2000 Dolly the sheep had been born, and embryo research was more and more desired by scientists as it increasingly seemed that embryonic stem cells might have therapeutic use. On issues concerning embryos, the primarily religiously based anti-abortion movements in the USA and the UK were attempting to mobilize ordinary citizens to oppose technological developments that harmed embryos such as embryonic stem cell research, reproductive and therapeutic cloning, pre-implantation genetic diagnosis and the creation of hybrid embryos.

As an example of an end-run around traditional elite bioethical debate, consider how public influence was exercised on end of life issues. Instead of creating academic articles about the right to life of people in vegetative states and presenting these to academic conferences, or trying to get religious conservatives on government commissions, the religious conservatives instead generated grassroots pressure on elected officials who could, because they are elected, use thick arguments. For example, in 2005 the US Congress intervened in the case of a comatose woman in Florida named Terri Schiavo, ultimately passing laws to stop her ex-husband from removing her feeding tube. Similarly, as of the end of the George W. Bush presidency in 2009, the US government did not pay for embryonic stem cell research except in extremely limited situations because of political pressure from these social movements in Congress and the executive branch. Both of these actions argued for an end that was not part of the dominant principlist theory (for example, protecting certain forms of human life) in the context of biomedical technologies. The bioethics agenda of religious conservatives is being achieved, not through academic and public deliberation of public bioethics, but through ordinary political power.

My conclusion about public pressure by religious conservatives on these beginning and end of life issues in the USA and Europe is that in both religious conservatives are able to slow down the development of technologies they do not like, but that the US religious conservatives are much more successful than their counterparts in Europe. In general, Europe is much more permissive with these technologies than is the USA, with the exception of Germany and a few other countries.

RELIGION RE-EMERGES INTO PUBLIC BIOETHICS

In the USA, this social movement activity of religious conservatives has in turn resulted in religious voices being forced upon the mainstream public bioethical debate from which they had previously been excluded. For example, the US bioethics commission of the Clinton presidency (1993–2001) held a series of hearings about cloning in 1997, which included testimony from representatives of religious traditions. The publicly stated reasons for including these voices were essentially that the public was very concerned about cloning, and the public is religious, so these voices must be included.[33] Interviews of staff members of the commissions reveal that an additional reason why elite religious voices were brought back to the table after years of exile was 'the concern that some Congressional staff members expressed over the fact that there were no "religious people"... on the Commission'.[34] I think it is safe to say that the congressional representatives who pressured the commission to include religious voices were being influenced by the religious right, as there would be no other constituency that would have wanted religious voices to be involved with the cloning debate.

Even more striking evidence of how social movements have forced, to some degree, a return of religion to elite debates is the national bioethics commission of President George W. Bush (2001–9). When it came to appointing his commission, it is clear that the president was pay-ing attention to the needs of his base of political support among con-servative evangelicals and Catholics, and he appointed a commission that was much more amenable not only to the conclusions of religious conservatives about embryos, but also to the use of religious language than recent public bioethical debate had been. The gulf between the earlier government commissions is clear when we realize that the Bush commission was fairly evenly split on the morality of embryo research, but not one member of the commission of the preceding Democratic Clinton administration was opposed to research that resulted in the destruction of embryos.[35] While accepting explicitly theological dis-course in its hearings, the writings of the Bush commission are secular, but secular in the thick sense I described earlier.[36] Thus, the Bush com-mission was open to secular translation of theological concerns.

In the early years of public bioethics, the debate was generally thick, and then it became thin. But the thick and thin participants were, for a time, in the same debate. Upon close examination, the contemporary political pressure from ordinary citizens has actually not resulted in a reintegration of religious voices into public bioethical debate, but has rather created parallel thick and thin public bioethical debates, with religious voices shunted into the thick debate.

The result is that we now have a culture war in public bioethical debate. Arthur Caplan describes the culture war as concerning 'what role ideology and religion ought to play in determining the policies and practices of biomedicine'. 'On one side is an alliance of neoconserva-tive and religiously oriented bioethicists' who 'speak in terms that are religious or quasi-religious.' 'On the other side stand a loose amalgam of left-liberal bioethicists tenuously allied with a far smaller number of more libertarian bioethicists' who 'speak primarily in secular terms drawn more from philosophy or the law. Explicitly religious arguments get them nervous.'[37] In my terminology, the first side is thick, and the second is thin.

The thin debate of the left-liberal bioethicists is, I would argue, dedicated to enforcing the ethical system that meets the approval of scientists. Of course, the self-image of the bioethics profession is that it is an opposition movement to the power of scientists and physicians, and it did truly force its ethical system on scientists and physicians in the 1960s and 1970s.[38] But I concur with historian Charles Rosenberg that 'as a condition of its acceptance, bioethics has taken up residence in the belly of the medical whale; although thinking of itself as still autonomous, the bioethical enterprise has developed a complex and symbiotic relationship with this host organism. Bioethics is no longer (if it ever was) a free-floating, oppositional, and socially critical reform movement.'[39]

Uncharacteristically for a social scientist, and for the sake of brevity, for evidence in support of this claim I will rely upon a thought-experiment. If the ethical system used in the thin public bioethical debate was truly oppositional to the ethics endorsed by scientists, scientists would have already tried to destroy bioethics. With many prominent bioethics centres embedded in medical schools, dependent upon their legitimacy and largess, it seems unlikely that if public bioethics and medical science were really combatants, one combatant would allow the other to live in its house. Indications of what would happen if mainstream bioethics were to become critical of the mainstream scientific agenda can be found in the scientific and bioethics establishment's extremely negative reaction to Bush's President's Commission on Bioethics, which has brought into question some activities that mainstream science would like to conduct.

I must emphasize that the ethical system endorsed by scientists and bioethicists is important, and it does deter scientists from acts that are probably nearly universally considered to be wrong. Whereas we can imagine some scientists wanting to conduct surreptitious medical research on poor people (if only because they have done it before in the infamous Tuskegee experiments), the dominant ethics in the mainstream bioethical debate would definitely stop this occurring (autonomy). Similarly, nobody is going to be allowed to clone a person until it can be reasonably shown to be safe (non-maleficence). These are the ethics that scientists have agreed to, at the original prodding of bioethicists, and bioethicists are an effective enforcer of these professional ethics.

The thick debate, as Caplan describes it above, is more likely to question the entire purpose of the scientific enterprise. The bioethics commission of the George W. Bush administration was keen to ask such questions as: what is the purpose of science? Or, to take a typical question in contemporary theological bioethics: should we value the health of rich people over the health of poor people?[40] These are debates that scientists do not want to have. They have the ends they have agreed to – primarily autonomy, beneficence and non-maleficence. They do not want to have a debate about whether these are or are not the appropriate goals for their actions. Therefore, when theologians and other participants in the thick debate try to make these thicker arguments, the mainstream bioethicists ignore them.

Religious influence on bioethical debate now exists on two tracks. On one, citizens mobilized by social movements try to influence their elected officials to pass policies forwarding their ethical views of issues having to do with the body, such as reproduction and end of life issues. On the other, an elite, thick, public bioethics that includes religious voices tries to influence policy through persuading elected officials and educating the public.

IMPLICATIONS

This account of the relationship between science and religion provides us with some broader lessons. In general, discussions of bioethics – that realm where the morality of scientific issues is discussed – tend towards idealism. On the one hand, this makes great sense because by and large the field is normative – the point is to come up with the best or most persuasive moral position on, for example, embryonic stem cell research. Participants in these debates whose moral positions win out tend to conclude, quite naturally, that their position won because they made the best argument, which means that it was the most logical or made the most sense. A standard narrative in bioethics is that bioethicists and philosophers displaced theologians because their arguments were better.[41]

The sociology of knowledge rejects the view that the quality of argumentation is determinative. In one strand of this tradition, the intellectual position that tends to displace the others is the one that garners enough resources to be spread the most widely. While this is a longstanding tradition, it has been supported by the cognitive psychology of recent decades which has shown that ordinary citizens can hold at the same time a number of beliefs that an expert would consider to be contradictory,[42] so the logic of the elites is not something that will make a position win out among the public.

A simple motto for the sociology of knowledge would be that he who controls the printing press gets to write the history. In bioethics, thick arguments originally lost out not because they were worse, but because they were not useful to the people who were providing the resources. If the audience for bioethical arguments – those who indirectly pay for them – is the public, then thick arguments would be the best. If the audience is the bureaucratic state, then thin arguments would be the best. Since it is analytic philosophy and bioethics that makes thin arguments, the rise of these professions in these debates is not because their arguments are better than those from theology, but because their arguments fit the interests of the primary (indirect) resource provider, the bureaucratic state. If we are to focus on ideas in future analyses of ethical conflict between religion and science, we should not presume that one set of ideas will make more sense to people than another.

Similarly, the focus upon the quality of the ideas in religion and science can also lead to a Whiggish history, where science inevitably triumphs over religion because of its superior abilities to explain nature and so forth. At least in sociology there has long been the assumption that science and religion are in epistemological conflict, and that secularization will continue as science grows in its explanatory power and citizens cannot handle the logical contradiction between believing in religion and believing in science. The most recent sociological studies of religion and science have avoided this assumption, and have tended to take a sociology of knowledge perspective, asking how the resources were garnered to persuade the public at a particular time that religion was true and at another that science was true.[43]

A second broader lesson from this chapter is that there are multiple ways that science can impact the morality of a society. It is common to think that scientific discoveries challenge existing morality. For example, discoveries in neurology make us ask whether human moral agency actually exists; evolutionary psychology attempts to show that behaviour is not necessarily guided by what would normally be called morals, but by our genes, determined millions of years ago in the age of evolutionary adaptation; and the discovery of nuclear weapons requires the development of game theoretical ethical systems. More prosaically, the standard narrative in bioethics is that scientific discoveries raise moral issues that society must develop ethical systems to address.[44] A classic example is the development of artificial respirators, which ultimately led to a debate about whether a person was dead or not. This chapter shows that science contributes to the creation and growing influence of a thin ethics for society not due to the content of any of its discoveries, but because of its interests in not having the public able to debate the purposes of science. At least in this instance it is the institutional interests of science that challenge the morals of society, not its discoveries.

A final contribution is that while historians have long critiqued the idea that religion and science are inevitably in conflict,[45] and epistemological conflict is on the decline,[46] this chapter has focused on a conflict between religion and science that is not about epistemology but rather about values. In the social scientific study of science, the dominant strand has been the sociology of scientific knowledge, and the values of science went out of consideration with the eclipsing of the perspective of Robert Merton in the 1970s. While many scholars have discussed value conflict – for example, it is often mentioned that William Jennings Bryan of Scopes monkey trial fame was primarily concerned about values not epistemology[47] – the focus has remained on scientific knowledge. At least in the contemporary world, science should be viewed not only as a knowledge producer, but as an institution with values, interests and resources that competes with many others, including religion.

Notes

1   Albert R. Jonsen, *The Birth of Bioethics* (New York: Oxford University Press, 1998), chapter 8.
2   Brock Chisholm, 'Future of the Mind', in Gordon Wolstenholme (ed.), *Man and his Future* (Boston: Little, Brown, 1963), p. 315.
3   Pippa Norris and Ronald Inglehart, *Sacred and Secular: Religion and Politics Worldwide* (New York: Cambridge University Press, 2004), p. 74.
4   For limited exceptions, see Michael Mulkay, *The Embryo Research Debate* (Cambridge University Press, 1997), ch. 7; Melanie Latham, *Regulating Reproduction: a Century of Conflict in Britain and France* (Manchester University Press, 2002).
5   John H. Evans, *Playing God? Human Genetic Engineering and the Rationalization of Public Bioethical Debate* (Chicago, IL: University of Chicago Press, 2002), p. 34.
6   Wolstenholme (ed.), *Man and his Future*, p. v.
7   The next three paragraphs summarize the argument in John H. Evans, 'After the Fall: Attempts to Establish an Explicitly Theological Voice in Debates over Science and Medicine after 1960', in Christian Smith (ed.), *The Secular Revolution* (Berkeley, CA: University of California Press, 2003), pp. 436–41.
8   Howard L. Kaye, *The Social Meaning of Modern Biology: From Social Darwinism to Sociobiology* (New Brunswick, NJ: Transaction, 1997), p. 42.
9   Wolstenholme (ed.), *Man and his Future*, p. 372.
10   Paul Ramsey, *Fabricated Man: the Ethics of Genetic Control* (New Haven, CT: Yale University Press, 1970), p. 144.
11   Helmut Thielicke, 'The Doctor as Judge of Who Shall Live and Who Shall Die', in Kenneth Vaux (ed.), *Who Shall Live? Medicine, Technology, Ethics* (Philadelphia, PA: Fortress Press, 1970), p. 172.
12   M. Therese Lysaught, 'And Power Corrupts...: Religion and the Disciplinary Matrix of Bioethics', in David E. Guinn (ed.), *Handbook of Bioethics and Religion* (New York: Oxford University Press, 2006), p. 101.

13 Albert R. Jonsen, 'A History of Religion and Bioethics', in Guinn (ed.), *Handbook of Bioethics*, p. 33; Carla M. Messikomer, Renee C. Rox and Judith P. Swazey, 'The Presence and Influence of Religion in American Bioethics', *Perspectives in Biology and Medicine* 44, no. 4 (2001), 485–508; James F. Childress, 'Religion, Theology and Bioethics', in Franklin G. Miller, John C. Fletcher and James M. Humber (eds.), *The Nature and Prospect of Bioethics* (Totowa, NJ: Humana Press, 2003), pp. 43–68.

14 Evans, 'After the Fall', p. 437.

15 Evans, *Playing God?*

16 Evans, 'After the Fall', p. 441; John H. Evans, 'Public Vocabularies of Religious Belief: Explicit and Implicit Religious Discourse in the American Public Sphere', in Mark Jacobs and Nancy Weiss Hanrahan (eds.), *Blackwell Companion to the Sociology of Culture* (Malden, MA: Blackwell, 2005), pp. 398–411.

17 The thick and thin distinction is partly inspired by Habermas' modification of Weber's categories of substantive and formal rationality, respectively, which are themselves the institutionalized version of his more famous distinction between value and instrumental rationality. In value rationality, ends and means are considered together, towards what Weber interpreter Talcott Parsons called ultimate meaning. In instrumental rationality, the question is whether the means maximize the ends in question. To make rough philosophical analogues, value rationality is similar to deontological reasoning, and instrumental rationality is similar to consequentialism or its special case, utilitarianism.

18 This and the next eight paragraphs in this section are taken directly or modified from Evans, 'After the Fall', pp. 451–3.

19 Cited in Albert R. Jonsen, 'Foreword', in Edwin R. DuBose, Ronald P. Hamel and Laurence J. O'Connell (eds.), *A Matter of Principles? Ferment in US Bioethics* (Valley Forge, PA: Trinity Press International, 1994), p. xiv.

20 Renee C. Fox and Judith P. Swazey, *Observing Bioethics* (New York: Oxford University Press, 2008), pp. 169–70; Raymond Devettere, 'The Principled Approach: Principles, Rules and Actions', in Michael A. Grodin (ed.), *Meta Medical Ethics: the Philosophical Foundations of Bioethics* (Dordrecht: Kluwer, 1995).

21 Tom L. Beauchamp, 'The Origins and Evolution of the Belmont Report', in James F. Childress, Eric M. Meslin and Harold T. Shapiro (eds.), *Belmont Revisited: Ethical Principles for Research with Human Subjects* (Washington, DC: Georgetown University Press, 2005).

22 Tom L. Beauchamp and James F. Childress, *Principles of Biomedical Ethics*, 6th edn (New York: Oxford University Press, 2009).

23 Fox and Swazey, *Observing Bioethics*, p. 168.

24 Evans, *Playing God?*, pp. 85–9; Courtney S. Campbell, 'On James F. Childress: Answering that God in Every Person', in Allen Verhey and Stephen E. Lammers (eds.), *Theological Voices in Medical Ethics* (Grand Rapids, MI: Eerdmans, 1993).

25 Edwin R. DuBose, Ronald P. Hamel and Laurence J. O'Connell, 'Introduction', in DuBose et al. (eds.), *A Matter of Principles?*, p. 1.

26   K. Danner Clouser and Bernard Gert, 'A Critique of Principlism', *Journal of Medicine and Philosophy* 15 (1990), 219–36.

27   Fox and Swazey, *Observing Bioethics*, p. 216.

28   Warren Thomas Reich, 'The Word "Bioethics": the Struggle over its Earliest Meanings', *Kennedy Institute of Ethics Journal* 5, no. 1 (1995), 19–34, p. 22.

29   Theodore M. Porter, *Trust in Numbers: the Pursuit of Objectivity in Science and Public Life* (Princeton University Press, 1995), p. 195.

30   James Q. Wilson, *Bureaucracy: What Government Agencies Do and Why They Do It* (New York: Basic Books, 1989), p. 303.

31   Sheila Jasanoff, *Designs on Nature: Science and Democracy in Europe and the United States* (Princeton University Press, 2005), pp. 262, 266.

32   John H. Evans, *Contested Reproduction: Genetic Technologies, Religon and Public Debate* (University of Chicago Press, 2010).

33   James F. Childress, 'The Challenges of Public Ethics: Reflections on NBAC's Report', *Hastings Center Report* 27, no. 5 (1997), 9–11; Evans, *Playing God?*, p. 190.

34   Messikomer *et al.*, 'The Presence and Influence', p. 502.

35   Leon R. Kass, 'Reflections on Public Bioethics: a View from the Trenches', *Kennedy Institute of Ethics Journal* 15, no. 3 (2005), 221–50, p. 227.

36   Kass, 'Reflections on Public Bioethics'.

37   Arthur Caplan, '"Who Lost China?" A Foreshadowing of Today's Ideological Disputes in Bioethics', *Hastings Center Report* 35, no. 3 (2005), 12–13.

38   David J. Rothman, *Strangers by the Bedside: a History of How Law and Bioethics Transformed Medical Decision Making* (New York: Basic Books, 1991).

39   Charles E. Rosenberg, 'Meanings, Policies, and Medicine: On the Bioethical Enterprise and History', *Daedalus* 128, no. 4 (1999), 27–46, p. 38.

40   Lisa Sowle Cahill, *Theological Bioethics: Participation, Justice, Change* (Washington, DC: Georgetown University Press, 2005).

41   'There is a sense in which the most esteemed religiously trained and oriented figures in the early history of bioethics were regarded more as sages than as clear and clarifying thinkers. To the extent that they are remembered today, it is as much for their moral stature as for their intellectual contributions.' Fox and Swazey, *Observing Bioethics*, p. 38.

42   Paul DiMaggio, 'Culture and Cognition', *Annual Review of Sociology* 23 (1997), 263–87.

43   John H. Evans and Michael S. Evans, 'Religion and Science: Beyond the Epistemological Conflict Narrative', *Annual Review of Sociology* (2008), 87–105.

44   Fox and Swazey, *Observing Bioethics*, pp. 23–5.

45 Colin A. Russell, 'The Conflict of Science and Religion', in Gary B. Ferngren (ed.), *Science and Religion: a Historical Introduction* (Baltimore, MD: Johns Hopkins University Press, 2002), pp. 3–12.

46 Evans and Evans, 'Religion and Science'.

47 Mark A. Noll, 'Evangelicalism and Fundamentalism', in Ferngren (ed.), *Science and Religion*, pp. 274–5.

Part III

Philosophical perspectives

11 Atheism, naturalism and science: three in one?

MICHAEL RUSE

> The more the universe seems comprehensible, the more it also seems pointless.
>
> (Steven Weinberg, Nobel laureate in physics)[1]

The past few years have seen a spate of books arguing that God does not exist and that religion is one of the most pernicious and dangerous aspects of modern culture.[2] As it happens, the arguments of the new atheists are all over the place, ranging from criticisms of the traditional proofs of the existence of God to moral exhortations not to follow the prescriptions of the religious. However, the authors all presume to write in the name of science and certainly it is in that sense that most readers, receptive and antagonistic, have taken them. This chapter is offered as a reflection of the interest that these writers have obviously sparked. In the light of today's science, what can be said about the intellectual status of religion and the central claims that are made in its name?

Defining and constraining the discussion, I shall focus on Western religion and of that primarily on Christianity. This is not unfair or mere chauvinism. Modern science emerged in a Christian context and much of the discussion today is framed explicitly in terms of Christianity.[3] Where appropriate, the discussion can easily be extended. I shall consider science to range from the physical sciences through the biological sciences and on to the social sciences, and I shall understand it as an attempt to understand the world of experience in terms of causes, things which presuppose the universal rule of natural law. I take it therefore that modern science is rooted in naturalism. This last term can mean a number of things. I distinguish methodological naturalism, meaning that in doing science one assumes that there are no God-directed supernatural causes like miracles, and metaphysical naturalism which is equivalent to atheism, meaning that there are no supernatural factors or entities, full stop. It is therefore methodological naturalism that I link to science. I recognize that in the past this was not necessarily the case but since the early nineteenth century at the latest this has been so. My link therefore is lexical and not stipulative. I distinguish naturalism from scientism, meaning by the latter the belief that science can solve all problems. This is a very dubious claim.

WARFARE

The physicist-theologian Ian Barbour distinguishes four possible science–religion relationships:[4] warfare, independence, dialogue and integration. Not everyone is completely happy with this typology,[5] but, for our purposes here, it can serve as a framework for thinking about positions that have been taken on the boundaries and interactions between science and religion. The late nineteenth-century critics of religion such as Thomas Henry Huxley were great supporters of the warfare model and this sentiment is shared by the new atheists.[6] Supposedly, science and religion compete for the same territory and although battles as such do not determine the winner, in this case science wins. There is obviously much truth in this claim. If you are a young-earth creationist, thinking that Genesis is literally true and that everything was created about six thousand years ago and shortly thereafter there was a worldwide flood, then you are in direct conflict with modern physics, modern biology, modern geology, modern anthropology, and probably modern everything else in science if you think hard about matters. And you are wrong. In a million years, you cannot reconcile the true theory of plate tectonics with the Noachian Deluge and in ten million years you cannot reconcile the true claims of modern palaeoanthropology with the story of Adam and Eve. The same is true of specific claims by specific religions. Allowing for the sake of argument that the Mormons are a variety of Christianity, there is no way to reconcile their claim that the native peoples of America are the lost tribes of Israel with the true findings of genetics about the origins of the native people from folk who crossed the Bering Strait about twelve thousand years ago.

However, before the discussion is ended right here, it must be pointed out that young-earth creationism is far from traditional Christianity, Protestant or Catholic, and the same is even more true of the Church of the Latter Day Saints of Jesus Christ. Traditional Christianity, going back at least to St Augustine around 400 CE, has always had clauses about the way in which the Bible was written in language that common people, nomadic people like the ancient Jews, could understand.[7] In the words of that canny lawyer John Calvin, God accommodates his speaking to the uneducated and ill-informed.[8] The Christian position has always been that truth cannot be opposed to truth; that our understanding of the natural world comes through our senses and our reason, the very things that make us in the image of God; and that hence if Scripture and science clash it can only be apparent and must be resolved, quite possibly by reading the Bible in a metaphorical way.

This does not mean that people like Augustine subscribed to modern evolutionary theory or anything like that – although given that Augustine (believing that God lies outside time) thought that God created organisms potentially and that they then developed in time, there are those who claim Augustine as the theologian for evolutionists. What accommodation does mean is that the warfare thesis is true only up to a point. It is the case that much claimed in the name of religion does clash with modern science. It is not the case that this spells the end of traditional religion, specifically traditional Christianity.

INDEPENDENCE

The argument that science and religion cannot really clash because they speak of different things is a very popular position. Known in theological circles as neo-orthodoxy, it owed much to the theology of the Swiss thinker Karl Barth. The leading American theological exponent, Langdon Gilkey,[9] would explain the difference as between knowing how or what and knowing why. 'What did you do yesterday?' 'My family and I went to the seaside in the car and got home late.' 'The kids and I took my wife to the seaside to celebrate her birthday and to show our love.' Two different responses, of kinds that simply cannot clash. The first response is equally compatible with: 'I engineered a family trip to the seaside to upset my wife whose father died of drowning, in order to get her to hate me and give me a divorce.' The same sorts of factors separate science and religion. Consider an ecosystem. A biologist might discuss it in terms of patterns of equilibrium, for instance invoking the MacArthur–Wilson hypothesis of island biogeography showing why, after a devastating fire, an isolated area built up new species, and why the species number topped out after a while. A theologian or a religious person (not necessarily mutually exclusive!) might talk of the ecosystem in terms of God's providing for his children and of our obligations to use the system but not to destroy it. A developer with very different intentions, intending perhaps to build a new Las Vegas in the desert, might equally subscribe to the scientific description.

The most-publicized, recent enthusiast for the independence position (without the theological commitments of the neo-orthodox) was the late Stephen Jay Gould, palaeontologist and popular writer supreme. In his book *Rocks of Ages* (1999), he introduced the idea of a magisterium, a kind of world picture and associated approach, and argued that science and religion being different magisteria cannot interact and hence cannot clash.[10] Unfortunately, Gould's position pointed to the big weakness in the independence position, namely ambiguity about what belongs to science and what belongs to religion. For Gould, religion could have ethics, moral thinking and behaviour, but not much more. Ontological claims, for instance about the resurrection and about eternal life, apparently are claims falling under the science magisterium and hence must be judged false. A conclusion which is satisfying to a new atheist no doubt but hardly to a person of faith. At a minimum the traditional Christian will want to say that God exists, that he created the universe from nothing, that we are made in the image of God and are fallen, that Jesus was the son of God and died on the cross for us, and that he rose from the dead and that his sacrifice and triumph makes possible our eternal salvation. If these are part of science and are judged false then we are right back with the warfare position.

INTERACTION

There are two ways forward here, and many believers endorse a combination of the two. On the one hand, you can deny that the just-listed claims really are scientific. Take the question of origins. It is true that science has an origin story. The Big Bang and then organic evolution. But this is not really what the believer is talking about when he or she speaks of God as creator. The religious belief rather is about God as a necessary, eternal being – in some sense being the support or guarantee of a very contingent world. The technical theological term is 'aseity' and it means that God is not dependent on others for his being – he is from himself (*a se*) – and the world depends on him. God answers the question: Why is there something rather than nothing? He does not answer: Where did this planet or this cabbage come from?

On the other hand, you can argue that the domains of science and religion really are not so different and that they can either speak to each other (dialogue) or even overlap into one whole (integration). People who take natural theology seriously – proving the existence of God and that sort of thing – fall at least into the dialogue camp. Today, it is true, many believers do not much care for natural theology. Barth loathed it, and he was far from the first. The great English theologian John Henry Newman wrote in correspondence about his seminal philosophical work, *A Grammar of Assent*: 'I have not insisted on the argument from design, because I am writing for the 19th century, by which, as represented by its philosophers, design is not admitted as proved. And to tell the truth, though I should not wish to preach on the subject, for 40 years I have been unable to see the logical force of the argument myself. I believe in design because I believe in God; not in a God because I see design.'[11] Continuing: 'Design teaches me power, skill and goodness – not sanctity, not mercy, not a future judgment, which three are of the essence of religion.' Note that Newman and those in his footsteps do not separate the worlds of experience and of faith completely. It is rather that we move from faith to experience instead of the other way. The German theologian Wolfhart Pannenberg speaks of this as a theology of nature.[12]

There are still people who think you can go from the world of science to the world of religion and of God. Supporters of so-called intelligent design theory (IDT) – people who think the organic world so intricately organized that blind law could not have produced it – fall into this camp.[13] So also do supporters of strong versions of the anthropic principle, believing that the physical constants of the universe are so precise and so necessary that they cannot exist by mere chance. Hence, there must be a designer.[14]

It goes almost without saying that there are vehement scientific critics of both these positions. Biologists flatly deny that life's intricate organization is such that it could not have been produced by blind law, and they delight in showing that the paradigms of the ID supporters – for instance, the bacterial flagellum and the blood-clotting cascade – are readily explained in conventional evolutionary terms.[15] Many physicists likewise deny the claims of the anthropic principle enthusiasts. On the one side, there is the possibility of multiple universes with different constants. That we live in a universe with constants that makes our life possible is true but unsurprising. On the other side, perhaps the constants are not as exact or necessary as often supposed. There may be far more slack and less need to invoke God than is suggested.[16]

It should be added also that, theologically, both of these positions are problematic.[17] The problem of evil still looms. If there is a designer, why did he not prevent evil? This is particularly troublesome for IDT. If God is needed to explain the ferociously complex, then why did he not also clean up the simple but horrific? Many genetic diseases have simple causes – one bit of DNA gone astray. Could God not have put things right or was he too busy with the bacterial flagellum? Also there are the other traditional problems. Is there one designer or many? Is this world of ours the end of a long line of earlier attempts and will there be better worlds after ours?

Of course, none of this disproves the existence of God and it is still possible for the believer to think that science illuminates theological claims even if it does not prove them. The Christian doctrine of original sin is a nice example. In the light of modern science, it is hardly plausible to think of two initially created humans, hanging about in a garden, finally succumbing and eating an apple. But modern evolutionary biology, especially the evolutionary biology of human beings, stresses that we are the result of conflicting forces. If, as biologists believe, the main motive force for change is natural selection – the survival of the fittest – then human features (adaptations) are going to be shaped in the direction of helping their possessors to survive (and to reproduce). Richard Dawkins,[18] incidentally one of the leading new atheists, speaks metaphorically of selfish genes, meaning that features had better serve their owner's ends or the owners will be biological failures. However, today we realize that major adaptations, especially for intelligent beings like humans, are directed towards co-operation with fellows.[19] Getting together to hunt or to forage or to fight attackers pays big dividends. Helping others can lead to help for ourselves – when we are young or old or sick we need help and the best way to obtain this is to be prepared to help others in their hours of need. You scratch my back and I will scratch yours. So, thanks to our evolution, we are a rather tense melange of selfishness and of friendliness or altruism, to use the biologists' term for giving help. And this is surely close to what religious people mean by original sin. We are made in the image of God, so we are naturally good. But we are fallen – this is now part of our nature – and so we are also bad. An uneasy hotchpotch of selfishness and altruism.

Note that, as with design arguments, there is no proof here. There is no literal substitution of evolutionary biology for Genesis. Just an attempt to make sense of puzzling religious claims through modern science. But what if you want to go further and want full integration of science and religion? This would be the sort of move that followers of Alfred North Whitehead, process philosophers, would make, seeing both God and the creation in evolutionary terms. God supposedly has emptied himself of his powers – kenosis – and can influence but not determine the world. Everything, including God, is in a state of flux.[20] Integration was also the aim of the French Jesuit palaeontologist, Father Pierre Teilhard de Chardin. He saw the whole of life in a progressive evolutionary march up to humankind, and thence on to the Godhead, Jesus Christ, whom Teilhard referred to as the Omega Point.[21]

Some people, scientists especially, have been very critical of any such thinking. The Nobel laureate Peter Medawar wrote of Teilhard's synthesis:

> I have read and studied *The Phenomenon of Man* with real distress, even with despair. Instead of wringing our hands over the Human Predicament, we should attend to those parts of it which are wholly remediable, above all to the gullibility which makes it possible for people to be taken in by such a bag of tricks as this. If it were an innocent, passive gullibility it would be excusable; but all too clearly, alas, it is an active willingness to be deceived.[22]

Historically, we can now see that this judgement was a little harsh. It is true that Teilhard claimed that his position was purely scientific, which it clearly is not. However, he did this hoping thereby to escape the censure of his church, since if his thinking was pure science there could be no theological objections. As it is, the church did judge his ideas heretical, so he ended by being the scorn of both science and religion.

Today more charitably we can say of Teilhard, as we might of process philosophy, that if one is a believer and wants to accept modern science, integration certainly does not seem *a priori* foolish. Why should not the two facets of God's world come together as one? Nevertheless, there are serious questions, both theological and scientific. Many would argue that the idea of a God in flux is simply not the God of Abraham, or Jesus or Mohammed. Their God is eternal, unchanging, good and all powerful. Many would also argue that the progressive world picture of Teilhard is simply not well taken. Evolution rather is a slow, meandering process going nowhere. It is true that there are scientific supporters of biological progress. Sociobiologist Edward O. Wilson writes: 'Progress, then, is a property of the evolution of life as a whole by almost any conceivable intuitive standard, including the acquisition of goals and intentions in the behavior of animals.'[23] Others disagree. Stephen Jay Gould spoke of the idea as 'a noxious, culturally embedded, untestable, nonoperational, intractable idea that must be replaced if we wish to understand the patterns of history'.[24]

NATURALISM

What about the related philosophy of naturalism? You might think that methodological naturalism at least is fairly innocuous. Deliberately, it does not take a stand on the ultimate questions. However, there are strong critics, notably the *éminence grise* of the ID movement, Phillip Johnson,[25] who thinks that it is a slippery slope that ends with metaphysical naturalism and full-blown atheism. Actually, this seems not to be true and is indeed a classic case of the *post hoc ergo propter hoc* fallacy. One grants that many have started as methodological naturalists and ended as metaphysical naturalists; but, apart from the many who have not, the reasons for the move rarely depend on the naturalism as such. Biography after biography of nineteenth- and twentieth-century believers show that what led to non-belief was theological not scientific.[26] People worried about the problem of evil or eternal damnation or the stories of the Old Testament or such things and decided that enough was enough – they wanted no more of such stuff. By and large – by and very large – they did not read Newton or Darwin or Einstein and declare that God is dead. Darwin himself moved to agnosticism (he was never an atheist) because he could not stand the idea of his father – the man he admired above all others – being condemned to eternal torment for his non-belief.[27] In Richard Dawkins' case, reading the *God Delusion* gives the strong suspicion that it was the dictates of the God of the Jews that turned him away from religion. Many English public school boys have found that, having had one headmaster in this life, they would prefer not to have another in the next. (This last sentence has intentional autobiographical undertones.)

Yet surely even methodological naturalism will not permit subscription to the Christian faith – or Judaism or Islam or other faiths for that matter? The methodological naturalist believes that everything in this world goes according to unbroken, blind law. What place then for miracles? If no miracles, then no resurrection – or parting the Red Sea or splitting the moon into two or whatever. Basically, especially in the Christian tradition, there are two counter-strategies here, usually associated with Augustine and Aquinas respectively.[28] You can argue that the miracles are to be taken metaphorically. Or you can simply invoke the distinction between the order of nature and the order of grace, and say that miracles, in the sense of breaking the laws of nature, did really occur but that these are taken on faith and claims about them are simply not scientific.[29]

There are arguments in favour of both strategies. Some of the miracles, if literally true, are a bit iffy theologically. Did Jesus really turn water into wine to keep the party going? Even the resurrection might be better understood less as a physiological event and more as one of the psychology of the disciples after the crucifixion, uplifted when they might have been expected to have been downhearted. Analogously, invoking the order of grace gets you away from tedious and surely problematic discussions of whether there is evidence that the stone was really moved and so forth. You simply accept it on faith and leave matters at that. With this second, Thomistic strategy are you nevertheless breaking from methodological naturalism? Well, in a strict fashion perhaps you are, but not in a sense that gives you absolute licence or that opens the way for IDT and the like. Miracles still have to be understood in the context of salvific history. The resurrection was part of the story of God's making possible our eternal glory with Him. It was not a bit of biological engineering. One can still argue that normally God works through unbroken law. Bacterial flagella do not need miracles. Miracles are or were needed only for the ultimate drama of the Fall and the atoning sacrifice.

Recently, the philosopher Alvin Plantinga has been highly critical of what here is being called methodological naturalism.[30] He argues that it collapses in on itself and hence cannot be an adequate philosophy, and much the same applies to anything dependent on it, specifically a science that excludes the possibility of miracles. Basically Plantinga's argument depends on the claim that evolutionary theory, Darwinian evolutionary theory centring on natural selection in particular, does not guarantee truth. At most, it guarantees that we can get through life successfully. But it is quite compatible with success that we are totally mistaken about everything, including evolutionary theory itself obviously. Hence, everything degenerates into paradox. Of course, we think that our senses and powers of reason as produced by natural selection lead us to the right order of things. But we would think that, wouldn't we?! Plantinga tells us of a dinner at Oxford, where there were many courses and much conversation, including Richard Dawkins telling the philosopher A. J. Ayer the conditions under which one could be an atheist. (Coals to Newcastle one would have thought.) Perhaps our senses and reason deceive us so much that we could project being at this dinner to other, very different circumstances. We could be in the jungle fighting crocodiles but the features that lead to croc fighting also lead to illusions about what we are doing – illusions that we are putting Freddie Ayer right on matters of religious commitment. 'Under this possibility ... beliefs wouldn't have (or needn't have) any purpose or function; they would be more like unintended by-products, and the likelihood that they are mostly true would be low.'[31]

I doubt any Darwinian evolutionist is going to find this argument very convincing. Evolution just does not work that way. It is true that sometimes we are systematically deceived (or open to being deceived) by our biology. I will note shortly that some would argue this of convictions about the truth of religion. But we only know about evolution's deceptions because we are not deceived all of the time – we use the non-deceived instances as touchstones to judge difficult or problematic cases. And there have to be good reasons for the deception. As, we shall see, are suggested in the case of religion. There is nothing in evolutionary theory suggesting that such a radically mistaken notion as thinking you are at high table in Oxford when you are really in the jungle under threat of your life could possibly have an adaptive value, and it is so counterproductive that it is hardly possible that it could be a by-product of something that was working to our benefit. By-products have to be pretty minimal or selection will eliminate them.

Plantinga counters that perhaps we are deceived all of the time. It could be that there is systematic deception even of the supposed touchstones. Think of an analogy. Looking at an assembly line in a factory, we think that the produced widgets are red. Then, taking off our rose-tinted protective glasses we realize that we were mistaken. Perhaps, however, we can never take off our glasses. This does not mean that the widgets in the factory are really red. The same could be true of the deceptions of evolution.

One suspects that at this point the naturalist, of whatever stripe, has to concede. But what does the concession mean? It does not mean that we do not have a coherent system of thought, including evolutionary thought. It means that we can never get outside our sensing and thinking to tell if the world is really as we think it is. In other words, we cannot prove an ultimate correspondence between our seeing and thinking and absolute reality. However, many philosophers are dubious about absolute realities anyway.[32] At the best, we can have a kind of coherence of our beliefs. Within the system we can have correspondence. There is none between the thinking you are at the dinner but really being in the jungle. Overall, however, we must accept that we are prisoners of our own, evolved selves. And as a *tu quoque*, most naturalists would argue that someone like Plantinga is really no better off. If he would appeal to God as a guarantee of his beliefs, then he is caught in the circle of Descartes' *Meditations*. How can we be certain that an evil demon is not deceiving us about God? We need God to guarantee our thoughts but cannot get to God to do this. In short, no good reason has been given to jettison methodological naturalism.

EXPLANATIONS

To conclude, let us turn briefly to the question of origins and to the explanations offered by science. At least since David Hume,[33] if not earlier, philosophers and scientists have been offering naturalistic explanations of religion and of claims, particularly moral claims, made in the name of religion.[34] For Hume, and then a century later for Charles Darwin,[35] religion was something that came about as a by-product of other aspects of life. 'We find human faces in the moon, armies in the clouds; and by a natural propensity, if not corrected by experience and reflection, ascribe malice or good-will to everything, that hurts or pleases us.'[36] Darwin likewise told stories of his dog being upset at a parasol moving in the wind, thinking it more than it was – the implication being that religion is much the same sort of thing.

Both Hume and Darwin denied that they were actually disproving the truth of religion. Today's thinkers in this tradition are less inhibited. Philosopher Daniel Dennett likens religion to the lancet fluke (*Dicrocelium dendriticum*), a parasite that corrupts the brain of an ant, causing it to strive to climb blades of grass, where it is eaten by a sheep or cow, thus allowing the fluke to complete its life cycle, producing offspring that are excreted and taken up again with ants.[37] No more argument is needed about the truth status of religion. Edward O. Wilson is less causally hostile to religion – for him, it is an adaptation promoting group solidarity – but he too thinks that a causal explanation negates truth claims. He writes that 'sociobiology can account for the very origin of mythology by the principle of natural selection acting on the genetically evolving material structure of the human brain'. Continuing: 'If this interpretation is correct, the final decisive edge enjoyed by scientific naturalism will come from its capacity to explain traditional religion, its chief competition, as a wholly material phenomenon. Theology is not likely to survive as an independent intellectual discipline.'[38]

Two comments are in order. First, although these types of speculations (about the origins of religion) may have been around for more than two hundred years, today no one could say that they are part of firmly established science. Indeed, those writing on the subject are (let us say gently) not entirely unanimous in their thinking and inferences. We have just seen that Dennett thinks that religion is a harmful parasite whereas Wilson thinks religion has beneficial societal effects. For this reason, Dennett wants to eliminate religion entirely whereas Wilson wants to substitute a kind of secular humanism. Other differences pertain to the causal units behind religion. Richard Dawkins thinks that religion is all a matter of culture – he has invented the term 'meme' to talk of units of culture akin to genes, the units of biological heredity.[39] Others think that there might even be God genes.[40] The Pope has them and Dawkins does not. The jury is out on whether Anglicans have them or not.

Second, because you can explain something it does not follow that it is false. One can give an evolutionary explanation of the origin of eyes and an anatomical-physiological explanation of how they work, but (Plantinga notwithstanding) it does not follow that the train I see bearing down on me is non-existent. If science works, one would expect to be able to give a scientific explanation of religion. And to say that because religion is a parasite or a by-product means that it must be false is a bit like copying those nineteenth-century prudes who said that because humans are produced by one kind of genital going into another kind this means that sex must be bad and not something that God really wanted. In any case, not all parasites are bad – where would we be without *E. coli*? – and the same is true of by-products. It is not long since many a patch of rhubarb flourished because of droppings from the milk-man's horse.

What about morality? A number of enthusiasts for evolutionary explanations of human behaviour think that now moral thinking and action can be shown to be a function of the genes.[41] The arguments run along the lines of those sketched above in the discussion of original sin. There are good biological reasons for co-operation and there are equally good biological reasons for thinking that our urges in this direction are more than mere feelings – that they are objective norms laid upon us. If we think that morality is objective or absolute we are going to be much less willing to break it than otherwise.

Does this mean that morality therefore is without foundation – an illusion imposed upon us by our biology to make us good co-operators, as it has been described?[42] Not necessarily, for the same reasons just given as to why explanations of religion do not automatically make it false. However, one might well argue that although the formal structure of co-operation cannot change, the content of moral claims is somewhat contingent. If, for instance, we could be persuaded to co-operate with a moral norm along the lines of 'hate your neighbour but co-operate because you know he hates you' – a kind of Cold War morality – then science surely starts to make you wonder about some of the absolutist claims that are made in the name of religion. But this is hardly more than the wonder one has already about the different forms that religion takes and the consequent suspicion that not all of them can possibly be quite as true as they individually claim. You hardly need science to notice this and to draw the obvious conclusions.

This is a good note on which to end. Science and religion do interact and there is no doubt that science makes some religious claims untenable. Given modern science, out-and-out biblical literalism is untenable and the same is true of some more specific claims, such as the belief that the native people of North America are the lost tribes of Israel. However, this clash between modern science and various facts insisted on in the name of religion does not prove the impossibility of any kind of meaningful religious faith. Most obviously, science hardly destroys the total moral dimension of religious commitment. Also, it is far from certain that science makes impossible central ontological claims: about the existence of a necessary being; about other features of this being, for instance about its power and goodness; and about interventions in the order of nature. Obviously, because there may be room for faith, it does not follow that one can or should have such faith. The main thing to keep in mind is that we should be wary of simplistic dismissals of the claims of religion – for instance, because we can give naturalistic explanations of belief systems that this means that they must necessarily be false and misleading. This may be true of some (or all) such systems, but if it is then proper arguments must be given for their demolition. Most particularly, we should be careful in talking about naturalism. Methodological naturalism is a powerful approach to understanding with many great successes to its credit. Do not assume, however, that it is identical to metaphysical naturalism or that the one leads easily to the other. Overall, the one sure conclusion that we can draw is that there are many other factors beyond science, most certainly philosophical but also surely including those within religion itself, that are going to influence the final position anyone takes on these matters.

Notes

1 Interview, *New York Times*, 25 January 2000; Steven Weinberg, *The First Three Minutes* (New York: Basic Books, 1977), p. 154.
2 Notably S. Harris, *The End of Faith: Religion, Terror, and the Future of Reason* (New York: Free Press, 2004); Harris, *Letter to a Christian Nation* (New York: Knopf, 2006); D.C. Dennett, *Breaking the Spell: Religion as a Natural Phenomenon* (New York: Viking, 2006); R. Dawkins, *The God Delusion* (New York: Houghton Mifflin Harcourt, 2008); C. Hitchens, *God is Not Great: How Religion Poisons Everything* (New York: Hachette, 2007); V.J. Stenger, *God: the Failed Hypothesis. How Science Shows that God Does Not Exist* (Buffalo, NY: Prometheus, 2007).

3   M. Ruse, *Can a Darwinian be a Christian? The Relationship between Science and Religion* (Cambridge University Press, 2001).

4   I. Barbour, *Religion and Science: Historical and Contemporary Issues* (San Francisco: Harper, 1997).

5   See Mikael Stenmark's contribution to this volume.

6   For Huxley, see A. Desmond, *Huxley, the Devil's Disciple* (London: Michael Joseph, 1994); A. Desmond, *Huxley, Evolution's High Priest* (London: Michael Joseph, 1997); M. Ruse, *The Evolution–Creation Struggle* (Cambridge, MA: Harvard University Press, 2005).

7   E. McMullin, 'Introduction: Evolution and Creation', in E. McMullin (ed.), *Evolution and Creation* (Notre Dame: University of Notre Dame Press, 1985), pp. 1–58.

8   D. A. Young, *John Calvin and the Natural World* (Washington, DC: University Press of America, 2007).

9   L. B. Gilkey, *Maker of Heaven and Earth* (Garden City, NY: Doubleday, 1959); L. B. Gilkey, *Creationism on Trial: Evolution and God at Little Rock* (Minneapolis: Winston Press, 1985).

10 S. J. Gould, *Rocks of Ages: Science and Religion in the Fullness of Life* (New York: Ballantine, 1999).

11 J. H. Newman, *The Letters and Diaries of John Henry Newman, XXV*, ed. by C. S. Dessain and T. Gornall (Oxford: Clarendon Press, 1973), p. 97.

12 W. Pannenberg, *Towards a Theology of Nature* (Louisville: Westminster/ John Knox Press, 1993).

13 See especially M. Behe, *Darwin's Black Box: the Biochemical Challenge to Evolution* (New York: The Free Press, 1996).

14 See especially J. D. Barrow and F. J. Tipler, *The Anthropic Cosmological Principle* (Oxford: Clarendon Press, 1986); J. C. Polkinghorne, *The Faith of a Physicist* (Princeton University Press, 1994).

15 K. Miller, *Finding Darwin's God* (New York: Harper and Row, 1999).

16 S. Weinberg, 'A Designer Universe', *New York Review of Books* 46, no. 16 (1999), 46–8.

17 E. McMullin, 'Fine-tuning the Universe?', in M. H. Shale and G. W. Shields (eds.), *Science, Technology, and Religious Ideas* (Lanham: University Press of America, 1994), pp. 97–125; W. A. Dembski and M. Ruse (eds.), *Debating Design: Darwin to DNA* (Cambridge University Press, 2004); M. Ruse, *Darwin and Design: Does Evolution Have a Purpose?* (Cambridge, MA: Harvard University Press, 2003).

18 R. Dawkins, *The Selfish Gene* (Oxford University Press, 1976).

19 E. O. Wilson, *On Human Nature* (Cambridge, MA: Harvard University Press, 1978); M. Ruse, *Taking Darwin Seriously: a Naturalistic Approach to Philosophy* (Oxford: Blackwell, 1986).

20 John Haught writes eloquently on these topics. See especially J. F. Haught, *The Cosmic Adventure* (New York: Paulist Press, 1984); Haught, *The Promise of Nature* (New York and Mahwah, NJ: Paulist Press, 1993); and Haught, *God after Darwin: a Theology of Evolution* (Boulder: Westview, 2000).

21 P. Teilhard de Chardin, *Le phénomène humain* (Paris: Editions de Seuil, 1955).

22 P.B. Medawar, 'Review of *The Phenomenon of Man*', *Mind* 70 (1961), 99–106, p. 106.

23 E.O. Wilson, *The Diversity of Life* (Cambridge, MA: Harvard University Press, 1992), p. 187.

24 S.J. Gould, 'On Replacing the Idea of Progress with an Operational Notion of Directionality', in M.H. Nitecki (ed.), *Evolutionary Progress* (Chicago: The University of Chicago Press, 1988), pp. 319–38, p. 319.

25 P.E. Johnson, *Darwin on Trial*, 2nd edn (Washington, DC: Regnery Gateway, 1993).

26 S. Budd, *Varieties of Unbelief: Atheists and Agnostics in English Society 1850–1960* (London: Heinemann, 1977); Ruse, *The Evolution–Creation Struggle*.

27 C. Darwin, *Autobiography* (New York: Norton, 1969).

28 Ruse, *Can a Darwinian be a Christian?*

29 E. McMullin, 'Plantinga's Defense of Special Creation', *Christian Scholar's Review* 21, no. 1 (1991), 55–79; E. McMullin, 'Evolution and Special Creation', *Zygon* 28 (1993), 299–335.

30 A. Plantinga, 'An Evolutionary Argument against Naturalism', *Logos* 12 (1991), 27–49; A. Plantinga, *Warrant and Proper Function* (New York: Oxford University Press, 1993); A. Plantinga, 'Methodological Naturalism', *Perspectives on Science and Christian Faith* 49, no. 3 (1997), 143–54.

31 Plantinga, 'An Evolutionary Argument', 34.

32 R. Rorty, *Philosophy and the Mirror of Nature* (Princeton University Press, 1979); H. Putnam, *Reason, Truth, and History* (Cambridge University Press, 1981).

33 D. Hume, 'The Natural History of Religion' [1757], in R. Wollheim (ed.), *Hume on Religion* (London: Fontana, 1963).

34 M. Ruse, *Charles Darwin* (Oxford: Blackwell, 2007).

35 C. Darwin, *The Descent of Man, and Selection in Relation to Sex* (London: John Murray, 1871).

36 Hume, 'The Natural History of Religion', pp. 40–1.

37 Dennett, *Breaking the Spell*.

38 Wilson, *On Human Nature*, p. 192.

39 Dawkins, *The Selfish Gene*.

40 D.H. Hamer, *The God Gene: How Faith is Hardwired into our Genes* (New York: Doubleday, 2004).

41 Ruse, *Taking Darwin Seriously*; M. Ruse (ed.), *Philosophy after Darwin: Classic and Contemporary Readings* (Princeton University Press, 2009); M. Hauser, *Moral Minds: How Nature Shaped our Universal Sense of Right and Wrong* (New York: Ecco, 2006); R. Joyce, *The Evolution of Morality* (Cambridge, MA: MIT Press, 2007).

42 M. Ruse and E.O. Wilson, 'The Evolution of Morality', *New Scientist* 1478 (1985), 108–28.

12   Divine action, emergence and scientific explanation

NANCEY MURPHY

Philosopher Richard Rorty claims that it is 'pictures rather than propositions, metaphors rather than statements, which determine most of our philosophical convictions'.[1] The picture that has predominated in discussions of the topics of this chapter, throughout the modern era, has been that of a hierarchy of sciences, each higher science studying more complex entities made up of the entities studied by the science below. Today the hierarchy is taken (unproblematically) to include various levels of physics, chemistry, and the many levels of biology from molecular biology to scientific ecology. Whether the human and social sciences can be added to the hierarchy has remained a contentious issue, one closely tied to debates about human nature.

This chapter will explore the consequences of this picture for understanding scientific explanation, human freedom and God's action in the physical world. We shall see that when causal reductionism (the idea that all causation occurs at the bottom of the hierarchy of complexity) and the idea of deterministic laws of nature are added to the picture, it produces (apparently) insoluble problems in understanding human and divine action. In short, the combination of these three assumptions suggests that the determinism of physical laws 'works its way up' the hierarchy of complex systems, resulting in a fully determined natural world. In consequence it is difficult to see how God might act in the world without contravening those laws, and how human agents might exercise free choice. We shall then explore a change that is occurring in the present generation: the rejection of reductionism in favour of the recognition that complex wholes often have reciprocal effects on their components.

REDUCTIONISM AND SCIENTIFIC EXPLANATION

Modern thinking was launched by developments in science. The acceptance of Copernican astronomy required an entirely new approach to physics as well, since the physics developed by the ancient philosopher Aristotle (384–322 BC) was so closely tied to the Ptolemaic conception of the universe. Early modern physicists such as Pierre Gassendi (1592–1655) revived ancient Epicurean atomism as a replacement. The essential assumption of atomism is that everything that happens is a consequence of the motions and combinations of atoms. The indestructible atoms ('atom' meant uncuttable) are not affected by these interactions. The atoms' characteristics were speed and direction of motion (and sometimes shape). When modern scientists combined atomism with Isaac Newton's laws of motion, it was then reasonable to assume that these deterministic laws governed the behaviour of all physical processes. Thus, all causation is bottom-up, and all physical processes are deterministic because the atoms obey deterministic laws. The consequence is that complex, higher-level entities are not causal players in their own right.

So far I have focused on causal reductionism. However, a number of related versions of reductionism have been developed. One is methodological reductionism, the view that the proper way to do science is to analyse or decompose an entity or system into its parts, and then to study the behaviour of the parts. This has been an enormously fruitful approach to science. Another version is epistemological or theoretical reductionism. This is the assumption that the laws or theories of higher-level sciences can and should be reduced to the next level below, and ultimately to physics. This was the goal of many twentieth-century philosophers and scientists. Because the laws at higher levels are couched in different language from those of lower levels, principles for translation, called bridge principles, would be needed. So, for example, the gas laws of chemistry should be reducible to underlying atomic physics by defining temperature and pressure of gases in terms of the mean kinetic energy of the atoms and the consequent frequency of collisions with the walls of the container. Mid-twentieth-century philosophers Carl Hempel and Ernst Nagel worked out the most elegant theories regarding the nature of scientific explanation. The phenomena of any scientific field should be deducible from strict, deterministic scientific laws and theories.[2] And ideally higher-level theories would be explained by reducing them to lower-level theories.[3]

This atomist-reductionist-determinist picture of science had powerful consequences for understanding human freedom and divine action. The ancient Epicureans had already recognized the implications of their views for human freedom. Atomism applied to human bodies and also souls, since they held a materialist account of the soul. So human beings, too, are merely temporary combinations of atoms and their behaviour is a result of the motions of the atoms. Early modern responses are best represented by the contrast between Thomas Hobbes' (1588–1679) acceptance of a determinist account of human behaviour and the radical substance dualism devised by René Descartes (1596–1650). Descartes accepted a mechanistic account of all of nature, including animals and human bodies, but argued that the mind or soul (thinking substance) was entirely free. Dualism and materialism were the primary options in the twentieth century as well. However, by this time, quantum indeterminacy had disturbed the worldview of early modern science, and so there have been attempts to show that quantum events play a role in human freedom.[4]

As modern physics developed it became increasingly difficult to understand God's role in the natural world. It is ironic that the concept of the laws of nature was developed as an account of how God's will was manifested in the natural world, but these laws later came to be seen by many as obstacles to God's action. With Newton's laws of motion came the image of the universe as a giant clockwork mechanism. Newton's concept of inertia (bodies at rest and bodies in motion remain so unless a force is impressed upon them) provided, for Newton (1642–1727), an argument for God as the necessary first mover. Also, observed planetary motions did not fit perfectly with predictions based on Newton's laws, so Newton hypothesized that the Clockmaker occasionally intervened to adjust their motions.

One hundred years later, Pierre-Simon Laplace (1749–1827), with better calculations and data, said that God was a hypothesis he did not need. If the state of the entire universe could be described, along with all relevant laws, all future states could (in principle) be calculated.

There were three major responses to this Laplacean notion of the closed causal order. One was Deism, a widely held view in the eighteenth century. According to deists, God created the universe and set up the laws according to which it operates, but has no further engagement with it. Deists, in consequence, rejected traditional Christian concepts such as providence, incarnation and revelation.

Conservative Christians developed an interventionist account of divine action: if God is the creator of the laws of nature, then he can intervene. He can interrupt or override the laws so as to perform special divine acts. Miracles came to be defined as violations of the laws of nature.

Friedrich Schleiermacher (1768–1834) is said by liberal Protestants to be the father of modern theology. He developed what might be called an immanentist account of divine action. Schleiermacher and his followers argue that God is acting within all of the created order, and so it does not make sense to distinguish any particular events as actions of God. The notions of special providence and miracles were abandoned, and revelation was redefined in terms of human religious awareness. I have argued that this difference between interventionist and immanentist accounts of divine action is responsible for the sharp split between conservative and liberal Protestants, respectively, in the USA.[5]

This extremely influential atomist-reductionist-determinist worldview has been called into question in many ways during the past century. The atoms themselves are now understood to be composed of more basic entities, whose particle-like character is not always in evidence. Quantum physics, on the most widely accepted interpretation, has challenged the determinism that had been taken to apply at the bottom of the hierarchy of the sciences. Perhaps most important is the questioning of causal reductionism expressed in development of the concepts of emergence and downward causation.

EMERGENCE AND DOWNWARD CAUSATION

The most significant criticisms of causal reductionism (and thereby of epistemological reductionism) fall into three stages: an early emergentist movement (from approximately 1920 to 1950); the exploration of the concept of downward causation or whole-part constraint (beginning in the 1970s); and, currently, an account of causation that combines both downward causation and emergence.

The idea of emergence was proposed in the philosophy of biology as an alternative both to mechanist-reductionist accounts of the origin of life and to vitalism. The vitalists claimed that in order to get life from inorganic matter something like a vital force or entelechy (a quasi-Aristotelian notion) needed to be involved. Emergentists, such as Roy Wood Sellars, argued that the increasingly complex organization, as one ascends the hierarchy of systems, accounts for the appearance of new kinds of entities with causal powers that cannot be reduced to physics. The organic emerges from the physical; so too do the levels of the mental or conscious, the social, the ethical, and the religious or spiritual.

Sellars claimed that '[t]he ontological imagination was stultified at the start by [the picture] of microscopic billiard balls'.[6] In contrast, he argued: 'Organization and wholes are genuinely significant'; they are not mere aggregates of elementary particles. Reductive materialism overemphasizes the stuff in contrast to the organization. But matter, he claims, is only a part of nature. 'There is energy; there is the fact of pattern; there are all sorts of intimate relations.' 'Matter, or stuff, needs to be supplemented by terms like integration, pattern, function.'[7]

With hindsight we can see that Sellars and some of the other emergentists were exactly right; however, their arguments did not prevail against the reductionist philosophers of science.

In the 1970s psychologist Roger Sperry and philosopher Donald Campbell both wrote specifically about downward (or top-down) causation. On some occasions Sperry wrote of the properties of the higher-level entity or system *overpowering* the causal forces of the component entities.[8] The notion of overpowering lower-level causal forces rightly raised worries regarding the compatibility of his account with adequate respect for the basic sciences.

Donald Campbell's work has turned out to be more helpful. Here there is no talk of overpowering lower-level causal processes, but instead a thoroughly non-mysterious account of a larger system of causal factors having a *selective* effect on lower-level entities and processes. Campbell's example is the role of natural selection in producing the remarkably efficient jaw structures of worker termites.[9] His example is meant to illustrate four theses. The first two give due recognition to bottom-up accounts of causation: first, all processes at the higher levels are restrained by and act in conformity to the laws of lower levels, including the levels of subatomic physics. Second, the achievements at higher levels require for their implementation specific lower-level mechanisms and processes. Explanation is not complete until these micromechanisms have been specified.

The third and fourth theses represent the perspective of downward causation. Third, '[b]iological evolution in its meandering exploration of segments of the universe encounters laws, operating as selective systems, which are not described by the laws of physics and inorganic chemistry'. Fourth:

> Where natural selection operates through life and death at a
> higher level of organization, the laws of the higher-level selective
> system determine in part the distribution of lower-level events
> and substances. Description of an intermediate-level phenomenon
> is not completed by describing its possibility and implementation
> in lower-level terms. Its presence, prevalence or distribution
> (all needed for a complete explanation of biological phenomena)
> will often require reference to laws at a higher level of organisation
> as well.[10]

It appears that little was written on downward causation until the idea was taken up by philosophers of mind in the 1990s. Robert Van Gulick made two important contributions. First, he spelled out in more detail an account based on selection. The reductionist's thesis is that the causal roles associated with the classifications employed by higher-level sciences are entirely derivative from the causal roles of the under-lying physical constituents. Van Gulick argues that even though the events and objects picked out by the special sciences *are* composites of physical constituents, the causal powers of such an object are not deter-mined solely by the physical properties of its constituents and the laws of physics. They are also determined by the organization of those con-stituents within the composite. And it is just such patterns of organiza-tion that are picked out by the predicates of the higher-level sciences.

These patterns have downward causal efficacy in that they can affect which causal powers of their constituents are activated. 'A given physical constituent may have many causal powers, but only some subsets of them will be active in a given situation. The larger context (i.e. the pattern) of which it is a part may affect which of its causal pow-ers get activated ... Thus the whole is not any simple function of its parts, since the whole at least partially determines what contributions are made by its parts.'[11]

Such patterns or entities are stable features of the world, often in spite of variations or exchanges in their underlying physical constitu-ents. Many such patterns are self-sustaining or self-reproducing in the face of perturbing physical forces that might degrade or destroy them (for example, DNA patterns). Finally, the selective activation of the causal powers of such a pattern's parts may in many cases contribute to the maintenance and preservation of the pattern itself. Taken together, he says, these points illustrate that 'higher-order patterns can have a degree of independence from their underlying physical realizations and can exert what might be called downward causal influences without requiring any objectionable form of emergentism by which higher-order properties would alter the underlying laws of physics. Higher-order properties act by the selective activation of physical powers and not by their alteration.'[12]

Van Gulick's second contribution is to provide a classification of the various emergentist theses that have been proposed, and to point out that they are all roughly equivalent to the denial of various reductionist theses. He makes a helpful distinction between emergentist theses that pertain to objective real-world items and those that appeal to what we as cognitive agents can or cannot know. He further distinguishes, on the objective, metaphysical side, between two classes of emergents: properties and causal powers or forces. Within the category of epistemological theses he further distinguishes those pertaining to prediction and those pertaining to understanding.[13]

I mentioned above methodological, epistemological and causal reductionism. Van Gulick notes that ontological emergentist theses proposing the emergence of new causal powers are the converse of causal reductionism, and epistemological theses are the converse of epistemological reductionism. Note that if either sort of emergentist thesis is true, it means that while methodological reduction has been essential to science, it cannot provide a complete understanding of emergent phenomena.

The focus of this chapter is on causal reductionism versus causal-ontological emergentism, for two reasons. First, epistemological emergence is relatively uninteresting because we know of cases where we can neither predict outcomes nor explain known facts at the higher levels simply because the level of complexity or the need for fine-scale measurements goes beyond human capacities. Thus, if there are instances of epistemological emergence they do not necessarily tell us anything about the real world. Second, it is causal reductionism that has had dramatic consequences for understanding human and divine action, so its inverse, causal emergentism, is most likely to be relevant to these issues.

We can see from the foregoing that evading causal reductionism requires the recognition that higher-level entities and systems have emerged (evolved) from lower,[14] and that these entities can be somewhat independent of the causal processes of their constituents, thereby manifesting new, higher-level causal capacities. The sort of organization and selection of lower-level causal processes that Van Gulick describes calls for new concepts, and, in fact, represents something like a paradigm change across the sciences. This is the shift from thinking in mechanistic terms to thinking in systems terms.

Alicia Juarrero describes the changes required to understand complex systems. One has to give up the traditional Western philosophical bias in favour of things, with their intrinsic properties, for an appreciation of processes and relations; the components of systems are not things, but processes. Systems are different from both mechanisms and aggregates in that the properties of the components themselves are dependent on their being parts of the system in question. So, for example, from a systems perspective, a mammal is composed of a circulatory system, a reproductive system, and so forth, not of carbon, hydrogen, calcium. The organismic level of description is decoupled from the atomic level.[15]

Notice how far we have come from Descartes' hydraulic animal bodies and Newton's clockwork mechanisms. The world is now seen to be composed not only of things but also of complex systems, which organize spontaneously and constrain the behaviour of their own components in such a way as to preserve themselves and operate in the world as causes in their own right.[16]

HUMAN FREEDOM

I pointed out above that two early modern options were to accept the determinism of human behaviour that followed from a reductionist view of the hierarchy of complexity, or else to posit a non-material mind or soul, to which free will could be attributed. These were the primary options available to philosophers in the mid-twentieth century as well. In light of the development of the concepts of emergence and downward causation a new option has recently appeared, usually called non-reductive physicalism. This is the view that humans are entirely physical and that they nonetheless exhibit all of the higher human capacities once attributed to the mind: rationality, morality, spirituality and free will.

Philosophers often speak of the free-will problem. However, it would be better to realize that there have been numerous sources of worry about free will: divine determinism; divine foreknowledge; social determinism; and a variety of forms of physical determinism, based on the roles of physics, genetics, neurobiology. The aspects of the problem that are relevant to this chapter involve physical determinism. Although genetic determinism is treated as a legitimate worry by some, there is little, if anything, in human life that is strictly determined by the genes; also the human genome contains nowhere near enough information to determine the precise wiring of an individual's brain. So a more interesting question is whether human thought and behaviour are determined by the laws of neurobiology.

Recognition of downward causation, however, allows for a clearer focus on this issue. The critical issue is not whether neural processes are deterministic, but rather whether neurobiological reductionism is true. This is a particular instance of the question of whether complex wholes (human beings) are entirely governed by their parts (their neural systems).

It is said that the human brain is the most complex of all known systems, yet it is only a part of the entire human body, and an individual is only a part of a vast system of social, cultural and historical relations. In so far as it can be shown that even simple complex systems self-organize, select and form their own parts, selectively attend to external constraints, and thereby exhibit varying degrees of autonomy from the causal processes of both their parts and their environments, there are extremely good reasons to expect humans in society to exhibit (a degree of) causal autonomy.

Mere lack of bottom-up determination, however, is not equivalent to free will. What needs to be added to the sort of flexibility and autonomy possessed by other higher animals (and even small children) to constitute free will? The major obstacle to answering this question is that there is no agreement on how free will should be defined. Most of the current philosophical literature is structured by the compatibilist–libertarian debate. All agree that if determinism is true, then all human choices are determined by prior causes. Compatibilists argue that determinism may well be true, but it is a conceptual error to suppose that this rules out free will. Libertarians argue that free will requires that our choices, somehow, not be determined. A variety of authors agree that this debate has reached a stalemate. For example, Galen Strawson sees little chance of progress in settling this issue: 'The principal positions in the traditional metaphysical debate are clear. No radically new option is likely to emerge after millennia of debate.'[17]

This chapter proposes that recognition of the existence of emergent systems with (some) autonomy from both their environments and their parts in fact breaks the stalemate. Downward causation involves selection among lower-level variants, and it does not matter whether these variants are produced by deterministic or indeterministic processes. For example, evolution selects among organisms with variations in their genomes; some of these variations are produced by deterministic processes, others by indeterministic, quantum-level events.

If determinism versus indeterminism is not the defining issue for understanding free will, then it is helpful to look at alternative proposals. There are a number of valuable contributions to be found in the long history of the free-will literature. For example, a major tradition defines free will as being able to act for a reason. There are also various accounts of free will defined as autonomy, and these are distinguished by the authors' perceptions of the greatest threats to human autonomy. One threat, of course, is the threat of external control, but there are also various internal factors such as passions and appetites. A final example: Harry Frankfurt has helpfully distinguished first-order and second-order desires, and claimed that we are free when we have the second-order desire to have our own first-order desires. For instance, if I have a desire for revenge, but my higher-order desire is not to have this first-order desire, then I am not free.[18]

Alasdair MacIntyre's understanding of the capacity for morally responsible action incorporates the roles of reason, autonomy and self-evaluation that have been highlighted in the free-will literature. He argues that the capacity for morally responsible action depends on the ability to evaluate that which moves one to act in light of a concept of the good.[19] Spelling this out more fully, he says:

> as a practical reasoner I have to be able to imagine different
> possible futures for me, to imagine myself moving forward
> from the starting point of the present in different directions. For
> different or alternative futures present me with different and
> alternative sets of goods to be achieved, with different possible
> modes of flourishing. And it is important that I should be able
> to envisage both nearer and more distant futures and to attach
> probabilities, even if only in a rough and ready way, to the future
> results of acting in one way rather than another. For this both
> knowledge and imagination are necessary.[20]

Notice that this description incorporates the ingredients in various concepts of free will drawn from the literature. One ingredient may be called self-transcendence, the ability to make oneself the object of observation, reflection and evaluation. This is what Frankfurt called attention to in his recognition of our ability to evaluate our own desires. MacIntyre broadens this insight to include an evaluation of all of the sorts of factors that shape our actions. He notes the role of sophisticated language in enabling this ability. In order to evaluate a motive for acting, one must be able to formulate sentences complex enough not only to describe the motive, but also to state an evaluation of the motive so described.

A second ingredient, of course, is reason – not the mere reasonableness of higher animals, but the ability to enunciate principles against which to judge our own lower-level cognitions and motivations. Regarding autonomy, MacIntyre focuses on development of the ability to form our own moral judgements independent of social conformity – that is, not only the ability to evaluate our motives in light of social norms, but also to evaluate social norms themselves. This is an instance of third-order self-transcendence.

MacIntyre's description of morally responsible action, then, requires at least the following (more basic) cognitive components: (1) a symbolic sense of self (as MacIntyre says, the ability to imagine 'different possible futures for me'); (2) a sense of the narrative unity of life ('to imagine myself moving forward from ... the present'; 'nearer and more distant futures'); (3) the ability to run behavioural scenarios ('imagination') and predict the outcome ('knowledge'; 'attach probabilities ... to the future results'); (4) the ability to evaluate predicted outcomes in light of goals; (5) the ability to evaluate the goals themselves in light of abstract concepts ('alternative sets of goods ... different possible modes of flourishing'); and (6) the ability to act in light of (1) to (5).[21]

Note that the arguments of this section do not constitute a solution to the free-will problem. They do, however, shift the terms of debate regarding the worry about physical determinism – the worry that human behaviour is entirely determined by our parts, be they ultimate physical constituents, our genes or our neurons. The question is no longer whether processes at these lower levels are deterministic, but rather whether higher-level systems, in general, are entirely governed by the behaviour of their parts. We see now that this is often not the case, and this recognition opens the door for investigation of how humans' neural and social complexity gives them (a degree of) control over their own bodies and behaviour.

DIVINE ACTION AND THE INTEGRITY OF NATURE

Interventionist accounts of divine action have been criticized for a variety of reasons: it would be irrational for God to set up natural laws and then violate (contradict) them; God's acting in the world reduces God to one cause among many; or God's intervention violates the functional integrity of the created order. The immanentist account evades all of these difficulties, but it is functionally equivalent to Deism, in that it does not allow for designating any particular events (for example, the exodus from Egypt, the birth and life of Jesus, the formation of the church) as God's acts in any stronger sense than, say, the migration of any people group to new territory. Worse, how can one avoid describing the birth of a Hitler as any less an act of God?

Much effort has been invested in recent decades in finding clues in contemporary science that allow for an account of special, providential divine actions, without postulating violation of natural laws or of the integrity of nature more generally. There are two strategies relevant to the present discussion of reduction, emergence and downward causation.

Arthur Peacocke was instrumental in assembling and developing resources for understanding downward causation and emergence.[22] He preferred to speak of whole–part constraint rather than downward causation because it disallows the illusion of the whole somehow being other than its parts, and because the term 'constraint' involves relations within the system other than the push and pull of physical causes.[23]

Peacocke also provided an illuminating model for picturing the relations between theology and the sciences. If it is the case that, as one ascends the hierarchy of the sciences, one studies not only more complex systems but also more comprehensive systems, then theology ought to be considered the science at the top of the hierarchy, because it is the discipline that studies the most complex system possible, that of the relation between God and all of the rest of reality. He called his account of the relation of God to the world (a version of) panentheism, meaning that God is immanent in the whole of creation, but also transcends creation. Thus, he wrote that God is in the world, but the world is also, in a sense, in God. God's action, then, is to be understood by analogy to the whole–part constraint that occurs within the created order.

This account of divine action is appealing owing to its consistency with the paradigm or worldview changes described in this chapter. However, there may be a crucial disanalogy between God's relation to the world and the relation of a physical entity or system to its parts.

Juarrero offers the following as an illustration of the sort of context-sensitive constraints that operate in complex systems. At the beginning of a card game with four players, the probability of being dealt an ace is one in thirteen. However, the progress of the game changes the probabilities.

> [O]nce players A, B, and C have already been dealt all four aces, the probability that player D has one automatically drops to 0. The change occurs because within the context of the game, player D's having an ace is not independent of what the other players have. Any prior probability in place before the game starts suddenly changes because, by establishing interrelationships among the players, the rules of the game impose second-order contextual constraints (and thus conditional probabilities).

> ... [N]o external force was impressed on D to alter his situation. There was no forceful efficient cause separate and distinct from the effect. Once the individuals become card players, the conditional

probabilities imposed by the rules and the course of the game itself alter the prior probability that D has an ace, not because one thing bumps into another but because each player is embedded in a web of interrelationships.[24]

So it is certainly the case that the laws of physics and biology do not determine D's being dealt an ace. Nonetheless, ordinary physical processes need to be in operation for the players to exist, to be able to move the cards, and so forth. It is because the players, the cards, the table are composed of matter, with its regular sorts of processes, that the card game can take place at all. The disanalogy in the case of divine action is that, unless one wants to hold a position comparable to pantheism (God and the world are identical), God is not literally (partially) composed of the entities in nature.

Peacocke's account, however, could be supplemented by the second major approach to divine action, called the theory of quantum divine action (QDA). This approach also emphasizes God's immanence in all of nature; thus, necessarily God is immanent in the events and entities at the quantum level. Robert John Russell has been the most prolific defender of QDA. He argues that God acts directly at the quantum level both to sustain the development of elementary processes and also to determine otherwise indeterminate quantum events. This latter sort of action is the means by which God brings about special, providential and revelatory events at the macro-level.[25] God's action is in co-operation with natural causes: it involves 'a continuous creative (divine) presence within each (quantum) event, co-determining the outcome of these elementary physical processes'.[26] So this is not a picture of God occasionally acting from outside the world, but rather a very precise way of providing scientifically informed specification of the nature of immanent divine causation. Because of the (widely accepted) ontological indeterminacy of events at the quantum level, there is no violation of natural laws or causal overdetermination.

This account of divine action has many critics. One criticism is that action only at the quantum level would entail almost no possibility for noticeable events at the macroscopic level. Other criticisms turn on technical disagreements about issues in quantum physics, which cannot be addressed here.[27]

The first objection can be addressed by pointing out that QDA does not postulate that God can act in only one quantum event at a time. Hence, the charge that individual quantum events have limited effects because all are averaged out at the macro-level is beside the point.

Second, there are in fact very important points at which individual quantum events do have significant effects, such as in causing some of the mutations that drive the evolutionary process.[28] It is also likely that quantum events play a direct role in brain processes, thus potentially affecting human thoughts and emotions.

Finally, if one divine action problem is to explain how God acts at all, a second problem is the question of why, in the face of so much suffering, God appears to do so little. If God does restrict divine activity to the quantum level in order to preserve the integrity of nature, this criticism of the limited scope of possible divine acts is actually a help in addressing one aspect of the problem of evil: the question of why God so often appears not to act.

Note that divine action as here understood will always be invisible to science, since it will originate in events that can only appear to scientific investigation as chance occurrences. The claim that the role of chance in nature (especially evolution) rules out divine creativity actually puts the matter backwards. It is the absence of deterministic explanations that makes an account of non-interventionist divine action possible. Note also that Russell's proposal is not a contribution to the intelligent design movement, since the movement assumes an interventionist account of divine action such that ruling out a natural cause is grounds for postulating a non-natural designer.

I suggested above that Peacocke's account and QDA might be seen as complementary. QDA fills in the specifics of how God influences the world-as-a-whole, namely by immanent action at the quantum level. Furthermore, it is in agreement with Van Gulick's emphasis on downward causation via selection: God selects among the causal powers of lower-level entities.

Peacocke's final work was an essay employing the concepts of emergence and downward causation to explore Christian doctrines. If we countenance divine action via quantum events in the human brain, then it can be worked into a synthesis with, for example, Peacocke's account of the Eucharist or Lord's Supper as an emergent phenomenon, with downward effects on the participants. Peacocke emphasizes a distinctive complex of interrelations here: individual believers obeying Jesus' teaching; the authorization of the church to carry on the ritual; the use of bread and wine, not only parts of the material world, but the material world made over by created co-creators; the tie to Jesus' self-sacrifice; Jesus' promise to be present again in this recalling of the events of his death and resurrection; the presence of God; and the transformation of the community. He writes, 'Do we not have in the eucharist an exemplification of the emergence of a new kind of reality requiring a distinctive ontology? For what (if one dare so put it) "emerges" in the eucharistic event *in toto* can only be described in special non-reducible terms such as "Real Presence".[29]

If we think of the God–world relation as the highest of complex systems, then God's action is downward, in the first instance, to the lowest levels and, via bottom-up causation, up to the levels of the human and the social, which in turn have downward effects in individuals' lives and in the ways humans reconfigure the world in light of their religious beliefs.

So the overturning of the causal reductionism that characterized much of modern thought has immense consequences for religion. It helps to defuse some of the most significant objections to traditional views of humans as free and morally responsible. It offers promising, scientifically informed ways of understanding God's immanent divine action in nature and human life. And note that there is no conflict between the theories of divine action presented here and the thesis of human free will, since the point of these accounts of divine action was to flesh out the theological intuition that God respects the integrity of nature. *A fortiori* these accounts assume that God's action in human life is largely to uphold our capacity for free action. In so far as greater capacity to imagine future behavioural scenarios contributes to free will, God's action at the neural level might account for that still, small voice that has long been taken to provide invitation to a fuller, freer life.

Notes

1 Richard Rorty, *Philosophy and the Mirror of Nature* (Princeton University Press, 1979), p. 12.
2 Carl Hempel, *Aspects of Scientific Explanation* (New York: The Free Press, 1965).
3 Ernst Nagel, *The Structure of Science* (New York: Harcourt, Brace, and World, 1961).
4 The most impressive is Robert Kane, *The Significance of Free Will* (Oxford and New York: Oxford University Press, 1998).
5 Nancey Murphy, *Beyond Liberalism and Fundamentalism: How Modern and Postmodern Philosophy Set the Theological Agenda* (Valley Forge, PA: Trinity Press International, 1996).
6 Roy Wood Sellars, *The Philosophy of Physical Realism* (1932; reprint New York: Russell and Russell, 1966), p. 5.
7 Roy Wood Sellars, *Principles of Emergent Realism: the Philosophical Essays of Roy Wood Sellars*, ed. by Preston Warren (St Louis, MO: Warren H. Green, 1970), pp. 136–8.
8 Roger W. Sperry, *Science and Moral Priority: Merging Mind, Brain, and Human Values* (New York: Columbia University Press, 1983), p. 117.

9   Donald T. Campbell, '"Downward Causation" in Hierarchically Organised Biological Systems', in F.J. Ayala and T. Dobzhansky (eds.), *Studies in the Philosophy of Biology* (Berkeley and Los Angeles: University of California Press, 1974), pp. 179–86.

10 Ibid., p. 180.

11 Robert Van Gulick, 'Who's in Charge Here? And Who's Doing All the Work?', in John Heil and Alfred Mele (eds.), *Mental Causation* (Oxford: Clarendon Press, 1995), pp. 233–56, p. 251.

12 Ibid., p. 252.

13 Robert Van Gulick, 'Reduction, Emergence and Other Recent Options on the Mind/Body Problem: a Philosophic Overview', *Journal of Consciousness Studies* 8, nos. 9–10 (2001), 1–34, pp. 16, 17, 20.

14 For an account of how pre-organic systems can self-organize, see Ilya Prigogine and Isabelle Stengers, *Order Out of Chaos* (London: Heinemann, 1984).

15 Alicia Juarrero, *Dynamics in Action: Intentional Behavior as a Complex System* (Cambridge, MA: MIT Press, 1999).

16 For a more extensive account of emergence and downward causation, see Nancey Murphy and Warren S. Brown, *Did my Neurons Make me Do it?: Philosophical and Neurobiological Perspectives on Moral Responsibility and Free Will* (Oxford University Press, 2007), ch. 2.

17 Galen Strawson, 'Free Will', in Edward Craig (ed.), *Routledge Encyclopedia of Philosophy* (London and New York: Routledge, 1998), vol. III, pp. 743–53, p. 749.

18 Harry Frankfurt, 'Alternative Possibilities and Moral Responsibility', *Journal of Philosophy* 66 (1969), 829–89.

19 Alasdair MacIntyre, *Dependent Rational Animals: Why Humans Need the Virtues* (Chicago: Open Court, 1999), chs. 6 and 8, *passim*.

20 Ibid., pp. 74–5.

21 This analysis is argued in Murphy and Brown, *Did my Neurons Make me Do it?*, pp. 243–4.

22 See, for instance, Peacocke's *Theology for a Scientific Age: Being and Becoming – Natural, Divine and Human*, 2nd enlarged edn (Minneapolis: Fortress Press, 1993).

23 See Juarrero, *Dynamics in Action*, ch. 9 on the definition of constraints and their role in complex systems.

24 Ibid., p. 146.

25 Robert John Russell, *Cosmology from Alpha to Omega: the Creative Mutual Interaction of Theology and Science* (Minneapolis: Fortress Press, 2008), ch. 5.

26 Ibid., p. 156.

27 Ibid., ch. 5 for an overview and response.

28 Ibid., ch. 6.

29 Arthur Peacocke, 'A Naturalistic Christian Faith for the Twenty-First Century: an Essay in Interpretation', in Philip Clayton (ed.), *All That Is: a Naturalistic Faith for the Twenty-First Century* (Minneapolis: Fortress Press, 2007), p. 43.

13 Science, God and cosmic purpose

JOHN HAUGHT

> ... what exhilarates us human creatures more than freedom, more
> than the glory of achievement, is the joy of finding and surrendering to
> a Beauty greater than man, the rapture of being possessed.
>
> (Teilhard de Chardin)[1]

> The teleology of the Universe is directed toward the production
> of Beauty. Thus any system of things which in any wide sense is
> beautiful is to that extent justified in its existence.
>
> (Alfred North Whitehead)[2]

Jews, Christians and Muslims all believe that the universe is the temporal and spatial expression of an eternal meaning or purpose. In these traditions, authentic human life begins with a steady trust that something of everlasting significance is going on in the universe and that our own lives are connected to this larger drama. However, these same faith traditions are also aware that whatever purpose the universe might have can never be made completely clear to mortals. Why not? Because if there is a pervasive purpose in the universe, in order for it to give meaning to our own lives it would have to be larger and deeper than any human mind could fathom. At least, this is the teaching of all traditional theologies. Purpose, if real, would grasp us more than we could grasp it. We could encounter purpose only if we let it take hold of us and carry us away, just as we may have allowed a great symphony or poem to carry us away in its intoxicating beauty. We cannot appreciate a great work of art or allow it to have any impact on us unless we abandon the need to control it intellectually. The same would be true of cosmic purpose.

However, in the age of science can we honestly believe that the universe has any purpose? Is it credible to claim that something of everlasting importance is working itself out in the universe? Of all the questions in science and religion, many of which are discussed by other authors in this volume, I believe the most fundamental is whether the universe has a purpose.

But what do I mean here by purpose? In a general sense, purpose means simply the bringing about of something good. Purpose is the actualizing of a value. Another word for purpose is teleology, from the Greek word *telos*, which means goal or end. What makes any process teleological is that it is on the way towards realizing an objective, goal or end that is self-evidently good. For example, I take my writing this chapter to be purposeful, or teleological, since I have the goal of sharing with readers some ideas that I consider important. Even opponents of theology can understand what I am talking about here. Suppose they take issue with religious and theological claims and bother to write a rebuttal. Their efforts would be just as purposeful as a theologian's since the goal of their arguments, one may presume, would be to serve the larger enterprise of seeking and submitting to something incontestably good and truthful to them. Even their criticism of a faith tradition's belief in purpose would be for them a most purposeful activity, since their efforts would be directed towards the goal of delivering their readers from what they consider to be unnecessary ignorance.

However, the question I am considering in this chapter is whether the universe may in some analogous way also be in the business of 'bringing about something undeniably and everlastingly good'. I say 'everlastingly' because, for the universe to be purposeful, it is not enough that it be in the process of producing something good. This good must also be imperishable in some sense, for no matter how many valuable outcomes the evolving universe may have – such as living, thinking and moral beings – if everything is swallowed up by nothingness in the end, then the universe, even if it exists for trillions of years, can hardly be called purposeful. As a matter of fact, nowadays many scientifically educated people are quite certain that the universe can have no overarching purpose since science predicts that it is heading irreversibly towards a decisive and final death at some point in the future. Physics and astronomy together claim that the entire universe, along with each one of us, is drifting slowly toward an abyss in which everything, including life, consciousness and culture, will perish utterly. The end of all things is zero. Consequently the universe must be purposeless.

This, of course, is not how religions, especially the Abrahamic traditions, see things. They have no trouble agreeing that everything physical, including our own bodily existence and the universe that sustains it, will perish. But they also believe in something eternal. Not everything, in other words, is subject to non-being. In order for anything to exist at all, theologians have argued, there must be a creator, a being that is not capable of non-being. This being believers have called God.

Accordingly, the purpose of the universe is to disclose the infinite divine resourcefulness that gives being to all beings. Simply by existing and witnessing to the infinite creativity of God, the totality of beings is full of purpose.

Moreover, believers trust that the creator's eternal remembrance of everything created will allow the world to be transformed and renewed everlastingly in the form of a new creation. Clearly, then, for theistic faiths nothingness is not the final word, as it is for contemporary scientific sceptics. As long as God exists there is the possibility that whatever perishes, be it an organism, a person or the entire universe, can somehow be rescued from absolute oblivion.

The intuition of biblical faith is that the eternal and infinitely inexhaustible mystery named God has also drawn near to the created universe in love and providential care. In an age of science this latter point, as we shall see below, is especially hard for many to accept. Nevertheless, all three theistic faiths teach that God is personal and responsive rather than impersonal and apathetic. In fact, Christian theology even maintains that the infinite divine mystery of God is also self-emptying love. Christians are taught not to think about God without first thinking of the man Jesus whose selfless laying down of his life is considered to be the decisive manifestation of what God is like.[3] It is this God whom Christians profess to be the ultimate environment, ground and destiny of all being. Out of God's humility and self-giving love the universe has been given its being and its purpose. From a Christian point of view the purpose of the universe is to give expression in space and time to the infinite love that is the ground and source of all being. In their traditional form the God-religions have conceived of the entire cosmos, not just human history, as pulsing with sacred meaning. To think of the universe as purposeless would be inconceivable to most people who have ever believed in God.

COSMIC PESSIMISM

However, this religious and theological way of understanding the world had its origins long before Galileo, Darwin and Einstein. Today many thoughtful people sincerely doubt that trust in divine purpose can survive the age of science. These cosmic pessimists, as I shall be calling them, are scientifically educated people who are convinced that science makes it harder than ever to think of the universe as having any overall meaning to it.

The renowned physicist Steven Weinberg, for example, claims that as the universe has grown more comprehensible to science 'the more pointless it also seems'.[4] Pondering Weinberg's sentiments, astronomer Margaret Geller essentially agrees: 'Does [the universe] have a point? I don't know. It's not clear that it matters. I guess it's a kind of statement that I would never make … It's just a physical system, what point is there?'[5] Also responding to Weinberg, physicist Marc Davis reflects: 'I try not to think about the question [of cosmic purpose] too much, because all too often I agree with Steven Weinberg, and it's rather depressing.' However, he continues, 'That doesn't mean that you can't enjoy your life.'[6] Likewise in agreement with Weinberg, the astronomer Sandra Faber says that the universe appears to her to be 'completely pointless from a human perspective'.[7]

The natural sciences, cosmic pessimists claim, have given us an entirely new picture of the world, one that is impossible to square with the hopes of religious believers. In their personal lives cosmic pessimists are usually not paralysed by melancholy and grief. They may not be optimistic about the long-range future of the universe, but they are generally not gloomy in a pathological way. They cherish life, which they consider precious because it is so precarious. They enjoy participating in communal life with their fellow mortals, and more often than not they are environmentally sensitive and morally altruistic. They typically face the loneliness and sadness of death fatalistically and courageously. But they are convinced that the natural sciences today are inconsistent with the hopeful outlook of their religiously deluded sisters and brothers.[8]

But is science really incompatible with a religious trust in cosmic purpose? Science, it is important to remember, is not formally concerned with the question of cosmic purpose in the first place. What science has to say about the universe is not irrelevant to our question, of course, but science, as a self-limiting method of understanding, cannot even ask, let alone answer, the question of purpose. Modern scientific method, which looks at the world without asking about God, values or meaning, is simply not wired to detect any signals of purpose should the universe be transmitting any.

If scientists express opinions, as they often do, on whether the universe is pointless or not, they are no longer speaking as scientists strictly speaking, but as persons who have turned momentarily into philosophers, pundits or even propagandists. Reflection on the discoveries of science may lead a person to cosmic pessimism, but such reflection is not itself scientific. For example, reflection on Darwin's

evolutionary theory has led many biologists to reject as illusory the idea
of a providential deity. But it is not a prerogative of biology itself to
arrive at such a conclusion. If it were, then scientists and the courts
would hardly be justified in censoring those US public school biology
teachers who instruct their students that subcellular complexity points
to the existence of an intelligent designer.

This is in no way to deny that the life of a scientist or even a cosmic pessimist, since ideally it is oriented towards the discovery of
truth – the most undeniable of all values – may be filled with meaning.
However, this meaning is discovered not by scientific method itself, but
by a pre-scientific faith or trust that truth is worth seeking. Scientific
method does not provide the grounds for the belief that seeking truth is
worthwhile. Rather a faith in the importance of truth-seeking is what
initiates and energizes the actual practice of scientific method.

Even if cosmic purpose is real, therefore, scientific experimentation
as such could never know anything about it. Purpose, in order to give
meaning to our lives, must grasp us more than we could ever grasp it.
We cannot capture or possess purpose scientifically, but we can be captured and possessed by it, and it can motivate us to do science. Purpose
is something we can never wrap our minds around, but we can let it
wrap itself around our minds. We can allow purpose to take hold of us
and fill our brief lives with meaning. But we cannot control it or invent
it by an act of will. It comes in the form of a gift, not as an object to be
mastered. As theologian Paul Tillich insists, ultimate meaning (or purpose) lies outside the boundary of any purely scientific comprehension
or verification.[9]

After Galileo, Einstein and Darwin, however, it seems a considerable stretch for many scientific thinkers to connect ancient ideas of
God and cosmic meaning to the recent discovery of a still unfolding
universe now some 13.7 billion years old. Before the age of evolution
and astrophysics, it was much easier for people to view the universe as
purposeful. This was partly because Western thought took the universe
to be a stationary hierarchy of levels, a Great Chain of Being connecting the world to its creator.[10] The bottom link of the chain consisted of
lifeless matter. Then, higher up came the domains of plants, animals,
humans and angels in ascending order. Above the whole hierarchy of
levels, but infinitely beyond human reach, dwelt the purpose-giving,
eternal and infinite source of all being known as God.[11] The whole of
creation emanated from God on high. Every created level in the hierarchy had the purpose of existing for those above it, and ultimately for

the glory of God. All beings participated, in different degrees, in the eternity of God who was said to exist far beyond the realm of perishable beings. As long as people could think of the created universe and our fragile human existence as tied somehow to the divine permanence, they could also believe that they would be rescued from eventual oblivion and that the cosmos has an eternal meaning to God in spite of the fact that it is perishable.

The question of purpose, we should emphasize, is inseparable from that of perishing. And, as theologian Paul Tillich has observed, the human fear of perishing is at heart the fear of eventually being forgotten. People have always found it hard to bear the thought that their lives will be thrust deeper and deeper into the past and then totally lost to all memory. The search for purpose, therefore, includes the quest not to be forgotten. This is why even morally sensitive non-believers want to leave a permanent mark on the world. They do not want to leave behind at death a world that has been unchanged by their presence. So they seek immortality in many ways, not just through religious faith:

> The Greeks spoke of glory as the conquest of being forgotten. Today, the same thing is called 'historical significance.' If one can, one builds memorial foundations. It is consoling to think that we might be remembered for a certain time beyond death not only by those who loved us or hated us or admired us, but also by those who never knew us except now by name. Some names are remembered for centuries. Hope is expressed in the poet's proud assertion that 'the traces of his earthly days cannot vanish in eons.'[12]

Nevertheless, as Tillich goes on to say, 'those traces, which unquestionably exist in the physical world, are not we ourselves, and they don't bear our name. They do not keep us from being forgotten.'[13] So we ask whether there is anything that can keep us from being totally forgotten. And is there anything that can also keep the whole universe from being pushed into the past and lost forever? Religious luminaries claim there is. Jesus, for example, taught that the hairs of our head are numbered, that our suffering is not in vain, and that the God of life cannot forget us. The psalmist cries out to God: 'Record my lament; list my tears on your scroll – are they not in your record?' (Psalms 56:8 NIV). Our sufferings, as well as our joys, are remembered forever by God. Indeed everything that exists, including the whole universe, can be renewed and redeemed everlastingly by the living God. Tillich once again captures the essence of this religious hope:

> Nothing truly real is forgotten eternally, because everything real comes from eternity and goes to eternity ... Nothing in the universe is unknown, nothing real is ultimately forgotten. The atom that moves in an immeasurable path today and the atom that moved in an immeasurable path billions of years ago are rooted in the eternal ground. There is no absolute, no completely forgotten past, because the past, like the future, is rooted in the divine life. Nothing is completely pushed into the past. Nothing real is absolutely lost and forgotten. We are together with everything real in the divine life.[14]

Today, however, new scientific knowledge about the evolution of life, the depth of time and the ongoing expansion of the universe has apparently demolished the static, vertical hierarchy that had reached upward to eternity and given so much comfort to anxious religious believers here below. Science, we might say, has flattened, temporalized or horizontalized the Great Chain of Being. Plants, animals and humans are now understood to have evolved only gradually, over an unimaginable span of time, out of an impersonal matrix of lifeless matter. Lowly matter, the bottom rung in the classical ladder of levels, now seems to be the ultimate origin and final destiny of everything – including beings endowed with minds. Purpose, it now appears, is nothing more than an illusion fabricated by pre-scientific imaginations to make the cosmos seem more imperishable and less hollow than it really is.

As if the mindless dragging on of time and the fading of everything into the past were not enough to establish a sufficient basis for cosmic pessimism, the ragged story of life as told by evolutionary biology appears to do so decisively. During the past century and a half Charles Darwin's science has made it plain to many naturalists that life has flourished not because of any divine supervision or purpose, but simply because of the combining of blind accidents with the impersonality of natural selection. Life scientists now realize that only relatively few organisms have been selected by nature to survive and produce offspring. Evolution, they insist, is completely devoid of any foresight. The emergence of life's extravagant diversity of species has occurred over an immense expanse of time with no goal or purpose in mind. Even purpose-oriented human minds are the result of an adaptive but mindless process. According to many if not most contemporary biologists there is nothing inevitable about the appearance of human beings. If sufficient time is available, small variations blindly selected by nature can eventually lead to all the diversity and design evident in the life-world.

Contemporary cosmology and Darwinian biology, then, have seemingly ravaged the sacred hierarchy prized by traditional theistic faiths. The natural sciences have made the universe seem devoid of both principle and purpose. Heartwarming religious accounts of a purposeful universe must now give way to the coldness of scientific realism.[15] Evolutionary biology and Big Bang cosmology have conspired to wrest the world free from any entanglement with eternity. Accordingly, the inanimate material realm, which was the lowest and least real level in most religious cosmologies, has now usurped the status of ultimate origin and explanation of life and mind alike.[16] For cosmic pessimists, matter, the lowest level in the classic hierarchy, has currently become the quasi-eternal origin and destiny of all being. And everything that has ever materialized out of this ground state of being must eventually return to and lose itself forever in the blank dumbness from which it arose.[17]

In the process of divesting the cosmos so completely of meaning, scientific thought has simultaneously atomized everything as well. Atomism is the method of mentally decomposing complex entities into elemental units such as quarks, electrons, atoms, molecules, genes or cells. The method of atomistic analysis is entirely proper to science, but atomism has also fostered the worldview I am calling cosmic pessimism. Atomism decomposes the exquisitely layered hierarchical and purposeful universe of religious cosmology into the dust of elementary, incoherent fragments. In the wake of such granulation, the ancient and medieval sense of discontinuity between inanimate matter and living beings fades away completely.[18] As a result of atomism the theistic conviction that divine wisdom pervades the universe dissolves as well.

THE SIGNIFICANCE OF INFORMATION

Even so, at least to many scientifically enlightened religious thinkers, the implicit assumption that natural science necessarily entails a purposeless universe has no basis in reality. The horizontalizing and atomizing of the cosmos may be useful as far as scientific method is concerned. But, logically speaking, it is no less possible today than it was for religious people in the past to embrace a religious intuition of cosmic purpose. Before jumping to the conclusion that science inevitably entails cosmic pessimism it may be instructive to look first at how the recent emphasis on information by a number of scientific thinkers allows, at least in principle, for a hierarchical and teleological universe.

The philosopher and scientist Michael Polanyi, for example, has argued that the recent discovery by science of the role of information in nature is enough to demonstrate that science is not logically incompatible with the idea of a hierarchically organized universe and a sense of purpose in nature. Hierarchy, after all, need not be vertical and static, as traditionally understood. Rather, it may be thought of as emerging stepwise over the course of a long span of time. In an emergent universe the discontinuity between various levels of being consists, in part at least, of informational differences operative at each level of organization. These informational differences are not washed out by nature's gradualism or by the unbroken historical flow from material, to living, to mental states of being.[19]

Nature, as it turns out, is composed not only of matter and energy but also of information. The most conspicuous instance of information in nature is the configuration of DNA molecules in the nuclei of living cells. After specifying the role of nucleic and amino acids in cells and organisms some scientists and philosophers were seduced into thinking that life, since it is made up of molecules and atoms, is just chemistry. This was the conclusion of both Francis Crick and James Watson, the co-discoverers of the double helix formation in cellular DNA.[20] However, even though a biochemist may view genetic DNA strictly as an interesting chain of chemicals, an informational point of view will see something more: the DNA in a living cell is arranged in a specific sequence of triadic arrangements of four letters (A, T, G and C). Any particular distribution of letters is consistent with chemistry, but chemistry itself cannot specify in any particular case why the letters are arranged just so. Indeed the chemical processes that create DNA are the same from one organism to another, no matter what pattern the letters follow.

Chemistry, one might say, is indifferent to the sequence of letters that encode the particular species and unique traits of an organism. According to Polanyi, it is the specific sequence of the letters in DNA, not neutral chemical processes, that makes one organism turn out to be a human being rather than a monkey or frog. So obviously there is much more to life than just chemistry. The informational aspect of DNA (and RNA) is what places an organism in a distinctive species and outlines the unique identity of each living being. Viewed materialistically, DNA may be just chemistry, but from an informational point of view the specific sequence of nucleotides is logically distinguishable from, and undetermined by, the material processes operative in all living beings.

To avoid any misunderstanding, this is nothing like the proposals made by advocates of intelligent design. Here Polanyi is not suggesting that an invisible divine hand somehow directly arranges the sequence of letters in the cell's nuclear DNA. His point is simply that a chemically unspecifiable informational pattern enters unobtrusively into nature and brings about sharp ontological (hierarchical) discontinuity between levels of being without interrupting physical, chemical or evolutionary processes. Informational discontinuity can exist at one level of understanding while physical gradualism and continuity are seen to be operative at another. Both the historical (evolutionary) and atomistic understandings of nature are perfectly compatible with an informational reading.[21]

By analogy, meaning or purpose could in principle be quietly and effectively present in the physical universe without ever showing up on scientific registers. Knowledge of chemical laws alone is not enough to equip a scientist either to observe or to read the informational aspect of a cell or organism. Only an informational kind of reading allows human observers to take note of the fact that there is a non-chemical aspect to living beings. It takes a special kind of training of the human mind to recognize the hierarchically emergent levels of being. Chemical expertise is not enough. In an analogous way, most traditional religions and philosophies have insisted that being able to read a purpose in the universe requires that one first undergo a personal transformation that would prepare one's consciousness to be grasped and carried away by ultimate reality and meaning. Science by itself cannot provide the instructions needed to read and interpret such a momentous experience. But nothing in science forbids it either.

COSMIC PESSIMISM AND THE NEW COSMOLOGY

My next consideration in this discussion of science and cosmic purpose is that contemporary astronomy, astrophysics and cosmology have now weakened and possibly destroyed one of the linchpins of cosmic pessimism. Belief that the cosmos is pointless has been closely associated with the assumption that the physical stuff of the universe is essentially mindless and that the eventual emergence of beings endowed with minds is the result of a series of mere flukes. Science itself, however, has now challenged this materialist assumption. As a result of increasingly more precise measurements, and the blossoming of relativity theory and quantum mechanics, it has become increasingly evident that the physics of the Big Bang universe has a much tighter connection to the existence of living and thinking beings than scientists formerly thought. In order for our universe to become alive and, at least in human beings, conscious of itself, the physical characteristics of this universe had to be remarkably right from the beginning. The mathematical values associated with the physical constants and initial conditions that would allow for the eventual emergence of life and mind billions of years after the Big Bang seem to have been fine-tuned very precisely at the very start. Even the slightest variation in these mathematical values, and life and mind could never have appeared.[22]

What is the scientific basis of this rather surprising claim? In order to have mind (in the sense of human consciousness), science now realizes, there had to be brains with sufficient physiological complexity to engage in what we call thought. However, in order to produce brains capable of thought, a long process of Darwinian evolution was needed to bring about a cerebral complexity sufficient to allow thought to occur. But, of course, evolution requires the existence of life, and life in turn requires carbon and other chemical elements. Astrophysicists have learned recently that in order for the universe to give birth to life, massive stars are needed to cook primordial hydrogen and helium into carbon, nitrogen, oxygen and other elements needed to make living cells and organisms. Moreover, one cannot take these massive stellar furnaces for granted. Astrophysicists now realize that such huge celestial bodies would never have formed at all except for a very precise rate of cosmic expansion (Hubble constant) and gravitational pull. And we must remember that these exact values had to have come into play at the very first instant of our universe's existence. An infinitesimally slower or faster rate of cosmic expansion, or a slightly weaker or stronger gravitational pull at the start, and the door to the emergence of supernovae, carbon, life and mind would have been closed. The existence of life and mind, therefore, seems to be tied in a non-arbitrary manner to the precise way in which the whole universe has been configured physically from the outset.[23]

Can we make anything of this remarkable set of coincidences as far as the question of cosmic purpose is concerned? I have no intention here of turning the new astrophysical knowledge directly into an argument for the existence of God or cosmic purpose, even though others have done so. It is sufficient for now to acknowledge that the existence of life and mind are inseparable from the general make-up of the universe. This would not be surprising except for the fact that, as astronomer Martin Rees has pointed out, the general features of the universe could very well have been otherwise physically speaking, at least as far as we know.[24] Given only an infinitesimally different set of physical values, life and mind would not have existed and evolved in our Big Bang universe. Given the physics of the early universe, the emergence of mind in our cosmos now looks a lot less improbable than it has to most modern cosmic pessimists. There is still plenty of room for contingency in the life process, but the physical stuff of the universe is such that it would be rash to keep claiming that universe is essentially lifeless and mindless. And since most modern scientific materialists and cosmic pessimists still base their rejection of cosmic purpose on the belief that the universe is essentially mindless, contemporary science provides ample reason to question that assumption.

Of course, one may always respond by imaginatively conjuring up, as the backdrop for our own universe, the idea of a multiverse. A multiverse, if it exists, would be an enormously large plurality of mostly lifeless and to us unobservable universes. The existence of an unimaginably large number of universes would increase the chances that a mind-bearing universe such as our own would pop up once, or perhaps occasionally, without having to be planned. So our own universe, which from our narrow human point of view seems to be fine-tuned for life, would really be a purely pointless accident in a natural process of blind cosmic experiments. Of course, there is no way, at least so far, of either proving or falsifying the multiverse theory. Nonetheless it has become a favourite refuge for contemporary cosmic pessimists since it seems to deny any essential connection between nature and consciousness.

In order to address this increasingly common, but so far unconfirmed conjecture, I propose that readers take a new look at the evolutionary ideas of Pierre Teilhard de Chardin (1881–1955). More earnestly than almost any other important thinker in the late modern world, this famous Jesuit geologist argued that the cosmos and consciousness are inseparable from each other. The universe is fundamentally conscious – even though scientific method conventionally avoids any formal acknowledgement of subjectivity and conscious experience. The emergence and intensification of consciousness, Teilhard proposes, is not a local terrestrial accident, even if our planet is the only place where life and mind have actually blossomed. Even if the emergence of consciousness is only local it requires a root system that is cosmic in scope.[25]

Teilhard's cosmic vision, I believe, is wide enough to accommodate a multiverse as well, if indeed there is any such larger array. In our own universe the existence of consciousness anywhere, even if only on earth, still requires the fermentation of a whole universe. So in a parallel way Teilhard's thought allows in principle that the existence of one life-bearing universe may also require the fermentation of a multiverse. The presence of consciousness in only one very local region or epoch of a multiverse may still have a tight connection to the larger panorama. Consider the fact that astronomers are right now extending their own minds out over a hypothesized plurality of worlds so as to pull this enormity into the sphere of what is intelligible. This expansiveness is enough to demonstrate that consciousness can in a sense be everywhere. The leap of our minds in the direction of a multiverse is not one that Teilhard actually made, but it is perfectly consistent with his wide vision of a world now awakening to consciousness.

To the scientific naturalist, of course, it seems obvious that life and mind are unintended accidents, simply because their emergence is apparently both late and local. However, as Teilhard rightly remarked in 1931, 'even if life was, and had to remain, peculiar to the earth, it would not follow that it was "accidental" to the world' as such. Life and consciousness may seem to be 'peculiar to the earth', but they would still be 'the life and thought of the world' as a whole.[26] If necessary, the idea of world, or theologically speaking the idea of creation, can easily be extended so as to embrace a multiverse as well.

Long before recent astrophysics tightened up the linkage between the existence of mind and the fundamental physical features of the Big Bang universe, Teilhard had already written:

> Man 'the thinker', generally regarded as an 'irregularity' in the universe, is precisely one of those special phenomena by which one of the most basic aspects of the cosmos is revealed to us with a degree of intensity that renders it immediately recognizable ... We must make up our minds, by virtue of the general perspectives of evolution themselves, to make a special place in the physics of the universe for the powers of consciousness ...[27]

Again, the same line of reasoning could easily accommodate the idea of a multiverse even if consciousness breaks out only on one planet in one of countless universes. So I suggest that it is consistent with Teilhard's cosmic vision that we read multiverse wherever he uses the terms 'world' and 'universe'. By insisting that 'the physics of the universe' is not completely intelligible apart from the existence of mind, Teilhard is not offering us an offensively anthropocentric perspective. His purpose is not to hoist our species or planet above the rest of nature, but instead to understand the whole of nature by starting with a most conspicuous outcome of natural process, namely, the emergent fact of consciousness. Any cosmology that aspires to be comprehensive must not ignore the phenomenon of consciousness as though it were alien or accidental to the character of the universe. The dimension of thought on our planet is seamlessly connected to the process of sidereal, terrestrial and biological evolution. Mind is the most important key we human beings have to understanding what the universe is really all about. It may also be at least one key to understanding what a multiverse is up to as well.

But is there purpose here? For a process to have purpose it must be oriented towards achieving something undeniably valuable. According to Teilhard, in as much as the cosmic process gives birth to consciousness, it exhibits the character of being purposeful, at least as I defined purpose earlier. Purpose means the actualizing of something undeniably treasurable, and consciousness is self-evidently an example.[28] Purpose in the universe may mean much more than the birth of consciousness, but any universe that conspires throughout the totality of its being to bring forth and intensify consciousness could be called purposeful – at least in a minimal sense. And for all we know a multiverse may be required to bring forth only one living and conscious universe. If so, this makes consciousness, which can in principle penetrate the totality of universes and gather them into its expansive sweep, all the more to be treasured.

THE BEAUTY OF IT ALL

Finally, a discussion of cosmic purpose after Darwin and Einstein would do well to consider several ideas of Alfred North Whitehead. Like Teilhard, Whitehead (1861–1946) was both a scientific and religious thinker. He taught at both Cambridge and Harvard universities, and towards the latter part of his productive life he thought he could make out something momentous going on in the universe, something that a cosmic pessimist may have missed altogether. Again like Teilhard, Whitehead was most impressed by the relatively recent scientific discovery that nature is an ongoing, evolving and unfinished process. According to contemporary science the universe has never stood still indefinitely. Whitehead was inquisitive enough to ask why. What is the ultimate reason, he wondered, why the cosmos is a process rather than a state? Science as such could have been quite content with a perfectly static universe, so why is the universe forever restless? Along with scientific answers to that question Whitehead thought there is room for a theological explanation as well. The universe has a purpose. It is that of aiming, under the stimulus of a divine persuasive love, towards ever more intense instances of beauty.[29]

In Whitehead's philosophy beauty means, quite simply, the 'harmony of contrasts' or the 'ordering of novelty'.[30] Beauty requires for its actualization a synthesis of these polar elements. Contrast or novelty, without some degree of harmony and order to balance it, amounts to mere chaos or discord. But harmony or order without contrast and novelty is mere triviality or monotony. Neither chaos nor monotony is aesthetically satisfying. Beauty is composed of elements forever in tension and in danger of falling apart altogether. Beauty risks disorder on the one side and tedious uniformity on the other. Its existence is both precious and precarious.

Though ignored by science as such, at the heart of cosmic process there lies an aim towards beauty. This aim, according to Whitehead, is enough to give purpose to the universe. For if purpose, as I defined it earlier, means the actualizing of something self-evidently valuable – and beauty is such a self-evident value – then the universe can rightly be said to be purposeful. Moreover, Whitehead's cosmological vision is also wide enough to include a multiverse, so when I use the term 'universe' below I take it to include a possible plurality of universes or what Whitehead sometimes called cosmic epochs.

The universe, in any case, has now shown itself to be something more than an aimless drifting through time. Even if a cosmic aim towards beauty is not obvious to most of us, it is undeniable that there has been a net increase in the intensity of ordered novelty in the universe. There has been an increase, for example, in the organic complexity of living beings and in the capacity of organisms to feel. Your own consciousness – as you read this chapter and raise questions and criticisms and experience different emotions about what I have been saying – is clear evidence of what Whitehead is claiming. After all, what is more beautiful and fragile than a mind? But it takes a whole universe to make something as exquisitely beautiful as a mind.

The universe may at times appear discordant, monotonous or insensate, but in making minds, and in making minds that in turn can make endlessly beautiful products, it has given birth to a grandeur that is always open to novelty. Within his expansive cosmic vision Whitehead is also proposing that there is plenty of room for the central insights of religious faiths that profess belief in a cosmic purpose. Even the struggle and suffering that occur in the evolution of life is not inconsistent with the idea of a general cosmic aim towards more intense beauty.[31]

I propose, then, that the general features of the universe are configured in accordance with what might be called the aesthetic cosmological principle. Unlike the anthropic cosmological principle, which typically interprets initial physical conditions and cosmic constants as predicting the emergence of human consciousness, the aesthetic cosmological principle suggests, much more broadly, that the fundamental properties of the universe are oriented towards the ongoing production of instances of beauty and the intensifying of a capacity in some organisms for aesthetic experience. In a comparable way, the physicist Freeman Dyson once conjectured that the universe is fashioned by a principle of maximum diversity. According to this principle, Dyson noted, 'the laws of nature and initial conditions are such as to make the universe as interesting as possible'.[32] Similarly, on the basis of a joint reading of Whitehead and contemporary astrophysics, I am suggesting here that the universe (or multiverse) is bounded by an aesthetic cosmological principle and that the purpose of this totality is, at least from one point of view, that of maximizing beauty. Accordingly the meaning of our own lives may be that of participating in and prolonging the cosmic aim towards intensifying beauty in whatever way we can.

In conclusion, then, we do not have to view science as the frustration of religious hope or as antagonistic to the human search for meaning. Our need for meaning is one of the traits that distinguish human beings, including scientists, from other living entities. Human beings are most fully alert and alive when they are trying to make sense of things and when they are being drawn towards what is good, true and – perhaps above all – beautiful. Science is an important part of this adventure, but it is not all there is to it. To scientific and religious thinkers such as Polanyi, Teilhard and Whitehead, human vitality, unlike that of other organisms, depends upon our feeling our way towards an inexhaustible goodness, truth and beauty – that is, towards what some religions call God.

Notes

1   Pierre Teilhard de Chardin, *Hymn of the Universe*, trans. by Gerald Vann (New York: Harper Colophon, 1969), p. 119.
2   Alfred North Whitehead, *Adventures of Ideas* (New York: The Free Press, 1967), p. 265.
3   The late Pope John Paul II put it this way: 'The prime commitment of theology is the understanding of God's *kenosis* [self-emptying], a grand and mysterious truth for the human mind, which finds it inconceivable that suffering and death can express a love which gives itself and seeks

nothing in return.' Pope John Paul II, *Encyclical Letter Fides et Ratio* (1998, 9/14), # 93.

4   Steven Weinberg, *The First Three Minutes* (New York: Basic Books, 1977), p. 144.

5   Alan Lightman and Roberta Brawer, *Origins: the Lives and Worlds of Modern Cosmologists* (Cambridge, MA: Harvard University Press, 1990), p. 340.

6   Ibid., p. 377.

7   Ibid., p. 340.

8   See Richard Dawkins, *The God Delusion* (New York: Houghton Mifflin, 2006); Sam Harris, *The End of Faith: Religion, Terror, and the Future of Reason* (New York: W. W. Norton, 2004); Sam Harris, *Letter to a Christian Nation* (New York: Knopf, 2007).

9   See, for example, Paul Tillich, *Dynamics of Faith* (New York: Harper Torchbooks, 1958), p. 76; Paul Tillich, *Systematic Theology*, 3 vols. (Chicago: University of Chicago Press, 1967), vol. i, pp. 3–159.

10   Arthur O. Lovejoy, *The Great Chain of Being: a Study of the History of an Idea* (New York: Harper and Row, 1965).

11   See E. F. Schumacher, *A Guide for the Perplexed* (New York: Harper Colophon, 1978), pp. 18–34.

12   Paul Tillich, *The Eternal Now* (New York: Charles Scribner's Sons, 1963), pp. 33–4.

13   Ibid.

14   Ibid., p. 35.

15   For example, E. O. Wilson, *Consilience: the Unity of Knowledge* (New York: Knopf, 1998).

16   For example, Daniel C. Dennett, *Consciousness Explained* (New York: Little, Brown, 1991).

17   See Hans Jonas, *The Phenomenon of Life* (New York: Harper and Row, 1966), p. 9.

18   Pierre Teilhard de Chardin refers to this point of view as the 'analytical illusion' which falsely supposes that we can explain the phenomena of life and mind fully by breaking them down into mindless units of matter. *Activation of Energy*, trans. by Rene Hague (New York: Harcourt Brace Jovanovich, 1970), p. 139.

19   See Michael Polanyi, *The Tacit Dimension* (Garden City, NY: Doubleday Anchor, 1967); Michael Polanyi, *Personal Knowledge* (New York: Harper Torchbooks, 1964); Michael Polanyi and Harry Prosch, *Meaning* (University of Chicago Press, 1975).

20   Francis H.C. Crick, *Of Molecules and Men* (Seattle: University of Washington Press, 1966), p. 10; J.D. Watson, *The Molecular Biology of the Gene* (New York: W. A. Benjamin, 1965), p. 67.

21   Michael Polanyi, *Knowing and Being*, ed. by Majorie Grene (University of Chicago Press, 1969), pp. 225–39.

22   See Martin Rees, *Just Six Numbers: the Deep Forces that Shape the Universe* (New York: Basic Books, 2000); Martin Rees, *Our Cosmic Habitat* (Princeton University Press, 2001).

23   John Barrow and Frank Tipler, *The Anthropic Cosmological Principle* (Oxford: Clarendon Press, 1986).

24 Rees, *Just Six Numbers*.
25 The most accessible introduction to these ideas is Pierre Teilhard de Chardin, *The Future of Man*, trans. by Norman Denny (New York: Harper and Row, 1964).
26 Pierre Teilhard de Chardin, *Human Energy*, trans. by J.M. Cohen (New York: Harcourt Brace Jovanovich, 1969), p. 25.
27 Ibid., p. 21.
28 For a more thorough development of this point, see my book *Is Nature Enough? Meaning and Truth in the Age of Science* (Cambridge University Press, 2006).
29 Whitehead, *Adventures of Ideas*, p. 265.
30 For the following, see Whitehead, *Adventures of Ideas*, pp. 252–96; *Process and Reality*, pp. 62, 183–5, 255 and *passim*; *Modes of Thought*, pp. 57–63. See also Charles Hartshorne, *Man's Vision of God* (Chicago and New York: Willett, Clark, 1941), pp. 212–29.
31 I have set forth these points in more detail in my books *God after Darwin: a Theology of Evolution* (Boulder: Westview Press, 2000); *Deeper than Darwin: the Prospect for Religion in the Age of Evolution* (Boulder: Westview Press, 2003); and *Is Nature Enough?*
32 Freeman Dyson, *Infinite in All Directions* (New York: HarperCollins, 1988), p. 298.

14 Ways of relating science and religion
MIKAEL STENMARK

The number of books and articles written during the past twenty years on the relationship between science and religion is truly amazing, and new ones are coming out almost every day. The ideas propounded vary widely and the question arises of whether it is possible to classify these differing viewpoints in any meaningful way. An important challenge in the science–religion discussion is therefore to categorize the main ways of relating science and religion. How might this be done in an illuminating and unbiased way that is neither too simplistic nor too complex?

The best-known attempt to offer such an account is Ian Barbour's four-fold typology: the conflict view, the integration view, the dialogue view and the independence view.[1] Others scholars such as Willem B. Drees, John Haught, Ted Peters and myself have responded to Barbour's work and suggested modifications or alternative typologies.[2] In this chapter I shall try to take these discussions a step further.

FOUR SCIENCE–RELIGION MODELS

Nowadays there is a common view that although science and religion were once compatible, and perhaps even mutually supportive, this is no longer true. According to this view, science and religion are in serious tension, even in direct conflict with each other. We have to make up our minds and pick one of them: it is no longer possible to embrace both. Nobel laureate Francis Crick writes: 'Not only do the beliefs of most popular religions contradict each other but, by scientific standards, they are based on evidence so flimsy that only an act of blind faith can make them acceptable.'[3] The philosopher of science John Worrall is even more forthright: 'Science and religion are in irreconcilable conflict ... There is no way in which you can be both properly scientifically minded and a true religious believer.'[4] The promulgations of science are in relentless conflict with those of religion. Let us call this view the irreconcilability model. It says this: Science and religion cannot be reconciled whilst still maintaining their respective identities, the distinctive features that characterize them as science or as religion, and not some other human activity.

Science and religion are incompatible. They compete on the same turf and in the end one will emerge victorious.

Other equally distinguished scholars hold a very different view. Francis Collins, leader of the Human Genome Project, writes: 'In my view, there is no conflict in being a rigorous scientist and a person who believes in a God who takes a personal interest in each one of us ... I will argue that these perspectives not only can coexist within one person, but can do so in a fashion that enriches and enlightens the human experience.'[5] According to the reconciliation model: Science and religion today can be combined or reconciled whilst still maintaining their respective identities and distinctive features.

Science and religion are compatible. However, advocates of the reconciliation model are not the only ones to think that science and religion are compatible. According to the independence model: Science and religion are compatible because today they are two completely separate but legitimate practices with no overlap at all.

The reconciliation model then, in contrast to the independence model, presupposes the existence of some kind of overlap or contact between the two practices. This is why I have sometimes referred to this model as the contact view.[6]

Stephen Jay Gould is one well-known proponent of the independence model. He writes that 'the net, or magisterium, of science covers the empirical realm: what is the universe made of (fact) and why does it work this way (theory). The magisterium of religion extends over questions of ultimate meaning and moral value. These two magisteria do not overlap, nor do they encompass all inquiry ...'[7] Science and religion each has its own distinctive domain and characteristic methods, and each can be justified on its own terms. There are two jurisdictions and each party should keep off the other's turf.

A fourth possibility is the replacement model. Perhaps the best-known advocate of this view is biologist Edward O. Wilson. According to this model: Science could today or in the near future replace religion: that is, the domain of science can be expanded in such a way that science might become our new religion.

On this view, traditional religions are so full of falsehoods and superstition that they have to go, but the mental processes of religious belief represent programmed predispositions whose components were incorporated into the neural apparatus of the brain through thousands

of generations of genetic evolution. As such, they are powerful, ineradicable and at the centre of human social life. Therefore we have to find
a substitute for religion. Wilson writes:

> We are obliged by the deepest drives of the human spirit to make
> ourselves more than animated dust, and we must have a story
> to tell about where we came from, and why we are here. Could
> Holy Writ be just the first literate attempt to explain the universe
> and make ourselves significant within it? Perhaps science is a
> continuation or new and better-tested ground to attain the same
> end. If so, then in that sense science is religion liberated and writ
> large.[8]

One problem is that science lacks the primal source of power that religion, for genetic reasons, is hooked into. This is partly because the evolutionary epic denies immortality to the individual and divine privilege
to society. Moreover, scientific naturalism will 'never enjoy the hot
pleasures of spiritual conversion and self-surrender; scientists cannot
in all honesty serve as priests'.[9] But Wilson, nevertheless, believes that
a way exists to divert the power of religion into the service of science,
even if it will be for the future to tell us how exactly this should be done.
The evolutionary epic is probably the best myth we shall ever have.

REFORMATIVE AND SUPPORTIVE VERSIONS
OF THE RECONCILIATION MODEL

If we survey the extensive science–religion literature we discover that
most of the ideas expressed presuppose an acceptance of the reconciliation model. That is to say, most of the scholars engaged in the dialogue
today maintain or assume that science and religion can be combined
or reconciled in some way or other; yet they differ on how exactly this
should be done, and develop a variety of different standpoints. The
challenge we face, then, is to adjudicate between these views in an
objective way.

Let us go back a step for a moment before we try to respond to this
challenge. Barbour talks not about the irreconcilability model but about
the conflict model. Are these different names for the same core model?
Barbour thinks there are two paradigmatic examples of advocates of the
conflict view: scientific materialists and religious literalists.[10] This is so
because both groups claim that science and religion make rival statements about the same domain, the history of nature, so that one has

to choose between them. This seems like an appropriate classification when it comes to scientific materialists such as Richard Dawkins and Edward O. Wilson, and my examples Crick and Worrall. But why does Barbour classify a religious literalist like Phillip E. Johnson as an advocate of the conflict view? Johnson does indeed believe that the current theory of evolution conflicts with Christian faith.[11] But his further view is, in short, that most contemporary evolutionary biologists have got their theories wrong and, once they get them right, there will no longer be any conflict between science and Christian faith. These practices are, on this particular issue, on the same turf, but the idea is not that in the end one or other will emerge as the winner. Johnson would surely reject Worrall's view that science and religion are in irreconcilable conflict.

What causes confusion is that the notion of conflict between science and religion is, in fact, compatible not only with the irreconcilability model (Barbour's conflict view) but also with the reconciliation model (Barbour's integration and dialogue views). If there is an area of contact or overlap between science and religion there is always the possibility that a conflict might arise, but equally there could be harmony or even mutual support there as well. It follows that although a necessary condition for being a proponent of the irreconcilability model is to claim that there exists a conflict between science and religion, it is not a sufficient condition, since this claim is something that a protagonist for the reconciliation model could maintain just as well. The additional requirement of the irreconcilability model would consist of the idea that religion can never be reconciled with science – one and only one of the two will stand victorious in the end. To avoid any ambiguity on this issue, the suggestion is that we talk about the irreconcilability model rather than the conflict model.

William A. Dembski, Phillip Johnson and other creationists or members of the intelligent design movement embrace one particular version of the reconciliation model, which belongs to the family of reformative views.[12] But Gordon Kaufman and many other liberal theologians also espouse the reconciliation model, albeit from a very different reformative standpoint. Kaufman argues that changes in scientific theory make it necessary to reconstruct the conception of God that has traditionally been endorsed by Christians, Muslims and Jews. There is a conflict between a personal conception of God and scientific theories about cosmic and biological evolution. Instead we should think of God in terms of the metaphor 'serendipitous creativity', that is, roughly, in terms of the coming into being of something new conditioned by an inscrutable mystery of surprise.[13] What characterizes any reformative view of the reconciliation model is the idea that: Science and religion today can be reconciled if one (or both) of them changes (or is modified or reformulated) in some way or another.

Johnson embraces a religion-priority reformative view: there is a conflict or tension between science and religion, but if science were to modify significant parts of evolutionary theory, science and religion could be reconciled. Kaufman's account rather assumes a science-priority reformative view: there is a conflict or tension between science and religion, but if religious believers were significantly to reformulate their conception of God, science and religion could be reconciled.

Arthur Peacocke claims that those attempting to develop a Christian theology which takes into account contemporary science have been content to leave intact relatively traditional formulations of the Christian faith, but he thinks that we have to realize that 'radical revisions ... are necessary if coherence and intellectual integrity are to be achieved'.[14] Although Peacocke regards his view as radical, and like Kaufman rejects the supernaturalism of traditional Christianity, he still understands God not merely as a symbol of a profound and unknowable mystery, but as a personal being with specific intentions. This makes his view of religion less revisionary than Kaufman's. On the other hand, John Polkinghorne, who like Peacocke is a scientist-turned-theologian, would argue that traditional formulations of the Christian faith can be left relatively intact.[15] Theologian Keith Ward would probably be of a similar opinion, for he contends that Peacocke's alternative to traditional theism, theistic naturalism, would make any personal theist wince.[16]

There are two issues here. First, in the area of overlap between science and religion, do both need to change or just one of them? Second, how much do religion and/or science need to change? What is evident is that some scholars think that the overlap between science and religion is fairly limited, whereas others reckon that it is more substantial, although they too would maintain that the major part of both these practices lies outside this intersection. It might therefore be fruitful to distinguish between weak and strong versions of the reconciliation model. How should one make such a distinction? What, more precisely, is it that they are weak or strong about?

One idea is to suggest, as Barbour does, that someone who limits the area of contact to metaphysical presuppositions, methods of inquiry, conceptual tools or models and the like, exemplifies the weak view, whereas the strong view adds to these the theoretical content of science (theories) and religion (beliefs and stories). The weak view characterizes his dialogue view and the strong one his integration view.[17] But what if someone claims that the methods of the two practices are, or should be, the same in the sense that the only evidence that ought to be allowed in both science and religion is observational evidence of the kind that is used in the natural sciences? Such an overlap at the methodological level between science and religion might entail far more radical changes in religion than would result if we were to claim that, for instance, the Christian doctrine of original sin must be modified in the light of changes in scientific theory. When it comes to theories of language, similar radical outcomes would follow if one embraced the positivist idea that the only cognitively meaningful statements are empirical propositions verifiable by sense data. Many religious statements would then lose their cognitive status, failing even to be true or false.

The foregoing discussion suggests rather that we should focus directly on the need to reformulate one of the two practices in the light of the other. So if one claims that only minor reformulations or changes to religion (typically, but not necessarily; because it could be science that needs to change instead) are called for in the area of conflict, then one holds a weak view. If more substantial reformulations or changes to religion (again typically, but not necessarily; it could be science that needs to change) are called for, then what we have is a strong view. Ward and Polkinghorne would then be regarded as advocates of a weak reformative reconciliation model, whereas Kaufman and Peacocke would support a strong reformative reconciliation model.

However, there is still something missing from our typology. So far we have assumed that the only kind of relationship between science and religion in the area of overlap, when expressed in more negative terms, is one of conflict or tension, or, if expressed in more positive terms, one of change or reformulation. But the relationship could just as well be one of support, reinforcement or confirmation. While there is potential for conflict (and therefore need for reformulation), there is also potential for mutual support. The emphasis is now on not science or religion needing to change or undergo reformulation, but rather the suggestion that each supports, reinforces or affirms the other. What, then, characterizes the supportive view of the reconciliation model is the idea that: Science and religion today can be reconciled, not because one (or both) of them can change its content without losing its identity, but because they can actually support or confirm each other in one way or another.

One aspect of contemporary science that has frequently been suggested as supporting religion (or, at least, some forms of religion) is the fine-tuning argument (discussed in chapter 8). Science has discovered that many of the fundamental parameters of physics and the initial conditions of the universe must be finely tuned in order for intelligent life to occur. The fine-tuning of these parameters and initial conditions is just what one would expect if life and consciousness were among the goals of a rational and purposeful God. It is not what one would expect if the cosmos is merely the outcome of chance. These remarkable coincidences seem to give some support to beliefs found in at least the Abrahamic religions. But how much support? Barbour thinks that this fine-tuning is merely consistent with belief in God, so we should think about a relationship of consistency rather than of support.[18] Polkinghorne disagrees. Although he does not think that the theistic conclusion is logically coerced by these scientific discoveries, he believes they still offer support for theism and promote a revival of a cautiously revised form of natural theology.[19] Oxford philosopher of religion Richard Swinburne seems ready to go yet one step further when he writes: 'The very same criteria which scientists use to reach their own theories led us to move beyond those theories to a creator God who sustains everything in existence ... The very success of science in showing us how deeply orderly the natural world is provides strong grounds for believing that there is an even deeper cause of that order.'[20] So then, when it comes to supportive views, it might again be helpful to divide them into weak and strong views.

Another example of a supportive view is Fritjof Capra's conception of the relationship between modern physics and Eastern religions. Newtonian physics was in conflict, or at least tension, with Eastern religious beliefs, but with the development of the new physics things have changed. Capra's conclusion is that 'a consistent view of the world is beginning to emerge from modern physics which is harmonious with ancient Eastern wisdom'.[21] To a limited but still significant extent the theories of contemporary physics confirm the Eastern wisdom – a wisdom which Hindus, Buddhists and others have acquired in different ways and by different means.

I have so far presented the reformative view and the supportive view as mutually exclusive. It is probably true that someone like Kaufman would not go further than endorsing the (science-priority) reformative view, and this would also be true for many of the scholars engaged in the science–religion dialogue. But one could, of course, both think that religion might have to reformulate some of its content (in the light of recent scientific discoveries or theoretical development) and at the same time believe that one practice can support the other in some other area of common interest. For instance, on the one hand, the traditional

Judeo-Christian view held that the first human beings, Adam and Eve, were created in the Garden of Eden. But evolutionary theory undermines the idea that there was a paradise without conflict, death and suffering, and says that we are the descendants of earlier, pre-human beings. So the traditional doctrine of the Fall must be reinterpreted. On the other hand, Robert Wright says that 'the idea that John Stuart Mill [and many modern social scientists after him] ridiculed – of a corrupt human nature, of "original sin" – doesn't deserve such summary dismissal'.[22] A tendency to sin, or to do evil, or to be selfish might be a fatal flaw in our nature that we cannot overcome by social engineering. Wright thinks that this is something that evolutionary psychology can confirm. Is this Christian idea then something that theories in evolutionary psychology can, at least to a limited extent, support? John T. Mullen thinks so. He argues that all but one of the versions of the doctrine of original sin that he identifies can 'be rendered more epistemically probable upon the addition of evolutionary psychology to one's belief structure'.[23]

Be that as it may, it is important to distinguish between two sub-models of the reconciliation model: the reformative view which states that science can change, undermine or cause reformulation of religion in the area of contact, or vice versa; and the supportive view which rather entails that science can support, reinforce or confirm religion in the area of contact, or vice versa. These two views can then also be combined, and we would then have a third sub-model, the reformative-supportive view.

Keith Ward's account of the relationship between theism and science would exemplify this last view, but would do so more on the level of principle than do the examples given above. He claims that, according to the theist,

> there exists a supremely perfect creator, since that is the only proper object of unlimited devotion. That in turn entails that any created universe will have a specific character – it will be intelligible, morally ordered and goal directed. Consequently, a demonstration that this universe is not rationally ordered, or that it is non-purposive or morally cruel or even indifferent, will undermine belief in God. It is clear, then that theism is falsifiable ... It is also confirmable, if the universe, as experienced, mediates, at least in part, a personal presence; if it is rationally ordered; if it seems purposive; if it seems conducive to the realization of beauty and virtue, understanding and creativity; and if the idea of God seems coherent and plausible.[24]

The Dalai Lama seems also to advocate a reformative-supportive view in respect to the relationship between Buddhism and science. Although the Dalai Lama thinks that certain aspects of Buddhist thought will have to be modified in the light of scientific discoveries, he also believes that 'it is possible for Buddhism and modern science to engage in collaborative research in the understanding of consciousness . . . By bringing together these two modes of inquiry, both disciplines may be enriched.'[25]

These three views could, moreover, be either strong or weak views, in that they might assume either a substantial or a merely narrow over-lap between science and religion.

COMPLICATING FACTORS

Let us now focus on some elements in the science–religion debate that either complicate the picture so far painted or seem to have been left out of it. Notice first that until this point I have not really said anything about what science and religion actually are. I have just written 'science' or 'religion', assuming perhaps that everyone knows and agrees on what these notions entail. But of course neither in society at large nor within the community of science–religion dialogue do all people agree on these issues. However, the intention behind the typology is actually to leave things quite open at this level of generality. It is only when we move in closer that we need a more detailed map of the terrain than I have given to this point.

On this closer scrutiny, religion could be explicated not merely in terms of different traditional religions such as Christianity, Islam or Buddhism, or more recent phenomena such as Baha'i or what is some-times called the New Age spirituality, but also in terms of traditions or denominations within one religion, such as Orthodox, Catholic and Protestant Christians (or more narrowly still, distinguishing between Lutherans and Calvinists). Hence the relationship between science and Christianity at any one time might look quite different from the rela-tionship between science and Buddhism at the very same time. Suppose for the sake of argument that Dawkins' criticism of Christianity in *The God Delusion* (2006) is correct. The irreconcilability model would then most likely be the best one to use to characterize the relation-ship between science and Christianity today. But Dawkins' arguments would hardly have much impact upon the Eastern wisdom that Capra presents in *The Tao of Physics*. So if we assume that Capra's character-ization of both Eastern wisdom and modern physics is correct, then the relationship between science and say Buddhism would probably be best understood in terms of the supportive view of the reconciliation model. This possibility reveals a danger with the typology proposed – it might give the impression that the relationship between science and religion would be the same for all religions; that one model is the correct one to fit all cases – but this is most likely wrong.

CONSERVATIVE, TRADITIONAL, LIBERAL AND CONSTRUCTIVIST RECONCILIATION MODELS

Further, it might sometimes be necessary to distinguish between more conservative and more liberal groupings within these religions traditions, or denominations. At any particular time there could be major differences between the views held by conservative and liberal Christians on any of these issues. Moreover, it is possible that, at that point in time, there might be greater similarity of view between conservative Christians and conservative Muslims than between conservative and liberal Christians (even though the latter two camps share the same religion).

For instance, conservatives within both Islam and Christianity have argued for a reintegration of science and religion and for a rejection of the Western modernist idea of a religiously neutral science.[26] Zainal Abidin Bagir points out the similarities when he writes: 'For this group [of Muslims], science is not value-free; modern science is coloured by Western secular values; thus Muslims need their own science loaded by Islamic values ... [This] idea is similar in some senses with the idea of "theistic science" which has been intensively discussed among certain American Christian groups ...'[27] But a warning flag needs to be raised here: within a Muslim context is Medhi Golshani, for instance, really a conservative? Rather, would he not be counted as a liberal? Consider what Seyyed Hossein Nasr writes. Nasr tells us that he is at a loss to explain to fellow Muslims why Christian theology seems, at least in liberal circles, to undergo major changes: 'There is nothing in Islam to compare with innovations on the understanding of God from the traditional manner in which Catholic and Protestant theology has understood Him, and to certain current views of the Divinity in evolutionary theology *à la* Teilhard de Chardin or process theology *à la* John Cobb via Alfred North Whitehead.'[28] The answer to the question of whether Muslim scholars such as Golshani and Nasr are conservatives depends on whose scale we are applying. Consider, for example, a parallel case: many people on the right wing of the political scale in Sweden would end up on the left wing of the political scale in the United States; but which scale should be used?

Let us now return to Richard Dawkins. If he is right about the relations between science and religion (it is a big if, but that is beside the point), then, for example, John Polkinghorne's understanding of Christianity would be seriously challenged, whereas Gordon Kaufman's Christian naturalistic theology would remain relatively intact and undisturbed. Again, the typology might give the impression that the relationship between science and Christianity would be the same for all Christians, that is, that one model would correctly represent them all; but this is almost certainly wrong.

If we stick to how the labels 'liberal' and 'conservative' are used in the United States and Europe, and limit ourselves to Christianity, we can formulate four versions of the reconciliation model that would help us locate many of the participants active in the contemporary science–religion dialogue. The idea is to picture a scale with two poles and four suggested stops along the scale, but with no clear-cut boundaries between. One could very well question whether some of the persons I take to exemplify particular views should actually be moved along towards another stop, so to speak. But be that as it may, the important point is that, hopefully, it might illuminate a vital section of the dialogue.

According to the conservative reconciliation model, it is primarily science that needs to change its content, whereas traditional Christianity is to a very large extent satisfactory as it is. Conservative Christians who are severely critical of evolutionary theory would exemplify this view, for instance, Johnson, Dembski and, to a lesser extent perhaps, Alvin Plantinga. Plantinga argues that the theory of evolution is by no means religiously neutral and he is therefore ready to reject parts of it. Science needs to be reconciled with Christianity so that something we might call theistic science is born: 'what we [Christians] need when we want to know how to think about the origin and development of contemporary life is what is most plausible from a Christian point of view'.[29]

According to the traditional reconciliation model, science might need to change some of its content whereas Christianity certainly needs to change some but not most of its traditional content. Situated here, but perhaps positioned somewhat towards the previous model, would be Alister McGrath and Nancey Murphy, whereas Polkinghorne and Ward would be located further along towards the other end. Francis Collins would also be one of the advocates of this view. These scholars read the Bible much less literally than the advocates of the conservative reconciliation model and accept biblical criticism without much question. They are not ready to privilege Christianity to the extent that the advocates of the previous model do, but neither do they privilege science to the extent that the proponents of the next model are typically willing to do. Polkinghorne's comment about such people is significant. He writes that there is in their thinking too high a degree of one-way assimilation and accommodation: 'this stance will always carry the danger of the subordination of the theological to the scientific. It is theology that will tend to be assimilated into science.'[30]

The third model is the liberal reconciliation model. According to this model science is fine as it is; it is rather Christianity that needs to change most (but not all) of its traditional content. Peacocke illustrates this stance well when he writes that the aim of his work 'is to rethink our "religious" conceptualizations in the light of the perspectives on the world afforded by the sciences'.[31] Liberal reconciliationists, again roughly, read the Bible essentially symbolically, privilege science without question, and reject, or at least significantly modify, the traditional theistic notion of God. They instead want to embrace, for instance, panentheism or yet further naturalize the notion of God and to speak about theistic or religious naturalism, or alternatively to talk about an unknowable transcendent mystery named the 'Real' or the 'Ultimate'. To varying degrees, Barbour, Drees, Kaufman, Peacocke and Sallie McFague exemplify those scholars whose work assumes the liberal reconciliation model. The elevated view of science presupposed in the model becomes explicit when, for instance, Ted Peters writes that science's 'ruthless dedication to empirically derived truth renders science brutal in its disregard for previous beliefs, even sacred beliefs'.[32] This is in sharp contrast to the non-privileged, perhaps even debunking, view of science that we shall see exhibited in the next model.

There is also a fourth model worth exploring, although I would hesitate to identify names of scholars in the dialogue who would presuppose it in their writing. According to the postmodern or constructivist reconciliation model, neither science nor (traditional or liberal) Christianity is acceptable as it is; rather, both need to change radically. The starting point would be with radical postmodern literary theory and scholars such as Nietzsche, Derrida, Foucault and Rorty, and with philosophers and sociologists of science such as Thomas Kuhn, Barry Barnes, David Bloor and Sandra Harding. Their ideas are then applied to the science–religion dialogue. What we are invited to understand is that both science and religion are social constructs developed to satisfy certain needs or interests. Consequently, the natural world has a small to non-existent role in the construction of scientific knowledge. Not only religious truth, but also scientific truth, is a reflection of power relations at a particular time. There is no objective truth to be found. In the words of Don Cupitt, a philosopher of religion: 'The world as such – if indeed we can speak of such a thing at all – is no more than a featureless flux of becoming, which different cultures simply order in different ways.'[33] When applied to science, this means that the universe has no inherent structure for scientists to task themselves to discover. All our stories about the world are just transient constructs, and a scientific and a religious perspective are just two among many. If we understand science and religion in this or a similar way it is quite possible to reconcile them with each other. Again, the views could be more or less radical, although all would contain the idea that scientific theories and religious beliefs are social constructs in the sense that they are influenced by cultural and social interests and do not capture a reality independent of human beings.

VIEWS OF SCIENCE

It is true that the participants in the science–religion dialogue hold views about religion that are more diverse than are their views about science, but the accounts of what science is can also vary quite widely. It is therefore a mistake to think that the relationship between science and religion would be the same for all of the sciences or for all accounts of science. This further complicates the whole picture of the dialogue, but the typology is nevertheless available for different understandings of what science is. Let us for a moment move closer to the subject matter on this point and draw a slightly more detailed map.

First, science could be explicated in terms of a particular discipline like physics or biology, or in terms of all the natural sciences, or the natural sciences and the social sciences, or perhaps even more widely to include the humanities – as the usage of the term for science in Swedish or German allows. Clearly religion as a whole is not a science. But some have argued that theology is a science.[34] Ideas of how science should be demarcated would therefore affect how the relationship between science and religion is perceived.

Second, much of the discussion about how science and religion are related assumes a realist view of science. Scientific realism is, roughly speaking, the view that the theories of science are true or false, or at least approximately so, by virtue of the way in which they capture features of the world, independent of language or observer. According to this view, scientists can often tell of a theory whether it is (approximately) true or is false, by testing it against empirical reality. Theories attempt to give an account of what is going on behind the phenomena we experience, so science is not merely in pursuit of a careful, methodological description of the observable aspects of the world. But of course it is possible instead to hold some kind of non-realist or anti-realist view of science, and this would influence how science and religion are related.

One option to take is scientific instrumentalism. Instrumentalists maintain that scientific theories should not be thought of as making true or false assertions about the underlying non-observable structure of reality, but should simply be regarded as either useful or not. Theories are intellectual tools for organizing observation data and predicting future phenomena, and nothing more. The best-known instrumentalist in the science–religion debate is perhaps Pierre Duhem, who argues that because physical theories can be neither true nor false they have no part to play in theological discussion. These scientific theories, properly understood, have no 'ability to penetrate beyond the teachings of experiment or any capacity to surmise realities hidden under data observable to the senses'.[35]

A third possibility would be to adopt scientific empiricism and to claim that scientific theories intend to be telling the truth but should only be accepted as empirically adequate and not believed to be true, because of the problem of determining their truth value. Theories attempt to give true descriptions of a reality underlying the phenomena experienced, but we cannot say whether any such description is indeed true or whether it is false.

Constructivism in the sense described earlier would give yet a fourth option. Advocates of scientific constructivism would not deny that scientific theories can be true or false and that we can legitimately talk as if we know them to be true, but scientific truth is always a social construct. Scientific theories can never be true or false in virtue of the way of the world, independent of language or observer. Rather, they are always deeply embedded in language, social practices and political structures, but nonetheless are about what is real. It is just that truth is always truth-for-us or truth from one or other perspective, and science is no exception to this rule.

TWO FURTHER COMPLICATING FACTORS

One could easily be led to conclude that this typology presupposes science to be a set of theories and religion to be a set of beliefs or doctrines, and that these are the things that we ought to try to bring into relationship. But that is not the case: the typology is consistent with the idea that we might understand science and religion as social practices with many layers, including perhaps propositional content but not excluding other types of content. For instance, if we understand science and religion as two social practices, then an overlap between the two does not have to consist in scientific theories being of relevance for religious beliefs, but can, for example, consist simply in a person being both a scientist and a religious believer, or in a religious foundation supporting a particular scientific research programme.

In fact, the starting point for a more detailed account should be that science and religion are not merely sets of beliefs or theories plus certain methodologies, but are two social practices. That is to say, whatever else science and religion might be, they are complex activities performed by human beings in co-operation within a particular historical and cultural setting. We could roughly say that a practice is a complex and fairly coherent socially established co-operative human activity, through which its practitioners (for instance, religious believers or scientists) try to achieve certain goals by means of particular strategies. A practice can thus be distinguished by identifying the goals that its practitioners have in common and by the means that they develop and use to achieve these goals. Science and religion conceived in this way consist of all the activities that scientists and religious people participate in when pursuing the goals of their particular practice; and since these two practices have existed for a long time, they each have a history and constitute traditions.

Another difficulty with typologies is that they might give the impression that the science–religion relationship is static; it is always the same.[36] The typology proposed is, however, compatible with the idea that science and religion can change (and indeed do change, as the study of the history of science and of religion reveals). If we accept that science and religion are social practices then, like all other social practices, they can change over time. As a result, it is possible that at time t_1 there is no overlap between science and religion, but owing, say, to scientific theory development, at time t_2 there is an area of contact between these two practices, and perhaps at time t_3 there will be a union between science and religion.[37] This could be a development that would come at the expense of traditional religion and not of science, if we are to believe an advocate of the replacement model, such as Wilson. Alternatively the impact could be in the opposite direction, as Golshani, Marsden and Plantinga maintain, with religious beliefs influencing the direction of scientific research and the justification of scientific theories more than they previously did.

It is therefore important that we link the distinction between the irreconcilability model, the independence model, different versions of the reconciliation model, and the replacement model to the notions of expansion and restriction, indicating that the relationship between science and religion could be dynamic and evolving over time.[38] But notice if we accept that science and religion are practices that change over time and use the terminology of expansion and restriction as a means of characterizing changes in the relationship between science and religion, then we cannot immediately identify what Loran R. Graham has called scientific restrictionism, with the independence model.[39] This is so because restriction or expansion is always relative to the previous situation and that situation could be characterized by a particular kind of overlap between science and religion, and not by two autonomous, non-overlapping practices. A restrictionist would in such a situation be someone who argues against the attempt of expansionists to expand the overlap further either at the expense of religion or at the expense of science. Hence there is no immediate risk that the typology I am proposing would turn out to be too a-historical and static to provide a useful map of the relationship between science and religion as advocated throughout the ages. Having said that, however, the notion of a reconciliation model does, in one sense, presuppose the contemporary situation in which many people think that science and religion are in competition, and that just one will stand victorious in the end. In this situation it does indeed seem appropriate to attach the label of 'reconciliation' to approaches that hold that both practices might in fact co-exist, or be combined, or be of some relevance to each other. However, if we go back through history, the prevailing presumption would probably have been that science and religion are supportive of each other. In such circumstances it might be more fitting to call the model the contact model rather than the reconciliation model.

Notes

1 Ian Barbour, *Religion and Science* (San Francisco: HarperSanFrancisco, 1997); Ian Barbour, *When Science Meets Religion* (San Francisco: HarperSanFrancisco, 2000).

2 Willem B. Drees, *Religion, Science and Naturalism* (Cambridge University Press, 1996); John F. Haught, *Science and Religion* (New York: Paulist Press, 1995); Ted Peters, 'Theology and the Natural Sciences', in David F. Ford (ed.), *The Modern Theologians*, 2nd edition (Oxford: Blackwell, 1997), pp. 649–67; Mikael Stenmark, *How to Relate Science and Religion* (Grand Rapids, MI: Eerdmans, 2004); Mikael Stenmark, 'Religion and Science', in Chad Meister and Paul Copan (eds.), *The Routledge Companion to Philosophy of Religion* (London: Routledge, 2007), pp. 692–701.

3 Francis Crick, *The Astonishing Hypothesis: the Scientific Search for the Soul* (New York: Charles Scribner's Sons, 1994), p. 257.

4 John Worrall, 'Science Discredits Religion', in M.L. Peterson and R.J. Vanarragon (eds.), *Contemporary Debates in Philosophy of Religion* (Oxford: Blackwell, 2004), p. 60.

5 Francis S. Collins, *The Language of God* (London: Pocket Books, 2007), p. 6.

6 Stenmark, *How to Relate Science and Religion*, p. 9.

7 Stephen Jay Gould, *Rocks of Ages: Science and Religion in the Fullness of Life* (New York: Ballantine, 1999), p. 6.

8 Edward O. Wilson, *Consilience* (New York: Knopf, 1999), p. 6.

9 Edward O. Wilson, *On Human Nature* (Cambridge, MA: Harvard University Press, 1978), p. 193.

10 Barbour, *Religion and Science*, pp. 77–84.

11 Phillip E. Johnson, *Reason in the Balance* (Downers Grove, IL: InterVarsity Press, 1995).

12 William A. Dembski, *Intelligent Design: the Bridge between Science and Theology* (Downers Grove, IL: InterVarsity Press, 1999).

13 Gordon D. Kaufman, 'On Thinking of God as Serendipitous Creativity', *Journal of the American Academy of Religion* 69 (2001), 409–25.

14 Arthur Peacocke, 'A Naturalistic Christian Faith for the Twenty-First Century', in Philip Clayton (ed.), *All that Is* (Minneapolis: Fortress Press, 2007), p. 6.

15 John Polkinghorne, *Belief in God in an Age of Science* (New Haven: Yale University Press, 1998).

16 Keith Ward, 'Personhood, Spirit, and the Supernatural', in Clayton (ed.), *All that Is*, pp. 152–62, p. 153.

17 Barbour, *Religion and Science*, pp. 90–105.

18 Ibid., p. 205

19 Polkinghorne, *Belief in God in an Age of Science*, p. 10.

20 Richard Swinburne, *Is there a God?* (Oxford University Press, 1996), pp. 2, 68.

21 Fritjof Capra, *The Tao of Physics*, 4th edn (Boston: Shambhala, 2000), p. 12.

22 Robert Wright, *The Moral Animal* (London: Abacus, 1996), p. 13.

23 John T. Mullen, 'Can Evolutionary Psychology Confirm Original Sin?', *Faith and Philosophy* 24 (2007), 268–83, p. 269.

24 Keith Ward, *God, Chance and Necessity* (Oxford: Oneworld, 1996), p. 98.

25 Dalai Lama, *The Universe in a Single Atom* (London: Abacus, 2005), pp. 6, 146.

26 Medhi Golshani, 'How to Make Sense of "Islamic Science?"', *American Journal of Islamic Social Sciences* 17 (2000), 1–21; George M. Marsden, *The Outrageous Idea of Christian Scholarship* (Oxford University Press, 1997).

27 Zainal Abidin Bagir, 'Islam, Science and "Islamic Science": How to "Integrate" Science and Religion', in Zainal Abidin Bagir (ed.), *Science and Religion in a Post-colonial World* (Adelaide: ATF Press, 2005), pp. 37–64, p. 40.

28 Seyyed Hossein Nasr, 'Islamic–Christian Dialogue: Problems and Obstacles to be Pondered and Overcome', *Islam and Christian–Muslim Relations* 2 (2000), 213–27, p. 224.

29 Alvin Plantinga, 'When Faith and Reason Clash: Evolution and the Bible', *Christian Scholar's Review* 21 (1991), 8–33, p. 29.

30 John Polkinghorne, *Scientists as Theologians* (London: SPCK, 1996), p. 7.

31 Arthur Peacocke, *Theology for a Scientific Age* (Minneapolis: Fortress Press, 1993), p. 3.

32 Ted Peters, 'Theology and the Natural Sciences', in Ford (ed.), *The Modern Theologians*, pp. 647–68.

33 Don Cupitt, *Lifelines* (London: SCM Press, 1986), p. 133.

34 Nancey Murphy, *Theology in the Age of Scientific Reasoning* (Ithaca, NY: Cornell University Press, 1990); Peacocke, *Theology for a Scientific Age*; Alister E. McGrath, *The Science of God* (Grand Rapids, MI: Eerdmans, 2004).

35 Pierre Duhem, *The Aim and Structure of Physical Theory* (Princeton University Press, 1954), p. 279.

36 John Brooke and Geoffrey Cantor, *Reconstructing Nature* (Edinburgh: T. and T. Clark, 1998), p. 275; J. Wentzel van Huyssteen, *Duet or Duel? Theology and Science in a Postmodern World* (Harrisburg, PA: Trinity Press International, 1998), p. 3.

37 But it is also possible that at time t_4 there is merely overlap again, and at time t_5 science and religion are completely separate practices, and so on.

38 Stenmark, *How to Relate Science and Religion*, pp. 257–8.

39 The terms 'scientific restrictionism', and 'scientific expansionism' are introduced in Loren R. Graham, *Between Science and Values* (New York: Columbia University Press, 1981), and further developed in Mikael Stenmark, *Scientism: Science, Ethics and Religion* (Aldershot: Ashgate, 2001).

A guide to further reading

Introductory

Ian Barbour, *Religion and Science: Historical and Contemporary Issues*, San Francisco: Harper, 1997.

John Hedley Brooke, *Science and Religion: Some Historical Perspectives*, Cambridge University Press, 1991.

Philip Clayton and Zachary Simpson (eds.), *The Oxford Handbook of Religion and Science*, Oxford University Press, 2006.

Thomas Dixon, *Science and Religion: a Very Short Introduction*, Oxford University Press, 2008.

Gary Ferngren (ed.), *Science and Religion: a Historical Introduction*, Baltimore: Johns Hopkins University Press, 2002.

David C. Lindberg and Ronald L. Numbers (eds.), *When Science and Christianity Meet*, University of Chicago Press, 2003.

Ronald L. Numbers (ed.), *Galileo Goes to Jail and Other Myths about Science and Religion*, Cambridge, MA: Harvard University Press, 2009.

John Polkinghorne, *Belief in God in an Age of Science*, New Haven: Yale University Press, 2003.

Keith Ward, *The Big Questions in Science and Religion*, Philadelphia: Templeton Press, 2008.

Science and religion in the middle ages

John Baldwin, *The Scholastic Culture of the Middle Ages, 1000–1300*, Lexington, MA: D. C. Heath, 1971.

Marcia L. Colish, *The Foundations of the Western Intellectual Tradition, 400–1400*, New Haven: Yale University Press, 1997.

Edward Grant, *Science and Religion, 400 BC to AD 1550: From Aristotle to Copernicus*, Baltimore: Johns Hopkins University Press, 2004.

David C. Lindberg, *The Beginnings of Western Science: the European Scientific Tradition in Philosophical, Religious, and Institutional Context, Prehistory to AD 1450*, 2nd edn, revised, University of Chicago Press, 2007.

David C. Lindberg, 'Science as Handmaiden: Roger Bacon and the Patristic Tradition', *Isis* 78 (1987), 518–36.

Fernand van Steenberghen, *Aristotle in the West*, trans. by Leonard Johnston, Louvain: Nauwelaerts, 1955.

Religion and the Scientific Revolution

I. Bernard Cohen (ed.), *Puritanism and the Rise of Modern Science: the Merton Thesis*, New Brunswick: Rutgers University Press, 1990.

Amos Funkenstein, *Theology and the Scientific Imagination: From the Middle Ages to the Seventeenth Century*, Princeton University Press, 1986.

Stephen Gaukroger, *The Emergence of a Scientific Culture: Science and the Shaping of Modernity, 1210–1685*, Oxford: Clarendon Press, 2006.

Peter Harrison, *The Bible, Protestantism, and the Rise of Natural Science*, Cambridge University Press, 1998.

Peter Harrison, *The Fall of Man and the Foundations of Modern Science*, Cambridge University Press, 2007.

David C. Lindberg and Ronald L. Numbers (eds.), *God and Nature: Historical Essays on the Encounter between Christianity and Science*, Berkeley: University of California Press, 1986.

Ernan McMullin (ed.), *The Church and Galileo*, University of Notre Dame Press, 2005, pp. 117–49.

Margaret J. Osler, *Divine Will and the Mechanical Philosophy: Gassendi and Descartes on Contingency and Necessity in the Created World*, Cambridge University Press, 1994.

Steven Shapin, 'Understanding the Merton Thesis', *Isis* 79 (1988), 594–605.

R. S. Westfall, *Science and Religion in Seventeenth-Century England*, New Haven: Yale University Press, 1958.

Natural theology and the sciences

John Hedley Brooke, *Science and Religion: Some Historical Perspectives*, Cambridge University Press, 1991.

John Hedley Brooke and Geoffrey Cantor, *Reconstructing Nature: the Engagement of Science and Religion*, Edinburgh: T. & T. Clark, 1998.

Pietro Corsi, *Science and Religion: Baden Powell and the Anglican Debate, 1800–1860*, Cambridge University Press, 1988.

John Gascoigne, 'From Bentley to the Victorians: the Rise and Fall of British Newtonian Natural Theology', *Science in Context* 2 (1988), 219–56.

Dov Ospovat, *The Development of Darwin's Theory: Natural History, Natural Theology, and Natural Selection, 1828–1850*, Cambridge University Press, 1981.

Jonathan R. Topham, 'Beyond the "Common Context": the Production and Reading of the Bridgewater Treatises', *Isis* 89 (1998), 233–62.

Religious reactions to Darwin

Mariano Artigas, Thomas F. Glick and Rafael A. Martinez, *Negotiating Darwin: the Vatican Confronts Evolution, 1877–1902*, Baltimore: Johns Hopkins University Press, 2006.

Peter J. Bowler, *Reconciling Science and Religion: the Debate in Early-Twentieth-Century Britain*, University of Chicago Press, 2001.

Geoffrey Cantor and Marc Swetlitz (eds.), *Jewish Tradition and the Challenge of Darwinism*, University of Chicago Press, 2006.

Alvar Ellegard, *Darwin and the General Reader: the Reception of Darwin's Theory of Evolution in the British Periodical Press, 1859–1872*, University of Chicago Press, 1990.

David N. Livingstone, *Darwin's Forgotten Defenders: the Encounter between Evangelical Theology and Evolutionary Thought*, Grand Rapids, MI: Eerdmans,1987.

James R. Moore, *The Post-Darwinian Controversies: a Study of the Protestant Struggle to Come to Terms with Darwin in Great Britain and America, 1870–1900*, Cambridge University Press, 1979.

Ronald L. Numbers, *The Creationists: From Scientific Creationism to Intelligent Design*, expanded edn, Cambridge, MA: Harvard University Press, 2006.

Jon H. Roberts, *Darwinism and the Divine in America: Protestant Intellectuals and Organic Evolution, 1859–1900*, University of Notre Dame Press, 2001.

Science and secularization

Peter L. Berger, 'The Desecularization of the World: a Global Overview', in Peter L. Berger (ed.), *The Desecularization of the World: Resurgent Religion and World Politics*, Grand Rapids, MI: Eerdmans, 1999, pp. 1–18.

John Hedley Brooke, 'Science and Secularisation', in Linda Woodhead (ed.), *Reinventing Christianity*, Aldershot: Ashgate, 2001, pp. 229–38.

John H. Evans and Michael S. Evans, 'Religion and Science: Beyond the Epistemological Conflict Narrative', *Annual Review of Sociology* 34, no. 5 (2008), 1–19.

David Martin, 'Does the Advance of Science Mean Secularisation?', *Science and Christian Belief* 19 (2007), 3–14.

Ronald L. Numbers (ed.), *Galileo Goes to Jail and Other Myths in Science and Religion*, Cambridge, MA: Harvard University Press, 2009.

Charles Taylor, *A Secular Age*, Cambridge, MA: Harvard University Press, 2007.

Scientific creationism and intelligent design

Nathaniel Comfort (ed.), *The Panda's Black Box: Opening Up the Intelligent Design Controversy*, Baltimore: Johns Hopkins University Press, 2007.

Barbara Forrest and Paul R. Gross, *Creationism's Trojan Horse: the Wedge of Intelligent Design*, New York: Oxford University Press, 2004.

Karl W. Giberson and Donald A. Yerxa, *Species of Origins: America's Search for a Creation Story*, Lanham, MD: Rowman & Littlefield, 2002.

Edward J. Larson, *Trial and Error: the American Controversy over Creation and Evolution*, 3rd edn, New York: Oxford University Press, 2003.

Ronald L. Numbers, *The Creationists: From Scientific Creationism to Intelligent Design*, expanded edn, Cambridge, MA: Harvard University Press, 2006.

Robert T. Pennock, *Tower of Babel: the Evidence against the New Creationism*, Cambridge, MA: MIT Press, 1999.

Andrew J. Petto and Laurie R. Godfrey (eds.), *Scientists Confront Intelligent Design and Creationism*, New York: W. W. Norton, 2007.

Michael Ruse, *Darwin and Design: Does Evolution Have a Purpose?*, Cambridge, MA: Harvard University Press, 2003.

Evolution, human uniqueness and religious belief

Simon Conway Morris, *Life's Solution: Inevitable Humans in a Lonely Universe*, Cambridge University Press, 2003.

Simon Conway Morris (ed.), *The Deep Structure of Biology: Is Convergence Sufficiently Ubiquitous to Give a Directional Signal?*, West Conshohocken, PA: Templeton Press, 2008.

T. Crean, *A Catholic Replies to Professor Dawkins*, Oxford: Family Publications, 2007.

John F. Haught, *Deeper than Darwin: the Prospect for Religion in the Age of Evolution*, Boulder, CO and Oxford: Westview Press, 2003.

Alister A. McGrath, *The Open Secret: a New Vision for Natural Theology*, Malden, MA and Oxford: Wiley Blackwell, 2008.

Kenneth R. Miller, *Finding Darwin's God: a Scientist's Search for Common Ground between God and Evolution*, New York: HarperCollins, 2007.

Nick Spencer, *Darwin and God*, London: SPCK, 2009.

David Stove, *Darwinian Fairytales: Selfish Genes, Errors of Heredity, and Other Fables of Evolution*, Aldershot: Encounter Books, 2006.

God, physics and the Big Bang

Paul L. Allen, *Ernan McMullin and Critical Realism in the Science–Theology Dialogue*, Aldershot: Ashgate, 2006.

David B. Burrell, *Freedom and Creation in Three Traditions*, University of Notre Dame Press, 1993.

William E. Carroll, 'Divine Agency, Contemporary Physics, and the Autonomy of Nature', *The Heythrop Journal* 49, no. 4 (2008), 1–21.

George F. R. Ellis, *Before the Beginning: Cosmology Explained*, London: Boyars/Bowerdean, 2001.

Robert John Russell, Nancey Murphy and C. J. Isham (eds.), *Quantum Cosmology and the Laws of Nature: Scientific Perspectives on Divine Action*, Vatican City State and Berkeley, CA: Vatican Observatory Publications and the Center for Theology and the Natural Sciences, 1993.

Robert John Russell, William R. Stoeger, SJ and George V. Coyne, SJ (eds.), *Physics, Philosophy and Theology: a Common Quest for Understanding*, 2nd edn, Vatican City State: Vatican Observatory Publications, 1995.

Psychology and theology

Ian Barbour, *Nature, Human Nature, and God*, London: SPCK, 2002.

D. S. Browning and T. Cooper, *Religious Thought and the Modern Psychologies*, 2nd edn, Minneapolis: Augsburg Fortress, 2004.

M. A. Jeeves, *Human Nature at the Millennium*, Grand Rapids, MI: Baker Books, 1997.

W. W. Meissner, *Life and Faith: Psychological Perspectives on Religious Experience*, Washington, DC: Georgetown University Press, 1987.

P. Morea, *In Search of Personality*, London: SCM, 1997.

G. R. Peterson, *Minding God: Theology and the Cognitive Sciences*, Minneapolis: Augsburg Fortress, 2003.

F. Watts, *Theology and Psychology*, Ashgate Science and Religion Series, Aldershot: Ashgate, 2002.

Science, bioethics and religion

Dena S. Davis and Laurie Zoloth (eds.), *Notes from a Narrow Ridge: Religion and Bioethics*, Hagerstown, MD: University Publishing Group, 1999.

David E. Guinn (ed.), *Handbook of Bioethics and Religion*, New York: Oxford University Press, 2006.

Lisa Sowle Cahill, *Theological Ethics: Participation, Justice and Change*, Washington, DC: Georgetown University Press, 2005.

Allen Verhey (ed.), *Religion and Medical Ethics: Looking Back, Looking Forward*, Grand Rapids, MI: Eerdmans, 1996.

Science, atheism, and naturalism

W. A. Dembski and Michael Ruse (eds.), *Debating Design: Darwin to DNA*, Cambridge University Press, 2004.

L. B. Gilkey, *Maker of Heaven and Earth*, Garden City, NY: Doubleday, 1959.

John Haught, *God after Darwin: a Theology of Evolution*, Boulder: Westview Press, 2000.

Ernan McMullin, *Evolution and Creation*, University of Notre Dame Press, 1985.

Michael Ruse, *Can a Darwinian be a Christian? The Relationship between Science and Religion*, Cambridge University Press, 2001.

Michael Ruse, *The Evolution–Creation Struggle*, Cambridge, MA: Harvard University Press, 2005.

E. O. Wilson, *On Human Nature*, Cambridge, MA: Harvard University Press, 1978.

Divine action, emergence and scientific explanation

Alicia Juarrero, *Dynamics in Action: Intentional Behavior as a Complex System*, Cambridge, MA: MIT Press, 1999.

Robert Kane, *The Significance of Free Will*, Oxford University Press, 1998.

Nancey Murphy, *Beyond Liberalism and Fundamentalism: How Modern and Postmodern Philosophy Set the Theological Agenda*, Valley Forge, PA: Trinity Press International, 1996.

Nancey Murphy and Warren S. Brown, *Did My Neurons Make Me Do It?: Philosophical and Neurobiological Perspectives on Moral Responsibility and Free Will*, Oxford University Press, 2007.

Arthur Peacocke, 'A Naturalistic Christian Faith for the Twenty-First Century: an Essay in Interpretation', in Philip Clayton (ed.), *All That Is: a Naturalistic Faith for the Twenty-First Century*, Minneapolis: Fortress Press, 2007, pp. 3–56.

Robert John Russell, *Cosmology from Alpha to Omega: the Creative Mutual Interaction of Theology and Science*, Minneapolis: Fortress Press, 2008.

Robert John Russell, Nancey Murphy and Arthur R. Peacocke (eds.), *Chaos and Complexity: Scientific Perspectives on Divine Action*, Vatican City State: Vatican Observatory Press, 1995.

Nicholas Saunders, *Divine Action and Modern Science*, Cambridge University Press, 2002.

Science, God and cosmic purpose

Paul Davies, *The Mind of God: the Scientific Basis for a Rational World*, New York: Simon & Schuster, 1993.

John F. Haught, *Is Nature Enough? Meaning and Truth in the Age of Science*, Cambridge University Press, 2006.

Arthur O. Lovejoy, *The Great Chain of Being: a Study of the History of an Idea*, New York, Harper & Row, 1965.

Jürgen Moltmann, *God in Creation: a New Theology of Creation and the Spirit of God*, trans. by Margaret Kohl, San Francisco: Harper & Row, 1985.

Michael Polanyi and Harry Prosch, *Meaning*, University of Chicago Press, 1975.

Martin Rees, *Our Cosmic Habitat*, Princeton University Press, 2001.

Ways of relating science and religion

Ian Barbour, *Religion and Science*, San Francisco: HarperSanFrancisco, 1997.

Paul Draper, 'God, Science, and Naturalism', in William J. Wainwright (ed.), *The Oxford Handbook of Philosophy of Religion*, Oxford University Press, 2005.

John F. Haught, *Science and Religion*, New York: Paulist Press, 1995.

Alvin Plantinga, 'Religion and Science', *Stanford Encyclopedia of Philosophy*, 2007, http://plato.stanford.edu/entries/religion-science.

Mikael Stenmark, *How to Relate Science and Religion*, Grand Rapids, MI: Eerdmans, 2004.

Topics not covered in this book

Science and the World Religions

Philip Clayton and Zachary Simpson (eds.), *The Oxford Handbook of Religion and Science*, Oxford University Press, 2006, Part 1.

Noah J. Efron, *Judaism and Science: a Historical Introduction*, Westport: Greenwood Press, 2007.

Donald S. Lopez Jr., *Buddhism and Science: a Guide for the Perplexed*, University of Chicago Press, 2008.

Ronald L. Numbers and John Hedley Brooke (eds.), *Science and Religion around the World*, New York: Oxford University Press, 2010.
George Saliba, *Islamic Science and the Making of the European Renaissance*, Cambridge, MA: MIT Press, 2007.

Science and the Advocacy of Atheism

Richard Dawkins, *The God Delusion*, London: Bantam Press, 2006.
Daniel C. Dennett, *Breaking the Spell: Religion as a Natural Phenomenon*, New York: Viking, 2006.
Christopher Hitchens, *God is Not Great: the Case against Religion*, London: Atlantic, 2007.
Victor Stengler, *God: the Failed Hypothesis: How Science Shows that God does not Exist*, Amherst: Prometheus, 2007.

Religion, Anthropology and Cognitive Science

Justin Barrett, *Why Would Anyone Believe in God?*, Walnut Creek, CA and Oxford: AltaMira, 2004.
Pascal Boyer, *Religion Explained*, New York: Basic Books, 2001.
Todd Tremlin, *Minds and God: the Cognitive Foundations of Religion*, Oxford University Press, 2006.
Harvey Whitehouse and James Laidlaw (eds.), *Religion, Anthropology and Cognitive Science*, Durham, NC: Carolina Academic Press, 2007.

Science, Religion and the Environment

Robin Attfield, *Creation, Evolution, and Meaning*, Aldershot: Ashgate, 2006.
Robin Attfield, *The Ethics of Environmental Concern*, 2nd edn, Athens: University of Georgia Press, 2004.
R. J. (Sam) Berry (ed.), *Environmental Stewardship: Critical Perspectives – Past and Present*, London: Continuum, 2006.
Robert S. Gottlieb (ed.), *The Oxford Handbook of Religion and Ecology*, Oxford University Press, 2006.
E. O. Wilson, *The Creation: an Appeal to Save Life on Earth*, New York: Norton, 2006.

Index